America's Quest for the Ideal Self

AMERICA'S QUEST
FOR THE IDEAL SELF

Dissent and Fulfillment
in the 60s and 70s

PETER CLECAK

New York   Oxford
OXFORD UNIVERSITY PRESS

Copyright © 1983 by Oxford University Press, Inc.

Library of Congress Cataloging in Publication Data
Clecak, Peter.
America's quest for the ideal self
  Includes index.
    1. United States—Social conditions—1945–1970.
  2. United States—Social conditions—1970–
  3. United States—Civilization—1945–
  4. United States—Civilization—1970–
  I. Title.
  HN59.C57   1983   973.92   82–14532
  ISBN 0-19-503226-8
  ISBN 0-19-50544-5 (pbk.)

16.10

Printing (last digit): 9 8 7 6 5 4 3

Printed in the United States of America

69503

For my mother,
Jean Peter Clecak

Acknowledgments

I began this book unwittingly in the spring of 1978, after accepting an invitation from Betty Chmaj to give a brief talk on the seemingly tidy topic of decades, in particular on "America in the Sixties and Seventies," at the California Conference on American Studies, Annenberg Center, the University of Southern California. Robin Brooks, John Brazil, and Betty offered cogent criticisms of that early fragment, but in spite of them I persisted, hoping to produce an essay of reasonable proportions and then sensibly to let the matter rest. The projected essay got out of hand, and by the fall of 1978 I was captivated by the project. Sheldon Meyer of Oxford University Press read the expanded essay and decided that with another year's work it might make a useful short book. The present version, which overshoots this mark in length, has been through more revisions than I care to recall. At each major juncture, Sheldon has provided encouragement and sound advice, exhibiting admirable patience and just the right amount of editorial prodding along the way.

My work on this project has been supported generously. From the summer of 1979 through 1980 I had as much leisure as anyone could dare to hope for: a one-quarter sabbatical and a year-long NEH Senior Fellowship strung together by two summers. Dean Linton Freeman of the School of Social Sciences at the University of California, Irvine, protected the domain of research, scholarship, and criticism through stringent times. I have been helped immeasurably by the work of two research assistants, John Mohr and Jock Eggers, who tracked down references and supplied valuable critiques of early drafts. Rosemary Johnson typed some portions of the manuscript, proofed others, and supplied warm encouragement along the way. Helen Wildman dragged me into the age of the Wang word processor, preparing the bulk of the manuscript—typing, editing, and proofing it. Cheryl Larsson had a go at it during one summer when Helen sought refuge in the country.

Along the way I have acquired a wonderful string of intellectual debts. I am especially grateful to Howard R. Bowen, intellectual mentor and friend, who not only read the manuscript with his usual critical care but also provided me with an example of responsible intellectual optimism over the past several years. Other friends have inspired me. David Sandberg has challenged and enlarged my theological under-standing of liberal Christian theology. Dr. John Rodino, biochemist and nutritionist, helped me discover the gift of energy and in so doing has made it possible for me to forgive a string of inept medical practitioners.

Several people have been kind enough to comment on my manuscript at one stage or another of its growth: Arthé Anthony, Daniel Bell, Norman Birnbaum, Richard Busacca, Francesca Cancian, Stanley Coben, Darrell Hamamoto, Samuel Hines, Laurel Hollowaty, Irving Howe, David Johnson, Seymour Martin Lipset, William O'Neill, Ross Quillian, Dickran Tashjian, and Albert Wlecke. I wish to thank Dave Bruce, John Diggins, Barbara Glenn, Alan Lawson, Julius Margolis, Spencer Olin, Myron Simon, and Pamela Steinle for detailed written critiques that exceeded any reasonable expectations I might have held. I have learned from each of these people and have often shamelessly transcribed their ideas—not often enough, I should guess, to suit some of them, but with sufficient regularity to make me painfully aware of their contributions. I hope that I have discharged at least some of my other debts in the notes to each chapter. But a subject such as mine has elicited ideas from people and from the media almost any time I have been prepared to listen. It would bring out the scavenger in anyone.

Once again, Vivian Clecak has been a constant source of encourage-ment. Still my best friend and often my best critic, she is the intellectual other of this book, my principal source of dialogue about its large struc-ture and small textures. She has managed to be all this while putting her own career ahead of my book, a cause for joint celebration. Aimée, and more recently Lisa, the joys of my life, have treated my project with bemused tolerance, indulging me in many ways; at times with silence, and often with visits to the study to "color while you work," as Aimée puts it. These sessions inevitably turn into conversations, often useful ones. Aimée has helped me on matters of perspective in more ways than she knows or that I can say.

This book is dedicated to my mother, Jean Peter Clecak, who nurtured me well and sent me on my way at the proper time. She has become a good friend, but still an indulgent one—sufficiently indulgent to accept a book whose main contentions strike her as simply wrong. She will be in good company.

June 1982   P. C.

Contents

Contents

III *Misreading the Signs*

America's Quest
for the Ideal Self

The real cycle you're working on is a cycle called "yourself."
ROBERT PIRSIG
Zen and the Art
of Motorcycle Maintenance

Self, self, has half filled Hell.
Scottish proverb

1
Prologue

An advertisement for "A New Magazine for the '70s" published in 1977 featured a cropped photograph of a crowd of young people. They could have been listening to a speech or to a rock concert, attending a love-in or staging a political demonstration. All one can tell from the photograph is that they are together—and that their cultural moment has passed. Superimposed on this icon is the question, "What's Left of the '60s?" The answer: "MOTHER JONES, Finally . . . . A Magazine for the Rest of Us," for the veterans of "the generation that got back in touch with our world, in the most basic ways." The copywriter then rehearses a familiar litany of personal and cultural achievements: "We rediscovered ourselves. Music opened us up, and took off. The Beatles. The Stones. Dylan. We found our own literature, with a tough cosmic, comic vision . . . *Catch 22. Slaughterhouse Five. Cuckoo's Nest.* We identified with a handful of writers. Pynchon. Grass. Barthelme. Vonnegut. Barth." The political dimension follows: "We put our stamp upon the world by fighting Vietnam [*sic*], by working in the Peace Corps. And by confronting racism, sexism and militarism." With the promise of a lively exploration of current alternatives, the reader is urged to subscribe: "After all, there's no sense in living the '70s alone."[1]

Here, in a revealing if jumbled and sentimental caricature, are the chief elements of a perspective on the recent American past that grew increasingly popular in the seventies. Proposed by certain radical sur-

vivors of the sixties, played with significant reservations by a range of
left-liberal critics, and amplified by media journalists, this perspective
turns on a vague centering of postwar American cultural history in
the succession of decades and decennial generations.[2] The sixties form
the centerpiece, a hopeful moment between the sterile, conformist
fifties and the constricted, lonely, self-absorbed seventies. In this perspective, the sixties are represented as a morally generous, energetic
time of political, personal, and communal action—or at least a time
when concerted action against the ills of civilization seemed to be a
live possibility. The seventies, in contrast, are an apolitical, devitalized
decade of intense, morally debilitating preoccupation with the self.[3]
Although important disagreements separate those who accept the main
terms of this guiding cultural fiction, its dominant contours are by
now painfully familiar. Thriving on contrasts, which control the fashionable rhetoric of decadism, this fiction operates within a larger
framework of nostalgia. Every *other* decade may be viewed as a moment of hope, but the overall direction of the historical spiral is downward. Within the framework of nostalgia, the present typically is assumed to be inferior to the past—either actually worse, or worse by
virtue of a collapse of previous hopes and expectations. This perspective informed nearly all of American social and cultural criticism in
the late seventies. And it dominated commentary in much of the print
and electronic media as well.

Thus, when their dreams of dramatic political and social action began to fade in the early seventies, many critics and participants on the
left inverted themes that only a few years earlier had been assigned a
prominent place in constructions and preliminary reconstructions of
the sixties: the seventies became the sixties turned inside out, and in
some readings a replay of many themes of the fifties. Above all, critics
stressed what they considered perversions of the idea of personal fulfillment. When stripped of its left communal and political contexts,
the search for fulfillment was said to divide individuals against one
another, intensify loneliness, and promote greed. Under these altered
circumstances, it was supposed, the search for self-fulfillment yielded
illusions of gratification and liberation that could neither satisfy individuals (for long) nor advance the cause of social justice. In the
seventies, then, America allegedly deliquesced into a squalid time of
personal "selfishness" (Tom Wolfe's "Me Decade"); "narcissism"
(Christopher Lasch); "decadence" (Jim Hougan); political incoher-

ence and political "reaction" (Henry Fairlie, speaking, one supposes, for *The New Republic*).[4] This decade was supposed to have been marked by a rise of selfishness and a further decline of all forms of authority: theological, cultural, ideological, textual, political, institutional, patriarchal, and paternal. As a consequence of these associated developments, American culture was judged by many critics to have been balkanized, fragmented beyond repair. And American politics was said to have been plunged into a seemingly permanent stalemate, a stand-off among self-interested forces.

At worst, critics on the left declared the seventies a time in which American life turned nasty and brutish, lacking even the compensating Hobbesian grace of brevity. By the late seventies, Irving Louis Horowitz observed, America had "become a Hobbesian rather than a Marxian nation, a place where the war of all against all is conducted with a ferocity that makes nineteenth-century class warfare seem tame in comparison."[5] Even those critics on the left who managed to hold a more balanced view described the salutary features of the seventies as mere survivals of what they had judged promising beginnings in the sixties.[6] Before the end of the seventies, less ideologically constrained and less discriminating critics were wishing the decade away, dismissing it as a time in which nothing was happening. "The perfect Seventies symbol," Howard Junker remarked, "was the Pet Rock, which just sat there doing nothing."[7] As Charlie Haas put it in *New West*'s premature obituary, published in 1979, the seventies turned out to be a "Pinto of a decade" whose characteristic disease was "hypoglycemia."[8] For those disappointed in one way or another by the apparently entropic seventies, the only sensible course was to "cool out" and "wait for the Eighties." After all, considering the parade of contrasting decades fashioned by critics, the eighties could be expected to reverse the seventies: the "me decade," some observers contended in a facile turn of phrase, might be succeeded by the "we decade."

I take a quite different approach to the sixties and seventies, an approach that emphasizes thematic and ideological continuities and connections instead of the usual disjunctures. Rather than apprehending the sixties as a hopeful political and cultural drama that ended some time between 1968 and 1974 and then characterizing the remaining years of the seventies as a dead space or a time of rampant selfishness and reaction, I view both decades as aspects of a single, uncompleted chapter in American civilization. Despite clear differences in mood and attitude, as well as substantial changes in the political economy, I believe that this episode was unified by a central cultural theme: a quest for personal fulfillment, a pursuit of a free, gratified, unalienated self within one or more communities of valued others. Although it was variously defined, the ideal self was endowed with sufficient energy and resources to explore a range of possibilities, both on its own and with others. The quest itself is as old as the American enterprise, although the meanings of its key terms have changed often enough. In the sixties and seventies, however, the quest for fulfillment was pursued with particular intensity. It was pursued on a far wider scale than ever before, touching nearly every sector of society, albeit unevenly. And it was pursued, I shall argue, with impressive overall results. During these years, Americans within every disadvantaged biological and social category, from race to social class, sought—and found—ways to define and enact various visions of the self within small communities of others. The main *social* effect of this multifaceted search was a rapid democratization of personhood. By "democratization of personhood" I mean to indicate the substantial extension of the many facilitating conditions for fulfillment of the self: enhanced cultural options, rising economic resources and rewards, strengthened legal guarantees, and augmented personal and political rights.

Of course, no sensible observer of American affairs would claim that the sixties and seventies marked a period of uninterrupted improvement in every sphere—in the economic well-being of all citizens; in their political and personal rights; in their capacity to influence public decisions; and in the quality of their social, personal, and cultural lives. Nor could anyone plausibly claim that everyone in any disadvantaged social category gained the material accouterments to fulfillment, or even that the average level of every group had risen. There nevertheless were important advances: stunning cultural gains, significant political gains, and even measurable economic progress. All of these advances have been slighted or only grudgingly (and belatedly) acknowledged in the higher circles of social criticism—for good if finally not sufficient reasons. These gains were uneven. They were inadequate, especially when judged against any ideal standard, but also when measured against earlier hopes. They were distributed unevenly, even inequitably, among the various social groups and categories. By the end of the seventies, some of these advances—especially those in the economic condition of citizens—seemed precarious. And all of the advances appeared potentially trivial when seen in the larger context of global nuclear insecurity. Still, the cumulative effect of these changes was to permit significant numbers of Americans to discover (or hope to discover) a satisfactory synthesis of the main elements of fulfillment, which I shall refer to as "salvation" and "a piece of social justice."

I shall not insist that Americans were generally "happier" at the end of the seventies than they were in the late fifties, or even that they thought themselves happier. In fact, such survey research as is available suggests that the state of the nation's perceived happiness has remained remarkably stable in the postwar years despite cultural, social, and political change and even dislocation.[9] There are variations among social categories, of course: women, for example, typically rate themselves as happier than men, whites as happier than blacks, married people as happier than single people, spiritually active citizens as happier than their inactive counterparts. Overall, however, Americans claim to be quite satisfied with their personal lives. In the summer of 1981, for example, a Gallup survey showed that 83 percent of respondents were satisfied with the course of their personal lives, whereas 81 percent were dissatisfied with "the way things are going in the U.S. at this time." This paradox of a people who maintain high levels of reported personal happiness in the midst of perceived dissatisfaction with larger events and trends can be read variously as a triumph of optimism or as a reign of self-deception. At the very least, this paradox seems to indicate the cultural centrality of the quest for personal fulfillment in the sixties and seventies.

In any case, my argument does not hang upon reports of happiness. For progress in self-fulfillment cannot be discerned unambiguously in survey research into what social scientists (and others) conventionally call "happiness." Although they are related, "happiness" and "fulfillment" (as I use the terms) are not synonymous. In many instances, these notions may be inversely related, as when augmented expectations of fulfilling personal relationships are subverted by limited resources: an ideal mate, friend, lover, or community of others does not exist to meet the wishes of every individual. In the chapters ahead, I explore a more reasoned set of claims. I argue that the quest for fulfillment represented the central, energizing thrust of American culture in the sixties *and* in the seventies. I contend that the material, political, and cultural prerequisites for achieving full personhood were democratized significantly during these years. And I take seriously the subjective reports of tens of millions of citizens who claimed some degree of success in their search for fulfillment—reports that on the whole suggest a significant increase in available cultural space and a healthy thickening of individuality. Progress (small *p*) was registered within American civilization as the quest unfolded during these decades, even though the future of the whole enterprise may seem (and may be) more problematic in the early eighties than it was in the late fifties.

2

The Argument

A quest for personal fulfillment within a small community (or several communities) of significant others: this strikes me as the dominant thrust of American civilization during the sixties and seventies. This metaphor of a quest obviously fits the well-publicized case of the therapeutic search for self, whose company, Daniel Yankelovich estimates, had grown to nearly one-fifth of the American working population, or about seventeen million citizens, by the end of the seventies. But it is not confined to this sizable body of people, many members of which are upwardly mobile, relatively young, liberal, college-educated professionals who tend to embrace what Irving Howe has called "the psychology of unobstructed need." Nor do such seekers of the expressed self, however influential, set all of the terms of fulfillment for the 63 percent of working Americans whom Yankelovich believes to be involved less intensely in the quest.[1] The quest, as I imagine it, is rather a multifaceted search conducted with varying degrees of intensity and different specific aims by elements of the population as diverse as born-again Christians and atheistic feminists, gay-rights activists and red-neck males, mainline Protestants and hard-line conservatives. The metaphor of a quest thus permeated American culture so thoroughly that it could not be construed as the property of any single ideological faction or group, whether its members fancied themselves arbiters of the future or guardians of the past. To bring sub-

9

sequent discussions of various, often contradictory manifestations of this quest under minimal control, I have chosen to emphasize two complexly related dimensions of fulfillment: salvation and social justice.

Dimensions of Fulfillment

What must a person do to be saved? This ancient question posed by Nicodemus emerged repeatedly during the sixties and seventies. It cropped up everywhere, from the cultural revolt of Beat artists in the middle fifties to the revival of evangelical and charismatic Christianity belatedly noticed by intellectuals in the middle seventies. The question was evident in the quasi-religious overtones of radical and even much left-liberal activity. It preoccupied exponents of the counterculture. It haunted the secularized therapeutic search for spiritual, mental, and physical wholeness through diet, exercise, meditation, and psychother-apy. Answers ranged from "nothing" to surrender to one god (or idol) or another; they ranged from merely personal effort to collective action—from reform of self and society to revolutionary annihilation of one, the other, or both. Throughout the dense regions of cultural discourse, however, one expectation recurred: the hope, to recall a phrase from the Gospel of John, of a more "abundant life" character-ized by an individual's opportunity to define and enact possibilities of feeling and mind as freely and as fully as possible. In the sixties and seventies, this pervasive desire to realize individual "potential" domi-nated what remained an essentially individualistic culture.

The category of salvation doubtless will seem arcane to those un-believers—and believers—who cling to the notion that the evocative power of religion, especially of religion in the Judeo-Christian tradi-tion, has been exhausted. It is true, of course, that the most vital con-temporary forms of Christianity are less ascetic and frequently less other-worldly than those interpretations that prevailed over most of the first three centuries of American history. This de-emphasis of what Hume termed "the monkish virtues," however, does not signify the demise of Christian vision, only the demise of its ascetic variants. In their popular contemporary forms, Christian notions of salvation have taken on much of the hedonistic and therapeutic cast of secular American culture. Retaining its claim to triumph over death, the idea of salvation also has come to include the promises of temporal self-fulfillment, of release from the seemingly more tractable facets of alienation: from divisions within the self, and from conflict with others, society, nature, and God. Salvation, as I shall use the category, may occur within the world, apart from the world, or in both realms. It may appeal primarily to the authority of Scripture, or, following a strong antinomian tradition in America, to the authority of individual sensibility and conscience.

However unpalatable such beliefs had grown in intellectual and academic circles, variants of the old model of evangelical Protestantism—traditional metaphors and all—were claimed or reclaimed by tens of millions of Americans during the sixties and seventies. Yet for purposes of definition, the extent of literal belief in Christian paths to salvation is not decisive. Indeed, a majority of Americans may dismiss or take lightly the specific symbols of the Christian paradigm of salvation. A majority also may conclude that the model does not deliver all the material and psychic goods its various exponents promise. No matter: during the sixties and seventies the Judeo-Christian metaphor of salvation continued to delineate the outer limits of individual hope and desire in America. For many, it did so in a more or less literal fashion. For a larger number of citizens, it did so in abstract, indirect, and highly metaphorical ways, supplying therapeutic expectations of wholeness and fulfillment historically grounded in theological categories. Thus, in one sense or another, the Judeo-Christian metaphor of salvation informed the personal searches of Pentecostal Christians and adherents of Arthur Janov's primal therapy, of mainline Protestants, of devotees of *est,* and of many political and cultural radicals.

Despite its fundamentally personal and cultural appearance—its focus on personal salvation—the search for self-fulfillment was tied increasingly to a second dimension: the idea of social justice. As the notion of salvation acquired a more secular, even sensuous cast, social components of the quest for self-fulfillment took on ever greater significance. During recent decades, the interpenetration of theological and therapeutic categories of thought pushed expectations of personal fulfillment to ever higher levels. For many people, enlarged psychic expectations were inseparable from rising material and public expectations—expectations of more goods, more services, wider opportunities, ample private space, pleasant public surroundings, more leisure, and a rich mix of cultural offerings. The belief that present affluence would evolve into abundance—that more of everything would become available to everyone—was a staple element of the postwar rhetoric of democracy versus communism. But if the anticipation of material abundance informed American visions of the future in the fifties, sixties, and through a part of the seventies before it became problematic, the idea of personal liberty remained constant: it comprised the core of present conceptions of social justice throughout the postwar period.

Of course, liberty (and the related notion of liberation) serves multiple contexts. Liberty is a crucial dimension of salvation, since fulfilled individuals claim to want freedom in the form of psychological and spiritual wholeness; release from guilt, anxiety, and despair; and community in the form of equality and fraternity in voluntary groups of believers. But psychological and spiritual liberty also presuppose at least the rudiments of personal and political liberty: even the most apolitical of fundamentalist Protestant sectarians acknowledge these as preconditions of their versions of salvation. Moreover, in a nonascriptive society, the notion of personal liberty entails commitment to some version of the idea of equal opportunity (in other words, to the liberty of others). Otherwise, nobody's liberty could be defended plausibly, at least not in instances marked by conflict of interest. Nor could the actual inequalities in the distribution of wealth, income, status, and responsibility be justified—or even convincingly rationalized. Although other, stronger notions of equality—equality of access and equality of result—gained some currency during these years, the concept of equal opportunity remained the common denominator. The belief that each citizen ought to be free to follow intelligence, talent, and affective capacities to the limits of his or her potential—indeed, to decide which potentials ought to be realized and which forgone—informs all popular versions of social justice in America.

In the sixties and seventies, then, *general* (or distributive) conceptions of social justice based on some elaborated synthesis of liberty and equal opportunity for everyone served as an ideal. But less heroic *particular* conceptions of social justice held by individuals and groups served increasingly as animating notions in a flawed world: here the achievement of "my" liberty and "my" equality, as well as the acquisition of liberty and equal opportunity for persons within "my" disadvantaged social category (or categories) dominated individual consciousness. Thus multiple specifications of the meaning and terms of the quest for fulfillment included some mix or other of salvation and a piece of social justice.

The Structure of Disadvantage

What sets the sixties and seventies apart from the fifties (or at least the early and middle fifties) is this: the expanding idea of personal fulfillment was diversified and extended to include significant numbers of citizens within every social category. During these years, sociopolitical categories assumed growing public importance as people sought redress for historical injustices by identifying themselves as members of disadvantaged groups. At the same time, fixed social roles lost much of their authority as individuals sought authentic identities outside of such roles, or at least at a playful distance from them. Living at greater psychic distances from institutions, individuals took up and discarded lightly a greater variety of roles than ever before, even as they assigned decreasing importance to the *idea* of social roles.

A growing assertion of the self through and beyond the many facets of its accidental phenomenal and social appearances characterized these two decades, linking diverse cultural and political attitudes to the general construct of the quest for personal fulfillment. Biological and sociopolitical categories of race, ethnicity, sex, sexual inclination, physical appearance, physical condition, age, religious preference, region, occupation, and social class were challenged actively and discredited as legal and de facto barriers to fulfillment of the self. In the sentimental fiction *Franny and Zooey* (1961), J. D. Salinger's Franny comes to realize that she must learn to love the "Fat Lady," to see the face of Jesus in her. Loving the fat lady—a type of the disadvantaged—remained optional two decades later. For the main advance lay not so much in love, although this, too, was an important if abused keyword in the sixties and seventies: as David Riesman observed, these years witnessed "a rising standard of loving." Progress was expressed primarily in the variety of legal, institutional, and attitudinal changes that enhanced political and cultural rights—the degree of respect individuals command, and the degree of self-respect that they may claim.

The indeterminate equation of fulfillment, then, entailed ever larger measures of social justice. It presupposed, moreover, a growth of cultural pluralism and a corresponding widening of personal options. In the early postwar period, notions of liberty, equality, and fulfillment existed primarily as abstractions for a majority of Americans. In their pure forms they still do, of course, but beginning in the late fifties these abstractions were translated increasingly into diverse, concrete, felt aspirations and demands. It is true that during the forties and fifties economic growth established the context for a rapid democratization of the quest for fulfillment. Between 1940 and 1960 the gross national product rose by a factor of five, from $100 billion to $506 billion, and per capita income climbed from $592 in 1940 to $2216 in 1960.[2] This growth of affluence probably would have established fresh opportunities for millions of Americans even if the structures of inequality had remained intact. It is also true that during the fifties political and legal efforts were made to lower the social and cultural barriers that precluded a majority of Americans from living, or even imagining themselves, as persons with full political and cultural rights: the Supreme Court's school desegregation decision of 1954 (*Brown* v. *Board of Education*) provides an obvious example. But these efforts were weak and scattered by comparison with those of subsequent decades. Moreover, in the fifties, efforts to democratize personhood unfolded within a culture of restricted possibilities. These efforts were launched and pursued within a constellation of power—raw and symbolic—thoroughly dominated and typified by middle-aged white males.

Interpenetrating spheres of economics, politics, and culture reinforced a structure of disadvantage (or advantage) that affected a decisive majority of Americans.[3] I do not have in mind here simply the arrangement of classes, which, in spite of its fluidity, enforces inequalities of wealth, income, status, and power and sets limits on the life chances of groups of Americans from birth. I assume rather that the quest for individual fulfillment can be conducted with reasonable prospects of success within a wide range of material, social, and cultural circumstances. After all, the quest might have gathered momentum in years of affluence, but it also managed to survive expectations of relative scarcity in the seventies. What individuals require minimally is this: a piece of social justice and cultural space that in their view is sufficient to enable them to pursue their disparate images of salvation. By "structure of disadvantage," then, I refer not only to social class, but also—often primarily—to the dominant cultural images and imperatives that hamper citizens in their quest for fulfillment. Even though the American class structure survived the sixties and seventies without undergoing massive changes, the structure of disadvantage, I shall argue, was ameliorated appreciably during these years.

Although it is far from precise, the vague notion of the white Anglo-

Saxon Protestant (WASP) will serve as the representative face of the dominant public culture of the fifties: for typical views and valuations of men, women, and children; youth and age; race and ethnicity; work and leisure; marriage and other states of existence. "Successful" persons usually fit at least a modified version of the WASP male. In the postwar era, "our man," as Peter Schrag describes him, "part Leatherstocking, part Teddy Roosevelt, part John Wayne, with a little Ben Franklin thrown in for good measure—frontiersman, cowboy, soldier, entrepreneur"—had become domesticated and disciplined by the organization. He appeared as an anonymous man in a gray flannel suit.[4] Not quite anonymous, however, for he still was typically white, male, and usually of Anglo-Saxon (or northern European) lineage. He was also, as a rule, middle-aged, married, the father of two children, and, more often than not, at least a nominal mainline Protestant (an Episcopalian, Congregationalist, Presbyterian, or refined Methodist). And he still exercised power and commanded authority, at least at the highest levels, although with rare exceptions he did so without much verve.

These norms and exemplars established a fairly narrow and rigid cultural hierarchy of possibility and success. Public success—usually construed as some combination of economic mobility and status—was considered generally a precondition to fulfillment. Measured against the standard of successful male WASPs, nearly everyone—including such unfortunate WASPs as poor Scotch-Irish-British Southerners— was found wanting, disadvantaged materially and culturally in one respect or another (or in some instances simply vanquished). Although WASP images might have dominated the popular cultural landscape, other groups made real social gains in the fifties, especially those of second- and third-generation European ethnic descent. Both Jews and Catholics made stunning social advances. Jews entered the professions and the academy in large numbers, while continuing to enliven literature and the fine arts. Catholics registered important gains in many areas—in the academy and in business, as well as in politics and government, as the election of John Kennedy in 1960 suggests. Indeed, by the sixties such groups were considered full participants in the dominant white culture by many members of racial minorities who themselves began to demand a larger slice of social justice, a chance to pursue fulfillment on reasonable terms. There was at least some economic truth to such perceptions, but in fact only segments of these ethnic groups had made it to the suburbs. Most of those who had arrived were still breathless from the journey and culturally uneasy.

There also were any number of subcategories in popular conceptions of the dominant WASP cultural hierarchy: the college jock, the blonde sorority girl, the well-to-do suburban wife and mother. But each stereotype occupied a distinctly subordinate place in the American pantheon of public success—either a dead end, as in the case of the housewife, or raw potential, as in the case of the college boy. Beyond these lay the multiple categories of disadvantage, ranging from race, ethnicity, and religion to economic position. These categories of disadvantage overlapped, of course. The more disadvantages an individual accumulated, the greater distance he or she was likely to be from the dominant WASP ideal and the fewer recognized cultural resources he or she possessed in the quest for self-fulfillment.

The Proliferation of Dissent

The traditional WASP fell into partial disfavor during the fifties. And in the sixties and seventies matters grew worse for him and his more commonly observed descendant, the organization man. By the middle fifties, there were visible cracks in the prevailing structure of advantage and disadvantage, cracks that widened in the sixties and seventies. The most publicized version of postwar fulfillment—the white, middle-class pilgrimage to the suburbs—was subject to growing criticism and harsh satire. In the middle to late fifties, one sociologist after another, from David Riesman and C. Wright Mills to William H. Whyte and Vance Packard, catalogued (and caricatured) the anxieties, fears, and feelings of emptiness of successful white males in such works as *The Lonely Crowd* (1953), *White Collar* (1951), *The Organization Man* (1956), and *The Status Seekers* (1959). With the publication of Betty Friedan's *The Feminine Mystique* in 1957, the disappointments of suburban housewives—their failure to experience fulfillment in spite of material advances—came into public view. These signs of distress did not suggest a decline of concern with the quest for identity, to borrow a phrase popular in the fifties: they indicated rather a diffusion—a widening and deepening of interest in the qualities of subjective life.

There were other portents of the quest in these years. Deviants—those rebels without clear causes—began to crop up here and there:

such Beat writers as Gregory Corso, Jack Kerouac, and Allen Ginsberg; comedians like Mort Sahl, the Smothers Brothers, and Lennie Bruce; hipsters and young rebels like James Dean. Rock 'n roll singers like Elvis Presley and Buddy Holly blended black rhythm and blues with country sounds to provide a cultural rallying point for restless teenagers. Moreover, with the emergence of large-scale protest among Southern blacks, the civil-rights movement was energized in the middle fifties. Cultural dissidence of various sorts quickly began to acquire a rough political edge, and vice versa. Music and candles, prayer and incense, recreational drugs and public demonstrations: these symbols and rituals were to lend a richness to the events of the next decades.

In the sixties and seventies, representatives from each of the less privileged categories moved against the prevailing structure of advantage to claim their piece of social justice and to seize their cultural space. To pursue their visions of salvation, they moved—personally, politically, culturally—to clear away contrived biological, social, and cultural obstacles to personal fulfillment. As they did, the hegemony of the public culture of the fifties was shaken, although its main themes persisted in force. It was as though many leading values of the dominant culture, from independence and pluralism to ideas of salvation and social fairness, had been released from the congealed, stereotyped WASP forms they had assumed in the public culture of the fifties. Cultural authority slackened. Ideological pluralism flourished. And the exercise of covert power by large public and private organizations became increasingly difficult. As a consequence of these changes, diverse images of fulfillment, charismatic centers of authority, and supportive subcultures emerged in every corner of society. The multi-faceted quest for fulfillment is most visible in the complicated patterns of dissent and protest that have grown exponentially since the middle fifties. During the sixties and seventies, as expectations of fulfillment rose, everything came to seem to be an obstacle to one group or another. And in a social atmosphere in which the claims of pleasure seriously rivaled those of duty, individuals grew increasingly willing to "make a scene," as Philip Slater puts it. Hence everything—values, attitudes, moods, sensibilities, structures of power, and institutions—came under attack from at least some quarter. Construed in this wide sense, dissent was essential to personal, political, and cultural facets of the quest.

Consider the scope of dissent as it was expressed in the proliferation of social criticism. Although aimed in many directions, the arrows of dissent fell within range of two inclusive and interrelated targets. There was considerable disaffection with various facets of industrial civilization, including science, technology, and the institutions of capitalist political economy: the dominant multinational corporations; big unions; the huge apparatus of the state; the professions; and unresponsive political institutions. By the middle sixties, there also was diffuse opposition to the dominant culture, especially to the thinned-out and confused versions of WASP standards of beauty, taste, morality, leisure, success, work, and sex, as well as to certain WASP patterns of spiritual conduct that survived the fifties. In a word, the postwar ideological shape of liberalism was challenged: its assumptions, values, and even its characteristic sensibility. Both targets—industrial civilization and contemporary culture—were broad. Both evoked a range of opposition and a bewildering variety of responses.

The beginnings triggered by dissent might represent the most important and far-reaching cultural and political legacy of the sixties and seventies. Indeed, dissent became the common denominator, the most visible popular expression of the search for fulfillment. Dissent moved Americans to think and feel in different ways. And it moved significant numbers of them to act. A brief recollection of the foci of protest in the sixties provides some initial sense of the range and essential logic of dissent and protest. Although not all the following groups mobilized their discontent into a coherent political force, individuals within each group were able to find symbolic shapes for their social and spiritual discontents and hopes, partly through public dissent and political action of one sort or another: (1) the civil-rights movement, beginning with blacks but quickly encompassing such other racial minorities as American Indians, Hispanic Americans, and Asian-Americans; (2) the young, especially college students and disaffected intellectuals; (3) the peace and anti-war movements; (4) the poor; (5) women; (6) the human-potential movement; (7) prisoners and other "outcasts"; (8) gays and lesbians; (9) consumers; (10) environmentalists; (11) the old; and (12) the physically different (the disabled, the very fat, the very tall, the very short).[5]

Groups within each of these categories created their own inner histories with distinctive stages of development, intramural conflicts, and ideological schisms. Within each focus, tensions developed between radical and left-liberal perspectives, and later between leftist and conservative dispositions. The radical forces within these various foci of protest were known collectively for a time as "the Movement," an umbrella term covering a range of political and countercultural attitudes and activity. (Chapter 9 contains a fuller discussion of the Movement.) Each group exerted influence in complicated ways, displaying structures of feeling, styles of dissent, and modes of protest that others adopted. Anti-war activists borrowed from the civil-rights movement. The radical wing of the women's movement, which took off in 1967, was inspired largely by the insensitive behavior of leading "revolutionary" men who believed that *their* women ought to serve coffee—and sex—on demand. The gay rights movement of the late sixties and seventies adopted styles of radical dissent. Through such synergistic processes of imitation, repetition, and variation, dissent and protest became dominant forms of cultural behavior during the sixties. In somewhat less dramatic, less well-publicized, and often more personalized ways, dissent and protest remained dominant throughout the seventies.

The overall impact of this activity was a rapid growth of dissent, which took publicly visible forms: criticism, marches, sit-ins, strikes, be-ins, boycotts, local political campaigns, class action suits—making scenes in various settings. Beginning with the civil-rights movement, the patterns of dissent and public protest grew steadily wider, affecting nearly every group in society. They grew deeper, creating what H. L. Nieberg termed a "culture storm" in the late sixties.[6] By the early seventies, the main force of this storm had abated. The idea of a "Movement" had paled, and its extreme cultural and political ideas and styles had faded from sustained public view. In spite of these developments—perhaps largely because of them—the Movement bequeathed a powerful legacy. Its radical countercultural dimensions were diluted and diffused throughout society. And many of its political dimensions persisted, blending into the left wing of the Democratic party, surviving in single-issue causes, and flourishing in community political organizations.

Moreover, leftist political and cultural activity bequeathed another important legacy, albeit an unintended one. It should be remembered that the visible and well-publicized political and cultural facets of the Movement and of left-liberal activity represented only one ideological side of dissent in the sixties and seventies. By the late sixties, elements of the Movement and of the liberal left had played a significant role

in activating other groups outside its amorphous precincts: (1) working-
and middle-class taxpayers (Middle Americans); (2) European ethnic
groups (Poles, Italians, Greeks, Slavs, and Jews); (3) disaffected Catholics; (4) Protestants who, in opposition to the mainline churches, became part of the evangelical and charismatic surge of the seventies;
and (5) neoconservative and New Right intellectuals.[7] These varied
forces were stirred into dissent and protest that survived the seventies
and in no small measure shaped attitudes in those years. They were
not simply reactionaries—ignorant and manipulated obstructers of what
critics on the left regarded as the only acceptable paths toward the future. Most of them, rather, were serious participants in political and
cultural life. They both complicated and further democratized the
quest for fulfillment by staking their own claims to a piece of social
justice and their own cultural space. In doing so, they ensured that the
near-term American future would be informed by older values as well
as by newly popular ones. Weighing and testing each proposed social
idea—from cohabitation to racial tolerance—the American majority,
so frequently dismissed by critics as culturally irrelevant or retrograde,
largely determined which notions would survive their fleeting moment
of fashion.

The Impact of the Quest

Radical challenge and conservative (frequently reactionary) response:
this is the tidiest ideological pattern of the sixties and seventies, the
one critics on the left most often lament. Although useful to a point,
this schema is finally too simple. During the sixties and seventies,
there occurred several overlapping ideological episodes: a rise and
rapid decline of marginal radical political perspectives; a growth, diffusion, and dilution of radical cultural perspectives; an ascendance
and partial eclipse of left-liberal outlooks from the early sixties through
the late seventies; and a swift growth of neoconservative and New
Right perspectives in the late sixties and seventies. None of these ideological episodes was conclusive, although some observers have claimed—
dubiously, I think—that the election of Ronald Reagan in 1980 represented a decisive moment in a long-term turn to the right. During
these decades, political change in America did not follow the lead of
any single ideological formulation. Every group and every ideological
tendency experienced fragmentary losses, reversals, and disappoint-

ments, as well as fitful gains. No group realized its particular vision of social justice (indeed, no group—blacks, white ethnics, Hispanics, women—held to a single view). During these years, the structure of disadvantage was both ameliorated and enlarged. Standards of personal dignity and personal rights rose. And economic, political, social, cultural, and psychological barriers to the achievement of one version or another of fulfillment fell, although not rapidly enough, evenly enough, or far enough to satisfy new, and newly democratized expectations.

Although they are important, ideological triumphs and reversals reveal only a part of the political and cultural story of America in the sixties and seventies. Dissent not only affected people in every part of the spectrum of American political ideology. It penetrated the regions of culture and personality—of individual consciousness—to such an extent that large numbers of citizens acquired the habit of dissent or at least exercised it with increasing frequency. The explosion of personal dissent greatly intensified cultural syncretism—the simultaneous presence of old and new, right and left, dominant and subordinate values and culture habits. In turn, this "mingling of strange gods," to borrow Daniel Bell's apt phrase, energized, enriched, and democratized the quest for personal fulfillment. This interplay of apparent opposites further pluralized and fragmented the cultural atmosphere in which the quest unfolded. Individuals sought identity and fulfillment by picking and choosing from among the ideological and cultural detritus of the culture storm. Even though traditional practices persisted, often in fragmentary forms, traditional modes of authority withered. Everyone had to compose his or her own story: autobiography threatened to displace history as a dominant way of making sense of things. Thus, by the middle seventies it was not impossible to run across "selective" Catholics who felt themselves exempt from Papal authority; radical lesbian Episcopal priests; politically radical Pentecostals; Jewish feminists defending the orthodox practice of ritual bathing (the *micvah*) as a means of preserving personal autonomy.

The semipublic sphere of domestic life was also reshaped in the sixties and seventies. Traditional options persisted, of course. It was still possible to graduate from college at twenty-one; marry after a year or two; become a wife, mother, and homemaker, or a husband, father, and worker (a "provider"). But this pattern no longer was dominant; it ceased to serve as the standard against which people in other circumstances had to be judged deviant. By the end of the seventies, options had widened considerably. It was culturally acceptable in many circles to skip college or to postpone it indefinitely; to remain unmarried or to marry and refrain from having children; or to marry and, after a few years, divorce (and in most cases, remarry). Indeed, the number of households composed either of individuals living alone or with others to whom they are not related grew dramatically between 1960 and 1980, as did single-parent households: together, these comprised 40 percent of American households by the end of the seventies. In the sixties and seventies, the bland configuration of Father, Mother, Dick, Jane, and Sally—those stick figures of school texts of the thirties, forties, and fifties—ceased to embody emerging norms.[8]

Rapid, disorienting, and confused changes accompanied and facilitated the quest for personal fulfillment during these decades. But the quest neither destroyed American culture nor immobilized American politics. The mixed American economic system survived. The political system continued to function, although it had become more complicated and unwieldy during these years. And the essential constituents of American ideology persisted, however severely they were tested by the proliferation of dissent, the growth of ideological pluralism, and the spread of cultural syncretism. By the end of the seventies, the three dominant facets of the bourgeois tradition—radical, liberal, conservative—had been questioned widely.[9] But in spite of challenges and substantial revisions—moments of promise and moments of defeat—these facets endured. They continued to function within the context of the central American ideological tradition, which is based on various mixes of personal liberty and equal opportunity.

The complicated patterns of dissent were formed mainly by the diverse aims of personal fulfillment as these were subjected to a variety of pressures: to the vagaries of international forces, the constraints of American ideology and American institutions, and, in the seventies, to declining expectations of abundance. As a consequence of these pressures and changes, the definitions and ratios of "salvation" and "social justice" were in constant flux. But these shifts, I argue in subsequent chapters, formed part of an overall direction: namely, a progressive democratization of personhood in America. As expressions of the many-sided quest for fulfillment, dissent and protest energized a largely irreversible, interactive pattern of cultural and political shifts that established fresh opportunities and fresh perils for self-definition and self-fulfillment.

However much one might wish it otherwise, judgments of gains in the quest for fulfillment finally are partial, matters of reasoned opinion. They depend upon qualitative assessments of the social and cultural costs of gains, as well as upon comparative assessments of expectations and achievements. Not everyone began the quest with the same advantages, the same hopes, or the same expectations. Nor did everyone come through the seventies ahead of the game, however they understood and defined the rules. Even at the end of the decade, millions of citizens had to deal with the quest at or almost below the elemental point of economic and, in some cases, physical survival. No doubt millions of others felt that they had barely weathered those years or had lost ground in one or more departments of their lives. In fact, since cultural gains outstripped the expansion of social roles, political participation, and economic opportunity, millions of individuals had to define fulfillment beyond, and against, previously accepted categories. Despite trials and defeats that plagued every individual and group, however, life for many Americans within each disadvantaged category, from blacks and women to gays and the handicapped, was more various, more full of possibility at the end of the seventies than it had been in the quieter, more stable middle fifties. This strikes me as the relevant mode of comparison, the most useful way to gauge short-term progress in the quest for fulfillment.

Such progress left traces in the impersonal tables of survey research. As Joseph Veroff, Elizabeth Douvan, and Richard A. Kulka suggest in their study *The Inner American: A Self-Portrait from 1957 to 1976,* "there has been a shift from a *socially* integrated paradigm for structuring well-being, to a more *personal* or *individuated* paradigm for structuring well-being." To substantiate this shift, the authors note three types of changes in "people's responses to questions of their well-being and coping styles: (1) the diminution of role standards as the basis for defining adjustment; (2) increased focus on self-expressiveness and self-direction in social life; (3) a shift in concern from social organizational integration to interpersonal intimacy."[10]

The salutary signs of the quest are even more evident in the eloquent testimony of distinct voices. In a poignant recollection of the postwar years, Marge Piercy observes that she "could not grow anywhere but through the cracks. I was," she continues, "not *for* anyone, my work burped in a void. I learned survival but also alienation, hostility, craziness, schizophrenia. Not until the slow opening of the sixties was I able to think I might begin to cease to be a victim, an internal exile, a madwoman." As the period unfolded, Piercy experienced "beatings, gassings, danger, repression, fear, separation, demands, condemnation, physical collapse, overwork, exhaustion, petty bickerings, factional fights, fanaticism . . ." Yet through it all Piercy discovered an enhanced sense of possibility, a chance to connect with other women and hence an opportunity to explore facets of herself that probably would have lain dormant or been stunted in the absence of the collective patterns of dissent and the emerging countercultural communities that marked the sixties and seventies. The "slow opening" of the sixties enlarged her sense of what she might become: "I might become an adult," Piercy realized. "I might become useful, I might speak and be heard, listen and receive . . . I might live in a community, however tacky and bleak at times, however scattered and faddish. I might conceive of my living and my working as a project forward in a struggle, however long and difficult and unlikely, tending toward a more humane society."[11]

Antecedents and Causes of the Quest

In the chapters ahead, I concentrate on cultural similarities between the sixties and the seventies, on the ways in which the quest for fulfillment and gains in the democratization of personhood marked both decades. My selection of the middle to late fifties as the moment of origin of, or rather as the point of transition to, this important episode in American civilization is to some extent arbitrary. Since this delineation of the postwar era may suggest a skewed view of differences between the sixties and seventies and what went before, it is worth recalling the obvious: neither the quest for fulfillment nor its democratization began in the sixties, or even in the middle to late fifties. The story covers several centuries of Western experience. "At a certain point in history," Lionel Trilling observes in his elegant study *Sincerity and Authenticity* (1972), "men became individuals." Of course, people had acquired consciousness of themselves as separate entities long before the early Renaissance. But this more recent historical juncture, which Trilling, following Durkheim, has in mind, defines the transition to modern senses of the difficult notion of the self, especially the many modes of self-consciousness. Before this, Trilling reminds us, people were not particularly attentive to "internal space." Lacking much psychological versatility, they did not imagine themselves "in more than one role, standing outside or above . . . their own personality." And they did not regard individuals as intrinsically interesting—automatically of consequence by virtue of their mere existence. Moreover, at least since the Industrial Revolution, there has been rapid if uneven social progress in the democratization of the idea and the reality of personhood, beginning with the stunning prolongation of life and the multiple opportunities for self-definition and expression it has created.

The contours of the quest do not appear only in the large structures of history: they are visible in the smaller textures, which also reveal important continuities. Although the emergence of the most recent phase of the black civil-rights movement in the middle fifties, for example, seemed dramatic—and was—it too represented but one moment in an odyssey whose beginnings were evident as early as the 1830s. Leaders of the NAACP had decided on the need for a politics of mass pressure several years before the Montgomery bus boycott supplied the spark in 1956. And from the Niagara Movement in the early years of this century, black civil-rights advocates have pressed their cause in a variety of public ways. Indeed, the many foci of protest—from blacks and women to consumers and taxpayers—embody variations of this theme. All have identifiable roots in the American, and Western, past. All display seemingly interrupted histories, moments of high drama, significant success (and failure), as well as times of quiet, subterranean existence.

In one sense, then, the episode of the sixties and seventies represents a continuation and partial fulfillment of earlier hopes and struggles. In this view, the early to middle fifties can be seen also as a pause or at least as a moment of relatively slow, unpublicized movement in the democratization of personhood. These years seem somewhat sluggish when recollected against the rapid cultural and social advances registered in the ensuing decades. Faced with a choice of emphasis, then, I have elected to explore continuities between the sixties and seventies, to consider these years as an essentially coherent cultural episode. I have done so not only because the continuities seem most significant but also because social critics who overstress differences between these decades usually minimize or obscure what strikes me as clear progress in the prospects for individual fulfillment.

If the existence of historical antecedents to the quest is clear, the problem of causation remains elusive. I do not advance a theory that purports to explain why the sixties and seventies should have witnessed such an intensification and democratization of the quest. A number of factors that must figure in such an explanation, however, were beginning to coalesce in the late fifties. The growth of affluence was central: it enabled ever larger numbers of people to take themselves seriously, to make a sustained project of the ordinary self. Affluence raised living standards, permitted an extension of educational opportunity, increased the time available for leisure, and facilitated occupational, geographical, and psychic mobility. By the postwar period, the long-term shift from a primarily agricultural to an essentially bureaucratic, service economy (via a major phase of industrialization) had led to significant changes in the occupational structure. As the processing of people and of information became central activities in the work place, individuals concentrated more than ever on understanding themselves and others, if often only in superficial ways.

The expanding advertising and consumer culture and the accompanying proliferation of media, especially television and stereophonic sound, reinforced notions of self-gratification and self-fulfillment in the here and now. Much of the rhetoric of domestic consumption centered on low-level appeals to self-indulgence—exhortations to "treat yourself." And much of it was aimed at associating particular products with improved personal appearance, health, and hygiene and greater versatility in one or another social role. Of course, quality-of-life issues had grown increasingly popular in the twenties. Although they persisted through the thirties and forties, the Depression intervened, and the pent-up consumer demand throughout World War II delayed full elaboration of the consumer culture until the late fifties and sixties.[12]

A variety of political factors also came together in the middle fifties. As the first Manichaean phase of the cold war ended after 1956, with the Soviet exposé of Stalin, the idea of self-denial for national defense lost much of its rhetorical edge. At the same time, America needed to appeal to the nonwhite majorities of developing nations. The requirements of foreign policy encouraged amelioration of the harshest domestic patterns of racism, prompting an official effort by the state to extend the minimal promises of personhood to blacks and other racial minorities. From the time of the New Deal, of course, fitful domestic progress registered in the struggle for extended economic, political, and cultural rights of working people resulted in steadily rising standards of personal dignity, albeit often only partially realized ones. Once begun, the practice of claiming full political and cultural rights took on a synergistic life of its own. There was no logical place for the quest to stop, no group willing to accept exclusion, or perhaps I should say no group willing to accept exclusion gracefully. The vague outlines of the political and cultural agendas of the sixties and seventies, then, were visible by the late fifties.

Any number of other cultural factors contributed to the quest. The most important ones, I suspect, were instances of the partial breakdown of older norms of self-denial. Child rearing became more intensive and more permissive, at least among educated people; traditional educational standards slackened. In both cases, discipline was relaxed by mutual consent: such arrangements made life easier (at least for a time) for subordinates *and* for authorities. Of course, fulfillment through subordination of the self to other people (children, husband, parents, friends, students) or to larger organizations and causes (the office, the union, the war effort, the church) remained possible, even usual, in the seventies. By the middle fifties, however, these roles had begun to seem less necessary and less inviting to increasing numbers of Americans of various ages. Moreover, such modes of self-denial violated the principal hedonistic imperatives of a consumer society. And they conflicted with the rhetoric employed by many people in the helping professions (educators, social workers, therapists). Under these circumstances, enhancement of the self—any self—became the cultural norm.

By the late fifties, then, the social stage was set for the drama of self-fulfillment that unfolded in the sixties and seventies. Although their weight and causal significance are by no means obvious, these related economic, political and cultural factors lent renewed energy to the old rhetoric of individualism, democracy, and fulfillment in these decades. There was a greater willingness on the part of Americans to make a scene and to make their own scenes: to engage in dissent and to create patterns of culture; to refuse inherited institutions and precast roles, and to widen and deepen their subjective space.

Parts of my central argument should be digested effortlessly, though
the whole of it, I suspect, may be rejected by a good many critics
and historians. Indeed, it has become a commonplace of criticism
to note the mixed economic, political, cultural, and personal gains
registered by substantial numbers of Americans in the overlapping
categories that comprise what I have called the structure of disadvantage. Acknowledgments of the salutary effects of one or another
facet of the quest are scattered throughout the body of American
social and cultural criticism. Typically, however, these limited acknowledgments are advanced grudgingly, as concessions or caveats that allow
a few bright streaks onto otherwise dark canvases of disappointed
hopes and unmet expectations. I argue rather that the quest for fulfillment constituted the central metaphor of American civilization in the
sixties *and* in the seventies; that this quest embodied and linked
personal salvation and a slice of social justice as inextricable aspects of
each other; and finally that this quest yielded stunning successes
evidenced in the widening and deepening of personhood and in an
enlargement of cultural space.

The chapters in Part I, "Defining the Framework of Nostalgia,"
outline the reasons why most American social and cultural critics
resist the main position I have sketched out, and especially why so
many of them resisted it with growing intensity as the seventies
wore on.

The chapters in Part II, "Searching for Fulfillment," take up my
characterization of the quest in a more detailed fashion. In these chapters I trace the principal shapes of the quest. I delineate the role of
dissent in assaults on the structure of disadvantage. And I assess the
main personal and social impact of dissenting modes of the quest
under the rubric of the democratization of personhood.

The chapters in Part III, "Misreading the Signs," explore what
strikes many people as the deficit side—the alleged links to the quest
of the much-discussed rise of selfishness and narcissism, and the corresponding intensification of a long-term decline of nearly all sorts of
authority. Both selfishness and an erosion of many modes of authority
are evident, of course. The difficult questions here, as elsewhere, come
down to reasoned judgments concerning the causes, extent, social
effects, and cultural significance of these phenomena. Both selfishness
and a degree of anomie, I believe, are largely unavoidable byproducts
of the quest for fulfillment. Both have been exaggerated by social and

cultural critics, often wildly so. And though both exact a social cost, neither commands anything like a fatal one. In the sixties and seventies at least, the main effects of the quest—the personal successes registered by millions of people and the democratization of personhood—far outweighed what I term, with deliberate prejudice, the untoward individual and social "side effects." Selfishness and anarchy simply amount to extreme instances of more salutary trends. In fact, I argue that certain modes of selfishness—or what might better be termed concerns with the self—and transformations of the locus, character, and intensity of authority are signs of the quest, evidence of its considerable success.

The Epilogue provides a retrospective glance at the main argument from the vantage point of the early eighties (after the election of Ronald Reagan) and contains a few speculative comments on the probable course of the quest for fulfillment in the years ahead.

An Autobiographical Note

Before getting on to the main sections of this book, let me add a brief autobiographical word. Although *America's Quest for the Ideal Self* continues a set of explorations into facets of American politics and culture begun more than ten years ago, it gives these probes a somewhat different focus. *Radical Paradoxes* (1973) and *Crooked Paths* (1977) were concerned primarily with understanding the spectrum of contemporary American ideology, especially its left bands. *Radical Paradoxes* illuminated the dead ends of utopian variants of communist vision from the perspective of a democratic socialism tinged with temperamental if not cultural conservatism. *Crooked Paths* surveyed American ideology, from communism (small *c*) to neoconservatism, in the light of the transition from relative affluence and the expectation of abundance to the onset of relative scarcity in the early seventies, a transition that changed the terms, prospects, and interrelationships of the major ideological formulations. I used democratic socialism as a touchstone, though in that instance less as an article of ideological faith than as a critical vantage point. And I placed heavier emphasis on conservative personal and cultural dimensions in my sketch of the crooked path of conservative democratic socialism.

To some extent, I suppose, I had simply drifted away from my earlier identification with a socialist vision of society which, due to my age and ideological lineage, was rooted in leading assumptions of the old Left rather than in the new radicalism of the sixties. I was not so much disillusioned (though this too) by the absence of a mature and significant American left in the seventies as I was increasingly convinced that the project of the socialist left was misconceived and in important senses overrated. The aim of social transcendence—the wish to replace one social system with another through political means—came to seem both impossible and in some senses undesirable, as it always had in sober moments. More important, perhaps, such a project struck me as an unnecessarily confining articulation of the egalitarian impulse that animates many sectors of the left—related perhaps to the achievement of a decent life, but surely not identical with it.

Such a turn of conviction, tardy as it was, led me in *Crooked Paths* to reconsider the value of liberal and conservative perspectives on American life, to insist on the need to recombine these disparate materials inherited from the past into a refracted vision of the present and near future. Ideologically deconstructed, or perhaps merely confused, I reverted to a more primitive intellectual state, giving a freer rein to a number of internalized impulses that contribute to formulations on both sides of the spectrum and in the middle as well. I did not lose faith in the egalitarian project, though I did, along with so many others, become skeptical about the capacity of the liberal state to advance this project justly and efficiently. Having rejected radical transcendence, I returned to a liberal branch of the Christian church, in spite of a Pentecostal heart, a Roman Catholic heritage, and a stubbornly skeptical sensibility. Wary of liberal efforts at reform, I began to explore libertarian sentiments that fit well with a long-standing personal distrust of certain modes of authority, but I did not pursue these into the political regions of the New Right, needless to say. By the middle seventies, then, I had moved away from leftward-leaning ideology although not away from leftward impulses or even from an essentially left-liberal politics. And I had lost faith in the supremacy of politics, although not in its high importance, in arranging the circumstances of a decent social life.

My interests thereafter widened from political ideology and politics to include the spheres of culture and subjectivity, again a familiar pattern among intellectuals in the seventies, as it had been in the forties and fifties. As I stopped trying to take the measure of American culture and society against some imagined socialist future, I began to see different shapes in the present. I came to appreciate not merely the various ideological strains, but even more the wonderfully rich, albeit cacaphonic possibilities for personal expression and democratic action that marked American culture by the late seventies. The ideology of the quest strikes me not only as central to American experience, permeating most articulations of native left, center, and right perspectives on politics and shaping attitudes about politics in general: this ideology also seems to me on the whole defensible, if not altogether admirable. Of course, I do not dwell exclusively on cultural matters: as I have said, the widening and deepening of subjectivity in the sixties and seventies required a vast economic transformation that began in the late nineteenth century, as well as a multifaceted politics—ordinary party politics, special-interest group politics, and an extraordinary politics of protest. And in this process, elements of the left, even some leftists bound to rigid views, made significant contributions. So did members of various American elite groups, including academics, intellectuals, and journalists. But these were not the only important voices: in a modern context, traditional positions became a matter of choice, a familiar though nonetheless important paradox.

In subsequent chapters I emphasize that the quest—the search for salvation and a slice of social justice—was pursued by nearly all elements of the population, elite and nonelite, leftist and left-liberal, and others on the right. Though much of what newly articulate people have had to say—about religion, culture, morality, politics, and economics—rubs me the wrong way, I consider the widening of subjectivity and the democratization of personhood gains of overriding importance. I find, for example, the Moral Majority preferable to silence, barely so at times, but preferable nonetheless if only because it allows a voice to many who never have spoken publicly or even endorsed the public pronouncements of others. Similarly, I find most specifications of the quest offered by women on the whole reasonable, despite the range of conflicting positions, from Marxist lesbian separatists to traditional homemakers. There are limits, to be sure: for example, feminist separatists must remain a minority if civilization is to survive. And members of the so-called Moral Majority must remain a minority if the rest of us are not to be bored to death. But these limits, I believe, ought not to be narrow.

Thus, I have tried to sustain what seems to me central—namely, the vision of the quest—without concealing my own particular views: to be inclusive about a range of reasonable alternatives without representing them as equally preferable. Such an effort requires a continuous juggling of contraries. Although this practice is voluntary, I suspect that it represents an expression of my own half-ethnic, half-native American heritage. At least, given my own syncretic background, it has proved the most convenient way to proceed. The case presented in these pages resists anything like a proof, but I hope to have set it out with sufficient clarity and representative illustration to make it intriguing. My effort is in the nature of a preliminary interpretation of the sixties and seventies, rather than a history of American civilization in these decades. It is, I trust, a useful way of re-viewing certain features of the recent past from an unremarkable angle of vision that, through steady and often stubborn use, may yield something of the neglected truth about these difficult and hopeful years.

I

Defining the Framework of Nostalgia

Too much questioning and too little active responsibility lead, almost as often as too much sensualism does, to the edge of the slope, at the bottom of which lie pessimism and the nightmare or suicidal view of life.

WILLIAM JAMES
"Is Life Worth Living?"

Intellectuals in the twentieth century have . . . found themselves engaged in incompatible efforts: they have tried to be good and believing citizens of a democratic society and at the same time to resist the vulgarization of culture which that society constantly produces. It is rare for an American intellectual to confront candidly the unresolvable conflict between the elite character of his own class and his democratic aspirations.

RICHARD HOFSTADTER
Anti-Intellectualism in American Life

3

The Seventies
versus
the Sixties

The idea of any decade, as everyone acknowledges, does not fit its historical chronology with any precision: "the sixties," for example, have their thematic and social origins somewhere in the middle fifties, and according to many accounts do not "end" until the early seventies. However skillfully it is employed and qualified, the convenient fiction of decade rhetoric structures historical vision by means of a series of contrasts. As Harvey Gross remarks in an essay on American poetry of the sixties, "our eye seems guided by the mysterious authority of the decade, by that fiction which identifies a change in sensibility—if not a scheduled apocalypse—every ten years."[1] Other points of contrast are associated frequently with the decades of twentieth-century American history. For example, ideological contrasts roughly fit the parade of decades. In a painfully oversimple way, the teens, the thirties, and the sixties might be classified as periods of heightened liberal and leftist activity, and the twenties, the fifties, and the seventies recalled as times of vaguely conservative ascendance. No serious historian or critic pushes such associations too hard. Nor does anyone deliberately assign intrinsic meaning to the chronological artifact of the decade. Still, the increasingly popular rhetorical structure of decadism (a term I shall not repeat) disposes critics to emphasize disjunctures and to neglect or minimize continuities.

"Nobody," declared a *Time* editorial published in the summer of

1979, "is apt to look back on the 1970s as the good old days."[2] As a piece of speculation, this assertion seems dubious. Before the quick rise and wide diffusion of nostalgic appreciations of "the sixties," it will be recalled, there were many jeremiads, so many in fact that the appearance of Charles Reich's naïve *The Greening of America* in 1970 was something of an anomaly. Etiological metaphors of "the sick society" littered left-wing criticism of the period. And in the late sixties, neo-conservatives like Norman Podhoretz and Lewis Feuer devoted considerable energy to sharp critiques of contemporary political and cultural radicals who, they seemed to believe, threatened the moral foundations of American civilization. Judging from this recent historical experience, I think it is reasonable to assume that the seventies will acquire at least a small company of defenders, especially if the grim intimations of the eighties expressed by certain critics should come to pass, or seem to.

Editorials in *Time,* however, need only survive the week's events. On this count, the statement cannot be faulted: it conveys a sense of the widespread pessimism about the state of American affairs that marked public discourse at the end of the seventies. Intellectuals from every point on the ideological spectrum judged the seventies an unattractive time. They did not bother to ask *whether* this decade was bleak, only in what senses and why. Negative perceptions of American culture and politics permeated the cultural apparatus, from such journals as *Partisan Review, Dissent, The New Republic, Salmagundi, National Review, Commentary,* and *The New York Review of Books* to the middlebrow regions of *Time* and *Newsweek* and even to the subliterate pages of *The Star* and *The National Enquirer.* A similar lack of enthusiasm for the American seventies pervaded the electronic media, especially in the closing years of the decade.

There are, to be sure, obvious reasons for such hypercritical judgments that must figure in any account of them. For one thing, the genre of social criticism itself enforces a bias toward negative views of the present—any present. And endings, especially of millennia or centuries, but even endings of such reified and arbitrary entities as decades, evoke a certain blend of anxiety, fatigue, and expectation. More important, no doubt, the seventies seemed particularly bleak because in many ways they were. Americans were chastened by a steady accumulation of unpleasant social facts, from the costly military defeat in Southeast Asia and the subsequent erosion of United States global power and prestige to energy shortages and impending scarcities of other nonrenewable resources. The mounting list of major and minor social problems seemed endless. Old problems persisted, and new ones took shape: apocalypse, the nuclear arms buildup suggested, had been wrenched from divine control and made possible by human arrangement. Selfishness, narcissism, and incivility appeared to be on the rise. Respect for authority and participation in public spheres appeared to be in decline. Even the salutary changes that many critics discounted, including a healthy proliferation of social criticism itself, augmented anxiety and disappointment, adding to an already rich stock of reasons for debunking the seventies.

In spite of all this, one is tempted to say that in certain ways the seventies improved upon the sixties. Such a claim is not simply perverse, though it is not one I should wish to press very far. Following the withdrawal from Vietnam in 1975, Americans did not fight abroad during this decade. The seventies was a period of comparative domestic peace and of relative prosperity, despite the deep recession of 1974–75, unmistakable signs of another in 1979, and the emergence of what may turn out to be a reasonably protracted period of economic dislocation and even decline. Life expectancy, which had increased by twenty years in this century, continued to lengthen: since 1950, life expectancy has increased by more than five years, from 68.2 years at birth to 73.8 (1979), an astonishing gain; and by the end of the seventies, three of four women who reached age sixty-five could expect to live another ten years.

I do not wish to paint a counterportrait of this period, but rather to suggest the availablity of sufficient materials from which essentially flattering or damning social portraits of both decades—the sixties *and* the seventies—could be drawn. Not everyone, it should be remembered, recalled the sixties in a haze of nostalgia. Recollecting these years, which Richard Rovere judged "a slum of a decade" and Richard Hofstadter dubbed an "Age of Rubbish," Meg Greenfield observes that "a time of so much terrible carnage—the death of Kennedy, the death of King, the police wars in the ghettos, the savagery of Tet, of My Lai—just does not qualify for me as a golden age of anything."[3] The business of social portraiture, this is to say, is wide open. As Arnold Rogow put it, "the supreme difficulty facing any interpreter of life in America is that almost any statement he wishes to make about the United States he can show to be at least half true."[4] If

Rogow's claim is roughly accurate—and I think it is—why was there such an imbalance of critical views at the end of the seventies? The question is in two parts. Why did American social critics register nearly universal dissatisfaction with the political shapes and cultural forms of the seventies? And why did so many of them—especially radicals and those on the liberal left—also express nostalgia for "the sixties" (or for some earlier moment of American history)?

No single answer can cover the varied activities of American social and cultural critics. Each critic submits different reasons, or different mixes of the same reasons, in support of qualified enthusiasm for the sixties and grim responses to the seventies. So do the loose associations of critics clustered along the main points on the continuum of American ideology. Despite the perils of premature historical generalization, I should like to suggest that disappointment and anxiety lie at the center of nostalgic readings of the sixties and excessively somber readings of the seventies: no longer committed to Judeo-Christian views of history which informed our civil religion, many intellectuals who commented on the American scene lacked even a perversely satisfying sense of certain, ultimate doom. Disappointed at the fate of their earlier visions, depressed by their perceptions of the present, and anxious about the future, American social critics became more nostalgic than usual as the seventies wore on. Many radicals and left liberals recalled "the sixties," or rather some cultural or political phase of that decade. Most conservatives looked to a more distant bourgeois past. And such Tory radicals as Christopher Lasch lamented the passing of radical possibilities that allegedly haunted that bourgeois past. In the remaining chapters of Part I, I examine the ways in which radical, left-liberal, and neoconservative critics constructed this framework of nostalgia. Before considering these ideological configurations serially, however, I want to sketch the main contours of the mood of nostalgia that informed much American criticism in the seventies.

The contrasting perspectives on these decades, I believe, arose in large part from a convergence of unfulfilled ideological hopes and frequently disappointed personal expectations that critics formulated in the sixties (or earlier). In the late seventies, critics from each major facet of the bourgeois tradition—radical, liberal, and conservative—recalled the failure, or the perceived failure, of their projected resolutions of economic, political, and cultural issues. A range of critics on the political and cultural left looked back to what many of them considered the central domestic event of these two decades: the radical Movement of the sixties. Some of them regretted its early directions; most of them lamented its decline in the seventies (or at least its failure to generate a mature politics of the left). Similarly, left liberals such as Arthur Schlesinger, Jr. remembered the Kennedy–Johnson years as their principal moment of hope in the postwar era—or at least as a moment of high domestic hope. Even formerly left-wing critics such as Daniel Bell, who found the adversary counterculture of the sixties "nihilistic" and the politics of radicals too contentious for their acquired neoconservative tastes, considered the late fifties and early sixties to have been a time of comparative innocence.

Toward the end of the seventies, social critics of all ideological backgrounds rushed to claim defeat. And they did so with some justification. Radicals and left liberals were convinced that the neoconservatives and, more importantly, the "reactionary" forces of the New Right, had registered major political and cultural victories. Neoconservatives contended that their own version of a left-wing "new class" of self-serving public servants had scored disturbing gains, probably irreversible ones. Although the welfare state itself survived and grew, nearly everyone considered the *ideology* of welfare-state liberalism moribund, even prior to the Republican victory in 1980. In no mood to forgo their own personal benefits derived from the welfare state, large numbers of Americans nevertheless were increasingly opposed to its size, clumsiness, impersonality, intrusiveness, and wastefulness. Deeply and probably unresolvably ambivalent about the state, many Americans found other temporal perspectives inviting. Under such circumstances, the habit of envisioning contemporary developments through the screens of past preferences spread. And it virtually ensured the jeremaic tone of much social criticism at the end of the seventies: compared with some past moment (often only an imagined one), the present seemed bleak and the future perhaps even more bleak than the present.

The personal and partisan sources of disappointment contributed importantly to the cheerless mood of public discourse at the end of the seventies. But the mood of pessimism represented more than the sum of disparate disappointments. It was synergized by the absence of a clear ideological and political winner in the seventies. Had such a group, coalition, class, or ideological tendency emerged, the losers would have had at least the consolation of a direction to oppose, as they did by the early years of the eighties. As it turned out, no group was satisfied, which is to say that nearly everyone was dissatisfied, affected by a suspicion of national drift rather than a perception of clear if misguided direction. "In the late seventies," as Michael Harrington observed, "the people of the United States were moving vigorously to the Left, the Right, and the Center, all at the same time."[5] If they did not move in these directions with anything like equal determination, they at least were proceeding along different paths. Cultural syncretism persisted. And an ideological pluralism of sorts had triumphed. As a consequence, no neat relation obtained between any received vision and power. Ironically, the political and cultural gains registered during the sixties and seventies by people within the various categories of disadvantage contributed significantly to what many judged a political stalemate. American politics was neutralized by a vast interplay of interests, which prevented decisive action against mounting national problems such as inflation, faltering productivity, energy, unemployment, housing, and urban deterioration. After the 1980 elections, of course, the New Right appeared to be the strongest recognizable ideological tendency, and several pundits proclaimed the advent of a firm and salutary direction for American foreign and domestic policy under President Reagan. Despite a major electoral victory, however, the divided forces of the new conservatism did not appear able to construct and enact lucid policies that commanded the strong allegiance of anything resembling a majority of Americans.

At the end of the seventies, then, the recent past of the sixties seemed distant and in many ways attractive. The present condition of the American economy, polity, and culture struck many critics as relentlessly depressing, especially so as it was represented through the verbal shorthand of social commentary and the visual compression of television and documentary film images. Both sorts of codes, which abstract the variety of American life and pile one catastrophe upon another, usually make matters appear worse than they are: "The actual texture of our daily activities," Michael Novak reminds us, "is not well represented by most of the theories about us, whether voiced by friend or foe."[6]

Even the future—that *deus ex machina* of the American enterprise—

appeared to offer little relief. Of course, anxiety about the American future was not new. Although they had been present as a persistent theme from the seventeenth-century prophecies of John Winthrop through the laments of Henry Adams, such misgivings began to permeate the intellectual community like a low-grade fever in the years before World War I. As Henry F. May observes in his elegant study *The End of American Innocence* (1959), a fundamental change in the perspective of many American intellectuals was beginning to take form during these years—a deliquescence of optimism, doubts about the notion of progress, and a rejection of idealism.[7] Although the labored mid-Victorian optimism of, say, an Edward Bellamy was impossible to sustain after World War I, a sense of confidence in the future of American civilization did persist among intellectuals through much of this century, except perhaps for a brief interlude of intellectual exhaustion in the late teens and twenties.[8]

In the thirties, the vague and for the most part sentimental Marxism popular among a significant minority of American intellectuals was informed by a confident view of a socialist future that would redeem the seedy capitalist present. And in the late thirties, a majority of American critics, who never turned to Marxism, also believed that the essential lines of the future could be drawn rationally within an evolving democratic capitalist framework. Commenting on a collection of thirty-six essays on the condition of American civilization published in 1938, Allan Nevins concluded that in spite of its impressive variety of views, the book "holds proof in almost every chapter of an undaunted American optimism. This optimism is at bottom the sense of promise in American life which has been noted by almost every foreign writer, which gave title to Herbert Croly's book, and which shines in Franklin D. Roosevelt's latest utterances."[9]

Derived from our peculiar blend of Judeo-Christian theology and civil religion, this sense of promise, which was shared by intellectuals and their primary audiences drawn from the educated middle classes, persisted during the patriotic years of World War II. And it survived in somewhat cooler versions thereafter. In the relatively satisfied and quiescent, if fitfully anxious and hysterical fifties, and through the middle sixties—years in which a broad liberal consensus governed intellectual and political life—social commentators maintained a quiet faith in the promise of American life. During what C. Wright Mills sarcastically termed "the Great American celebration," liberal and conservative intellectuals from David Riesman and David Potter to Richard Hofstadter and even to so deeply conservative a critic as Peter Viereck believed that in spite of large domestic problems, the American system of a mixed economy and political democracy "still contained potentialities for the greatest advance in the development of the human individual that the world had ever seen."[10] Progress was imperiled by what were classified (dubiously) as purely external threats: large-scale war and nuclear annihilation.

By the late seventies, however, the future appeared ill, perhaps terminally so, to many intellectuals. Rational maps to a usable future no longer seemed reliable, as faith in particular visions grew increasingly tepid. Socialist and communist visions, which a generation of radical critics had abandoned in the thirties and forties, remained only feebly alive in remnants of another postwar generation. Mainstream liberal projections seemed less plausible than ever in the light of the decline of reformist visions of a vigorous private economy enhanced and regulated by a beneficent welfare state. Fewer critics believed in a gradual realization of the promise of American life through the good offices of a "new class" of scientists, intellectuals, administrators, and other professionals. Even where this vision survived, doubts grew concerning the personal, political, and institutional means of its realization. Finally, conservative proposals to restore economic and political vitality by strengthening laissez faire practices amounted to exercises in nostalgia, at least insofar as they were represented as comprehensive cures to economic ills. Possessing the virtue of immunity from recent testing until the election of Ronald Reagan, these strategies appealed to conservative critics such as Milton Friedman and to many journalists and academics seeking a fresh direction. Anxiety about the future thus arose from overlapping sources. It grew out of the failure of particular visions, as well as out of the suspected inadequacy of all inherited visions: their flawed nature, their lack of sufficient public acceptance, or their distance from sources of power. Most importantly, I think, anxiety was heightened by a perception of the future as cramped. Doubts spread about the very idea of future space: the availability of raw materials, the capacity of the environment to bear unlimited industrial activity and population growth, and the possibility of maintaining international security in an age of revolution and insane nuclear arms buildups.

Between the middle sixties and the end of the seventies, Americans were pushed into a rediscovery of limits and limitations of all sorts. This rediscovery of limits was a haphazard affair, a piecemeal response to an accumulation of events and trends in evidence since the middle sixties. There was the tragedy of Vietnam, a war that, it now seems, nobody won. Still, Vietnam was in multiple senses a clear national defeat, one that led to deepening doubts about national security and international order. Exploding the hope of an "American century," Vietnam ushered in an era in which America's global power seemed markedly limited and tawdry rather than limitless and beneficent. Contractions of global space entailed swift domestic consequences. The era of plentiful sources of cheap energy ended, at least temporarily, with the rise of the OPEC cartel in 1973. By the end of the seventies, the belief that affluence would evolve into general abundance had ceased to be the controlling assumption of postwar American social criticism.

As this realization set in, the multivalent notion of limits and limitations spread to intellectuals' perceptions of institutions and, even more, to the men who manage them. Both the size and capacity of large institutions—the state, big business, the established political parties, the mainline churches—were subject to automatic skepticism, a disposition that for other reasons had belonged to radicals in the sixties. Above all Watergate, but also such episodes as Three Mile Island, the collapse of Skylab, and endless revelations of corruption in large corporations, unions, Congress, the FBI, the CIA, and the General Accounting Office provided dramatic instances of the apparent insufficiency of leaders and dominant institutions to deal with present issues and to shape a decent future. The large problems inherited from the sixties were complicated and perhaps even rendered permanent by the prospect of limited growth, intense foreign competition, growing unemployment, persistent inflation, high interest rates, low productivity, insufficient savings and investment, material shortages, and environmental stress.[11]

Thus by the end of the seventies American social and cultural critics questioned the central assumption of Enlightenment thought more thoroughly than ever. "The presumptuous control by reason of man's fate," to borrow another phrase from Mills, had come to seem just that: presumptuous. The shapes of the future were, as always, opaque, unpredictable, and perilous. And after the interlude of postwar optimism, another perennial source of anxiety resurfaced in the form of a spreading conviction that the future must be imagined as at best some shade of gray, if it could be imagined at all. As the idea of the future ceased to serve as a primary source of consolation, many critics wondered, along with Robert Heilbroner, whether it was possible any longer to "imagine . . . [the] future other than as a continuation of the darkness, cruelty, and disorder of the past." They wondered also whether it was possible to avoid foreseeing "in the human prospect a deterioration of things, even an impending catastrophe of fearful dimensions."[12]

For a variety of quite different intellectual, political, and personal reasons that I explore in the next few chapters, American social critics in the seventies created and inhabited a general framework of nostalgia. With few exceptions, radicals and liberals played the bleak seventies off against the hopeful sixties. Departing from this pattern somewhat, conservatives contrasted the gray seventies to what they regarded as the grimy sixties. But the dominant pattern and the neoconservative variant formed parts of an overall design informed by nostalgia: the present was assumed generally to be a disappointment— a departure from superior past realities or at least a refutation of past hopes and expectations. And the future was painted in dark tones: "deterioration" and "catastrophe," the flip sides of "reform" and "revolution," comprised the boundaries of a cramped critical vision.

4

The Radical Left

Whatever else they may agree upon—and usually it amounts to very little—radicals on the left always manage to be highly critical of present arrangements: the organization of the economy, the structure of politics, the shapes of culture. It doesn't much matter whether, by ordinary standards, things are going well or badly. In prosperous times radical critics may emphasize the evils of alienation, the ways in which present social arrangements inhibit salvation. And in times of relative scarcity, they may emphasize exploitation, the ways in which social arrangements inhibit social justice. During the late fifties and early sixties, for example, when American capitalism seemed to be on its way from affluence to abundance, many radical critics concentrated on exposing the spiritually deadening and politically repressive effects of a prosperous, post-Depression consumer capitalism. Herbert Marcuse characterized the American social order in *One-Dimensional Man* (1964) as a benign totalitarianism that bestowed a comfortable slavery upon a largely willing, if, in his opinion, stupefied population. "Advanced industrial society" (Marcuse's euphemism for late capitalism) had perfected the art of alienating citizens to the point where only a remnant remained even aware of its enfeebled condition. And they were powerless to do anything about it, since the entire system functioned so as to foreclose revolutionary options.

Even though the prospects for general abundance faded in the seventies, many radicals refined their analyses of the alienating power of advanced capitalist society during these years. Every stratum and social class was supposed to suffer in one way or another from this disease: the entire society displayed signs of infection. Indeed, the premier work of radical social criticism in the late seventies, Christopher Lasch's *The Culture of Narcissism* (1978), was largely a rewrite, in an American idiom, of *One-Dimensional Man:* both writers imagined the United States as a dystopia.[1] But other critics on the left placed renewed stress on more orthodox Marxist (and socialist) critiques of the exploitative arrangements of the American social order—the great systematic inequalities of wealth and power.[2] In this time of relative scarcity (which seemed to some observers to be as contrived as the affluence of the sixties had appeared to others), material inequalities became increasingly evident. The "ruling class" threatened to reverse the modest gains of working people and to reduce even further the precarious material circumstances of the underclass.[3]

For American radicals, then, it is always the worst of times in the larger society, even though some periods may seem (and be) less oppressive than others: the "hegemonic" system is relentlessly evil, and subtly so by virtue of its capacity to assume a variety of seductive appearances. Thus, in their changing assessments of American life in the sixties and seventies, radical critics regularly came to gloomy conclusions. Things were bad and growing worse, though not sufficiently so to stir the sluggish metabolism of the American working class (variously defined and redefined to include everyone except a few financial "parasites"). But radicals have their own conception of relatively good times, too: they are periods in which opportunities for substantial change seem bright. Not all sectors of the left agree on what sorts of change should be counted as "substantial" or "genuine." Nor do they share common perceptions of live possibilities at any given moment. With few exceptions, however, the fractious radical left perceived the sixties, or one or another phase of that decade, as a moment of high possibility, if not for political or cultural revolution then at least for significant movement on the left.

At the end of the seventies, some regarded the essentially left-liberal period of the Movement in the early sixties—the civil-rights movement, early SNCC (Student Nonviolent Coordinating Committee), and SDS (Students for a Democratic Society)—as the most promising phase. Others, probably a far larger number, located the high point in the more militant phase beginning in 1965, a year or so after publication of Marcuse's gloomy work, when the counterculture flourished and the scope of radical politics grew, modulating from dissent and protest to resistance and, for a tiny minority, open rebellion. Only a scattering of fanatics were nostalgic about the revolutionary fantasies and random violence that spanned the late sixties and early seventies, culminating in the bizarre destructiveness of the Symbionese Liberation Army.[4] In general, however, leftist critics recalled some part of the sixties as a time of opportunity, a period in which radical visions of the future flourished, and harsh, often telling critiques of American society and culture found small though willing audiences. Of course, the number of those who accepted the findings of radical criticism and endorsed radical strategies remained small in comparison with the larger numbers—perhaps as many as a quarter of the young—who were in full, though momentary, cultural revolt against the leading norms, figures, and institutions of American civilization: parents, schools, established churches, government (especially the Selective Service), work, competition, marriage, and so on. In this heady atmosphere of dissent and of soaring expectations not only among the privileged young but among all disadvantaged groups, many radicals harbored high, even revolutionary expectations of their own. Their expectations were raised further by events elsewhere: the flamboyance of Fidel Castro and Che Guevara, the cultural "revolution" in China, the Paris uprising of 1968.

During the seventies the major radical expectations of the sixties were subverted. No focus of left dissent and protest in the sixties—the black movement, the student movement, the new Left, the women's movement, the counterculture—fulfilled the impossible intentions of its most radical voices. None managed to trigger a full-scale redistribution of opportunity and reward in the sphere of political economy or a substantial redefinition of the values and sensibilities of a vast majority of Americans away from possessive individualism and toward a radical communitarianism. In their confessional history of the new Left, Greg Calvert and Carol Neiman conclude that the movement did not achieve "one single radical reform which transferred power from the corporate elite to the people."[5] To many of its participants and sympathetic critics, the left of the sixties appeared to repeat the tragic rhythm of twentieth-century American radicalism. Despite promising moments—in the early 1900s, the thirties, and the sixties—radical efforts always seem to yield paltry results, at least when measured against the high ambitions of their advocates.

Of course, the Movement must be counted as a success when measured against many less grandiose though equally important standards of performance. People on the left, from radicals to left liberals, literally rewrote the American agenda of social and cultural criticism for the sixties and the seventies. They brought the issues of discrimination into focus, prompting millions of Americans to begin to think about rules of fairness for people in every category, from blacks and women to gays, children, senior citizens, and the physically handicapped, and in every area, from such remote, exotic places as Watts and the South Bronx to the familiar regions of their own middle-class neighborhoods. Radicals called attention to the social mechanisms of advanced capitalism that had turned exploitation and a terrifying waste of human potential at every level of society into scarcely noticed features of daily life. The Movement of the sixties also played a significant part in certain major political and cultural changes in American life, from ending the war in Vietnam to augmenting the civil rights and civil liberties of millions of previously ignored citizens.

Still, the new Left came apart in the late sixties, and as it did, seasoned critics such as James Weinstein and Eugene Genovese took a longer view, hoping for the emergence of a vital socialist organizational presence in American politics and culture during the seventies.[6] Here, too, the radical thrust petered out. Organizations that took fragile shape in the sixties, for example, had all but disappeared by the end of the seventies—indeed, well before then. And no serious revolutionary party or preparty formation appeared in the seventies to discipline politically unruly radicals. At the end of the seventies, then, there was no shared radical dream, no viable radical institutional apparatus, no conspicuous popular demand for a new cultural and social order. Instead, a mood of discouragement and disillusionment, even futility, characterized the outlook of many critics on the left. "What ultimately disturbs me," Norman Birnbaum observed in 1975, "is that I can't easily recall a historical precedent for the universal bleakness of the intellectual landscape. There is no conviction that thought which is descriptively correct can have an impact, let alone belief that new ideas can in fact generate a different—or better —situation."[7]

If radicals recalled the sixties as a time of active possibility in the larger society and a time of intense experience of community at least *within* various warring factions, they perceived the seventies generally as a period of relative isolation, of living through one's subscription to *Mother Jones, Socialist Review,* and *In These Times.* It was for most of them a time of apparent defeat and loneliness, a scattering and decimation of the tribes. As the editors of *Socialist Review* wonder in their assessment of the seventies, "What does it mean to engage in a socialist project (in our case, producing a political journal) in a country where the socialist left does not exist as a major political force?"[8] According to most radical accounts, the seventies witnessed the triumph of political "reaction," a buzz word covering everything from the political center to the far right. And it was a period of radical default, a morally venal decade of personal selfishness, which to political types means a lack of interest in leftist theory and politics, and which to cultural radicals signifies a decline of interest in acceptable communitarian styles of life. "In the past two decades," Peter Dreier observes, "many radicals have shifted from false hopes of 'revolution now' to no hope at all."[9] At best, the seventies was seen as an interlude—a time to reconsider past mistakes and to plan for the future. As Tom Hayden put it, the radicals "who filled the streets in the '60s may yet fill the halls of government in the '80s, and if we do, I don't believe we will forget our roots."[10] In the meantime, many radicals of the sixties were settling in for a long season of theorizing and teaching, using criticism both as a lengthy prelude to more muscular sorts of action and as a substitute for more direct varieties of political action.

More than ideological, the pervasive (though perhaps temporary) mood of defeat sprang from deeply personal sources. Attempting to discover what went wrong in the sixties—why the radical moment seemed to end so abruptly and why it ended as it did—many surviving radical critics and activists found it hard to disentangle their depressed views of the present from their readings of the recent past. To one degree or another, the survivors were participants in the political and cultural left of the sixties, characters in a mass-mediated cultural drama of considerable scope and intensity. Actors who only a few years earlier seemed to have selected themselves (or to have been selected by the media) for important public roles—as the moral conscience of the nation, the political vanguard of a new historical dispensation, or the liberated innovators of fresh modes of personality and culture—found themselves cast out of Eden.

Forced to make their solitary ways, singly or in tiny groups, through bureaucratic mazes and cold psychic landscapes, they became so many figures in an Ann Beattie fiction, feeling victimized in what they considered a society of victims. For many the fall from momentary prominence was long, if not dizzying. In the late sixties, for example, Abbie Hoffman and Jerry Rubin, recently crew-cut college newspaper editors, became instant celebrities. Founders of the Yippies (Youth International Party), these clown princes of the counterculture were treated as gurus by their own fluid constituencies and as newsworthy figures by representatives of television and the press. Rennie Davis, a more dignified man, figured importantly in SDS and the anti-war movement, later becoming one of the celebrated Chicago Eight (along with Yippies Hoffman and Rubin). Bob Dylan, a competent musician, was cast absurdly in the role of prophet and folk hero in the tradition of Woody Guthrie. And Eldridge Cleaver, a convicted rapist, became minister of information of the Black Panther party and the presidential candidate of the Peace and Freedom party in 1968.

In the seventies, many of the prominent pop revolutionary figures of the sixties defected or found themselves socially naked, without a context: they sought new modes of ending alienation (their principal if not clearly understood agenda from the outset). To escape a charge of cocaine dealing, Abbie Hoffman went underground, although he managed periodically to call attention to himself for several years until he reappeared voluntarily in the early eighties, yet another manuscript in hand, and a stretch in jail ahead of him. Jerry Rubin, once ostensibly committed to social revolution, sought to revolutionize his own consciousness through a smorgasbord of ancient and modern therapies from Tai Chi to Fischer-Hoffman training; for the eighties, he came forth as a Wall Street investment counselor. Rennie Davis became a disciple of the Maharaj Ji, the young "perfect master" from India. Bob Dylan reportedly became a born-again Christian, a surmise strengthened by his 1979 album *Slow Train Coming*. And Eldridge Cleaver returned in the late seventies from a period of exile to declare his conversion to evangelical Christianity in *Soul on Fire* (1978), a thin volume that critics panned as injudiciously as they had overpraised *Soul on Ice* (1967) in the sixties.[11]

Irritated but unmoved by massive defections of former leaders and sympathizers, radical survivors persisted, hoping for better times in the eighties. In substantial agreement about the hard times of the seventies, they differed sharply over what went wrong in the sixties and hence over how to proceed. Did the sixties mark a time of political or cultural triumphs subverted in the seventies? Did radical cultural probes of the sixties, which were absorbed into the larger culture, undermine promising radical political beginnings? Did the sixties represent a failed opportunity (or only an apparent one)? Do they contain lessons that, if heeded, might lead to a revival of radicalism in the eighties? The varied answers to this puzzle depended largely upon whether survivors lived fully in one of several cul-de-sacs into which the left of the sixties drifted (and was pushed) or whether, as individual observers, they took a critical view of the difficult terrain in which all must make their way.

Between 1965 and 1970, it will be recalled, when left dissidence and protest reached their peak, the Movement confronted the old options that its founders and its sympathetic critic-participants had intended to avoid: sectarianism, withdrawal, and assimilation. First, those who pushed (or followed) their radical sentiments toward revolutionary ideological and political articulations ended up in possession of the principal organizations of the new left—SDS and SNCC. Rigid ideologues—a group of "new fogies," as one critic put it—gravitated toward the Maoist Progressive Labor party, which remained old Left in spirit. Others, driven by total radicalization of their sensibilities, drifted into underground terrorist cells. In the course of achieving control of the new Left organizations, however, "revolutionaries" soon destroyed them, driving the majority away and leaving themselves in possession of hollow organizational shells.

Second, those who followed their radical sentiments away from political metaphors and political action into personal and cultural domains participated, to one degree or another, in the counterculture, a carnival of youthful rebellion that embraced every conceivable negation of the dominant values and mores of the WASP culture of the fifties (except its commitment to individualism), from religious identity to musical taste, from sexual mores to conceptions of work. They did so along with a far larger number of people who short-circuited this process of choice by never acquiring a taste for political liberalism or political radicalism. Here, unmediated by the discipline of politics, the expressive side of the Movement displayed itself most fully. The theatrical and therapeutic dimensions of politics, which, to be sure, had infected "political" sectors of the Movement, dominated the counterculture, most of whose disparate constituencies never seriously concerned themselves with mundane questions of raw power or the changing shapes and possibilities of the welfare state. When countercultural themes were diffused through society, radicals judged this success a failure, a triumph of a reactionary though resourceful hegemonic culture.

Third, as the extremist dynamic of the Movement made its way toward the dead ends of political revolution and personal and cultural solipsism (Weatherman bombers and Timothy Leary at the end of his mantra), a significant minority of individuals affected by the Movement continued in politics. They sought conventional as well as new single-issue causes, worked in and around the Democratic party, and organized in local communities. Their activity helped to change the Democratic party in the early seventies, pushing its left-liberal constituencies several degrees to the left (measured, say, by the standards of 1960). As the visible energy of the Movement dwindled, however, many people ceased active participation in radical politics, in left-liberal politics, and in the counterculture, although they carried some of their acquired values, attitudes, beliefs, and styles of behavior into the seventies.

Of course, the main options of revolutionary sectarianism, withdrawal from politics, and participation in some version of a politics of reform, were not mutually exclusive. In an increasingly fragmented culture, individuals experimented with curious mixtures: there were revolutionary counterculture types, pot-smoking members of SDS, culturally straight Maoists, lesbian Marxist feminists, politically schizophrenic activitists who alternated between local radical activity and some semblance of coalition politics within the Democratic party. Nevertheless, the three main options of postwar American radicalism—indeed, of twentieth-century American radicalism—reasserted themselves in new forms during the sixties and early seventies. The most thoughtful of the surviving radical critics found each of these options unsatisfactory, though many apparently felt compelled to choose one, if only to avoid (or ameliorate) the *Mother Jones* syndrome of living one's political life through magazines.

For radicals, then, the seventies was an unusually intense decade of criticism. A significant portion of their energies went into criticism of American civilization. And a fair amount of attention was devoted to exploring the causes of radical failure in the sixties as a prelude to the charting of more promising paths through the eighties. Much of the blame for failure was assigned to "the times"—the unhappy conjunction of the sixties and seventies. It was claimed frequently that a combination of repression and cooptation (an empty formula that can cover every phenomenon) blunted the radical thrust in the late sixties. Or that the gains of the sixties—the enlargement of civil rights and civil liberties, the growth of the welfare state—were subverted by a resurgence of the New Right in the seventies. Or that the social bases of the Movement, composed mainly of middle-class young people, made it inevitably a fleeting phenomenon. Since previous defeats and current conditions in the larger society were beyond control, however, many radicals concentrated on diagnosing internal mistakes. They focused on the intellectual failure to see the limits of radical action, on the moral failure to press toward these limits, and on the temperamental inability to tolerate internal differences on the left. In a storm of recrimination, political radicals blamed cultural radicals and cultural radicals blamed political radicals.

A less abrasive tone marked the most intelligent of these debates in the late seventies. The experience of defeat, which left American radicals ten years older, led many to reassess the virtues of liberal values: individual liberty, moderation, tolerance, compromise, representative democracy, cultural pluralism. Thus, for example, Irving Howe, who in the sixties (and before) had irritated many people on the left by insisting on the crucial importance of democratic institutions to any genuine form of socialism, proposed in the seventies a series of articles of conciliation with, of all things, liberalism.[12] Responding to the disappointment of the sixties and seventies, intellectuals to the left of Howe moderated their views of liberal values, rejecting explicitly (or merely forgetting) their convoluted attacks on "repressive tolerance" during the sixties.[13] For example, in his retrospective analysis of the sixties, Eugene Genovese recommended the misplaced habit of tolerance regarding past mistakes and present differences. And Stanley Aronowitz, a spokesperson for a segment of the small New American Movement, proposed a "multitendency socialist movement," a pluralism within the far left.[14]

Tempered by age and by defeat, radicals of differing ideological commitments displayed a fuller appreciation of democratic values in the seventies, and even a wavering disposition to practice them. A lively, ecumenical newspaper such as *In These Times,* sponsored by such diverse people as Robert Allen, Noam Chomsky, Eugene Genovese, Michael Harrington, Dorothy Healey, David Horowitz, Staughton Lynd, and Carey McWilliams, would not have been possible in the later sixties. In those years the model of the *National Guardian,* a publication beset by a series of "splits" that left it increasingly unreadable, prevailed on the left. This reconsideration of liberal values by radicals represents a welcome turn. Without a genuine appreciation of these values, radicals must continue in a state of debilitating internal intellectual and political fratricide. Indeed, they may be consigned to this fate in any case. For the intellectual and social space in which liberal values can flourish among radicals seems cramped. In the absence of new and workable opportunities in the larger society, the options of revolutionary sectarianism, reform, and withdrawal from ordinary politics persisted in the seventies, forming the social basis of a continuing debate over what I have called radical paradoxes. The old paradox of powerlessness and the tensions between means and ends plagued leftists of the seventies, as it had their predecessors.[15] Moreover, no group or tendency was able to persuade a clear majority of people on the radical left to follow any unified political and moral course of action.

Hence, at the end of the seventies, the radical left remained fragmented, perhaps hopelessly so. This is hardly surprising, since throughout the twentieth century pursuit of any of the three main options has resulted in the apparent defeat of long-range aims, or at most in partial victories that frequently give American radicals a case of nerves.[16] The revolutionary option was discredited after a brief revival in the late sixties. Withdrawal from ideological wars into one variety or another of cultural rebellion struck most politically minded survivors as a form of acquiescence (and cooptation), an exercise in radical individualism without a useful political focus.

And the range of reformist options, which seemed to present the only reasonable alternative to revolutionary politics despite its tendency to deradicalize its practitioners, lost some of its earlier charm. The large left-liberal coalition of labor, left-out minorities, and the conscience constituency of professionals and intellectuals, which such critics as Michael Harrington, Michael Walzer, and Irving Howe believed might bend the welfare state in the direction of socialism during the affluent sixties, splintered, or rather never really took solid political form in the seventies. True, there flourished a scattering of communist and cooperative ventures, along with lively democratic political activity, ranging from union organizing and active participation in the Democratic party to local politics. And almost singlehandedly, Harry Boyte called the left's attention to the continuity of democratic *potential* that linked the seventies to the sixties: "The insurgent spirit born in the early sixties' civil rights movement," Boyte declares, "has subsequently spread, largely beneath the surface of media attention, among new groups in the population. In its course it has created enduring institutions, and generated profound changes in self-conception, sense of political possibility—and the very definition of what 'democracy' means—for millions of people uninvolved in any of the sixties' protests. In workplaces, families, neighborhoods—throughout the primary social structures—" Boyte continues, "the democratic hope has begun to mature that ordinary people can in fact control the institutions in which they live, and furthermore that they have a right to control such institutions."[17] Yet in spite of promising beginnings, these networks amounted only to a diffuse web without any radical or socialist design of national consequence. Although the parts were woven together easily enough, they were as easily ripped apart. Since each radical option remained alive, if only by virtue of the unattractiveness of the others, controversy on the left persisted in the seventies.

What makes the American scene seem paradoxical to radicals is their continued allegiance to a controlling assumption (or set of assumptions) that both binds and divides them. Although radicals place differing emphases on the economic, political, and cultural spheres, they are unified (if this is the proper term) in their opposition to much of the prevailing social order. The groups that make up this diverse collection of communists, socialists, anarchists, anti-ideological cultural radicals, communitarians, and intellectual Marxists of various stripes oppose the capitalist economy. They also fashion a variety of generally unenthusiastic positions on existing forms of representative democracy, from indicting them as "bourgeois shams" to criticizing their present capitalist economic matrixes. And radicals condemn the culture of advanced capitalism as either elitist, crassly popular, or more usually, an unattractive, alienating mix of both. Clearly, however, this elastic ideological bond is conceptually vague and politically often worse than useless: it forms the basis of a critical framework which ensures continuous internecine warfare over ends and means. Complicating the exercise of liberal values, this internal conflict is made more strident by what might be called a common radical sensibility.

Though hard to describe, even as an ideal type, radical sensibility is fairly easily recognized. It is a compound of moral anger, self-righteousness, and personal resentment that goes beyond ideology yet influences its conflicting shapes. The defining characteristic of radical sensibility is a crypto-Puritan desire for purity and a corollary impatience with obstacles to enacting vision. The radical sensibility releases itself in moral outrage at existing arrangements (and, sooner or later, at people) allegedly responsible for deforming human potentiality. This sensibility is expressed also in an impatience with slow social processes, even essentially salutary ones, and in a temperamental disregard, if not a plain contempt, for liberal values: moderation, compromise, individual rights, democratic procedures. By turns utopian and apocalyptic, the radical sensibility is not altogether without political resourcefulness. But it tends toward antipolitical extremes—toward purification of the self, others, the natural environment, and the structures of society. On the left, the theoretical limit of this emotional commitment to purity takes vague form in such concepts as "transcendence," "transformation," and "revolution." Heroic, fiery action—or hot rhetoric—permits the most uninhibited expressions of radical sensibility: its most energetic practitioners seem determined to outflank everyone to their left.

The radical sensibility informs the work of critics of such differing talents and outlooks as Timothy Leary, Ivan Illich, Jerry Rubin, Robert Allen, Adrienne Rich, Christopher Lasch, and Robin Morgan. It expresses itself in a particular style of social and cultural criticism marked by a casual pseudo-Hegelian assumption of the interconnectedness of all phenomena and by a relentless expressive psychology and rhetoric of exposure. Often less sophisticated than its Hegelian, Marxian, and

Freudian prototypes, this strategy of unmasking turns on disparities between surface appearances and hidden structures, between manifest meanings and latent implications. Rooted also in the American tradition of muckraking, it exposes disparities between pretense and performance, between the professed intentions and the "real" (usually the darkest imaginable) motives of elite groups in society.

Examples of this sensibility abound in the literature of the radical left. It animates even the most hardened figures and clichés of vulgarized Marxist thought. As Jeremy Brecher observes in one of those breathless sentences that attempt to evoke a world view, "Despite the false consciousness, the continuous official propaganda, and the narcotizing pacifiers of the media, consumption, national glory and the rest, as long as people are human and therefore able to respond to their own needs, they pose a potential threat to the functioning of the system—the threat of revolution."[18] Or, consider Mark Rudd's subtle meditation on American universities: "Whatever 'good' function the university serves is what the radical students can cull from its bones—especially the creation and expansion of a revolutionary movement. The university should be used as a place from which to launch radical struggles—anything less now constitutes a passive capitulation to social democracy and reformism, whatever the intention of the radicals involved."[19] Radical sensibility is also evident in more private modes of communication, such as Nadine Miller's "Letter to Her Psychiatrist," a misguided man, she claims, who persists in thinking of her as "crazy": "I have reached the point where I know there is only one solution for me as a woman—unity with other women and ultimately a revolution. I have also identified my oppressors. No, it is not society (that is too general). My oppressors are not institutions. My oppressors," Miller continues, settling down to specifics, "are MEN—and all the superstructures which are set up by men: I refuse to allow MEN TO DEFINE me anymore. I refuse to support a system which works against me and my sisters."[20]

Although this sensibility affects some radicals only periodically or weakly, it dominates the consciousness of others. But it is by no means the exclusive property of political and cultural leftists or of those who organize their experience in self-consciously ideological ways. On the broad left in America, radical sensibilities have been evident, though not necessarily dominant, in nearly every single-issue cause, from efforts to stay the execution of Caryl Chessman in the late fifties to the antinuclear protests of the late seventies. They receive their most un-inhibited expression in the left regions of the counterculture, where politics becomes a self-conscious metaphor for theater and therapy.

Those who act out this sensibility, rhetorically or otherwise, in tradi-tional far-left ideological forms constitute the small, antidemocratic component of the radical left. This ultraleftist remnant is also the most politically irrelevant (when not a positively destructive) element. Pur-suing purity through the Word (the special province of Trotskyist and neo-Stalinist sectarians) or through totally undisciplined spiritual or sensual liberation, those most thoroughly imbued with radical sensi-bility usually prove themselves temperamentally incapable of sustained practice of the liberal virtues in the larger society. For the most part, they cannot exercise these virtues in the cramped regions of the far left, either.

Why then do so many otherwise reasonable radicals persist in en-gaging the antidemocratic purists in endless debate? Why, one won-ders, do they consider sectarians important to the resuscitation of an American left? Delegates to the 1979 convention of the New Ameri-can Movement (NAM), for example, spent a portion of their time debating the claims of the August 7th Caucus, a sizable minority fac-tion that opposed even a serious discussion of merger with the Demo-cratic Socialist Organizing Committee (DSOC), a somewhat larger, nonsectarian, and largely non-Marxist group of moderate socialists headed by Michael Harrington. According to John Judis, "the August 7 Caucus attacked DSOC for its membership in the Socialist Interna-tional . . . its participation in the Democratic Party, its failure to en-courage rank-and-file revolts in the labor movement, its 'token anti-sexism,' and most important, its lack of commitment to socialism and revolution."[21] Such behavior, one gathers from this indictment, is pre-sumed to be beyond the pale.

Debate, of course, is essential to democratic decision making. And by all accounts, the controversy at the NAM convention was civil, at least when measured by the relaxed standards of such political gather-ings. (In this case it was fruitful, too, since plans were laid for a merger of NAM and DSOC in 1982 under the new name of Demo-cratic Socialists of America.) Moreover, since the extremists have often brought energy and organizing skills to single-issue causes of concern to the perennially small radical left and to the broader left as well, there is understandable reluctance to alienate them. Yet none of these ethical and practical reasons explains fully the willingness of many sensible radicals to waste their time and jeopardize their credentials in hopes of forming a "multi-tendency socialist movement" that includes sectarians—politically unaffiliated authoritarians, remnants of old Left sects like the Socialist Workers' party, and members of such newer organizations as the Revolutionary Communist party (1975) and the Communist Labor party (1974).[22]

The irony that far-left critics and activists must confront is this: ultraleftists, though politically bankrupt, claim possession of the most uninhibited secular theoretical articulation of radical sensibility. They are thus the guardians of orthodoxy, keepers of the tradition of revolutionary Marxism that, along with utopian analogues, remains the archetypal expression of the search for purity on the left. The ostensible enemy of purity, of course, is compromise. And many American radicals, who for a variety of compelling reasons abandoned or indefinitely shelved their vision of revolution in the seventies, wished to act politically, or at any rate professed such intentions. Since compromise remains essential to ordinary politics in America, however, they feared deradicalization, a loss of purity. And, I suspect, they also experienced a seizure of bad conscience upon entering into a series of accommodations that dilute the radical quest for purity. Such compromises represent the price of following a politics of reform or even of acting politically for "tactical reasons" with powerful groups seeking piecemeal change. Radical guilt and the plausible fear of deradicalization, I think, were largely responsible for keeping many critics and activists in an endless dialogue with antidemocratic sectarians. Though it is perhaps understandable, this seems a strange and self-defeating arena in which to exercise newly acquired or reclaimed liberal virtues.

By the end of the seventies (at the latest), the chief liberal values had ceased to be merely optional—desirable in some long range sense, perhaps, but dispensable in the interim. They had become indispensable to radical beginnings. The principal dividing line on the confused terrain of the radical left could no longer plausibly be said to lie in the hazy zone between revolution and reform. It no longer separated pro-Communists from anti-Communists. It did not even run through the question of democracy, though this remained a vital issue, inseparable from the main one. I believe, rather, that an acceptance and practice of the broad range of liberal values distinguished serious radicals from zealots, temperamental authoritarians, and essentially antipolitical people. This fundamental division, which John Dewey had proposed thirty-five years earlier in *Liberalism and Social Action,* was beyond debate by the end of the seventies.

The conflict over revolution and reform became obsolete in America not merely because a strategy of revolution proved once again to be antipolitical in its consequences. The very social framework in which the competing strategies of revolution and reform had once made sense to radicals (if not to others) had come apart. Although these differing strategies always presupposed a vague common end—a terminal (or transitory) social system toward which radicals aim—the very idea of an alternative social system had grown altogether problematic by the middle seventies. "Socialist" experiments abroad—in the Soviet Union, China, and Cuba—no longer could be taken seriously as models or even as culturally specific examples of the salutary potentialities of socialism. And domestic projections of one version of socialism or another remained vague or uninviting and certainly unpopular. Secular radical visions of the future survived, although they had become more tarnished and more hazy than ever, especially in the light of the accelerated nuclear arms race in the seventies. As a consequence, liberal values remained the only sensible point of departure, and an end to the arms race the most immediate issue of global concern in the early eighties.

A number of radical critics came to this realization in the seventies, or at least emphasized it in their writing during these years. A few, notably people associated with the journal *Dissent,* even questioned seriously the theoretical possibility of maintaining a political democracy in the midst of a socialist organization of the economy, the only sort of secular radical synthesis that may be superior to the capitalist disease. But almost none of those on the left who can be considered radical—who share both a radical sensibility and the minimal radical assumptions about the defects of the American social order—were able to confront an even more immediate possibility. They could not bring themselves to wonder openly whether the limited radical political and cultural probes of the sixties in which they had figured so importantly had been examined, revised, tempered, and partially adopted by the larger society in the seventies with essentially beneficial results.

Disappointment, radical guilt, and the fear of deradicalization precluded sustained inquiry into the positive effects of liberal and conservative pressures on radical ideas and initiatives. Nor could most radicals entertain the possibility that the ideological shifts of these years, which were unsettling when apprehended from any particular vantage point, expressed the cultural spirit of an essentially salutary and largely democratic quest for personal fulfillment. Such inquiry fell outside the temperamental, if not the ideological, range of most American radicals. The exercise of liberal values on the democratic potential in American culture nevertheless remained the only promising way for radicals to front the future. Of course, the democratic stirrings that Boyte underlined were largely without political shape, and many radicals, I suspect, instinctively understood that this democratic potential, even if it were to take political form, probably could not be pressed into ideological shapes of their own desire. For the bubbling of democratic sentiment from below was in fact a manifestation of the quest for personal fulfillment that many critics on the left regarded as a contaminating part of the American disease rather than as an element of a cure.

5

The Liberal Left

Left liberals suffered their own ideological reversals, political defeats, and personal disappointments in the sixties and seventies. By the end of the seventies, such prominent critics as Arthur Schlesinger, Jr. and John Kenneth Galbraith had lost a measure of the influence they exerted in inner circles of political power during the sixties. And the prevailing mood among less well-connected left-liberal critics was almost uniformly bleak. For evident reasons. As the late sixties and seventies unfolded, everything seemed to go wrong. Their vision of an abundant American future faded. Their amorphous ideology was attacked widely and tellingly by radicals and by conservatives. The foreign-policy initiatives that many left liberals had supported and indeed helped to formulate in the Kennedy-Johnson years yielded a series of stunning failures in Southeast Asia, Africa, Central America, and the Middle East. And the political base of the New Deal coalition, which held up their hopes, had been fractured beyond easy repair. By the end of the seventies, many critics concluded that left-liberal dreams had passed through the several stages of a prolonged death: denial, defiance, and bargaining, if not acceptance.

On the map of American political ideology, the left-liberal critics run from the near edges of radicalism on the left to the center. This unruly category includes democratic socialists like Irving Howe, Robert Heilbroner, and Michael Harrington, as well as such critics as Galbraith,

Schlesinger, and a diverse collection of people identified with the New Politics of the late sixties. Its practitioners have enough in common to distinguish them from radicals and conservatives, though not always easily: Howe and Harrington, for example, retain a large measure of loyalty to many socialist goals and values and hence live along the hazy political borders dividing radicals and left liberals. So does Galbraith, who in the seventies gravitated toward native American radical themes, drawn especially from Veblen. Weakened by critical assaults of political and cultural radicals in the sixties, critics on the liberal left were besieged by neoconservative and right-wing social commentators in the seventies. Partly as a consequence of these multifaceted assaults, the perspectives of critics on the liberal left became less clear and less compelling as the seventies wore on. Many liberals had lost a measure of their faith in the great domestic political "actors" of our time: the business community and the state.

Committed in varying degrees to a more equitable division of opportunity, responsibility, and reward through a growing welfare state and a democratic politics of reform, critics on the liberal left also tend to favor fairly strict governmental regulation of business and vigorous federal enforcement of civil rights and civil liberties. Of course, they differ somewhat among themselves on a range of political, social, and cultural issues: education, civil rights for minorities, women's rights, gay rights, civil liberties for dissenters, sexual permissiveness, recreational use of drugs, crime, law and order, abortion, pornography, prostitution, patriotism, military expenditures. And they display an even wider variation of sensibility. Imagine a guest list that includes the following people: Vernon Jordan and Bella Abzug, Norman Mailer and Eleanor Smeal, Ted Kennedy and Betty Friedan, Ralph Abernathy and Jacqueline Kennedy, Harvey Cox and Muriel Humphrey, Leonard Bernstein and Shirley Chisholm. For all their differences, however, left liberals remain committed to a tense interplay of values associated with personal freedom: conventional civil rights and civil liberties as well as certain forms of enforced equality (or reduced inequality) that permit individuals to flourish, to exercise their formal freedoms.

Not every critic in this amorphous cluster recalled the sixties in a mood of nostalgia: it was, after all, a difficult time in many ways, especially after 1966. For one thing, the growing counterculture threatened liberal political values and assaulted liberal sensibilities. For another, President Johnson's decision to pursue simultaneously the war abroad and the Great Society at home brought the ideology of the welfare state to a boil: Mr. Johnson's policy triggered inflationary pressures that, along with other causes of dissent, intensified ideological and political differences throughout America. Moreover, the atmosphere on campuses—the home turf of most critics—grew increasingly inhospitable toward the end of the sixties. No matter what they did— speak, write, petition, march, sit in, give in—left-liberal critics never were able to appease the radicals or gain their approval.

Still, these critics could recall parts of the sixties nostalgically, for it was a time of liberal triumphs in the domestic sphere. For many, the main dividing line was the assassination of President Kennedy in November of 1963. But the New Frontier, the civil-rights movement, and the first flowerings of the Great Society represented genuine political victories, most of which came about after Kennedy's death. The War on Poverty, expanded aid to education (especially higher education), Medicare and Medicaid, the Economic Opportunity Act, and the Voting Rights Act of 1965 all marked promising beginnings, enacted pieces of a larger dream. Writing with apparently deliberate simplicity at the end of the sixties, William Lee Miller described "the first part of the decade as the best period in American history that I have lived through, and the last part of the decade as potentially the worst."[1]

Events of the seventies only added to this nostalgic left-liberal view of the first part of the sixties. True, there were some acknowledged improvements, and much of the momentum liberals created in the middle sixties persisted into the seventies, at least in the growth of federal social spending. Domestic violence waned after the early seventies. The sharp edges of ideological politics were softened slightly, though not so much through a decline of ideological division as through a declining interest in politics. And a spate of legislation was passed, from measures to protect the environment and consumers to measures to secure the rights of handicapped people. For the most part, however, the seventies appeared to be a period of retreat for left liberals, a conservative beat in the rhythm of democratic politics. As the decade wore on, the possibilities of the sixties seemed increasingly poignant to left-liberal critics, serving as reminders of an unfilled and perhaps even impossible social agenda. Toward the end of the seventies Tom Wicker insisted that "developments of the 1960s and early '70s are being rolled back or endangered." Citing a loss of momentum in the civil-rights movement, the "ferocious attacks" on abortion rights, and the stubborn opposition to the Equal Rights Amendment, Wicker registered the general sense of disappointment of left-liberal critics in the late seventies. And he did so in typical left-liberal fashion, slicing the domain of political opinion and action into two parts, one "progressive," the other "reactionary."

This bifurcated view of ideology and politics exhibits the reluctance of left-liberal critics to acknowledge contributions of opposing forces to salutary social change. The schema illustrated by Wicker also helps to explain why so many critics in this mode underplay even their own triumphs: to stress limited progress in such long struggles as the movement for full social inclusion of blacks and other racial minorities apparently strikes them as a signal to relax future efforts rather than as the only practical reason to press ahead. Left-liberal political disappointment, then, amounted to this: their program, which seemed roughly compatible with their hopes through the middle sixties, had been thrown off course at least by the early seventies, and not merely by economic trends in the direction of relative scarcity. It had been slowed and in many instances redirected by conservative and reactionary forces, as well as by the spread of apolitical styles of life characteristic of the counterculture.

Although a simple pattern of rise and decline marks the period as a whole, the year-to-year course of left-liberal political fortunes was more complicated. Throughout the sixties and seventies hopes fluctuated rapidly. Recurrent periods of optimism punctuated the deepening gloom. In the sixties there was the election of John Kennedy, the promising domestic program of Lyndon Johnson in 1964, and the emergence of the New Politics during the first stages of Eugene McCarthy's bid for the Democratic nomination in 1968. In the seventies, bright moments were briefer and less luminous: the Pyrrhic victory of McGovern forces at the Democratic convention in 1972, the feeble resurgence of nervous optimism during the post-Watergate Carter campaign in 1976, and the entry of Edward Kennedy into the presidential race in 1979. In spite of these moments—perhaps even because of them—the cumulative effect of events and their own grim interpretation of events disheartened many critics on the liberal left. After 1968, Hubert Humphrey's "politics of joy" seemed grotesque in the context of war, domestic racial violence, and bitter divisions among

Democrats. The left-liberal program, such as it was, had lost its ideological coherence, its political base, and its moral force.

Consider first the ideological fate of left liberalism. In the postwar period, the vague social vision shared by left-liberal critics depended upon the central assumption that present affluence would evolve into abundance. Rising prosperity constituted America's secular equivalent of grace. It promised to finesse the philosophical issues associated with social justice, enabling liberty *and* equality to flourish. It promised to enable an amelioration, if not a resolution, of every major social problem—poverty and ignorance, disease and environmental decay, racism and other forms of discrimination. And it promised to do so without injuring anyone—by raising those at the bottom of the social structure and simultaneously adding to the fortunes of others.[2] The New Frontier and the far more ambitious program of the Great Society envisioned by Lyndon Johnson were the most vital political expressions of the liberal ideology in the sixties. In the spring of 1964, prior to his landslide election, President Johnson delivered a series of speeches outlining his vision of the American future. In Detroit (of all places) he declared, "We stand at the edge of the greatest era in the life of any nation. For the first time in world history we have the abundance and the ability to free every man from hopeless want, and to free every person to find fulfillment in the works of his mind or the labor of his hands." Johnson went on to say that "This nation, this people, this generation, has man's first chance to create a Great Society: a society of success without squalor, beauty without barrenness, works of genius without the wretchedness of poverty. We can open the doors of learning. We can open the doors of fruitful labor and rewarding leisure, of open opportunity and close community—not just to the privileged few, but, thank God, we can open those doors to everyone."[3] In these few lines Johnson manages to include every facet of the left-liberal view of the American future: freedom from the old ills of scarcity—poverty and exploitation—and genuine liberty and full equality of opportunity to pursue self-fulfillment in the new age of abundance. America possessed the material capacity, the institutional machinery, the technical knowledge (the 'ability'), and perhaps even the will to usher in the new age.

Meanwhile, such left-liberal endorsers of "The Triple Revolution" (1964) as Robert Theobald, Robert Heilbroner, H. Stuart Hughes, and Bayard Rustin foresaw in the early sixties an essentially cultural problem—an excess of leisure—clouding the medium-range American social agenda. By the year 2000, they believed, work would have become virtually obsolete and material scarcity a thing of the past. As David Riesman and Michael Maccoby put it in their essay on "The American Crisis," "In order for us to live with our abundance, there must be greater participation in the political life of the United States and of the world. The traditional American ideology which is concerned only with equality of economic and political opportunity and freedom from control—in other words with the major problems of scarcity alone—must readjust to face the problems that have suddenly become visible because of abundance: lack of participation in life and lack of opportunity and education for self-expression."[4]

Though subject to dispute, the main political and institutional means to this society of abundance were taken for granted by left-liberal critics. As Arthur Schlesinger, Jr. observed in *The Vital Center,* his early postwar attempt to stake out the left boundary of respectable social democratic opinion in America, "What the democratic parties of the developed nations have done . . . has been to use the state to force capitalism to do what both the classical capitalists and the classical Marxists declared was impossible: to control the business cycle and to reapportion income in favor of those whom Jackson called 'the humble members of society.' "[5] Echoing Schlesinger a decade later, in 1960, C. Wright Mills sarcastically summarized the main coordinates of American political and social vision: "The mixed economy plus the welfare state plus prosperity—that is the formula."[6] This formula also included less tangible factors: a traditional American capacity to solve technical problems and a measure of good will, especially within the relatively privileged middle to upper-middle sectors of society. As the prospect of abundance faded in the early seventies, however, this entire vision came to seem problematic. Social problems outpaced solutions. The war in Vietnam badly divided liberals. The nuclear arms race accelerated ominously in spite of the partial test ban treaty of 1963. The cold war heated up once again. State intervention in the economy for a variety of ends yielded, at best, mixed results. None of the major left-liberal hopes—sustained economic growth, full employment, reasonable rates of inflation, enhanced welfare, a hospitable environment—was achieved fully. Many left-liberal critics did not even claim reasonable progress toward these goals in the seventies.

Critics in this mold posited a variety of overlapping explanations for the alleged failure of the left-liberal political vision. External developments such as the extended war in Vietnam and the Arab monopoly on oil figured importantly in their accounts of stagflation. Some critics—Galbraith, for example—insisted that the programs of the Great Society had been too meager to be effective: the welfare state, in their view, never received a fair test. Others, like Sar Levitan, claimed that such genuine (if limited) successes as the Job Corps did not receive adequate recognition.[7] A major portion of criticism in the middle and late seventies was directed at those who, out of presumed ignorance or spite, refused to understand the left-liberal project, mainly, neoconservative, New Right, and more traditional conservative shapers of opinion. Finally, a number of left-liberal critics (along with some radicals and neoconservatives) emphasized the moral and psychological failures of Americans—their alleged loss of public spiritedness, their selfishness, their narcissism. Critics as diverse as historian Arthur Schlesinger, Jr., sociologist Herbert Gans, and Vernon Jordan, Jr., then president of the Urban League, lamented the unwillingness and declining capacity of people to press toward the mark of left-liberal vision despite the advent of relative scarcity and a near collapse of several crucial tenets of the faith.[8] The more optimistic among them—Schlesinger, for example—expected a revival of liberalism in the eighties. But in the late seventies, the anticipated revival seemed remote.

Political reversals added to ideological confusion and compounded the disappointment of left-liberal critics. By the seventies, their national political base, which probably was more imagined than real in the sixties, had come apart. The diverse coalition composed of elements of the underclass, the traditional working class, minorities, women, and a conscience constituency drawn from middle and upper-middle echelons did not gain majority strength and ideological coherence, or political control, after the electoral victories of 1964. When the idea of relative scarcity replaced the vision of abundance as the informing assumption of American social thought in the early seventies, tensions increased among various elements of the coalition. For example, blue-collar constituencies favoring growth despite certain environmental risks collided with predominantly middle-class environmentalists willing to sacrifice (without significant personal loss) future national economic gains in their quest for cleaner air, purer water, and more ample living space. As the costs of a fairer distribution of resources rose, the conscience constituency shrank.

Of course, not all conflicts within the potential left-liberal coalition were motivated by such narrowly and neatly defined class interests, though these concerns touched nearly everything. In the seventies, for example, differences among liberals over the size and role of the welfare state took on increasing importance. The welfare state evoked mixed attitudes. On the one hand, it was part of a governmental apparatus grown large, expensive, inefficient, and remote—or so it seemed to many Americans. On the other, it performed crucial services that a majority of citizens continued to need and want. The very prevalence of deeply ambivalent attitudes, however, weakened the thrust of the left-liberal vision and eroded its political base. People who considered themselves liberal on social and cultural issues from crime to gay rights felt increasingly free to support candidates who shared their social views, whether these figures represented themselves as fiscal liberals or fiscal conservatives. Or they could choose to withdraw from politics or even to refrain from such relatively effortless acts as voting.

Even successful left-liberal activism produced unintended consequences. For one thing, successes in the politics of inclusion—among women, blacks and other racial minorities, Jews and other ethnics of eastern and southeastern European descent—might have diluted the enthusiasm and shrunk the constituencies for further egalitarian reform. For another, a plethora of single- or multiple-issue constituencies—among racial minorities, women, gays, environmentalists, trade unionists—promoted internal turbulence within the liberal stream, further separating it from larger currents of opinion and further dividing the Democratic party. Thus the very constituencies that left liberals hoped to lead enjoyed a lively existence of their own in the seventies, splitting frequently over a range of social and cultural issues. To simplify the main class lines of this division: a significant portion of the better-educated, middle-class conscience constituency, as well as other elements of the left-liberal coalition, remained liberal on economic, social, and cultural issues. The traditional blue-collar class combined a measure of economic liberalism (perhaps a declining measure) with an assertion of its conservative inclinations on many social and cultural questions.

Using the dimensions of economic liberalism, economic conservatism, social liberalism, and social conservatism, Seymour Martin Lipset constructed a four-cell profile of factions in the American party system in the middle seventies: "The consistent conservatives (people who are economic and social conservatives) make up the Goldwater-Reagan wing of the Republican Party. Those who are consistent liberals on economic and social issues constitute the McGovern-New Politics wing of the Democratic Party." Each of these ideologically consistent and politically reliable groupings appears to comprise "about 20 percent of the electorate." Beyond these relatively stable groupings, the picture turns cloudy. Data from opinion polls, Lipset observed, suggested that another 30 to 35 percent of the electorate, based largely in the trade union movement and in the Democratic party, came to be classified as economically liberal but socially conservative. A much smaller faction—earlier identified as "liberal Republicans"—were economically conservative but socially liberal.[9] Rough estimates at best, the percentages attached to each of these categories were subject also to rapid fluctuations in the late seventies and early eighties, especially in the mercurial middle regions between ideologically consistent liberals and conservatives, the locus of the great American center. And allegiances to political parties were tenuous. My immediate point, however, does not depend upon precise measurements or settled patterns of public opinion. It is simply that in the seventies and the early eighties most signs pointed away from the emergence of a politically effective left-liberal majority. They pointed in other directions instead: toward a muddled, volatile, and comparatively conservative mix in the amorphous center, in the opinion of some observers; and in what strikes me as the more dubious view of others, toward a long-term shift to conservative Republican control of national politics.

In the course of their ideological disappointments and political defeats, many left-liberal critics searched for leaders who could absorb or minimize growing differences among their constituencies. But the chief liberal heroes—John Kennedy, Martin Luther King, Jr., and Robert Kennedy—were assassinated in their prime. And no one—not even the last of this generation of Kennedys—could take their place in the seventies. By the end of that decade, left-liberal recollections of their fallen leaders displayed a mixture of nostalgia and bittersweet memories of the sixties as a time of high possibility and, as the decade wore on, large disappointments. These disappointments went beyond public reversals: they stirred the sensibilities of left-liberal critics. For example, Benjamin Bradlee, Washington bureau chief for *Newsweek* in the early sixties and subsequently editor of the *Washington Post*, recalls that "Kennedy had never been a revolutionary in any sense of the word. Bobby was much more of a gut liberal than Jack. But life was never the same after President Kennedy was assassinated. That's for goddamn sure."[10] And for more than a thousand pages, Arthur Schlesinger's *Robert Kennedy and His Times* (1978) celebrates its hero and his family with frequently ill-disciplined enthusiasm.

Schlesinger's loss, like Bradlee's, was personal: a White House assistant during the Kennedy administration, Schlesinger later was an adviser (and friend) to Robert Kennedy. In varying degrees, left-liberal critics lost a measure of their intellectual and political influence after the middle sixties. Partly as a consequence of multiple reversals, many of them seemed to display a weakening of inner confidence in their vision. Sensitive to ambiguity, uncertainty, and paradox in the best of times, these critics became connoisseurs of irony in the seventies. Some, like Galbraith, also became by turns imperious and downright irritable.[11]

The private dimensions of this crisis of sensibility, I believe, led many left-liberal critics to accentuate their areas of agreement on matters of cultural belief and preference. Characterizing an apparent shift in the American political and cultural atmosphere from the sixties to the seventies epitomized by the election of Jimmy Carter, Richard Locke observes sourly: "We've exchanged radicals and wits for Jesus and grits."[12] This alleged exchange struck critics on the liberal left as an unhappy bargain. And they responded variously, though in a predictably negative fashion, to the Carter administration, first to its cultural style, and then, increasingly, to its political substance and operational incompetence. This was not surprising, for in spite of crucial differences in sensibility and cultural proclivities, left-liberal critics do exhibit certain affinities. They draw the line, often hazily, at the edges of cultural radicalism on the one side and at Jesus and grits on the other. Insofar as they articulate the economic and social needs of the underclass and working class in their own ideological terms, these critics may be said to side with the disadvantaged. They do so, at least tentatively, out of some ambiguous mixture of genuine concern and personal interest. But frequently they exhibit a set of cultural biases typically at odds with those of their presumed political allies. As one self-proclaimed anti-intellectual—an anonymous Polish-American machinist—put it in an interview with Robert Coles published in 1971:

The way I see it, you've got these people who run the big companies; and then you've got others who run the newspapers and the magazines and the television stations, and they're all full of themselves . . . The way they speak on those talk shows! The announcer, with his phony English accent! And the things they say, it makes you want to go and smash the damn set! They're full of long lectures, and they're always "reconsidering" something. They don't really like this country . . . that's one of the problems. There are times when I completely agree with what they'll say, but it's their *attitude* that gets you. They're conceited, that's what I'd call them. They make you want to go kick them you know where and tell them to come off it, cut it out. Like my wife says: "Jesus Christ, it can't be that complicated!"[13]

Left-liberal social critics, who for the most part inhabit the academy, generally favor intellectual and even academic life over ordinary life. They prefer the city or at least the idea of the city to the country, except perhaps in July and August when they flee to the Cape; and they detest the suburbs the year round. They prefer the Northeast, Washington, parts of California, and major academic outposts between the coasts to the rest of the country. And they disparage the midwest and the sun belt, especially Los Angeles and the deep South. Left-liberal critics tend to celebrate high—or at least middlebrow—culture, condescend occasionally to acknowledge certain facets of popular culture, and denigrate nearly all manifestations of mass culture. They take small doses of the adversary culture, preferring them sanitized and neatly packaged. They treat most religious expressions of Judaism as arcane, and they regard evangelical and charismatic manifestations of Christianity as hopelessly naïve, superstitious, and frequently reactionary.

This amounts to a powerful (though not really substantive) set of cultural biases that frequently has the effect of compromising the democratic vision of critics on the liberal left. Although they are not the sole property of left liberals, these cultural dispositions are practiced faithfully by even their best satirists—Woody Allen and Jules Feiffer.

When in full operation, these presuppositions prevent all but the most able critics on the liberal left from understanding the felt concerns of a decisive majority of their fellow citizens with any depth or sensitivity. *Gates of Eden* (1977), Morris Dickstein's well-received and in many respects competent study of American culture in the sixties, reveals these cultural predispositions in nearly uninhibited play. Dickstein concerns himself with some obviously important strains of American culture of the fifties and sixties, but he does not take account of the whole of it, or even of a part that can stand for the whole, as the subtitle of his book, *American Culture in the Sixties,* promises. Yet like so many other left liberals, Dickstein seems at ease with what he delivers, noting in his preface that he has "slighted cultural phenomena" for which he feels "little affinity, as well as others that were more conservative than innovative, and therefore tell us little about cultural change." However suitable it is for an examination of other intellectuals who share his parochialisms, Dickstein's curious logic makes him insensitive to larger currents in American society and culture, not to mention their nuances. The conflicts of the sixties, he writes, "unmasked another Old Regime whose convenient symbol was Eisenhower, and whose substance was the increasingly decayed and irrelevant traditions of rural or small-town America . . ."[14]

Because they are more than a pardonable shorthand, such pretension and insensitivity infect the center of left-liberal imagination, predisposing its exponents to celebrate one or possibly two thrusts of the sixties and to lament much of the seventies. It prevents them from dealing sympathetically with the conflicting range of aspiration in America during these decades. They may applaud the wish for political and social equality, personal dignity, and occupational opportunity on the part of women, blacks, and selected minorities. But they remain openly hostile to desires for affective religious experience and social respectability of Pentecostal and evangelical Christians. They are largely indifferent to the search for dignity and social space among less educated and less assimilated third-generation Jews and southern European ethnics. They lack cultural ties with the traditional working class and with large sectors of the middle class. And they disparage the revival of libertarianism, an idea once possessed by ascendant classes but now used loosely by relatively dispossessed individuals to express their opposition to the corporate system.

Blinded by their own vision, irritated by the defection of others, left-liberal critics had reached what many of them hoped would be only a temporary political impasse by the end of the seventies. The plight of people on the liberal left was complicated by the outbreak of philosophical debate advanced by such thinkers as John Rawls, Robert Nozick, and Ronald Dworkin over the proper role of the state and the relative importance of claims on behalf of liberty and equality. Though this debate testified to the survival of political philosophy, it proved unresolvable, especially in a social context increasingly apprehended as one defined by relative scarcity. In fact, the reemergence of political philosophy might have clouded political vision. The plight of left liberals was complicated further by an absence of any animating vision of culture. It is true that the collection of left-liberal cultural biases, which often unintentionally subverted the left liberals' political aims, served to keep various crowds at a distance. But these biases did not add up to a central or compelling view of American culture. Lacking a controlling vision beyond the idea of a democratic, pluralistic culture, left liberals were especially susceptible to cultural values, images, and ideas drawn from other areas of American life—especially the counterculture, minorities, and the underclass.

Left-liberal critics invoked a social gospel model of helping others. But it was an orientation grown cold, having been deprived largely of its invigorating spiritual and moral power: the authentic interests of left liberals were suspect among people who came to believe that such types specialized in helping themselves primarily and others only incidentally, if at all. Moreover, this orientation did not facilitate a growth of personal authenticity, since its adherents fed off the cultural vitality of other groups. Throughout the sixties and seventies critics from within the liberal left and beyond—from Norman Mailer and Leslie Fiedler to Andrew Kopkind and Edgar Z. Friedenberg—explored the cultural and spiritual hollow at the center of left-liberal perspectives. From Mailer's fascination with criminals, hipsters, and blacks to Kopkind's fascination with androgeny, left liberals searched for an authentic view of culture and personality that would illuminate their political concerns and themselves. Many claimed success, though they did so on terms other than those which bound left liberals in uneasy political alliances: as reform Jews, as independent humanists, as mainline Protestants, as progressive Catholics.

Others defected. But those who did not wander off to the radical cultural or political left or to the neoconservative (or "new liberal") right became increasingly aware of their narrowing critical options. They could learn to live with ideological confusion and political defeat and take solace in a return to a sort of Niebuhrean tragic vision. Or they could press ahead—on their own terms, of course—in pursuit of another round of economic growth, the key to any unfolding of left-liberal vision. As *The New Republic,* by all measures the best left-liberal periodical in the late seventies, put it in a major editorial published in 1979, "There is no reason why economic growth should be thought of as a conservative issue. But there is also no reason why liberals, in agreeing with conservatives about the importance of increasing prosperity, must accept the conservative prescriptions, which consist primarily of tax breaks for owners of capital. The most direct way to increase productivity is by putting unemployed people to work, something a government jobs program would achieve."[15]

Many left liberals seeking to wield political influence followed a more deliberately ambiguous path: they pressed ahead in search of power, promoting pieces of their dream while softening their overall vision. They hoped, that is to say, to reassemble a Democratic coalition that would give them a fragile electoral mandate. Power—or rather the degree of power they sought—eluded left liberals in the seventies. And they emerged from a decade most preferred to forget with only modest political hopes for the eighties. Even though their vision had faded and their postwar ideology had lost its overall coherence, however, left liberals, along with many radicals, came away from the seventies in possession of their values of liberty, a measure of equality, representative democracy, compromise, and tolerance. This was no small legacy, but it was one in disarray since pieces of liberal dreams and fragments of liberal values remained scattered with no clear prospect of imminent fusion into a compelling vision or a workable politics.

6

The Neoconservatives

"Even if we can't be happy," Irving Kristol advised, "we must always be cheerful."[1] Certainly the neoconservatives had reason to be cheerful in the seventies. In the span of a decade, these political intellectuals had gained a measure of respectability and public influence that, despite earlier successes, they could not have achieved on their own, even as editors and partisans of such lively journals as *The Public Interest* and *Commentary*. They had made it, to adapt Norman Podhoretz's phrase. As Peter Steinfels observed, "They dine with the President, advise his advisers, sit in the Senate, plot strategy for the political parties, tutor the media, philosophize for big business, and rally the forgotten cold warriors of the labor movement." Moreover, Steinfels continues, the neoconservatives "are solidly entrenched in the elite universities—the established church of our day—and they are rapidly constructing an independent intellectual base of imposing size: foundations, journals, and research institutes from which to launch their missionary activities."[2]

This swift rise disposed many neoconservatives to be personally cheerful, perhaps even a bit too buoyant to suit more traditional commentators such as Richard Weaver or Russell Kirk. But most of the leading figures in this cluster—such critics as Kristol, Daniel Bell, Robert Nisbet, Daniel Patrick Moynihan, Norman Podhoretz, Nathan

Glazer, Midge Decter, Seymour Martin Lipset, Aaron Wildavsky, Michael Novak, and Samuel Huntington—also made a decent if not altogether successful effort to be unhappy about American civilization in the seventies. Were it not for their mixed attitudes—their reserved enthusiasm for the contemporary American enterprise—it would be a simple matter to add neoconservatives to the list of radical, left-liberal, and more traditional conservative critics who for quite different reasons judged the seventies a bleak time. The neoconservatives, however, did not quite fit the dominant pattern of American social criticism in the seventies. Although they played the present off against a brighter past (as is the custom of conservatives of all varieties), they did not regularly contrast the dark seventies to the hopeful sixties in the manner of so many radicals and left liberals. Rather, neoconservatives tended to compare the beige seventies to the gray sixties. Reacting intensely to what they regarded as radical and left-liberal excesses of the sixties, these critics located their point of nostalgia vaguely in the American past.

Mostly white, male, middle-aged, moderately prosperous, Northeastern second-generation Jewish intellectuals, the important neoconservative critics share a distinctive sensibility. They neither created the growing national mood of temperamental conservatism in the seventies, nor were they altogether controlled by it. But they were its principal intellectual beneficiaries. Anticipating this mood in the sixties— or perhaps only finding it among middle American constituencies long neglected by the media—the neoconservatives gave it a particular shape and tone in the seventies. It is not the shape of traditional Burkean conservatism, or of the zealously urbane anti-Communism of a William F. Buckley, and certainly not of those caricatures of conservatism— the philistine, neopopulist politicians and fundamentalist preachers of the New Right who flourish in the sun belt. Nor did the neoconservatives themselves occupy a single piece of ideological turf. Daniel Bell characterizes himself as "a socialist in economics, a liberal in politics, and a conservative in culture," whereas others, like Kristol, who were more comfortable on the right, came to accept or at least tolerate the neoconservative label in the seventies.[3] Their odd compound of liberal and conservative notions acquired over several decades accounts, I think, for the central irony of neoconservative vision: a simultaneous celebration of the American experience and a curious reserve concerning its recent turns, especially the multifaceted quest for salvation and social justice that marked the sixties and seventies.

When approaching any network of conservatives, it is especially important to understand the intersections of biography and history. For American conservatism is primarily a personal and occasional affair. Conservatives never have been able to develop a unified social doctrine in an atmosphere of unending change: their constant factor is neither a stable class interested in preserving its status and culture nor even an evolving set of traditional habits and customs that persist through slow institutional change. American conservatism rather must discover and periodically rediscover its stable element in the idea of character. More adjective than noun, "conservative" refers primarily to personal attitude, mood, and cultural perspective. Hence, it is vital to understand *when* any cluster of critics became conservative and what they became conservative about.

Men like Kristol found themselves drifting into temperamentally conservative attitudes during the sixties (although Kristol claims to have been moving to the right since 1942). Doubtless there were many precipitating events, from the failures of socialist experiments abroad to the growing disorder at home, that added to the deepening worry that "democratic republics" were departing "from their original, animating principles," as Kristol put it in his influential collection of essays, *On the Democratic Idea in America,* published in 1972. But the student movement seems to have been central. It encompassed all of the cultural and political trends of the sixties that offended the neoconservatives. Student activists fronted the leading figures of this group along several dimensions. Sons and daughters rose up against fathers and mothers, as Lewis Feuer argued in *The Conflict of Generations* (1969), challenging them on grounds of sex and age, dismissing their intellectual assumptions and achievements, rejecting their authority in all spheres. The encounter could not have been more ill-timed. Just as many of the leading neoconservatives were ripening into the full maturity of their forties, gaining both success and respectability, the young rejected them in deeply personal ways. And they did so on the neoconservative intellectuals' turf: the academy.

Moreover, many of the young radicals left no nerve untouched. They adopted some of the worst authoritarian postures and practices of the old Left, thereby jogging memories of past battles between Stalinists and others on the left. To these, many new Leftists added a studied (and in some cases not so studied) anti-intellectualism, which drove their intellectual elders wild. They pressed for the most egalitarian social demands of racial minorities, and later of women, favoring as a device of redistributive justice the same quota systems that earlier had worked to the disadvantage of Jews in America. By the end of the sixties, sectors of the new Left supported or at least did not actively oppose latent sources of anti-Semitism. They tolerated and perhaps even encouraged the domestic anti-Semitism that surfaced among ghetto residents. And they endorsed a programmatic anti-Semitism among groups embracing caricatures of Israel as a reactionary appendage of American imperialism. The stench of an old and ugly disease was in the air.

Thus, the cultural and political radicals of the sixties did not merely challenge the narrow self-interest of those who were or were to become neoconservatives. Young radicals questioned their elders' developed sense of themselves, their deepest assumptions concerning personality, culture, and politics. This, I should think, accounts largely for the continuing preoccupation with the left of the sixties and the inability of critics like Kristol to approach the political and cultural radicals with the balance, detachment, and grace they often bring to other topics. Reawakening memories of earlier experiences, the new Left provided a metaphor for the Manichaean undersurface of the neoconservatives' social criticism, first expressed in the thirties as an opposition between the Stalinist enemy and the Trotskyist saving remnant, and then, after World War II, in the anti-Communist concerns among intellectuals, which reached their greatest intensity in the early fifties. Many neoconservatives acquired an enviable ease in dialectic during their bout with Marxism (especially its most virulent intellectual strains of Trotskyism). But they also learned, and retained at some level, a rigidity of mind and a sense of rectitude that they attribute, often accurately if somewhat cavalierly, to their latest opponents. Such people as Norman Podhoretz declared war on the Movement. Podhoretz proceeded to organize the troops around *Commentary* and to serve as an infantryman as well in, as he puts it, "the campaign against the Movement that began with the June 1970 issue and continued with great intensity for about three years. In the course of that time, the magazine ran articles critical of almost every important aspect of the radicalism of the sixties: its political ideas, its cultural attitudes, its institutional structures, and its literary and intellectual heroes; and I myself participated as a writer with a monthly column similar to the one I had done ten years before."[4]

Having passed beyond their youthful radicalism of the thirties, many of the intellectuals later identified as neoconservatives adopted large chunks of liberal political ideology in the forties, including the idea of the inevitability (if not necessarily the desirability) of a large welfare state, which embodied some of their early commitments to social justice. But they grew ever more wary of the state—and, I think, of politics as well. The philosophical liberalism of the fifties that influenced them—philosophical liberalism in the mode of Reinhold Niebuhr—was "realistic" and somber, alive to the complexities, ironies, and limitations of politics and history. It was altogether appropriate for intellectuals coming of age and participating, albeit diffidently, in the American celebration. And it was especially attractive to certain second-generation American intellectuals seeking a mature balance in their outlook, a counterweight to the apocalyptic dimension of their inherited immigrant sensibilities. Philosophical liberalism not only made good sense. It also fit well with the conservative antithesis of messianism within Jewish thought: an abiding concern for order, stability, evolutionary change, and tolerance. For most middle-aged neoconservatives, it seems fair to speculate, philosophical liberalism became a stabilizing element of their identity as Americans, a sign of acceptance and assimilation.

By the middle sixties, many neoconservatives were adding to their suspicions of the extended scope and degree of state intervention in American economic and social life. The expanding size and seemingly ubiquitous functions of the welfare state threatened to create a permanent imbalance between public and private spheres which, they believed, would produce an increasingly unhealthy concentration of power in the "new class" as well as a disturbing loss of respect for authority among citizens. At this point, certain intellectuals became temperamentally conservative about structural trends and highly critical of the left-liberal ideology that rationalized them. They reacted to the unruly political participation of minorities and of tiny elements of the Movement, concluding that the democratic system had become overloaded, strained by an infusion of what Samuel Huntington termed "credal passion."[5] They grew nervous about the capacity of government to enforce an extension of the idea of equal opportunity to include equal access, especially through affirmative action programs which often relied on quotas. And they adamantly opposed the notion of equality of result, as if it were more than a rhetorical flourish of the sixties, a weak tendency that never described or threatened to describe any substantial part of American public life.

Beginning in the late sixties, some members of this network—Glazer, Podhoretz, and Kristol, for example—deepened their criticism of left-liberal perspectives, borrowing and adapting, though not always fully integrating, notions from more traditional conservative thinkers: Aristotle, Burke, Michael Oakeshott. Not surprisingly, they have tended to approach proposals to extend the welfare state cautiously. But they remain at least ambivalent about the value of current welfare programs and often support those that benefit a majority of citizens. And they take various positions on fiscal matters, from libertarian economics to more structured, traditionally conservative approaches to political economy.

Most of the neoconservatives are not orthodox political conservatives or adherents of the neopopulist New Right. They are, rather, essentially cultural conservatives of a certain sort. Put simply, the neoconservatives express a nostalgic preference for the bourgeois ethos. The solid bourgeois virtues of "probity, thrift, self-reliance, self-respect, candor, fair dealing" are marks of a character type that thrives in the middle range of cultural possibilities, between the adversary culture of a postmodern, postreligious (at least post-Christian) intelligentsia and the vulgarities of mass-mediated culture. Kristol celebrates this bourgeois citizen. The individual who is well-educated, hard-working, ambitious, and above all, sensible, serves as an ideal cultural type, one Kristol believes to be fast disappearing in America. This nostalgia for the bourgeois ethos represents what might be termed a liberal cultural conservatism, a sentiment that distinguishes neoconservatives from their democratic socialist counterparts, men such as Irving Howe and Lewis Coser. It is, in fact, the genesis of their political and cultural differences with the comrades of their youth.

Neoconservatives may understand the idea of high culture and its modernist and postmodernist manifestations. They may consume some of its art and literature. But they profess a bourgeois cultural ideal in clear opposition to the moral and aesthetic canons of post-nineteenth-century high culture. Hence they display not only a distaste for attempts to act out the impulses of what Lionel Trilling calls the adversary culture. They also express deep reservations, even hostility, toward the aesthetic enterprise and moral implications of modernist culture. In the process of discovering their cultural métier, the neoconservatives became attached to the ideas of order and stability and uneasy about opposition and dissent, especially when presented in cultural styles beyond the middle range.

Beginning in the middle thirties, then, the neoconservative intellectuals—at least the founding fathers of the group—fashioned a distinctive sensibility rooted in their own encounter with American and world culture after, say, 1920. This sensibility is expressed partially in a hybrid ideology composed of philosophical liberalism, elements of the surviving New Deal political liberalism of the fifties and early sixties, and a developing commitment to liberal cultural conservatism. Although their high moment of public success was deferred until the late seventies, these critics seem most attuned to American life as they experienced it in the late fifties. Thereafter, the intellectual times changed more quickly than did the neoconservatives; hence, their political liberalism took on a conservative cast. The late fifties probably represents their moment of psychic ease: in retrospect, that time came to serve as the hazy dividing line between their nostalgia for the American past and the messy realities of the sixties and seventies. Defending the economic and political order of capitalism, neoconservatives lamented the apparent decline of its previous cultural strengths. Indeed, they contended that the economic and political consequences (and causes) of the deliquescence of character threatened the very stability of the republic.

Although Irving Kristol's *Two Cheers for Capitalism* (1978) consists of short occasional pieces written for *The Wall Street Journal* along with a few fuller essays that have appeared in *The Public Interest,* it provides one coherent and uncompromising version of neoconservative vision. As his coarse characterization of democratic socialism suggests, Kristol no longer believes it necessary to think strenuously about socialism, having elected to dismiss everyone on the left who questions "the key institution of liberalism: the (relatively) free market (which necessarily implies limited government)."[6] Ruling out all paths to the left, Kristol narrows his alternatives to one: some version of capitalism. Regarding himself as a realist, a man well aware of the irreversibility of the transition from competitive to corporate capitalism and the welfare state, he rejects as reactionary proposals to return to classical laissez faire capitalism. Classical liberal capitalism rather functions as a touchstone, a still point in a largely mythic past that helps to illuminate the present.

The chief virtue of capitalism, according to Kristol, is that it works, even through a series of massive institutional changes that stretch to the edges of plausibility his description of America as a "relatively" free-market economy. But capitalism considered as an economic mode does not entail civil or political liberty. It is rather the only economic organization in which liberty possibly can flourish. Nor is a free capitalist social order identical with Kristol's version of the good society. This larger vision includes the bourgeois ethos or rather some elusive equivalent of it that tempers the selfish imperatives and hedonistic consequences of an unrestrained capitalism.

Something like a satisfactory synthesis existed in the American past, although just when is not made altogether clear. But it turns out to have been an unstable synthesis. The citizens of liberal capitalist society developed a positive notion of liberty: the idea that men and women living moderately, with modest virtues, and expressing their prosaic preferences through the market, could create a good society. In the earlier stages, this notion of liberty was disciplined by the Judeo-Christian tradition and the Protestant ethic. But the idea of negative liberty prevailed, and the dynamic social order of capitalism also generated its own unsatisfactory excesses: the belief that the market translated the sum of private vices into the common good, the late-nineteenth-century equation of capitalism with the survival of the fittest, and a more recent emphasis on hedonism resulting from rising affluence and a presumed decline in the work ethic.

Ironically, then, liberal capitalism's success—its stunning economic performance and its enlargement of individual options—involved what Kristol terms a progressive depletion of "the accumulated moral capital of traditional religion and traditional moral philosophy." Following Daniel Bell, Kristol identifies the principal "enemy" of capitalism as nihilism—the ultimate consequence of the replacement of the holy by the profane—rather than socialism (old Marxist phrases turn up in odd corners of the text). For all its solid, sober virtues, the bourgeois social world came to seem dull, boring, prosaic, and progressively inadequate as the Judeo-Christian tradition exerted less authority among certain sectors of the population, mainly the better educated. Hence the emergence of an atheistic, amoral high culture that set artists and intellectuals, and later even political figures and bureaucrats, against bourgeois capitalism.

Kristol's central argument concerning the genesis and development of the present crisis of politics and culture leads him to a question neither he nor any of the other neoconservatives can answer. Unwilling to abandon his conception of individual liberty and voluntary association, Kristol realizes that his liberal stance is an insufficient means of coping "with the eternal dilemmas of the human condition." Because the bourgeois world is vapid and the adversary culture alienating, he argues, capitalism throws individuals back on their own inadequate resources. What seems to be called for is "the moral authority of tradition, and some public support for this authority." But Kristol recognizes also that the problem of assimilating this "authentically 'conservative,'" even precapitalist thought "into a liberal-capitalist society is perhaps the major intellectual question of our age."

Daniel Bell locates the sources of this problem within the evolving structures of American capitalism. "Without the hedonism stimulated by mass consumption," he concludes, "the very structure of the business enterprise would collapse. In the end, this is the cultural contradiction of capitalism: having lost its original justifications, capitalism has taken over the legitimations of an anti-bourgeois culture to maintain the continuity of its own economic institutions."[7] In Bell's view, whoever accepts the prevailing economic order must be prepared to endure its mixed political and cultural tendencies and consequences. Neoconservatives lived with these consequences during the sixties and seventies—or rather, they lived with their own generally somber readings of them. But they did so uneasily. Of course, they rushed to defend the entire American enterprise against its radical detractors: taking the long view, neoconservatives celebrated progress in the economy, the diminution of repression in the political sphere, and the vitality of pluralism in culture.

And against the world, they defended the American enterprise vigorously, arguing with rising success in the late seventies for a tougher foreign policy based on a renewed recognition of the continuing menace of the Soviet Union. Foreign policy provided an expansive arena for rhetorical excess. Here many neoconservatives could continue the long project of their own cultural assimilation by exercising once again the buried apocalyptic dimension of their sensibilities rather than hedging it about with devitalizing caveats. In the course of these exercises, they were able to assume their places as potent males in the dominant culture without having to focus on unsettling ambiguities associated with domestic matters: at the level of foreign policy, American civilization seemed capable of being put back together by transforming weakness into strength, both rhetorical and military. Not only would the righteous be vindicated. Those on the left who had committed cultural sins yet had eluded punishment in domestic spheres could be put in their place, taught a lesson in the symbolic locations of genuine power. The so-called cultural nihilists could be shown the real countenance of nihilism in the late twentieth century: the nuclear face.

Consider Norman Podhoretz's highly praised essay on the decline of American power, *The Present Danger* (1980). Using the rhetoric of the cold war to express a moralism barely distinguishable from a disquieting machismo, Podhoretz laments the erosion of American power in the world, identifying a combination of "pacifism, anti-Americanism, and isolationism" as the "malevolent legacy of the war in Vietnam."[8] The feared result of such impotence, Podhoretz warns, is a "culture of appeasement," which, if unimpeded, will end in "war or Finlandization." War seems less troublesome to Podhoretz than the subtle form of surrender he regards as the more likely outcome: no occupying troops in this scenario, just a growing imbalance of power in favor of the Soviets, rather like the one enjoyed briefly by Americans in the early postwar period. In these circumstances, the Soviet totalitarians would orchestrate the military, political, and economic tunes in Europe and throughout the Third World.

Against this effeminate drift, Podhoretz counterposes hope in the form of those policy makers and (neoconservative) intellectuals who set about articulating the "new nationalism," giving shape to rising popular (and right-wing) sentiment in the middle to late seventies. This new nationalism, of course, is little more than a rehash of old perspectives on the cold war: apparently a fair number of C. Wright Mills's "crackpot realists" of the fifties were alive and well and living in New York (or Washington) in the late seventies. Podhoretz calls for a revival of a policy of "containment," a resolve to regain military superiority over the Soviets so as to lift what he terms the "curse of Communism, or (to preserve the metaphor of containment) at least to keep it at a distance. "The reason Soviet imperialism is a threat to us is not merely that the Soviet Union is a superpower bent on aggrandizing itself, but that it is a Communist state armed, as Sakharov says, to the teeth, and dedicated to the destruction of the free institutions which are our heritage and the political culture which is our glory."[9] It is a hoary script, though not an altogether unreadable one. Elements of it have adequately described chunks of the postwar world for several decades.

Podhoretz, however, is cavalier about the nuclear complications that made his script both obsolete and dangerous—perhaps suicidal—by the end of the seventies. Acknowledging that "nuclear war would be a calamity beyond measure," he nevertheless attributes excessive nervousness over the prospects of such a war—the stubborn refusal to consider it even as an extreme alternative—to confused minds and feeble wills, nervous Nellies too anxious to think about the "unthinkable" (or even, perhaps, to smoke cigarettes). Podhoretz approvingly quotes an especially obtuse passage from another of his foreign-policy experts, Milovan Djilas, who observes that " 'the West has inflicted certain psychological wounds on itself which have no parallel in the Soviet Union. I have especially in mind the anti-nuclear propaganda of the Western Left. Their constant harping on mega-deaths and the prospect of doom descending on us unless SALT is signed, sealed and ratified has a debilitating impact on the NATO countries and especially on the United States.' " After citing the release of a lurid study of the probable consequences of a nuclear attack on the northeast corridor by the United States Congressional Office of Technology Assessment only a few weeks before the signing of SALT II, Djilas asks, " '*Cui bono?* The answer is obvious. No such accounts of the horrors of nuclear war ever reach the Soviet public, because the whole area of military planning is banned from discussion. This means that in the vital field of psychological confrontation the balance is strongly tilted in favor of Soviet interests.' "[10] This "constant harping" on nuclear danger (obviously the public equivalent of female nagging) may be the stuff of "Sunday-morning sermons in a little village community," but it surely is not the matter of serious, manly discourse. Only an effete weakling such as Jimmy Carter, the accidental president, or a person so unheroic as to prefer life in Finland to existence (if that) in some new Nagasaki could dish up such pap. If the *Soviets* are not deterred by contemplation of the consequences of nuclear war (a dubious assumption at best), Podhoretz reasons, *we* should not be either: it is simply unfair, a violation of playground rules.

Podhoretz's mock heroics seem to be the work of a man who reads his own magazine too faithfully. Those who perform the gritty work of writing about foreign policy in such journals, however, often wield finer brushes. In a *Commentary* symposium on "Human Rights and American Foreign Policy" published in November 1981, for example, Seymour Martin Lipset writes sensibly about the fashionable distinction between authoritarian and totalitarian regimes, a distinction occasioned by a partial collapse of the early cold war dichotomy between free societies and totalitarian ones (that is, the West versus international Communism). Lipset allows that the distinction "between totalitarianism and authoritarianism does not . . . correspond to that between Communist and non-Communist autocratic systems." Hungary, for instance, as well as Yugoslavia, and even, in a comparative sense, the Soviet Union after Stalin, may be considered authoritarian rather than totalitarian, fairly closed as opposed to shut tight. A page later, however, Lipset affirms the basic tenets of the neoconservative faith: reactionary, oppressive authoritarian regimes may change, he notes, but the leopard of Soviet Communism cannot remove its own spots. "Hence," Lipset writes, "as long as the Brezhnev doctrine is applied, we have no option but to resist Communist expansionism, to give aid and counsel to *every regime* threatened by Communist takeover."[11] The distinction between the authoritarian and totalitarian modes apparently makes only a theoretical difference when applied to "socialist" nations but a practical difference when used to justify American support for such tawdry regimes as those currently in El Salvador, Guatemala, and Chile.[12]

Relative degrees of sophistication aside, there appears to be a bottom line on neoconservative views of foreign policy: the need for a reassertion of American power, with conventional military and nuclear might as its centerpiece. It is a faith, quasi-religious in character and intensity, fueled by anti-Communism and unshaken by anything, not even the growing nuclear arsenals of both superpowers. Neoconservatives in the mold of Podhoretz come uncomfortably close to foreign-policy positions advanced by such New Right masterminds as Richard A. Viguerie, the genius of direct-mail fund raising, who declares that "the alternative to . . . an all-out American [defense] effort is simple. The Soviets will either force us into a war we will lose or we will be forced to surrender."[13] Perhaps neoconservatives are only hostages to the macho foreign policy rhetoric of the New Right. Surely there is more than a dime's worth of difference between, say, Viguerie and Podhoretz on the subject of United States foreign policy, since a strategy of containment promises to be less perilous than one of removing nuclear restraints on the conduct of war and peace and pursuing a first-strike capability backed up by a determination to use tactical and theater nuclear weapons in the right circumstances, as Viguerie proposes. But the differences may not be sufficient to put at ease neoconservatives able to think through the barriers of their anti-Communist faith. Politics may yet be the intellectual death of them. A pity, too, since their foreign-policy rhetoric serves so many other purposes: it confirms their membership in the dominant American culture while providing a release for apolitical, apocalyptic fear and anger; and it enables an assertion of macho sentiment in a universe of discourse uncluttered by the ambiguities, instabilities, and irritations of domestic affairs.

Although they managed a confident, even arrogant, rhetorical pose on the need for more American military "muscle," differing mainly on how, when, and where that muscle ought to be flexed, neoconservatives grew increasingly diffident about current domestic matters, especially about the success of the left-liberal project in the sixties and seventies. Considering their disposition to celebrate the American experiment—to serve as voluntary spokespersons for what they considered a beleaguered majority—neoconservatives exhibited a curious aloofness from the recent political, cultural, and personal aspirations of most Americans. Energetically defending the corporate sector and the defense establishment, many of them had little enthusiasm to spare for anyone else. The line of Kristol's villains forms to the left (in the broadest sense of this term). It includes, as one might expect, all ideologues (programmatic Marxists), cultural radicals, democratic socialists, and most left liberals. The main force of the attack is reserved for the more ideologically (and occupationally) diffuse "new class," located primarily in the influential middle and upper reaches of the public sector: "scientists, teachers and educational administrators, journalists and others in the communication industries, psychologists, social workers, those lawyers and doctors who make their careers in the expanding public sector, city planners, the staffs of the larger foundations, the upper levels of the government bureaucracy, and so on." What this class wants, Kristol insists, is "the power to shape our civilization—a power which, in the capitalist system, is supposed to reside in the free market."

Kristol regards large corporations, whose forming power he slides over, as the major counterbalancing force. These admittedly flawed institutions, he argues, constituted the key to preserving freedom of choice in the late seventies and beyond. But whose freedom? Neither Kristol nor most of his counterparts show much genuine concern for the underclass. For example, Kristol does not deny the existence of poverty in America. He rather tries to soften the phenomenon by concentrating on the logical difficulties of defining it, exposing the most hypocritical and self-serving motives of many of its middle-class opponents, and identifying the excessive costs of clumsy bureaucratic attempts to liquidate it. Little of the pain and suffering of people—poor people or people discriminated against on various other grounds—penetrates the clean, elegant, neoclassical rhetorical surface of these essays.

Who is left? These critics do tend to praise the traditional working class for its relatively recent assertion of cultural conservatism. Many neoconservatives themselves rose from poverty, and some, like Bell, Lipset, Novak, and Moynihan, have retained a decent sensitivity to the hopes and anxieties of various ethnic segments of the working class. Still, the neoconservatives, who share many left-liberal cultural biases, generally do not give detailed and sympathetic accounts of the varied political aspirations and cultural concerns of middle Americans. And they are for the most part insensitive to the continuing quest for salvation. Bell may be alive to religious concerns, and Nisbet fleetingly recognizes the power of evangelical and even Pentecostal religious experience.[14] Yet most neoconservatives treat religion in contemporary America as a superficial phenomenon. Leveling and then dismissing all forms of self-improvement from theosophy to bioenergetics as "intellectual rubbish that the demi-educated, when thrown back on their own resources, mistake for spiritual nourishment," Kristol registers a similarly facile judgment of stirrings within the Christian community. "It is true," he concedes, "that . . . there has been a marked upsurge in fundamentalist Christian activity," only to add with sophomoric cynicism that "both James Carter and Charles Colson have testified to its impact, and prayer breakfasts are becoming common events among businessmen (though not, as far as I can tell, among their secretaries)."

But Kristol wonders "how seriously the phenomenon is to be taken. At the grass roots level, in local communities, it seems to be more political than religious, deriving its fervor from an opposition to big government, pornography, and school busing. These are all excellent things to oppose—but they are not the stuff out of which true religious awakenings are made." Kristol's implied distinction between genuine and bogus religious activity illustrates a neoconservative penchant for contrasting the leading ideas and institutions of bourgeois culture—work, marriage, the family, religion, voluntary associations—to their own versions of contemporary realities. These comparisons typically flatten and obscure the actualities of life in America. By turns lamenting the apparent decline of such ideas and institutions, and finding their contemporary equivalents unsatisfactory, these critics finally construct a pale, half-hearted, platonic defense of the American enterprise.

With some exceptions, neoconservatives had considerable difficulty recognizing just how far their vision obscured the vitality and diversity of American life—left, right, and center—in the sixties and seventies.[15] At the end of the seventies, they defended some of the gains registered in the pursuit of social justice and salvation since 1960. They supported equal educational and employment opportunity. They advocated equal pay for equal work for minorities and women. And they stressed—perhaps too heavily—the decline of poverty and the growth of opportunity in the middling social ranges. But most of the neoconservatives tended to endorse these gains nervously, after the fact, while separating themselves from the turbulent political processes by which they had been secured. In the end, they hoped to find ways to moderate an essentially unruly social process by dampening high expectations of social justice and ridiculing most cultural manifestations of the quest for salvation that marked the sixties and seventies.

At the end of the seventies, however, these hopes remained in search of a viable politics. Despite their intellectual successes and their imprint on public policy, neoconservatives had not found a comfortable place on the political right, even though many of them welcomed the Republican electoral victory in 1980. Like the left liberals, the neoconservatives hoped for a majority coalition composed of people—from the poor and the traditional working class to professionals—whose genuine interests they claimed to articulate.[16] But the more thoughtful neoconservatives probably did not allow their political hopes an uninhibited play, for they were well aware of the qualities prominently displayed by many of the New Right activists in such organizations as the American Conservative Union and the Conservative Caucus, not to mention the operatives of even more provincial groups, such as the Moral Majority: their deep anti-intellectual biases; their neopopulist opposition to northeastern "elites" (especially Jews); their frequently mean-spirited opposition to civil rights and civil liberties for unpopular minorities; their primitive political witch hunts of senators and representatives who take the "wrong" position on a single issue.[17]

Despite apparent discomfort, however, many neoconservatives found themselves siding increasingly with forces on the right on such issues as tax cuts to corporations and lesser businesses, balanced government budgets, less governmental intervention in the economy, fewer environmental controls, reduced welfare spending, greater defense expenditures, and restrictions on organized labor. It was indeed ironic to have reached this bend in the road after their political and personal odyssey of nearly half a century. In the end, the prospect of political success seems to make neoconservatives nervous: apolitical in their truest instincts, ambivalent about the meanings and proper proportions of freedom and authority, many of them, I suspect, lack the stomach for a sustained political alliance with the authentic, native American conservatives of the New Right. Some of them, alas, do not.

7

The Ascendance
of Nostalgia

At the close of the seventies, then, a nostalgia that gave way easily to pessimism and even to cynicism defined the climate of American social and cultural criticism, just as a tepid version of the idea of progress had characterized such activity in the late fifties and early sixties. Of course, social critics did not invent the nostalgia of the seventies, nor did they articulate all of its principal forms. A mood of longing for a past moment pervaded the increasingly syncretic popular culture of the decade. For obvious reasons: nostalgia provided an aging population with a perspective on itself through the materials of a popular culture shaped around the fleeting values of youth. The convenient device of decades reinforced this practice, permitting a re-creation of youth as the mass-produced cultural artifacts of each generation were recycled, ten to twenty years later, when their original audience reached their thirties and forties. Nostalgia offered a source of apparent security, a refuge from a scattered present and an uncertain future.

The recollected past seemed certain; it had happened; it was *there—* elusive perhaps, but simplified for easy (and self-serving) access by the ruthless pruning of faulty memories. Musicals such as *Chorus Line* (1975) and *Annie* (1977); gangster films like *The Godfather* (1972); such fantasies of the thirties as *Superman* (1978) and *The*

Sting (1973); television comedies such as *Happy Days* (1974-) and *Laverne and Shirley* (1976-) which evoked the fifties, all conveyed the mood of nostalgia for the recent American past. The products of popular culture expressed nostalgia for each decade from the twenties through the sixties, filtered, of course, through the opaque screens of the seventies. Toward the end of the seventies, there even was an unexpectedly sympathetic revival of the Vietnam experience, conveyed in popular commentary and in such films as *The Deer Hunter* (1979). It was a nostalgic reconsideration not so much of the war itself as of neglected soldiers, marines, and sailors unable to find their way back into American life. Except for the most sentimental fare of popular culture, however, the nostalgic mood was not unalloyed: it mixed with guarded hope in the personal lives of most Americans.

By the middle seventies at least, the theme of nostalgia dominated popular culture: nostalgia for times past, for places either remote or undisfigured by technology, for family, and for an experience of community. Caught in the transition from industrial to postindustrial society, Americans in large numbers felt themselves losing their psychological, social, and moral bearings—their sense of time, place, and manner. In such circumstances the mood of nostalgia was appealing, for it sanctioned a tight, or what was more convenient, a loose hold on elements of the past. In the extreme, nostalgia serves as an exercise in primary narcissism, a longing to reverse biographical processes to an infantile state wherein security and wholeness are thought to reign. When biographical urges take on historical dimensions, however, an individual's longing for roots, for his or her own lost family, can turn into a social longing for the former shapes of *the* American family. In this nostalgic view, changes in the character of the family during the sixties and seventies were seen as a defeat of the old by the new. Thus, the narcissistic potential of nostalgia can also serve as one temperamental source of conservatism.

Despite the rhetoric of nostalgia, however, the American family did not break down. In fact, at the end of the seventies the most common type of family household still consisted of a married couple, with or without children. This is not to say that previous family norms—a working father, a housewife and children—did not undergo major alterations. In spite of changes in the composition of families, how-

ever, the idea of the family remained strong.[1] "Family" gradually
came to be redefined as a group of people living together with shared
commitments and responsibilities toward one another: instead of a simple reproductive model drawn from earlier decades, the possible structures became more ad hoc, including such variations as single mothers
and children, single fathers and children, lesbian couples, and unmarried
couples. Family life, then, survived and changed, growing more complex, more difficult, more problematic: it underwent a process of
evolution resulting from a number of factors, including rising rates
of divorce and cohabitation, lower birth rates, and growing numbers
of women in the work force. Its forms expanded considerably to
accommodate the expanded claims of personhood exerted by each
member: mother, children, and even father. Thus, metaphors of
decline may describe recent changes in family structure from some
largely imagined point in the past. Yet such metaphors obscure gains,
for many of the changes, such as the ease of divorce, probably reflect
progress in the quest for fulfillment and the democratization of
personhood.

In its most uninhibited forms nostalgia may represent a thoughtless clinging to the social past as well as to one's own biographical
past: such behavior makes adaptation to present realities difficult if
not impossible. Indeed, at the extremes, the academic and extra-
academic participants in the quest may be characterized in this way:
evangelical Christians who long to be swept away in the rapture;
radicals who long for a community of free, equal, and fraternal
revolutionaries; conservatives who long for the simplicities of a
laissez faire society; therapeutics who long for the experience of re-
birth, of re-enacting the primal scene; enthusiasts of the natural life,
from health foods to home births, who long to reverse the progress of
technology.

Such simplified images and set positions can be used as uncritical
modes of dissent against the present, as expressions of no confidence
in any plausible future, and as distorted recollections of the past.
Nostalgia can be used in these ways, and it often is. But nostalgia
also has been one means by which parts of the American past have
been preserved for use as materials for constructing the cultural
present and future. The American family at the outset of the eighties,
for example, was not the same as it would have been without the

long-term pressure of widespread nostalgia for traditional values associated with "family."

The exponents of pure nostalgia thus are stock characters in a cultural drama more sophisticated than any of its parts and more varied than most of its participants will allow. The parts are important, to be sure, but they are only elements of a more subtle story of adaptation, preservation, and change. Consider, for example (since we are speaking of the family), one of the most popular expressions of American culture in the seventies, Norman Lear's *All in the Family* (1971–79). In this classic video text of the decade, each of the principal characters represents a bundle of stereotypes. Archie Bunker is the conservative as bigot, the white male chauvinist who nostalgically protests nearly every aspect of the present, from open conversations about sex and bodily functions to the demands for full personhood on the part of women, minorities, European ethnics, Catholics, Jews, old people, young people, and homosexuals. Michael, his financially dependent son-in-law, represents knee-jerk liberal positions on every conceivable political and cultural topic. At least in the early phases of this series, Archie nearly always was proved either ignorant of the new (that is, of the progressive, the enlightened, the humane) or bigoted about every popular cultural and social development subsequent to the New Deal.

But the new does not triumph absolutely in *All in the Family,* although it may seem to do so in superficial ways. Gloria (Archie's daughter) and Michael often represent an ideological position inadequate to the complexity of life even among the Bunkers, let alone among other Americans. The young people may represent more appealing positions on most issues than Archie is able to manage, but they represent them in simplistic, often unappealing ways, lacking among other things the wisdom and grace that can accompany age. Nor does Archie's nostalgia, expressed at the top of each show in the theme song "Those Were the Days" and throughout in his character, really prevail. But nostalgia does serve as an important element in coming to terms with change and giving meaning to change. Even the setting of *All in the Family* evokes a bittersweet nostalgia: the Bunkers' modest frame house in a lower-middle-class section of Queens, with its overstuffed furniture, lace doilies, and noisy upstairs toilet. In this comfortably familiar if no longer typical setting, the popular drama of the interplay of older and newer values is played out to mixed conclusions.

So it was, more or less, with critics. Operating within the broad framework of nostalgia, social critics from each branch of the bourgeois tradition—radical, liberal, conservative—also tended to assess the seventies against expectations they had formed in earlier years. These expectations often were unreasonably high. They invariably were parochial. As a consequence, critics, especially those radicals and left liberals in descending phases of their influence, were apt to dwell on the failures of their particular visions. Many radicals lost their vision altogether; liberals lost firm control of their lever (the state); and, as some of their ideas began to see the harsh light of practice, even the more cheerful neoconservatives lost their trump card of powerlessness. Critics were disposed to overstress ideological, cultural, and political disjunctures between the sixties and the seventies. Most important, they were inclined to obscure, neglect, or even scorn the salutary features of what seems to me the most salient development of these decades: the widespread progress of millions of Americans in their search for fulfillment—for a subjective sense of salvation and a piece of social justice. At the very least, the framework of nostalgia prevented many American social and cultural critics from examining dispassionately such a heterodox notion of progress.

No cluster of critics proved temperamentally willing, intellectually disposed, and ideologically able to acknowledge the centrality and the overall rationality of the multifaceted quest for fulfillment. Such an appreciation would have required large and unlikely concessions. For one thing, it would have compelled critics to range freely across ideological borders. In the stress of ideological battle or even in calmer interludes, few American critics recognized all of these factors: the contributions of radicals to democratic political change in the sixties, the importance of the left-liberal political thrust in the sixties, the probably long-range cultural (and even political) impact of cultural radicals, and the tempering effects of conservative moods in the seventies. For another, it would have required critics to cross cultural borders and move more freely through zones of sensibility: to see the Movement, the Christian revival of the late sixties and seventies, and the therapeutic search as aspects of an overall quest for fulfillment—one that was largely successful in spite of its tawdry sides.

Many radical critics feared the emerging democratic constituencies; liberals could not organize these constituencies effectively enough to maintain national power; neoconservatives remained diffident toward them. In fact, critics as a group were largely out of touch with most of the extra-academic ranges of American culture and society—with the sources of limited progress in the quest for fulfillment, from blacks and other racial minorities to elements of the white working class, suburban European ethnics, Jews, old people, young people, and women. Nor were critics typically willing to gauge their own progress in the quest, to note (or rather to stress) the obvious: that their sizable company was itself drawn largely from social groups whose members a generation earlier would not have presumed to attempt to enter the academy in such numbers.[2] Yet nothing less than an ecumenical ideological spirit, I shall insist in Parts II and III, will permit a sympathetic understanding of the quest that brings the sixties and seventies together.

To gain such a perspective on these decades, critics would have had to acknowledge the particular contributions of each of the major strands of American thought and sensibility. And more: they would have had to accept the limited importance that Americans generally assign to *all* species of ideological and political activity. To most Americans in the sixties and seventies the enactment of any social vision—Marxist, democratic socialist, left-liberal, neoconservative—was an issue of comparatively minor significance. Although used fitfully by a variety of groups, criticism and politics in roughly ideological modes represented but one means to the more compelling aim of personal fulfillment within small communities. It was the vague ideology of the quest for personal fulfillment itself that dominated American cultural discourse and powerfully influenced American political thought in these decades.

Most critics resisted these concessions for good reasons as well as for self-serving ones. Such resistance is part of the nature of social criticism: partial, biased, and centered in the present, it tends toward myth and moral fable on the one side and toward self-justification on the other. Moreover, the intellectual vitality of democratic social criticism depends upon such differences in temperament and outlook.

So does whatever political influence social criticism may exert. Its immediate purposes, this is to say, differ from its retrospective uses. Lacking ample historical perspective, forgoing any hope of exercising direct political influence, the historian of contemporary culture who works with materials of criticism may gain a compensating advantage in the form of a useful license to wander across ideological, cultural, and social borders. The risk that attends such ecumenical exercises is obvious: parochial nostalgia may be exchanged for a generalized, uncritical sentimentality. The challenge lies in examining surviving fragments of thought, ideology, and sensibility cautiously. And the hope is to fashion preliminary interpretive mosaics that make fuller sense of the recent past than any single ideological vantage point can yield.

The framing idea of nostalgia also exerted troubling side effects in the larger society. It doubtless simplified the task of less constrained critics—those who place themselves beyond ideology and beyond academic discipline. Above all, the idea of nostalgia reinforced the widening mood of facile pessimism about the medium- and long-term prospects of American civilization. What Saul Bellow termed apocalyptic "junk from fashionable magazines" found a resonance among audiences. As Jim Hougan announced cynically in his meditation on *Decadence* (1975): "To diagnose the society as incurable, its malaise terminal, is something of a relief . . . Nero correctly understood that beauty, music, and irony can co-exist with disintegration, that the inevitable can be accompanied on the violin."[3] Pessimism about the larger world, Hougan assumes, can ease personal anxiety. Yet he neglects to mention that it also eases the requirements of thought.

As the work of serious critics and journalists was filtered and refracted through the cultural apparatus—television, radio, newspapers, journals, documentary film—its less ideologically constrained features strengthened currents of nostalgia in American culture and society. Detached from their respective intellectual contexts, radical sensibility, left-liberal cultural biases, and neoconservative removal from the textures of American life all affected popular social criticism in the sixties and seventies. These critical styles reinforced faulty, cynical perceptions of politics and culture that seriously underrated the achievement, vitality, and promise of American life. From tinny hysteria to an unearned weariness: this spectrum of tone became commonplace in popular social criticism of the seventies. Though far from negligible, the cultural, political, and personal fallout from the blasts of trendy pessimism was finally, I believe, a bearable side effect of a proliferation of criticism, dissent, and protest that facilitated and bore witness to an impressive democratization of personhood in these decades. For better *and* for worse, then, nostalgia has become a durable and important part of our syncretic culture. Its intensity may ebb and flow, but nostalgia does not seem likely to recede very far in the next decades.

II

Searching for Fulfillment

... where is what I started for so long ago,
And why is it yet unfound?

WALT WHITMAN
California Shores

For by grace you have been saved through faith; and
this is not your own doing, it is the gift of
God—not because of works, lest any man should boast.

Ephesians 2:8–9

8

Conditions of the Quest

The several varieties of disenchantment with American politics and culture in the seventies testify indirectly to the persistence and growth of a pluralism that many critics admire, at least to a point. Pluralism was nowhere more evident than in the quest for fulfillment and in the growth of dissent. Indeed, a fair estimate of the extent of the quest and its principal social manifestation, the democratization of personhood, requires an exploration of dissent in relation to the two dimensions of salvation and social justice. Dissent, I shall maintain in the chapters ahead, was most frequently an expression of the quest—in many ways its common denominator. Beginning in the late fifties, pursuit of that growing measure of social justice individuals believed necessary to their enactment of the quest for fulfillment required ever greater use of such modes of dissent as criticism and protest, self-assertion and a willingness to make scenes. Moreover, the open-ended search for salvation itself became an ever more fertile source of dissent during these years: it heightened material and political as well as psychic expectations, thereby widening perceived disparities between aims and achievements. Let me preview this exploration of dissent and fulfillment with a consideration of the search for salvation.

The search for salvation is an obviously important component of the quest. For many people in this essentially individualistic culture, it is a preoccupation that virtually eclipses the idea of social justice, the other central dimension of the search. At the very least, the pursuit of salvation offers a point of entry. Definitions of salvation are diverse and often incompatible. Yet I believe that in the sixties and seventies essentially evangelical Protestant forms of the Judeo-Christian exemplar remained the primary historical source of criteria (and even of images) of salvation in America. To be sure, the stern Calvinist formula, which stressed individual election and ascetic renunciation of earthly pleasures, had long ceased to define the ideal terms of salvation on anything like a national scale, if in fact it ever had. Since colonial times, American society has grown somewhat more secular and profane, though it is more religious now and was less religious then than is commonly supposed. Still, over time, Americans—including those professing one species of traditional Christianity or another—have become more openly concerned with immediate worldly satisfactions.[1]

Even the expressly Christian versions of salvation that persisted through the sixties and seventies did so more often than not in diluted or antinomian forms: most of them would have horrified Cotton Mather and Jonathan Edwards. Some of them, however, might have appealed to Anne Hutchinson, since they drew upon the antinomian spirit which has endured in the American experience from the early seventeenth century to the present. In this tradition, a sense of felt wholeness comprises the ground of salvation—an inner experience of grace beyond the capacity of either church or sect to arrange or validate. The idea of heaven survived the partial demise of the notion of hell among Americans. And as the terms of damnation were relaxed, the widening criteria of salvation came to include various mixes of spiritual enlightenment, psychological gratification, and material security. For some people, personal fulfillment was a by-product of Christian salvation, a consequence, they believed, of the sacrificial death and resurrection of Jesus. For others, salvation was identical with fulfillment, coextensive with some therapeutic variant of the realized self. Salvation encompassed the gift of life, the promise of afterlife, and the experience of more abundant life. It occurred in the world and apart from the world. And it was claimed in any number of variants by people who spent time in both realms.

In these circumstances, the authority of established churches—Catholic and mainline Protestant—was challenged increasingly, even from within the ranks of believers. Catholics became less and less distinguishable from Protestants in their modes of worship and their attitudes toward ecclesiastical authority. Even Protestants became more protestant in the root sense of the term: Episcopalians, Congregationalists, Disciples of Christ, and Methodists abandoned their mainline churches in significant numbers. Many of the earliest Christian heresies flourished—Antinomian, Gnostic, and especially, Pelagian.[2] Though it may be that doctrinal issues animated discourse in some circles, they yielded much ground to the subjective test of personal experience: salvation as a search for felt wholeness and acceptance within some religious (or secular) community, whether in the form of a personal relationship, in a small network of friends or relatives, or, symbolically, in some larger body such as "the Church," "the Nation," "the World." This, I believe, was the unifying cultural thread that ran through the many patterns of the quest in the sixties and seventies.

The diversified criteria of salvation informed non-Christian as well as expressly Christian visions of self-fulfillment. Freed to a greater degree than ever before as a consequence of more material security, enhanced leisure, and increased higher education, Americans pursued a seemingly endless number of sacred and profane variants of the Judeo-Christian exemplar. Many of these variants proved unacceptable to contemporary evangelical and fundamentalist theologians and even to more liberal mainline Catholic and Protestant theologians. The terms of the quest yielded many patterns and an even greater number of customized personal visions—so many, in fact, that the Judeo-Christian outline had blurred considerably by the end of the seventies. For all their differences, however, communitarian advocates of the counterculture, student rebels, twice-born Christians, radical feminists, joggers, health food enthusiasts, human potential advocates, and the more fervent environmentalists displayed a range of similar concerns: like so many of their fellow citizens, they were contemporary pilgrims, people in quest of a more abundant life.

What periodically surprised and disappointed many observers during the sixties and seventies—especially secular liberals and radicals—was the survival and intensification of the quest for salvation in the many spiritual and quasi-spiritual senses of the term. Most critics, echoing Daniel Bell, expected forms of evangelical and charismatic Christianity as well as antinomian radical ideologies to die quietly or to survive only marginally as more and more Americans achieved greater measures of social justice and enjoyed more goods and services.[3] Self-fulfillment, liberal critics supposed, was either a function of the American dream of material success, or it lay just on the far side of it. In these versions of the American civil religion, everyone had a right to pass through the zone of abundance, and in time, it was thought, everyone would. As the goal of general abundance was approached, the major social problems of discrimination, poverty, unemployment, divisive material inequalities, and environmental stress would become manageable. Some people might define abundance itself as the promised land; others might move on from material satiety to new psychological and spiritual frontiers.

It is true that during the late fifties and early sixties such able liberal critics as David Riesman worried publicly about the potentially corrosive psychological and moral effects of the expected reign of abundance.[4] These caveats notwithstanding, abundance was regarded widely as capitalism's covenant with the future, its store of grace sufficient to supply every need and want. Although a few Marxists such as Paul Baran and Paul Sweezy thought the advent of abundance— and its humane uses—would require a new social system and a new culture, most American critics did not.[5] In any case, utopian versions of social justice fashioned around the concept of anticipated abundance were either equated with salvation or considered its indispensable precondition. For leftist critics, then, the pursuit of general social justice virtually eclipsed the dimension of salvation in the equation of fulfillment.

Liberal and leftist social critics of the late fifties and early sixties, it now seems evident, were unsteady guides to the near future. For a variety of reasons, including their insensitivity to spiritual registers of experience, most intellectuals overlooked the continuing importance of the Judeo-Christian vision in America, especially the polysemous vitality of its leading idea of salvation. In the sixties and seventies, it turns out, this model of salvation provided metaphorical shape to the general quest for fulfillment for nonbelievers as well as for believers. However profane it had grown in some quarters, however diluted by the infusions of therapeutic notions, elements of the Judeo-Christian paradigm informed such diverse phenomena as the Movement, the Christian revival, and the therapeutic quest during these years. It permeated the concerns of the most active seekers as well as those of fitful participants in the quest. Despite important differences within and among these phenomena, they all represented, in my judgment, genuine manifestations of the common denominator of contemporary meanings of salvation: the quest for personal fulfillment within small affective communities.

The congested, criss-crossing paths toward salvation inevitably provoke intense, often fruitful disagreement among critics. In a pluralistic culture, of course, individuals may feel compelled to tolerate a variety of practices that are at odds with their own vision of salvation. They may even assume the validity of multiple paths or at least cultivate a genuine respect for alternate routes. During the sixties and seventies, modes of tolerance grew—among the indifferent, but also among the committed: Catholic theologians and sectors of the laity, as well as many mainline Protestants, reform (and conservative) Jews, secular humanists, and adherents of such Eastern disciplines as the Self-Realization Fellowship. Indeed, increasing numbers of people were able to commit themselves to one version of salvation without feeling compelled to condemn all others, a salutary and long overdue cultural innovation. At another less measurable level, however, metaphors of salvation still stir deeply personal feelings, frequently organizing them into exclusive views. Thus, when the search for fulfillment takes on a special intensity, as it did during the sixties and seventies, observers tend to dismiss large parts of the quest, or even all of it, as misguided, selfish, and bogus. Even tolerant critics lose patience with those who press their exclusive views beyond the elastic bounds of civility, or worse, as in the case of such cults as the Children of God, practice legally questionable and morally unconscionable forms of psychological coercion.

My own biases and reservations should become clear along the way. But I wish to begin with a more or less neutral summary of the traditional (or perennial) and contemporary conditions of the quest before reviewing the related shapes of salvation during the sixties and seventies in the next chapter. For I believe that critics have focused largely on the admittedly troubling side effects of selfishness and rejection of authority while neglecting the remarkable general features of the search for fulfillment: its pervasiveness, its variety, its vitality, and its effectiveness. Criticism of every part of the search—frequently even very able criticism—may have the cumulative effect of seeming to indict the entire phenomenon.

Consider then the main conditions of the quest. At first glance, the project of self-fulfillment seems to be located within the domains of personality and culture. Indeed, a large portion of it is, for individuals must discover or at least ratify the particular shapes of their own salvation. But even this exaggerated laissez faire formulation of the matter, which neglects intermediate organizations, implies a public dimension. For the conditions of salvation—its free pursuit within a democratic context—entail some minimal conception of social justice. However elusive definitions of individual salvation may be, most of them entail a social approximation of certain values in order to be regarded as plausible: first, the liberty of persons, including formal freedoms and legal guarantees against unjust invasions of privacy; second, equality of opportunity, a social order characterized (or at least idealized) by merit as opposed to ascription. These core values of individual liberty and equal opportunity, which weathered both decades, were accepted by most Americans even during the most radical moments of the late sixties.[6] They were, as might be expected, espoused in their more traditional meanings by those who identified themselves as moderate or as conservative. And they were accepted also as necessary though not sufficient conditions for any just pursuit of fulfillment by left liberals who advocated a stronger role for the state in securing liberty and equality of opportunity and access for every citizen.

Across the American ideological spectrum, then, from left liberal to at least middle right, the quest for self-fulfillment included a minimal ideological and political dimension.[7] In this range of opinion, of course, self-fulfillment cannot be guaranteed by the state. At most, the state can prevent needless interference, and in some liberal and even neoconservative views it can compensate for systematic discrimination and its corollary—unfair advantage. The quest then becomes a genuine though elusive possibility open on various terms to all citizens. Perhaps I should say it becomes a set of possibilities within American civilization, ranging from material and public success to physical and psychological well-being and spiritual wholeness.

The stress on individual responsibility is not accidental. For this traditional notion comprises an integral element of the amorphous and multivalent concept of individualism that lies at or near the core of most American value schemes. Individualism—and the even more vague notion of individuality—largely shapes personal, political, and cultural vision. The facets of American individualism, including autonomy; the individual as the rationale for society; and the individual's rights to inviolable private space, to equal respect, and to the development of his or her capacities: all these doctrines of the individual flourish in America, along with political individualism (government by individual consent), religious individualism (the individual's direct access to God), ethical individualism (the individual as the source of his or her own moral values and judge of personal conduct), and, to a lesser extent, economic individualism (laissez faire capitalism).[8] Even critics who construe individualism (or selfish interpretations of it) as a primary source of problems—social discord, gross inequality, alienation, and potential ecological disaster—must begin by assuming that most Americans are afflicted with some form of this disease.

Of course, the cliché that postwar America has become nothing more than a collection of isolated atoms goes too far. For in an increasingly technological era, individuals are continually forced out of their isolation by the demands of a large and complex network of social institutions. And they continually attempt to break out of their isolation because self-fulfillment depends upon various voluntary and semivoluntary forms of association. In addition to independence, fulfillment requires close relations with others as well as participation in shared cultural symbols and rituals that can lead individuals beyond themselves.

The confused and paradoxical issue of how individuals conceptualize and actualize their selves in the context of other persons and larger collectivities—families, communities, social institutions, traditions—was not resolved in the sixties or in the seventies. Nor, it seems safe to predict, will this issue, so deeply rooted in the American experience, be resolved as long as individualism, rugged or anemic, remains a pivotal assumption of popular social thought. But the problem of constructing a self that is a part of groups and yet in some senses remains apart from them moved quickly to the center of cultural concerns during the sixties and seventies, and it continues to fester there. For groups continued to be viewed variously as sources of community, as sources of oppressive conformity, and, more recently, as the bearers of confused and incoherent values.

From the twenties on, groups and institutions seemed—and were—
so powerful that the notion of individualism appeared to have fallen
into permanent decline. Nevertheless, the idea survived major institutional changes, though most of its nineteenth-century images—of one
man, one gun; one man, one woman; one man, one vote—diverged
steadily from postwar social realities. The idea of the self, too, was
variously perceived. Critics who have dealt with the problem of identity, from Whitman, Emerson, and Thoreau to Charles Reich, have
insisted that the self is the highest, or even, as Reich claims, the "only
true reality."[9] Post-Freudian psychologists as diverse in their social outlooks as Erich Fromm, Otto Rank, Abraham Maslow, and Carl Rogers
have emphasized versions of the growing self as central indicators of
cultural progress. Even more modest claims stressed the centrality of
individuals. At the very least, Americans clung to the belief that individuals are of primary importance: ideologies, institutions, even the
rule of law are presumed to exist in order to protect individual rights
and advance individual interests.

Although they are not identical, the diffuse ideas of individualism
and concern with the self do overlap in contemporary American culture. The many-sided notion of individualism remained pervasive in
the sixties and seventies. But its obvious incompleteness as a source of
salvation—an incompleteness persuasively recorded in more than twenty
centuries of Judeo-Christian scripture and commentary and rediscovered again and again through the medium of raw experience—ensured
the continuing relevance of an old American cultural dialectic. The
persistence of individualism thus guaranteed the survival of a perpetual
tension between libertarian and communitarian values. Communitarian
impulses in the direction of greater equality, fraternity, and a noble
national unity survived as partial images of fulfillment. In the sixties
and seventies they endured in religious and secular versions of the
Judeo-Christian exemplar; in the experimental communities of the
counterculture; in many therapeutic visions of salvation; in the search
for racial, ethnic, and family roots; and in the growth of Eastern religions. The charismatic radical kingdom of grace mixed uneasily with
the rule of law and the norms of democratic society. Important as
these communitarian impulses were, however, they still unfolded within
the immediate, lived quality of individualism.[10] For a defensible reason: Americans, I think, have not rejected the values of community.
They rather stress liberty as a precondition to the exercise of communal

values and as a means of avoiding the cloying underside of collective life: conformity, unbridled authority, lack of variety—in a word, oppressive *gemeinschaft*.

Viewed historically and structurally, individualism intensifies an apparently vicious circle, a historic tension between American political economy and American culture. Most commonly, the notion of liberty is linked to some version of capitalist political economy, either to the nostalgic image of a free market composed of small producers competing to supply the choices of consumers, or to the more plausible contemporary descriptions of the mixed American economy that emerged from the Depression and World War II. Each version of capitalism promises to satisfy the material needs and desires of individuals under conditions of liberty. In phases of growth characterized by relative scarcity and the long-term promise of abundance, the political economy encourages a prudent moral discipline based on hard work, sexual repression, and material sacrifice. Individuals are moved, or are supposed to be moved, to forgo present enjoyments in anticipation of future satisfactions. Since a principal aim of progress is steady economic growth, however, the inducement to defer gratification and sacrifice for ends remote in time or space lessens (but does not disappear) when the economy reaches a condition of peacetime affluence, as it did in the late fifties and early sixties. And the latent material and psychological hedonism observed by critics from Tocqueville to Tom Wolfe pushes toward the cultural surface.

In such circumstances, expectations of all sorts soared: material and psychological, personal and social. The perimeters of individual salvation enlarged and the timetable was telescoped to include immediate release from external and internal misery. Self-fulfillment—material, psychological, and spiritual—appeared to be available and imminent as it took on the strong hedonistic and affective cast of a consumer culture. At the same time, social injustice, including deprivation of basic liberty for some, persisted and seemed more glaring, since opportunities and rewards were distributed so unevenly, especially at the top and bottom regions of society. Individuals and groups came to feel entitled to larger shares of current affluence and a fairer chance to cash in on the anticipated abundance. They therefore pushed politically with increasing boldness against formal and informal barriers to liberty and equal opportunity. Thus, together with psychological expectations, material and political expectations rose, though to differing levels of intensity among various groups. And resentments of all sorts deepened, along with a willingness to express them through dissent and protest.

Tensions generated by the political economy may be displaced onto realms of personality and culture (and vice versa). They cannot always be resolved there, though resolutions occur more frequently than critics who overemphasize economic and political preconditions to fulfillment allow. Many individuals concluded a satisfactory separate peace, defining and acting out their particular secular or religious versions of salvation. Others got caught in the midst of the quest, feeling themselves neither saved nor lost. Still others became discouraged and cynical. As a consequence, there was no thorough resolution of the problem of alienation or exploitation in the culture, or even the prospect of a resolution. Indeed, the pivotal notion of individual liberty, which justifies various species of capitalism, also requires a cultural pluralism in part because each person must arrange his or her salvation, if only through an act of accepting one prepackaged plan or another.

But pluralism not only enables the quest for salvation: pluralism can complicate this quest, because "capitalism," as Kristol reminds us, "is the least romantic conception of a public order that the human mind has ever conceived. It does not celebrate extraordinary heroism in combat, extraordinary sanctity in one's religious life, extraordinary talent in the arts; in short, there is no 'transcendental' dimension that is given official recognition and sanction. It does not," Kristol continues, "necessarily denigrate such things either, but, in contrast to previous societies organized around an axis of aristocratic or religious values, it relegates them to the area of individual concern, whether of the isolated individual or of voluntary associations of individuals."[11] The pluralist culture entailed by modern, affluent, democratic capitalism sets the individual on his or her own to pursue the seemingly impossible task of coping with existential dilemmas without the moral authority of tradition or the consolations of an established religion.

In the sixties and seventies, the quest frequently was as complicated as Kristol suggests. For it had to be conducted under difficult social and cultural circumstances. The search had to proceed in a society undergoing an awkward transition from an industrial to a postindustrial phase; in a nation whose strong civil religion had lost much of its capacity to accommodate sacred and profane impulses; and in an unstable, syncretic cultural ambience in which the notion of belief and the possibility of salvation had become problematic. A confusing multiplicity of theological and psychological doctrines flourished, from established and revised varieties of Christianity and Judaism to fragments of Zen, Taoism, Buddhism, Hinduism, and Sufism imported from the Orient (via California), and from traditional and revised modes of Freudian theory to the latest therapeutic stew. But these doctrines existed in an ethos composed of high and conflicting expectations, which added to the anxiety, doubt, uncertainty, and unbelief. There was therefore no guarantee of success. Indeed, there was no generally accepted criterion of success in the pursuit of salvation that was more authoritative than individual testimony.

Though the quest was difficult, prospects for success were not as bleak as Kristol suggests. Formal separation of church and state does not preclude close ties between religion and society even in what critics and historians regularly refer to, with only partial accuracy, as a thoroughly secular and profane era. In fact, despite the many obstacles, tens of millions of Americans reported success in their search for salvation during the sixties and seventies. It was not only the therapeutics—those whom Daniel Yankelovich identifies as pursuing strong forms of the quest—who reported themselves saved. Large numbers of middle Americans also claimed to have found their way into deeper spiritual waters—mainly though not exclusively Christian. This was neither a once-born nor a twice-born confluence of generations: multiple births, including some spiritual and psychic thalidomides, were in fashion. Many people claimed to have been saved more than once. Such claims are observable, though the quality of the experience of salvation remains subject to dispute. The varied routes to personal salvation apparently do not appeal to Kristol or to a majority of social, cultural, and theological critics. Orthodox visions of salvation may seem unavailable or too infrequently practiced; revised and secularized versions may be unattractive. But this double bind, whether self-imposed or inherited, need not obscure the more salient fact that in an increasingly syncretic culture both ascetic and hedonistic—otherworldly and worldly —versions of salvation endured and generated a variety of hybrid visions.

In the sixties and seventies, then, traditional American values both survived and succumbed to the pressures of relentless change. Reflecting such perennial concerns as the interplay of libertarian and communitarian impulses, the pursuit of fulfillment was quickened by the fluid circumstances of the later fifties and sixties: rising affluence, a growing youth culture, expanding higher education, increased leisure, and the proliferating media of television and stereophonic sound. It was complicated in the seventies by the return of the perspective of relative scarcity and the idea of limits. Old possibilities of salvation persisted through change. And new possibilities took form.

9

The Shapes of Salvation

In record numbers during the sixties and seventies, social critics representing American intellectual elites judged both religious and secular derivatives of the Judeo-Christian exemplar of salvation harshly, finding them irrelevant, fraudulent, and simple-minded. Critics ignored the quasi-religious dimensions of the Movement until it had nearly exhausted itself as a semiorganized force in the late sixties. They belittled the spiritual ferment among evangelical Christians and observant Jews in the late sixties and seventies. And they considered the expressly therapeutic manifestations of the quest—the many paths to self-improvement—caricatures of both genuine salvation and secular modes of personal fulfillment. Above all, critics who chose to dwell on discontinuities between the sixties and seventies tended to minimize or disparage the important links among all contemporary seekers: their accent on personal experience; their wish for a community of affective, touching selves; and their comparatively light regard for authority, doctrine, and received institutions.

Such links, I believe, are more significant than any ideological or doctrinal differences for an understanding of the main thrust of American culture in these decades: personal fulfillment within small communities of significant others. These links call attention to the growing therapeutic dimension of salvation and to the salvific aspect of the therapeutic. To achieve fulfillment, individuals needed to adopt some concept or other of salvation. The choice of particulars grew ever wider, for even though the abstract criteria of salvation derived primarily from the tradition of evangelical Protestantism, particular models that flourished were articulated in both religious and therapeutic languages. In fact, the most visible loci of the search—the Movement, the Christian revival, and the expressly therapeutic quest—each displayed religious and secular, spiritual and therapeutic dimensions. Taken together, these phenomena suggest the centrality, the continuity, and the pervasiveness of the search for personal fulfillment that dominated American culture in the sixties and seventies. Let me illustrate.

The Movement

It was not until the late sixties that some left critics came to regard much of the youthful dissent and protest, both its political and cultural facets, as essentially a personal quest, a spiritual wish to end alienation. "For a long time," Paul Goodman observed in 1969, "modern societies have been operating as if religion were a minor and moribund part of the scheme of things. But this is unlikely." Beginning from the premise that the young were "in a religious crisis," Goodman concluded that "in the end it is religion that constitutes the strength of this generation, and not, as I used to think, their morality, political will, and common sense. Except for a few," Goodman declares, "like the young people of the Resistance, I am not impressed by their moral courage or even honesty. For all their eccentricity they are singularly lacking in personality. They do not have enough world to have much character. And they are not especially attractive as animals. But they keep pouring out a kind of metaphysical vitality."[1]

Goodman's judgment seems to me increasingly persuasive. Liberation of the self from an oppressive and alienating set of institutions, norms, and roles; and salvation of the self through or in a fraternal community of equals: these desires pervaded large parts of the Movement and the youth culture of the sixties. Secularized variants of the Christian paradigm of community were evident everywhere—in the "beloved Community" envisioned during the salad days of SNCC and SDS, in the tribal festivals of the counterculture, in varieties of utopian Marxism, and in the emergence of the radical thrust of the women's liberation movement during the late sixties. And there were specifically Christian analogues to the Movement among Catholic Workers (where

Michael Harrington learned his first radical lessons), as well as among such mainline Protestant civil-rights and peace advocates as Robert McAfee Brown of Stanford.

Moreover, an emphasis on personal salvation figured increasingly in Movement circles. Again and again, autobiographical accounts of radical awakenings took the form of conversion experiences. For example, Charles Perry, an organizer of the 1967 "gathering of the tribes" in San Francisco's Haight-Ashbury, observed that "it was like awakening to find that you'd been reborn and this was your new family."[2] And Gloria Steinem, recalling her early experiences in the women's movement, declared that "feminism is an enormous gift. It has given me life."[3] Through one or another mode of salvation, then, significant numbers of people in the Movement sought release from alienation. They differed seriously over the terms and proper symbols of salvation. They debated the meanings and mixtures of self, community, and politics that salvation required. They practiced very different rituals, from taking hallucinogenic drugs to living communally. Indeed, with such exceptions as early civil-rights advocates, whose strength derived largely from their Southern Protestantism, most people associated with the Movement rejected particular versions of Judaism and Christianity.[4] But they nonetheless sought salvation—some mode of commitment to others and to ideas beyond the self—as a central part of fulfillment.

I do not wish to deny the explicit political and social concerns of certain segments of the Movement: activists in the black civil-rights struggle, elements of the women's movement, antipoverty advocates. Nor do I wish to minimize the remarkable political impact of Movement activity in the sixties and seventies.[5] Here, however, I am concerned with an equally remarkable phenomenon: that within the entire spectrum of thought and activity called "the Movement," expressly political concerns existed fitfully, even secondarily. Because this is so, modes of inquiry that focus exclusively on the ends of general social justice and the means of social theory, protest, and political action reveal the Movement from restricted angles of vision. Such modes frequently predetermine pessimistic conclusions about its cultural, personal, and even political significance. I believe rather that the Movement is better understood as a manifestation of the many-sided quest for personal fulfillment in the sixties and seventies. It was not the only salutary expression of the search, as some of its disappointed defenders have maintained. But it was a crucially important phenomenon whose impact extends through these two decades. To illustrate this contention, let me begin by proposing a definition.

Just what *was* this elusive Movement? By most accounts, it began fitfully in the middle fifties with scattered cultural and political protests and ended, say, by 1973 when members of the Symbionese Liberation Army murdered Marcus Foster, the first black superintendent of schools in Oakland, California. No single definition fits the entire Movement. It did not display a wholly unified sensibility, a consistent set of attitudes toward self, others, society, and the future. Political activists and social dropouts of all sorts identified themselves in varying degrees with the Movement: liberals, Marxists (followers of Karl and Groucho), Maoists, libertarians, populists, anarchists, existentialists, and enthusiasts of the counterculture. As might be expected, the long-term aims of segments of the Movement were diverse, vague, and frequently incompatible: a reformed, more just democratic capitalism; democratic socialism; communism; anarchism; and a spate of semiarticulated, largely anti-ideological visions of self-fulfillment and community.

The scope of dissent, which matched ambitious social visions, ranged from a concern with particular injustices to inclusive condemnations of Western civilization. The targets were seemingly endless: nuclear weapons testing; the denial of civil rights to blacks; capital punishment; official harassment of dissenters, nonconformists, and marginals; *in loco parentis* on campuses; poverty and inequitable distributions of power and wealth; the consumer culture; the war in Vietnam; liberalism; capitalism and imperialism; discrimination against nonwhite minorities, women, children, and gays. Although they were clustered along the left side of the spectrum of American ideology, these targets of dissent were not encompassed in any overarching social theory or unifying social vision.

Moreover, there was no organizational unity and little organizational continuity to the Movement. The most common modes of organization were ad hoc committees, which sprang up by the hundreds, often dissolving as quickly as they appeared, and a lively adversary culture, including folk and rock music and an "underground" press, which gave scattered elements of the Movement some sense of a larger context. Coalitions of unstable groupings were attempted in the middle sixties, but none succeeded for long, as the divided 1967 Conference for a New Politics revealed. The principal new American organizations of the sixties—SNCC and SDS—were not very large even at their peak of influence.[6] And they were in disarray by 1970. Moreover, elements of older groups that harbored long-standing animosities of their own—the Communist party and Trotskyist and newer Maoist sects—functioned in and around the Movement along with such non-Marxist groups as the National Association for the Advancement of Colored People (NAACP), the Congress of Racial Equality (CORE), and Martin Luther King's Southern Christian Leadership Conference (SCLC).

If the political sectors of the Movement were wary about the "elitist" and "inegalitarian" implications of organization—and even about the ends of ordinary politics—the more amorphous counterculture stifled all impulses to organize.[7] Indeed, the Yippies reveled in parodies of the idea of organizations, whether of the larger society or of the new Left. As Paul Krassner put it, "The Crazies have a rule that in order to become a member one must first destroy his membership card."[8] Thus, styles of organization in the Movement ran the gamut from anarchistic to participatory to authoritarian. And styles of action were similarly eclectic, running from nonviolent protest to electoral activity to the "trashings" of the Weathermen, who roamed the streets of Chicago in the late sixties breaking windows, throwing Molotov cocktails, and shouting obscenities.

The Movement, then, eludes precise definition. But its diversity testifies to its vitality as a social force and a cultural presence in the sixties, as well as to the continuing influence of its central concerns in the seventies—for example, in the women's and the gay rights movements. A complete definition would require a complete history. In his massive documentary account of the new Left, Massimo Teodori underlines the frustration of characterizing the Movement by proposing this catch-all definition: "*Movement* (singular, with a capital M) signifies the complex of positions, actions and attitudes which have developed over the last ten years [1958–68], including not only political and social aspects, but psychological and cultural ones as well."[9] The "Movement," then, was an umbrella covering particular sectors that "developed around a specific theme or a particular period": for example, the civil-rights movement, the student movement, the new Left, the anti-war movement.[10] I am similarly inclined to construe the Movement broadly, to include aspects of the counterculture as well as the more obviously political sectors. Yet within this immense diversity,

I believe, there was a central thrust: a quest for personal fulfillment that stressed individual salvation and a piece of social justice. A felt sense of injustice and a sense of meaninglessness: these, I think, were the two principal sources of dissent that moved young people of all races to radical action throughout the sixties—to nonviolent protest, reformist political activity, and confrontation politics. These sources of dissent also disposed people to withdraw, in varying degrees, from the dominant culture; to form urban and rural communes; to explore the frontiers of consciousness through rock music and drugs; and eventually to engage in scattered violence.

Critiques of society, which sprang from visceral feelings and encounters with power, centered on the persistent material exploitation of so-called left-outs: the poor, blacks, and such other marginal people as dropouts, draft resisters, and even garden-variety criminals.[11] Critiques of culture, which emerged even more obviously from personal sources, centered on the persistence and growth of alienation in its several facets.[12] Throughout the sixties, elements of these two sorts of critique mixed, merged, and separated in the consciousness of people associated with the Movement. Politics became cultural; culture and personal life became political. By the late sixties, "the personal is political" had achieved the status of a popular slogan in some Movement circles. Early on, many student rebels and disaffected intellectuals applied the elastic category of "left-outs" reflexively, imagining themselves as politically powerless and culturally alienated: Jerry Farber's crude essay, *The Student as Nigger* (1969), whose title tells the story, was admired widely on campuses. By the end of the sixties, in fact, everyone could locate himself or herself at the bottom of one social or cultural heap or another. Whatever the relative social position imagined, the emphasis clearly was on the self.

This reflexive disposition became increasingly important in the sixties and seventies, though it was evident in the Movement from the outset. As the Movement grew rapidly in the middle sixties, the composition of its circles changed: the original core of activitists, drawn mainly from professional families, was enlarged by the addition of representatives of other social and ethnic groups.[13] This expanded base was partly responsible for the growing militancy and inflated radical rhetoric of the most publicized elements of the Movement after 1965: the Third World connection was forged in these years, as militant minority groups identified with their counterparts in Asia, Africa,

Latin America, and the Middle East. But in the early phases, the initial strategy of direct action emphasized by such organizations as SDS and SNCC was based on a politics of reform energized by communitarian vision. It produced both initial success and failure and set the direction of subsequent theoretical debate within Movement circles.

Reformist strategies of political coalition both within the Movement and beyond competed with schemes to build autonomous bases of power: community control, parallel institutions, and liberated zones. But by 1965, after the Free Speech episode at Berkeley, the election of Lyndon Johnson, and the expansion of the war, those within SDS and SNCC who favored coalition (and nonviolence) lost ground.[14] The social-gospel model of fulfilling oneself by assisting or consciously intending to assist disadvantaged others in their search gradually gave way to a more secularized evangelical model both in the Movement and in the larger society. Here the main accent fell on authenticity, on individual salvation within small communities of equals, and on some version or another of social justice for one's own group.

The principle of autonomous growth of the various foci of dissent gained ascendancy in the middle sixties. After the Mississippi summer of 1964, militant blacks told whites to work among their own people. Carl Davidson and Greg Calvert, who headed one segment of SDS, expressed the growing mood of separatism, arguing that "No individual, no group, no class is genuinely engaged in a revolutionary movement unless their struggle is a struggle for their own liberation."[15] By 1967, following the divisive National Conference for a New Politics, a group of women who had grown disillusioned with the attitudes of male radicals launched what was to become an influential current of the women's movement. In their paper, "To the Women of the Left," members of this group declared that " 'Women must not make the same mistakes the blacks did at first of allowing others (whites in their case, men in ours) to define our issues, methods and goals. Only we can and must define the terms of our struggle.' "[16]

Radicalized by the anarchist-communitarian dynamic of their own sensibilities, overwhelmed by the rapid acquisition of new participants and sympathizers after 1965, pushed into autonomous strategies of resistance by the perceived failures of coalition, certain elements of the Movement began to make a theoretical point of their separation before they had even come together. As separation along the lines of class, race, age, status, occupation, sex, and ethnicity grew, theoretically inclined activists sought new visions, new theories, and new agencies of change that ultimately would bring together disparate groups in a revolutionary movement. Disillusioned with left-liberal reform, a minority of radicals embraced sweeping revolutionary theories, new and used. Marxism (and its variants) was recovered, more or less by default. It was the only surviving grand theory acceptable to intellectuals that fused faith and science, personal troubles and public issues, communitarian vision and political activity. Marxist theories probably helped make sense of the intense feelings of alienation and the longing for salvation that were evident among many radicals. These theories explained the inadequacies of coalition politics. They articulated the short-range potentialities of autonomous strategies, including various forms of armed struggle. And they buttressed vain hopes for an even larger, long-term victory over majority social forces: the triumph that would follow a cleansing Armageddon.

Such Marxist and quasi-Marxist theorizing also provided a kind of specious rhetorical cover for what actually was happening in American culture from the middle to the late sixties: a new burst of cultural energy released in the course of "autonomous struggle." Under the principle of autonomous activity, radicals opposed to political coalitions on any terms other than their own found themselves working more and more among their own kind: students, blacks, women, gay men, lesbians, and so on. In the course of this activity, the Marxian notion of class struggle was once again undercut, despite frantic efforts to define a new revolutionary class. More important, the larger society's political and bureaucratic categorization of disadvantaged people by age, race, gender, and economic status was tacitly, though often unwillingly, validated. Variants of ordinary reformist politics, including dimensions of protest, were strengthened. In the late sixties, for example, left-liberal coalitions of the sort advocated in such early SDS manifestos as "The Port Huron Statement" (1962) and by such democratic socialist spokesmen as Michael Harrington emerged once again as the only workable national political direction for the left, even though such a politics had lost much of its appeal within the Movement and in the larger society. And single-issue and single-group politics flourished everywhere, in the Movement and beyond. To some extent, then, the main shapes of the politics of the seventies—even many of the conservative shapes—were fashioned in the Movement of the sixties.

Strengthening the category of reformist politics, the idea of autonomous struggle also facilitated growth of a *cultural* radicalism. From the point of view of many radicals, this ironic turn gave credence to the wrong sort of politics and at the same time discouraged much participation in any variety of politics at all. This notion of autonomous action intensified the search for personal authenticity and fulfillment, the central thrust of American culture during the sixties and the seventies: within each fragmented nodule of dissent, individuals could seek a community of equals among their own kind. The strategy of autonomous struggle supposedly ruled out arrangements that brought diverse people into systematically unequal and "inauthentic" relationships. Of course, tensions among social unequals marked all phases of the Movement: even in the early years, when communities within the Movement were small and relatively homogeneous, fragments of the social gospel idea persisted as privileged people went forth to help their less fortunate brethren. Nevertheless, the idea of autonomous struggle best fit the later, enlarged, more diverse, and more radical phase of the Movement. Not only was it consistent with single-group and single-issue politics; it also sanctioned what some sloganeers of the Free Speech movement called "the issue beneath the issues": the quest for personal fulfillment within a more narrowly defined community of equals than grandiose thinkers such as the early Tom Hayden had in mind. As Cathy Cade put it on joining the new women's liberation movement, " 'in the black movement I had been fighting . . . someone else's oppression and now there was a way that I could fight for my own freedom and I was going to be much stronger than I ever was . . .' "[17]

Thus the main course of Movement dissent after, say, 1965 underlined the commitment of participants and supporters to self-liberation, or the liberation of the self within the context of one's own special group: students, blacks, Hispanics, women, gay men, lesbians, and so forth. Political activity of various sorts—especially an expressive politics of protest—might have been formally consistent with the quest for self-fulfillment and self-actualization. And at certain points, as in the black civil-rights movement, political engagement was even perceived as a vital prerequisite to salvation by individuals in some groups, as I shall make clear in subsequent chapters. But early on, politics, especially noncommunitarian ordinary politics, came to be understood widely as accidental and occasional in many elements of the Movement. It was the search for salvation within small communities that formed an indispensable part of the quest, an organic component.

As Sara Davidson observes, recalling a scene from Berkeley in 1969: "Bob Dylan was singing from speaker vans. 'You can have your cake and eat it too.' Marvin Garson was writing: 'That high feeling—when you're relating to each other as brothers and sisters—that's the revolution. That's what's worth living and dying for.' "[18] The forms of politics that did flourish, from protest marches to sit-ins, then, emphasized and often parodied the elements of a crusade, a quest, from the initial awakening through trials to fulfillment. The secondary or accidental status of politics is confirmed by another fact: a majority of individuals sympathetic to one facet of the Movement or another never even took up the political search to universalize liberty and equality through politics—whether a hopeless antipolitics of revolution or a possible politics of reform. By the end of the sixties, even many activists who had once been drawn to politics had given up the search. Yet it remained possible for individuals who had gained or been bequeathed a degree of liberty and equality to continue the quest: to "do their own thing," to insist that nobody was superior to them, and to cultivate some community of essentially remissive and/or submissive personalities in which their hopes and fantasies of liberation and reconciliation might be nurtured. The quest for personal fulfillment within small communities survived the political pretensions and practices of the Movement.

Stripped of any vestiges of the discipline of political imagination, homologous visions of fulfillment as grandiose as the utopian Marxism of the late new Left spread, assuming forms that politically minded Marxists and left liberals found both alien and unacceptable: visions of divine light, of cosmic awareness, of inner enlightenment, and old-fashioned versions of Christian salvation. Though they were usually connected, at least imaginatively, to images of personal power, these visions remained more or less self-consciously detached from questions of class power. Such metaphysical forms were, of course, scarcely less removed from the levers of power in America than were the apparently hard-boiled Marxian schemes. In some instances, the new faiths provided small communities of refuge for those who had given up the long political battle for general social justice in America. And these new schemes served an old purpose that formerly prominent radicals must have appreciated: they kept their practitioners at the head of small, if usually motley, parades. Charismatic authority thus proved to be both protean and contagious, popular within the Movement and beyond.

Radicals who defined community in grandiose national and international leftist terms and then equated community building with political action frequently missed or pointlessly lamented an insistent American theme that characterized the Movement as well as much of the larger society: the centrality of the quest for fulfillment and its formative influence on the shapes of politics and culture in the sixties and seventies. Most Americans, including most of those touched by the Movement, simply rejected radical definitions of the notion of community. However inclusively they construed the *idea* of community, they did not, at least in large numbers, believe in a politics of revolution or a more plausible politics of reform as a primary means to fulfillment, to salvation, or even to social justice. Hence, in the sixties and seventies, Americans within the Movement and beyond typically limited the scope of the amorphous notion of community in practice to include only the self and select circles of significant others: a personal relationship, a small group of friends, a larger, symbolic collectivity. And a majority of minority groups viewed politics as at best a necessary evil—a means of advancing or protecting their immediate material interests and a means of securing or protecting their minimal rights to seek fulfillment and community. The search for salvation could and did spread as Movement politics and left-liberal politics—indeed, all politics—came to seem unsatisfying or even futile to millions of Americans in the late sixties and seventies. The Movement made more than a modest contribution to this apolitical and antipolitical drift. It succeeded in areas in which many of its radical advocates had hoped to fail.

The Christian Revival

If intellectuals recognized the spiritual and salvific dimensions of the Movement only tardily, they generally scorned the revival of expressly Christian modes of salvation that occurred during the late sixties and seventies. Diverted by the apparently irreligious character of the Movement of the sixties and confident that the new middle classes would give up old superstitious ways, highbrow critics refused even to acknowledge the existence of the Christian revival until it was well under way (and its main force perhaps very nearly spent). Even in the late seventies, when critics had begun to get hold of the elemental sociological facts of the case, they offered no sensitive treatments of the subject in such journals as *Partisan Review, The New York Review of Books, Dissent,* and *Commentary.*[19] As John Schaar observed in an essay on several works on contemporary American religion, "It is difficult for most intellectuals in this secular and enlightened age to take religion seriously. Many of us have grown out of it— if we ever had it—and we are pretty sure that the same progress will be followed by others . . . Religion is something that primitive, traditional, and simple-minded folk have and need, but it is bound to fade as they, too, are pushed into the 'modern world' . . ."[20]

If the general idea of religion struck such critics as Schaar as something analogous to an eradicable disease of childhood, such as polio, the particular doctrines of evangelical Christianity evoked their unrelieved contempt. And the related modes of Pentecostal and charismatic experience lay quite beyond their range of comprehension. Worst of all, many critics charged, evangelical and Pentecostal Christianity had become hopelessly cross-stitched with fundamentalist attitudes that took form as shallow, rigid responses to modernist culture.

The caricature of Pentecostal and charismatic phenomena that permeates middle- and highbrow social criticism goes something like this: evangelical doctrines of salvation are dying, if not dead, having passed into the hands of such shallow media merchants as Billy Graham. Pentecostal and charismatic modes may survive, but only on the social and cultural margins, mainly among lower-class Southerners and the urban poor—black, white, and, increasingly, Hispanic. These religious modes, many critics assumed, belong to a variety of quaint types: to scraggle-toothed, illiterate preachers (weary men who spend their weekdays repairing jalopies); to sweaty snake handlers who work the hills of Tennessee and Kentucky; and to obese women who beat tinny tambourines in urban storefront churches that are often too cramped to proclaim such elaborate names as "Christ the Solid Rock Church of God in Christ." The instances of condescension toward third-force Christianity are seemingly endless. For example, in the summer of 1980, Harvey Cox announced plans to turn several of his Harvard divinity students loose in the hills of West Virginia to study, in a sort of anthropological way, various churches and sects. "It's my conviction," Cox declared, "that while the classroom, the theory and the history are necessary, it leaves an awful lot out, namely the direct participation and observation of what people are doing."[21] A laudable intention, perhaps, though one whose prospective scholarly fruits hardly inspire confidence.

Critics often mix sentimentality and condescension with plain cynicism, characterizing evangelists and faith healers as knaves who prey on a host of hapless left-outs. These greedy confidence men are cast in the mold of Burt Lancaster's inauthentic *Elmer Gantry* (1960) or Marjoe Goitner's shallow, cynical semi-documentary self-portrait, *Marjoe* (1972). These caricatures often are off key (only Richard Pryor succeeds where other imitators fail), and they scarcely exhaust the genre. Occasionally an almost anthropological detachment pervades characterizations of the Christian revival, as when in the middle seventies critics and journalists tried to explain Jimmy Carter's born again experience to each other and to their incredulous educated audiences as if it were as alien to American culture as a Balinese cockfight. Evangelicals and charismatics, then, were viewed typically as ignorant, anti-intellectual, and uncultured. And they were classed—not altogether unfairly—either as apolitical creatures or as right-wing bigots. Above all, these Christians were judged to be beyond dialogue: they were in flight from modernity, "yearning," as Schaar puts it, to "be relieved of the anxieties and despair of our time, and to find shelter in simple belief and strong conviction."[22] Bearers of a social disease, evangelicals and charismatics were supposed to be ontological cripples, pursuers of an illusion who offered an easy target for serious critics occupying the firm ground of secular reality.

However amateurishly the phenomenon may have been apprehended, the evangelical idea of salvation not only survived the sixties and seventies. It flourished, along with charismatic styles of expression. To illustrate these phenomena, let me begin with a few pale statistics. The revival of evangelical and charismatic (or neo-Pentecostal) Christianity, which really did not surface in the media until the late sixties, had by the end of the seventies probably reached more than fifty million Americans, who claimed (or reclaimed) the traditional promises of salvation, old metaphors and all. At any rate, they professed them: liberty, in the form of psychological and spiritual wholeness; release

from guilt, anxiety, despair; victory over the fear of death; and community in the form of equality and fraternity among the born again.

Now this surge of evangelical Christianity may not have amounted
to a third (or fourth) Great Awakening, as some of its hyperbolic
publicists, like Charles Colson, reckoned.[23] Judging from public-
opinion polls, in fact, the perceived importance of Judeo-Christian
vision in America shows remarkable evidence of continuity and stability in the postwar era, despite a decline in the middle to late sixties.
According to a Gallup survey conducted in the middle seventies, 94
percent of those questioned professed belief in God—exactly the same
percentage Gallup found in 1948, though considerably larger than in
any comparable industrialized nation. Similarly, the percentage of
those affirming a belief in life after death remained the same from
1948 through 1977: nearly 70 percent.[24] In 1977, 83 percent professed
belief in the divinity of Jesus, 82 percent in his bodily and/or spiritual
resurrection, and 88 percent in the Bible as the actual (49 percent) or
inspired (39 percent) word of God. Revival, this is to say, presupposed
survival.[25]

There nevertheless were important changes in evidence by the seventies that suggest that religion had come to seem somewhat more
important to the conduct of American life than it had in the recent
past. For one thing, the number of respondents claiming that religion
was "increasing its influence on American life" tripled between 1970
and 1978, rising from 14 percent to 44 percent.[26] For another, significantly larger numbers of people once again defined their own search
for fulfillment in roughly theological metaphors. As the Gallup report
of 1977 put it, "People of all ages are searching for deeper meaning in
their lives . . . Many appear to be spiritually homeless and looking
for the particular faith or denomination in which they will feel at
home."[27] In fact, the framers of the *Connecticut Mutual Life Report
on American Values in the '80s* went so far as to conclude that the
high level of religious commitment in America at the end of the seventies "is a stronger determinant of our values than whether we are
rich or poor, young or old, male or female, Black or White, liberal or
conservative."[28]

Much of the searching for a spiritual home apparently took place
within the framework of organized religion: weekly attendance at
religious services rose to 42 percent of the population at the end of
the seventies, reversing a downward trend in evidence since the late

fifties. But the quest clearly spread beyond institutional boundaries.[29] In particular, there was a dramatic rise in evangelical and neo-Pentecostal forms of Christianity. The number of interviewees who reported a personal experience of salvation rose from about 24 percent who characterized themselves as "born again" in 1963 to between 35 and 40 percent—more than one in three Americans age eighteen and over—in 1978.[30] At the same time, interest in Pentecostal and charismatic modes of Christianity burgeoned in the late sixties and seventies. "In 1959," Martin Marty observes, "no map of American religion would include anything called Pentecostal except at the margins or in the ecological niches."[31] But by the late seventies, according to Gallup, Pentecostal and charismatic Christians made up "19 percent of adult Americans, more than 29 million persons" age 18 and over.[32]

There is, then, reasonably solid evidence of an important revival of expressly evangelical and charismatic concerns in the late sixties and seventies—a renewal or continued affirmation of belief in salvation through personal commitment to Christ. Although the Christian revival probably was the central religious event of these two decades, it was not the only one. There also was a renewal, albeit a comparatively small one, within American Judaism. Reform and conservative Jews emphasized *havurot,* extended networks of mutual support similar to efforts at intensive community building among mainline Protestants and Catholics. Hasidic Jews enjoyed a revival analogous in its experiential dimensions to the charismatic movement. And increasing numbers of Jews, especially young people, expressed a deepening commitment to traditional orthodox practices not altogether unlike fundamentalist Christian concerns with literal reading of Scripture.

Set against the major stirrings within the Judeo-Christian tradition, the growth of other forms of religious expression seems rather modest. According to the 1977 Gallup survey, 90 percent of Americans over eighteen identified themselves at least nominally with some facet of the Judeo-Christian tradition: Protestant (60 percent); Roman Catholic and Eastern Orthodox (28 percent); and Jewish (2 percent). Only about 10 percent classified themselves as atheists, advocates of no faith, or practitioners of religions outside the Judeo-Christian tradition, such as Scientology—a statistic that, if even remotely accurate, suggests that disproportionate attention might have been lavished on marginal religions. Still, there was an important if overpublicized rise in what Gallup terms "experiential" religious practices, from faith healing

(7 percent) and the charismatic movement (2 percent) to Transcendental Meditation (4 percent), yoga (3 percent), mysticism (2 percent), and other forms of Eastern religion, such as Zen (1 percent).[33] But even here, in this relatively new set of statistical categories, about half of the participants were engaged in expressly Christian activity (a majority of those in faith healing, as well as the charismatics, whose percentage was revised sharply upward by the end of the decade). Of the other half, a clear majority of about 10 million (the Transcendental Meditation and yoga groups) probably were only part-time practitioners, people who appropriated certain techniques of personal awareness as means of self-expression and self-development but neglected the theological and metaphysical contexts. Here the borders between the religious and therapeutic dimensions of fulfillment grow hazy and become more or less open to what purists regard as illicit traffic. In any case, activity along these overlapping frontiers quickened dramatically in the sixties and seventies. This increasing accent on experiential religion among Christians and non-Christians confirms the growing emphasis in American culture on personal salvation conceived in its broadest theological and quasi-theological senses of felt wholeness.

In these decades, then, large numbers of people—including better-educated, materially secure people—refused the journey from their childhood religious backgrounds to enlightened atheism. Contrary to the expectations and hopes of critics, many proceeded in the opposite direction. Although some pursued non-Western paths, most took up familiar Judeo-Christian themes, however uncongenial their parents might have found them. It thus was increasingly possible for children to rebel against the particular tradition of their parents, and, later on, to rejoin another branch of the same broad stream. At the end of the seventies, Dr. J. Gordon Melton reports in his *Encyclopedia of American Religions,* there were 1,203 groups from which to choose. Rather than attempt a full-scale discussion of the evangelical and charismatic surge here, I should like to recall the main characteristics of this diffuse movement and show how it represents an important manifestation of the quest for fulfillment.

Although it is not immune to the complications of systematic theology, evangelical doctrine aims to be simple: it calls attention to the essentials of New Testament Christianity. Above all, evangelicals concentrate on the idea of individual salvation made available by the sacrificial death and resurrection of Jesus. Salvation, by means of which individuals pass from spiritual death to new life, comes about through a personal experience of conversion (John 5:24).[34] Christianity, according to an evangelical cliché, is a "relationship, not a religion." This process of conversion can be dramatic and revelatory, like Paul's seizure on the road to Damascus, or it can be unemotional, even unnoticeable as a specific event. At any point along this continuum, individuals experience salvation when they are convicted of sin, believe in their hearts that Jesus rose from the dead in triumph over sin, disease, and death, and confess this faith openly (Rom. 10:9). Though all have sinned, salvation is open to everyone: the gospel of Jesus Christ, Paul observes, is "the power of God for salvation to everyone who has faith, to the Jew first and also to the Greek" (Rom. 1:16). Salvation is there for the asking. It is a gift, an act of grace that cannot be purchased, even through good works. As Paul put it in his letter to the church at Ephesus: "by grace you have been saved through faith; and this is not of your own doing, it is the gift of God—not because of works, lest any man should boast" (Eph. 2:8–9).

What an individual should become after he or she accepts the Christian plan of salvation is open to unending interpretation and speculation. But according to the New Testament scriptures, certain changes in attitude and behavior are to be expected. At the very least, the possibilities of self-fulfillment expand dramatically. Salvation promises eternal life in Christ, victory over the fear of death as well as over the fact of death: "Christ in you, the hope of glory" (Col. 1:27). In the end—whether a person dies of ordinary causes or is alive at the Second Coming—he or she, along with all redeemed persons, will live forever with Christ. Others must endure the fires of hell.[35] In the meantime, salvation is accompanied by a personal transformation, a freedom from various dimensions of alienation. As usual in this Paulinist reading of Scripture, Paul has the last word: "Therefore, if anyone is in Christ, he is a new creation: the old has passed away, behold, the new has come" (2 Cor. 5:17).

The shape of this new life—its duties, joys, and obligations—is indistinct. Biblical promises range from the open-ended notion of a more "abundant" life (John 10:10) to what may be construed as a more stoic guarantee that God's grace is sufficient to offset every burden and "to supply every need" (Phil. 4:19). Countless pieces of advice concerning the personal and social conduct of Christians are scattered throughout the Old and the New Testament. How closely these admonitions ought to be followed forms a subject of perennial interest among evangelicals. It is true that evangelicals regard the Bible, rather than institutions, experience, or progressive revelation, as the primary source and sole test of all doctrine.[36] But this ambiguous source of authority only sets up the context for interminable debate and division, often between fundamentalists, who take Scripture literally, and other Christians, who approach texts and people with greater suppleness and perhaps more grace. Even the majority of evangelicals who profess the rather narrow view of biblical inerrancy find sufficient vagueness—in Scripture and in the criteria governing literal readings of Scripture—to engage in unceasing controversy over doctrine, especially over comparatively minor points of conduct.

On central issues of faith, however, there is wide agreement among evangelicals. They accept the idea of one God in three persons (Father, Son, and Holy Spirit). They believe the doctrine of salvation through the atoning blood of Christ to be the only way to redemption. They believe in the importance of water baptism, they look for the imminent Second Coming of Christ, and they affirm the literal accuracy of Scripture. There is similar agreement on what to do about the good news of salvation. Evangelicals feel obligated to "witness" to others, to spread the gospel to every nation, kindred, and tribe (Matt. 28:19). In fact, however, the Gallup survey of 1977 suggests a curious conclusion. The number of Christian witnesses far exceeded the number of born again Christians: whereas upwards of 40 percent claimed to have been born again, 47 percent reported that they had "tried to encourage someone to believe in Jesus Christ or to accept him as his or her Savior."[37] Unless Christians who shun the "born again" prefix were witnessing on their own in larger numbers than it is easy to suppose, a fair number of Americans must have been dispensing second-hand theological advice.

If evangelicals concentrate on the revelation of God in Christ, charismatics (or neo-Pentecostals) focus on the indwelling of the Holy Spirit and the gifts of speaking in tongues, prophecy, and faith healing. The differences finally amount to matters of relative emphasis, since Pentecostals never have developed a distinctive theology. Indeed, they never have needed to, for in spite of their varied historical, class, and denominational origins, most old-line Pentecostals and newer charismatics (or neo-Pentecostals) accept at least the bare bones of evangelical doctrine. In America the classical Pentecostal movement can be traced to the early twentieth century. It arose out of "various Baptist bodies and 'Holiness' groups that were reacting against the secularism and rationalism then seemingly dominant in the institutional churches."[38] An almost wholly marginal phenomenon, classical Pentecostalism belonged to lower-class blacks and whites. Pentecostals were scorned by most elements of American society, including evangelical and mainline Christians. Their marginal status persisted into the postwar era, when Pentecostals gained a growing margin of respectability. As Martin Marty observes, "Two things had to happen to give Pentecostalism a place in the perceptions of the larger culture. The older churches in the movement had to make some compromises and accommodations to the culture, and some people in the mainstream churches had to produce some advocates themselves."[39]

Both developments were evident in the sixties and seventies. Shedding much of their incidental cultural baggage, many of the old-line Pentecostals moved uptown, or at least part of the way uptown. And there was a new manifestation of Pentecostal experience in the mainline churches—Protestant and Catholic—following the postwar revival within and on the fringes of classical Pentecostal circles led by such gifted preachers as Jack Coe, Oral Roberts, A. A. Allen, and William Branham.[40] By the middle sixties, Pentecostal power had spread from tents, temples, and tabernacles into the enclaves of better-educated Christians—to Episcopalians, Roman Catholics, and Lutherans. Though tensions born of class and cultural differences persist, traditional Pentecostals and new charismatics share a bias, a recognizable style of religious experience. Above all, Pentecostalism—old and new—is personal and experiential. Its advocates may slice up Christendom (and each other) in various ways, but they all distinguish "live" from "dead" Christians, spirit-filled congregations from those mired in ritual or simply stuck in the uncomplicated routine of evangelical worship. Though Pentecostals concentrate on evangelical modes of personal salvation, they emphasize a postconversion stage of Christian life: the baptism of the Holy Spirit.

In classical Pentecostal circles, the Holy Spirit could move at any time. But a special time—say Monday or Saturday night—often was reserved for such outpourings. The amorphous shape of the "Holy Ghost Rally," as it was then called, resembled an evangelistic meeting.

Following the first invitation, when sinners and "backsliders" were urged to accept the Christian plan of salvation, there was a second call aimed at those already saved who desired "a deeper experience," namely, the baptism of the Holy Spirit. At this point in the service the congregation was dismissed, and a relatively small group tarried with those who had "come forward." The evangelist often relinquished his or her central role to the circle of praying Christians—the remnant of the larger congregation. (This vintage formation is analogous to the basic unit of the newer charismatics, including Catholic charismatics, who typically meet in small, relatively unstructured prayer groups to seek the evidence of the Spirit.) While spirit-filled Christians laid on hands, the seekers prayed until there was some visible sign of the "baptism"—usually an utterance in tongues, or glossolalia. Following this experience of the second baptism by the "Holy Ghost and fire," believers were urged to cultivate the various gifts of the Spirit. In summarizing these gifts, which members of the first-century Church apparently displayed, Paul observes that "to one is given through the Spirit the utterance of wisdom, and to another the utterance of knowledge according to the same Spirit, to another faith by the same Spirit, to another gifts of healing by the one Spirit, to another the working of miracles, to another prophecy, to another the ability to distinguish between spirits, to another various kinds of tongues, to another the interpretation of tongues" (1 Cor. 12:8–10).

The division of labor that Paul proposes is amorphous (Rom. 12: 4–13). The gifts are parceled out to individuals in such a way as to supply the corporate needs of the church, the "body of Christ." Not everyone is to speak in tongues, the gift emphasized—indeed often overstressed—by Pentecostals. The only gift that everyone ought to claim is *agape:* "If I speak in the tongues of men and of angels, but have not love," Paul adds in a familiar passage, "I am a noisy gong or a clanging cymbal" (1 Cor. 13:1). Paul's advice—at least that portion of it pertaining to tongues—seems to have been heeded in contemporary charismatic circles. Only a small number of the estimated twenty-nine million Pentecostal/charismatics in America claim to have spoken in tongues, according to a 1980 Gallup survey—a statistic that might have heartened Paul, inasmuch as he devoted a good deal of his ministry to persuading first-century Christians to ignore inessentials and concentrate on the main requirements of salvation and evangelism.

Gallup's finding should come as no surprise, even though it is frequently supposed that speaking in tongues—a spontaneous activity—is a quintessentially democratic act that, like sex, nearly anyone except the physically incapable can perform at will. Both assumptions are naïve: many people cannot get loose enough to speak in tongues, despite encouragement and intense social pressure.[41] Although spontaneity served as a central cultural value in the sixties and seventies, it also constituted an elusive goal for many in the charismatic movement, as well as in secular and profane forms of the quest. Still, all the contemporary interest in glossolalia is not simply cultural foolishness. The resurgence of interest in expressive dimensions of religious experience, especially among neo-Pentecostals, testifies rather to the importance of the Christian revival as a major vehicle of the quest for fulfillment. The emphasis on expressive forms of charismatic worship centered on the "touch" of the largely feminine Holy Spirit, on individual salvation, on the search for affective communities of believers, and on a relative de-emphasis of doctrine, institutions, and ecclesiastical authority. These characteristics not only describe a majority of evangelicals and neo-Pentecostals but also fit the wider salvational criteria of the search for fulfillment that permeated other areas of American culture in the sixties and seventies.

Critics and historians who have little difficulty identifying non-Western religious manifestations of the quest regularly discount its socially far more important manifestations within the Judeo-Christian tradition. Writing in the Chicago History of American Religion series, Edwin Scott Gaustad declares that "religion that the head finds wholly agreeable the heart finds emotionally sterile." Despite mounting evidence of the emotional richness of evangelical and Pentecostal modes, Gaustad insists that his caveat fits contemporary forms of the Judeo-Christian tradition: "Western religion, having over many generations accommodated itself to scholasticism, to the Enlightenment, to the demands of the scientific method, and to the positivistic temper, has won an intellectual respectability—and little else. In rejecting all that," Gaustad continues, "the cult and occult fanciers have turned hungrily to another kind of religion—to the Jack Kerouacs, then the Alan Wattses and the Allen Ginsbergs, still later to the tantras, the sutras, the *I Ching,* to all the eroticism and mysticism and immaterialism of the Orient."[42]

There doubtless are varied reasons beyond a general hostility to religion why intellectuals at first ignored and then largely misread the

Christian revival of the sixties and seventies. But the main reasons also are the most evident ones. First, intellectuals—especially left and left-liberal intellectuals—despised the political beliefs, actions, and inaction they imputed to evangelicals and neo-Pentecostals. They did so often with good reason, at least from their points of view. At the fringes, born again Christians have participated in racist organizations such as the Ku Klux Klan and white citizens' councils. But there are more serious reasons for misgivings: as a social group, white evangelicals and neo-Pentecostals tend to be conservative or even right wing on domestic economic, political, and cultural issues. Leftist critics typically overstate the degree of conservatism—or fundamentalism—among such people, however. For one thing, they neglect the millions of black Americans (about one-fifth of born again believers) who identify themselves as evangelicals or Pentecostals and whose political views on many issues diverge from those of their white counterparts. For another, critics who deal in caricatures of these sectors of the Christian community emphasize their rather distinctive views on manners and morals but minimize their internal divisions on economic and political questions, from government spending for social purposes to firearms registration.[43] Nevertheless, in large numbers, evangelicals and neo-Pentecostals nostalgically affirm the premodernist ideology of an expanding competitive capitalism and celebrate the virtues of individual initiative, self-reliance, and material success. Many of them embrace a Manichaean view of foreign policy that disposes them to consider all adversaries, especially "Communist" ones, as agents of Satan and hence worthy of annihilation.

Second, intellectuals oppose the born again Christians' constricted theological range—and its most obvious political and cultural implications. To a large extent, the Christian revival represents a fundamentalist response to anxiety about the future occasioned by social and cultural dislocations: a response to rising economic expectations and satisfactions in the late sixties, and a reaction to an economic performance in the late seventies that fell below earlier expectations. It is not, of course, the varied social and cultural sources of renewed fervor that render the religious commitments suspect. It is, rather, the regressive and anti-intellectual character of common born again responses to cultural change and social uncertainty. Many evangelicals and neo-Pentecostals who embrace a premillennial vision refuse to participate in the public affairs of this world, preferring instead to concentrate on their heavenly mansions (and their personal earthly fortunes). Many others participate in hostile and mean-spirited ways.

Such infantile fantasies as that of Jesus returning on a cloud to "rapture" his church dispose many born again Christians to neglect issues of general social justice. Intellectuals—including many mainline Christians—have considered this asocial premillennialist theme essentially antipathetic to the Christian ethic of assisting the poor and the broken in spirit. Moreover, "postrevolutionary" visions that presuppose a cleansing apocalypse often dispose individuals to slide into nihilistic or fatalistic moods. Hence in the seventies many born again Christians eagerly endorsed an expansion of the American nuclear arsenal, just as a decade earlier many Marxist "revolutionaries" approvingly quoted the then-fashionable Mao on the survivability of the masses in a nuclear exchange.

The nearly exclusive emphasis on individual salvation and obsessive preparation for the celestial world constitutes a primary source of the central crisis of American Protestantism in evidence since the latter part of the nineteenth century. As Reinhold Niebuhr observed in the early fifties: "We can become converted. But the whole community will have to be converted from those mores and customs which defy the ultimate standards of Christian virtue. We have been too individualistic to come to terms with these social sins. The renewal of the church demanded of us now must therefore include encounter with the sins of the community . . . In a sense it is true that we cannot be saved unless we are all saved."[44]

Moreover, their premillennial inclinations affect more than attitude: they also seem to dispose many born again Christians to embrace charismatic, anti-intellectual, and antidemocratic modes of religious and political behavior that are similar in key respects to the apocalyptic strain found in much of the revolutionary left in the late sixties. Neo-Pentecostals are at once more democratic in a participatory sense and more authoritarian than their mainline counterparts. At one level, their styles of worship are more open-ended. The loose order of service can be interrupted by an outpouring of the Spirit—in the shape of spontaneous prayers, glossolalia, and prophetic utterances on the part of members of the congregation. The worshipers constitute in some real sense a "priesthood of believers" who share in various aspects of the ministry. Yet the wider freedom and spontaneous participation exacts a price, as it did in certain leftist sectors of the Movement. Routine

authority yields ground to charismatic authority vested in a central figure: the pastor who often rules a local congregation arbitrarily, en-
forcing tight discipline through his own narrow reading of Scripture.
In the course of such rule, the assumptions and ethos of representative
democracy are sacrificed to charismatic modes of behavior. And, as in
the case of left-wing sects, congregations and denominations often sub-
divide. Although such tendencies may be more pronounced among
neo-Pentecostals than among evangelicals—Southern Baptists, for example—they do permeate the born again regions of American culture.

Third, highbrow social critics feel themselves culturally superior to
most born again Christians, since evangelicals and neo-Pentecostals
typically inhabit middle and lowbrow ranges of American culture.
Wealthier as a group than they were in the early postwar years, most
born again Christians nevertheless shunned modernist discourse—
social, political, and artistic—in the sixties and seventies. Though often
comfortable in sarcastic modes, they are hostile, even impervious, to
complexity, irony, and paradox. Like so many radicals, born again
Christians display at best a labored sense of humor. A cursory tour of
any evangelical gift shop turns up a wide array of "Jesus junk" and
not much else: atrocious pastels of a soft-eyed Savior; cheap wooden
carvings of street signs featuring such slogans as "One Way"; a selection of insipid gospel records and tapes; Bibles surrounded by shelves
of books such as Hal Lindsey's *The Late Great Planet Earth,* a simple-
minded prophecy of the "end times" that sold over fifteen million
copies in the late seventies.

Though they are doubtless accurate to a point, these general impressions are both incomplete and misleading, ignoring as they do the social diversity of born again Christians. The Christian revival cut across
regional, ethnic, occupational, and educational lines: at larger gather-
ings in the seventies, old-line Pentecostals—middle-aged men in powder
blue leisure suits and matching patent-leather shoes—often stared un-
comprehendingly at libidinous young men wearing sandals, beards,
plunging necklines, and glittering gold crosses against the backdrop of
hairy chests. The revival also crossed denominational lines. The Gallup
survey of 1977 found predictably that 64 percent of evangelicals belonged to Baptist and other independent Protestant bodies. The mildly
surprising finding was that 36 percent were distributed among various

mainline groups: 12 percent were Catholic, 5 percent Lutheran, 15 percent Methodist, and 3 percent Presbyterians. One percent—or about 500,000—were Jewish.[45]

Moreover, the usual characterizations of born again Christians in highbrow journals slight dramatic exceptions and minor countertrends. They do not allow for such interesting evangelical thinkers as Carl Henry and John W. Montgomery or for such surprising leaders as Billy Graham, who in the late seventies and early eighties turned his attention to the antinuclear cause. They do not mention increasingly respectable centers of learning such as Fuller Theological Seminary in Pasadena, pockets of left-wing Christians like those involved in the antinuclear and disarmament movements, or the groups of radicals gathered around the journals *Sojourners, the Other Side,* and *Witness.* In his neglected study of born again Christians, *The Emerging Order: God in the Age of Scarcity* (1979), Jeremy Rifkin goes so far as to suggest that neo-Pentecostals and evangelicals may constitute the basis of an important two-part theological movement, a second reformation capable of guiding America into a postcapitalist age.[46] Rather than attempt simply to balance the usual portrait of evangelicals and neo-Pentecostals or to predict their future, I wish to underline a more mundane theme: that the Christian revival in the sixties and seventies represents a legitimate facet of the general quest for fulfillment. There is no sufficient reason to exclude the Christian revival from this quest. In spite of the constipated theology of most of its adherents, this vague and undefinable upsurge was culturally homologous in many respects to aspects of the Movement and the therapeutic quest. Like other seekers, born again Christians were full participants in the search for fulfillment—for personal salvation and a slice of social justice.

Most critical commentaries slide over the central possibility of evangelical and neo-Pentecostal experience—its imaginative power to release individuals from the bonds (and bondage) of alienation. Nevertheless, tens of millions of Americans were able to discover or rediscover a fuller sense of the possibilities of life through their encounters with evangelical and neo-Pentecostal modes of worship during the sixties and seventies. Their subjective testimony constitutes the most important evidence of the vitality of their faith. Not everyone, of course, can be expected to realize these promises fully: they comprise an uncompleted, and in some senses, utopian agenda. Yet the experience of salvation frequently is a deep and lasting one. It may initiate a psychological, moral, and even physical reorientation similar to the experience summarized in Marxist conceptions of "the new man" scheduled to emerge immediately in small communities of the elect and eventually in postrevolutionary communist communities characterized by freedom, equality, and fraternity. The evangelical paradigm also provides a controlling vision, albeit an impractical one, of what a complete resolution to the crisis of culture would look like. In the meantime, before the new age sets in, individual Christians, like radicals, may experience personal liberation and community with other believers through a process that is fundamentally antihierarchical, antibureaucratic, and charismatic in a secular sense.

In the sixties and seventies, then, the Christian revival was an instance—perhaps even the prime instance—of the search for fulfillment within a generally affluent, democratic, pluralistic, and individualistic culture. Indeed, it represented a multifaceted dissent against the institutional forms and structures of power that compromise and often subvert these cultural norms. It was not always an obvious dissent, or perhaps I should say, not a typically left-wing dissent: from most vantage points on the left, the "conformist" dimensions of evangelical and neo-Pentecostal political and cultural behavior are held to lie beyond dispute. These dimensions are especially evident in the generally conservative political positions the born again assumed on every issue from defense to welfare and abortion. This is not to say that their politics were despicable. Except at the fringes of the movement, born again Christians took positions on issues that fall within a reasonable or at least a debatable range, a concession often resisted by left and left-liberal critics.

Nor is their conservatism finally convincing evidence of an absence of political dissent within their ranks. Even the activities of such solid middle- and working-class Southern-based groups as the Reverend Jerry Falwell's Moral Majority, whose expressed aim is to bring America "back" to "Biblical principles" (and arm her to the teeth), contains elements of dissent: dissent from the culture of modernism, dissent from the social ethics of liberalism, and dissent from the politics of the welfare state. Instead of concentrating exclusively on spreading the good news of salvation, Falwell, a small-minded, mean-spirited man who doubts whether God hears the prayers of Jews, considers anti-war protest "immoral," and regards liberalism as an impediment to salvation, advises his colleagues to "get" their followers "saved, baptized, and registered" to vote.[47]

Such quasi-political initiatives testify to the widest thread of dissent running through the Christian revival, a dissent against what I have called "the structure of advantage." This dissent not only encompasses political efforts to achieve a piece of social justice—*my* liberty and *my* equal opportunity. It embraces more diffuse personal attempts to neutralize and disparage the social and cultural handicaps imposed by the structure of advantage. It is true that the evangelical tradition, which originated with the protest of Luther and Calvin, has formed something of an establishment of its own. But the tradition was not dominant in American culture of the sixties and seventies. Moreover, from their inception, the classical Pentecostal and Holiness sects constituted what Liston Pope termed "'a protest (couched in religious form) against social exclusiveness, and . . . a compensatory method (also in religious form) for regaining status, and for redefining class lines in religious terms.'"[48] Indeed, the parallels between many of the new charismatics and advocates of the counterculture are obvious: both sought personal authenticity and a release from inegalitarian social roles; both valued displays of personal energy; both were anti-institutional and in many respects antirational.

Thus, in large numbers, born again Christians, like participants in the Movement, encountered obstacles to fulfillment within organized Christianity and within the secular culture. These obstacles, ranging from bureaucracies in the churches to secular forms of cultural and political domination, became targets of dissent that Christians worked against in various ways. At least from their subjective points of view, then, participants pursued modes of fulfillment that emphasized the equal power of individuals to discover salvation—to define, express, and develop the self more or less independently of prevailing patterns of status, wealth, and power. Fulfillment thus required variously perceived measures of social justice, but it did not presuppose the advent of material abundance or even of great affluence. Born again Christians demonstrated that the mixes of salvation and social justice in the equation of fulfillment were far more varied than most social critics supposed.

Dissent, of course, was not confined to evangelical and neo-Pentecostal sectors of the Judeo-Christian tradition. The search for personal fulfillment triggered dissent within mainline Protestant and Catholic churches as well. The Protestantization of the Roman Catholic church in America represents the most dramatic instance of the impact of the quest on a major religious institution in the sixties and seventies. Shaken by changes initiated from above following the Second Vatican

Council (1962-65) and unsettled by dissent among the laity, the Church became a complex setting—or rather a collection of settings—for the drama of self-fulfillment. Catholics, at least "progressive" ones, moved toward less exclusive notions of revelation, and hence of salvation, than evangelicals held. This was an astonishing change in the nation's largest Christian denomination. It not only cleared ground for further ecumenical activity among Christians; it also augured better relations with other non-Christians whose different paths to salvation finally had come to be considered valid expressions of commitment to God.[49]

Catholics placed greater emphasis on the idea of personal salvation within their own tradition by removing or ignoring many of the Church's barriers to fulfillment of the self. The thick mediations of the institution were simplified, and the authority of the clergy was diffused. At Mass, for example, the celebrant faced the people and spoke mainly in English rather than in Latin. Laypersons—men and women—assumed more prominent roles in the various ministries of the church, including administering the sacraments under special circumstances. There was rising support among Catholics to include women in the priesthood. Weekly attendance at Mass became voluntary. And the sacrament of confession, like so much else, emerged from small, musty closets and became known as the Act of Reconciliation. All this brought individuals into a more direct, more classically Protestant relation with God and with each other. Moreover, Catholics tended to fashion their own variations of the rules of personal and social conduct. By the end of the seventies a majority of laypeople and a substantial percentage of priests had rejected the Church's prohibition on most forms of birth control. Thus Catholics began to pursue secular aspects of fulfillment in the context of smaller families. For similar reasons, opposition mounted to clerical celibacy. Indeed, in the seventies, Catholics and Protestants grew almost indistinguishable in their views on a range of social issues, from cohabitation and interracial marriage to legalized abortion and school busing for purposes of racial integration.[50] And the Catholic hierarchy assumed a prominent role among Christians in opposing the spread of nuclear weapons.

Because it was situated to the left of the center of the spectrum of American ideology, dissent within the mainline churches (Catholic and Protestant) proved more acceptable to intellectuals than the modes of dissent displayed by evangelicals and neo-Pentecostals. Such dissent often was concerned with such familiar issues of social justice as poverty and discrimination on grounds of race and sex. The quest for fulfillment among mainline Christians (and liberal Jews) was seemingly less offensive to intellectuals: these Christians did not seek to impose their own version of salvation on others through aggressive evangelistic campaigns. More important, such representatives of mainline Judaism and Christianity as Daniel Bell, Andrew Greeley, Peter Berger, Martin Marty, Michael Novak, Robert Coles, and J. Richard Neuhaus were familiar figures. They were practicing intellectuals—writers who contributed to major journals of opinion and mingled freely with those who place themselves beyond religion.

In spite of their tolerance of mainline Christian and Jewish intellectuals, social critics found it hard to imagine the value—even the contemporary possibility—of the experience of evangelical and neo-Pentecostal modes of salvation. They found it even more difficult to imagine that the saved self might be expressed or realized in ways that mattered. The cultural distances simply were too great. Even as sensitive a critic as Elizabeth Hardwick writes unsteadily on the subject. In her fitfully bright review-essay on several studies of Billy Graham, which includes comments on assorted electronic evangelists and faith healers (Rex Humbard, Oral Roberts, Ernest Angley, and Jimmy Swaggart), Hardwick concludes with "a remembrance from a story about Ruth Carter Stapleton and her therapeutic ministry. To a woman not looking her best, Mrs. Stapleton advised: 'Jesus wants you to have some conditioner put on your hair. He wants you to get some make-up. He wants you to look nice.' Poor He. Poor He."[51] Hardwick's coy irony misses the point. Forty years ago—even twenty years ago—the woman counseled by Mrs. Stapleton would have been urged not to "adorn" herself with lipstick and hair conditioner lest she breach prevailing standards of Christian decency. She might have displayed a powdery face, as so many Pentecostal women did, in silent testimony to an awkward compromise between desire and stern cultural dictates. But she wore no lipstick—a too obvious concession to the flesh. Those who set the cultural styles for classical rank-and-file Pentecostals simply did not care much about her appearance—at least not enough to have allowed her the materials to "look nice."[52]

Now the issue of makeup may strike someone like Elizabeth Hardwick as ludicrous. But the permission to cultivate a pleasing appearance that Mrs. Stapleton granted—albeit through an unnecessary bit of name dropping—suggests the considerably broadened cultural and personal options that born again Christians gained in the sixties and seventies. There are, to be sure, any number of cultural striations within evangelical and neo-Pentecostal circles. To an untrained eye, some of the electronic evangelists Hardwick discusses—especially the Southerners—frequently do seem of a piece with the pitchmen whose used-car commercials often appear before and after the televised services. But it is these various subcultures—not Elizabeth Hardwick and her circle—that provide the useful points of reference in any assessment of the Christian revival as a manifestation of the search for personal fulfillment. Mrs. Stapleton and those she counsels enjoy a far wider array of personal choices than did their counterparts of 1960—or 1940. And I suspect also that on the average the saved hold significant personal and cultural advantages over the unsaved in their search for fulfillment within these regions of American culture. If only by virtue of their religious experience, they are in a position to lay greater claims to personal dignity than their cultural and social counterparts.

At any rate, by the end of the seventies, born again Christians not only could look nice. They were urged to pursue other modes of self-expression and self-fulfillment, other measures to realize a more abundant life in the here and now. Their material circumstances had improved during these decades. Their occupational and educational opportunities had widened considerably. They were more active politically and hence more regularly heeded by politicians. And they were served by growing numbers of Christian and secular therapists, marriage counselors, and holistic health practitioners. Whatever such critics as Christopher Lasch may think, these professionals helped ordinary Christians cultivate facets of the self that would have been suppressed had they come to maturity in the forties, the fifties, or even the sixties. At the end of the seventies, then, the born again path remained theologically straight. But it was considerably less culturally narrow than it had been in earlier decades, and perhaps even somewhat less politically restricted.

The Therapeutic Quest

The strong therapeutic currents that ran through the Movement and the Christian revival usually were submerged in larger themes: salvation came either by good political works or by faith in a higher power.

In its raw forms, however, the therapeutic quest lacked such theoretical niceties: it was concerned more openly with the claims of the expressive self. Here, the dominant cultural theme of the sixties and seventies—the search for individual fulfillment—was articulated primarily in personal, sexual, and psychological terms, rather than in the languages of social theory, politics, or theology. Metaphors of individual salvation nevertheless figured importantly in expressly therapeutic conceptions of the self, from Gestalt to primal therapy. In fact, therapeutic modes of the quest for fulfillment probably came closest to fitting Irving Howe's conception of the "one uniquely modern style of salvation: a salvation by, of, and for the self."[53] Though it was perhaps more conspicuous than ever before during these decades, the style of salvation described by Howe was not new. It was rather a secularization of the ancient doctrine that individuals, though aided by God's grace, are the chief agents and beneficiaries of their own salvation. Declared heretical in the fifth century, the views of Pelagius are roughly similar to the leading assumptions of such ego psychologists as Abraham Maslow and Carl Rogers. Rejecting the idea of original sin, which, G. K. Chesterton observed, remains the only empirically verifiable tenet of the Christian faith, Pelagius asserted that individuals are essentially free and able to choose a more abundant life in spite of their psychic past and social present.

The therapeutic quest centers on salvation of the self from a variety of classic and contemporary conditions. The fulfilled self must be free from guilt and from the most debilitating aspects of alienation, including anxiety about death. Lacking faith in a traditional Christian doctrine of salvation, a high percentage of those pursuing therapeutic modes of fulfillment focused exclusively on the unused possibilities of this life—*their* lives—rather than on the prospect of a life after death. They concentrated on the length of life and the quality of life: according to one therapeutic cliché (lifted from a health food enthusiast), the goal was to "add life to your years and years to your life."[54] The fulfilled self, then, was an expressed self. Physical well-being, sexual amplitude, emotional intensity, and mental wholeness: these vague states were sought as ends in themselves. And they were pursued also as a means to expressing the self in the context of small communities—intimate personal relationships (especially sexual ones), family, voluntary associations, and what sociologists call "friendship groups."

Salvation thus came about by means of some synthesis of faith and good works. It frequently was necessary to believe in a therapist, in a supportive community, in a drug, in a diet, or in some ritual or routine. And it was imperative always to make a good, though not necessarily artful, work of the self. The definition and role of self-discipline in the project of self-fulfillment has been a subject of vigorous debate. Similarities and sharp differences between, say, the forms of therapy practiced at Esalan and *est* provide a compressed image of the overriding continuities and differences between the sixties and seventies. Both were popular forms of therapy, avenues toward self-fulfillment. Whereas encounter groups of the sixties operated on the premise of " 'letting it all hang out,' the lesson of *est* is 'Get your act together— and toe the line' . . ." One proceeds from a psychology of plenitude; the other from a perspective of relative scarcity.[55] Yet in spite of variations in popularity, both survived the seventies, demonstrating in yet another way that in a syncretic culture such as ours nothing seems to die. If the expressed self did not need to be especially well-crafted, it nevertheless had to be worked at, however fitfully and casually. It had to be taken seriously, since, as another therapeutic cliché put it, "Life is not a dress rehearsal." And the expressed self had to be talked about, in seemingly endless fashion.[56]

Set to secular music, this body of heretical assumptions was bound to elicit criticism from every quarter, much of it smug: from Freudians, Marxists, liberals, conservatives, secular humanists, and Christians of all persuasions. In their characterizations of "the seventies" as a time of unseemly preoccupation with the self, many critics professed an inability to distinguish therapeutic styles of salvation from pure selfishness and narcissism. There is obvious, if finally limited, truth to such charges. In most of its extreme forms—in Werner Erhard's *est* and Arthur Janov's primal therapy, for example—the Pelagian style of salvation lacked any serious reference beyond the self, whether to others, society, nature, or God. Other connoisseurs of the remissive self, no less extreme in their way, imagined connections between self-improvement and social issues that were as improbable as the links posited by sectarian leftists. Those who engaged in Transcendental Meditation, for instance, supposed that if a tiny percentage of the inhabitants of a city (or, what the hell, the world) were to concentrate hard enough, peace and prosperity would reign. Health food faddists told one another—and anyone else willing to listen—that if leaders would adopt their dietary prescriptions, or at least swallow a tablespoon or two of raw bran daily, conflict in the world would cease. Though they were obviously silly when projected on to whole societies, such prescriptions might have provided a measure of relief to an ailing President Carter, whose case of hemorrhoids was widely (and tastelessly) publicized in the spring of 1979. And it might have eased the presumed embarrassment of Tom Wolfe's distressed young woman who, when asked at an *est* gathering to think of "the one thing" she should most like to "eliminate" from her life, shouted over the microphone, *"Hemorrhoids!"*[57]

Excesses of self-regard provided suitable texts for any number of critical sermons, for enthusiasts of the therapeutic quest were especially susceptible to forms of idolatry, which Richard Rubenstein has defined aptly as "the confusion of a limited aspect of things with the ground of the totality." Reduced to the idolatrous confines of the self, the search for fulfillment frequently was turned into a celebration of alienation, a proclamation of "salvation" that went well beyond any conceivable meaning of this elastic term.[58] I do not wish to defend extreme manifestations of the therapeutic quest that roughly paralleled the forms and functions of isolated Christian and radical sects. Such formulations are theoretically thin and politically vacuous. They can be self-defeating and harmful to others. My aim here is rather to suggest that most expressly apolitical and areligious variants of the search for fulfillment were not primarily sectarian. In fact, they displayed enormous differences of degree and kind. By enlarging cultural options, these modes of enhancing the self contributed importantly, if haphazardly, to what I call the democratization of personhood in America. The therapeutic quest was not simply a diffuse cultural thrust that gained force at the expense of various modes of authority and species of political involvement. It was rather a mode of personal and cultural activity that enhanced the psychological options of millions of Americans, and, to one degree or another, their public options as well.

From the middle sixties through the seventies there flourished a bewildering variety of doctrines, disciplines, and therapeutic techniques aimed at self-fulfillment, especially among middle and upper-middle echelons of society. All sorts of alternatives rushed through the cracks in orthodox styles of treating mind and body. Freudian analysis, with its emphasis on extensive probing of repression and guilt in the patient's buried past, gave way to less intellectually demanding, less expensive, and less time-consuming alternatives. Allopathic medicine, which treats acute illness mainly through chemicals and surgery, lost some of its authority to a spate of techniques gathered (uneasily) under the umbrella of "holistic medicine." Neither psychoanalysis nor "organized" medicine was well suited to the felt needs of millions of Americans who sought greater measures of well-being—abundant physical energy, psychological ease, and personal "growth." Yet both survived in altered forms: psychoanalysis claimed a shriveling portion of a steadily expanding therapy market, and by the end of the seventies organized medicine was beginning to be enriched by holistic techniques.[59]

The range of the therapeutic search was astonishing. In the late sixties and throughout the seventies there was renewed emphasis upon the physical self, as millions of people experimented with a plethora of diets, from macrobiotic regimens (which produced an occasional case of malnutrition) and lacto-vegetarian schemes to revised standard versions of the four basic food groups stressing less red meat, less sugar, less salt, and fewer processed and chemically adulterated foods. Vitamins and other food supplements grew into a multi-billion-dollar business. More than thirty million Americans quit smoking cigarettes, and millions more switched to apparently less lethal varieties.[60] Many people "drank lighter," abandoning hard liquor in favor of dry white wines and Perrier. By the seventies, physical exercise also had become something of a national obsession: tennis, racquetball, swimming, cycling, hiking, and, above all, jogging were in vogue. In 1969, only 125 people entered the twenty-six mile marathon in New York City; in 1979, more than 11,500 began the trek. By then, more than forty million Americans jogged or ran, at least a bit.

In addition to heightened interest in the physical and sexual selves, the late sixties and seventies witnessed a spectacular rise of popular therapies—strategies designed to deliver the self from psychic impediments to fulfillment. Devitalizing stress, emotional numbness, sexual shyness, self-destructive habits, occupational burnout, and unfulfilling personal relationships: these were the chief complaints that clinically sane but personally dissatisfied people presented and sought to resolve through more than two hundred kinds of therapy, from transactional analysis and biofeedback to primal scream. It is impossible to gauge with any precision the meanings that Americans attached to this amorphous set of beliefs and practices. No doubt the therapeutic quest often got out of hand, as many critics charged. Though it was atypical, the pursuit of extremes seems to reveal in distorted forms the basic impulses of the quest. Many seekers took jogging or dieting or therapy to extremes, defining them as forms of salvation. In *Holistic Running* (1978), for example, Joel Henning declares that running is "indeed a form of worship, an attempt to find God, a means to the transcendent." Such views can easily constrict the criteria of salvation, eliminating serious theological dimensions on the one side and canceling social and political obligations on the other. Confusing means with ends, these small subsets of enthusiasts fit the broad labels of narcissism and selfishness that critics all too frequently affixed to the entire phenomenon.

Or consider Arthur Janov's primal therapy, which came into vogue in the middle sixties. For approximately $6000 (in 1975 dollars), a patient could be relieved of the accumulated psychic pain of his or her life. Janov took literally the question of Nicodemus—"What must I do to be saved?"—and led the initiate through a set of regressions that culminated in a reenactment of physical birth. Through a series of primal screams orchestrated by the therapist, the patient sloughed off the burden of guilt, anxiety, and hurt and emerged whole. Born again, or "rebirthed," to shift into therapeutic slang, the patient presumably became able to realize his or her mutilated potentialities. The ethos of Janov's institute is quite similar to that of certain Christian sects. Janov himself is by all accounts a charismatic figure, an impossible man who brooks no opposition. His pastiche of claims, he declares with characteristic immodesty, "renders all other psychological theories obsolete and invalid."[61] Janov does not submit his rash assertions to any disinterested group of scientists. Nor do social or political dimensions complicate his vision of the world. Theory and academic discipline are largely irrelevant activities to be left behind by a discoverer of *the* truth: only Janov's simple doctrine matters. Janov has become one of the "new messiahs," a revered figure who offers the promise of immediate personal salvation—a feeling of well-being, a sense of the expressed, authentic self—in exchange for mere submission: "Come, follow me."

If Janov concentrated on an individual's past, other therapists focused on the present, on a person's ability to realize his or her hidden potential for emotional intensity and emotional balance. The human potential movement—a loose configuration of therapies and well-known figures such as Abraham Maslow, Fritz Perls, and Carl Rogers— offered various plans of salvation through exercises in personal growth, which ranged from difficult techniques in the romantic tradition of personal struggle to easy ones packaged for mass consumption: encounter groups, nude marathons, guided fantasies, and more traditional individual sessions with a therapist/guru. Here, as in much of the counterculture, a romantic and essentially antimodernist notion dominated the rhetorical landscape: the creative self expecting release from social and psychic bonds.[62]

During the sixties and seventies, then, sectarian manifestations of the therapeutic quest abounded. When pushed to their limits, they frequently turned out to be silly and self-defeating, selfish and narcissistic. But this is not the only consequence of the therapeutic quest— nor is it the most important. I think it fair to say that despite their unvarnished rhetoric, therapeutic seekers were finally close cousins to many individuals in the Christian revival and the Movement, especially the counterculture. Consider the case of Michael Rossman, whose experience bridges these two decades, from Berkeley in the early sixties to a geographically indeterminate state of solipsism in the seventies. A veteran of the Movement, Rossman claims to have found his way from the radical political and cultural wars of the sixties to his own "essential and unalienable" body in the seventies: "I started out oppressed by social wrongs, tried to oppose them; learned that we had to clean up the operations of social power, tried to do this; learned that for this we had to reform the processes of power among ourselves, as radical political actors and as citizens, which meant to reform ourselves as human beings, not independently of the other projects, but in and by their processes and as their ground." Rossman comes to this conclusion somewhat tardily, a delay caused perhaps by his seemingly boundless capacity for self-absorption: "I shared . . . a key development of Movement consciousness in the white middle class: from action on behalf of unknown others who were wronged, to action on my own behalf, as well and first, through coming to recognize myself as victimized and oppressed in ways which ultimately were key to the oppression of those others."[63] So far as I know, Rossman did not join the Jesus movement in the late seventies. Judging from his odyssey, however, a decision on his part to do so would not have been surprising. At the extremes, then, the quest for fulfillment gave rise to a complex network of doctrines, practices, and rituals that many people took up cavalierly and then blithely discarded. Despite the competing character of these theoretical claims, many individuals found them compatible at some level of feeling and sensibility: they constituted alternate ways to express their authentic, buried selves.[64]

The profusion of modes of therapy suggests that dissent was as fundamental to the therapeutic quest as it was to the Movement and the Christian revival. Seekers of the fulfilled self were in revolt against traditional norms and values. They rebelled against the cultural hegemony of orthodox modes of treatment and the scientific epistemology that justified them. In the laissez faire world of the therapeutic quest, alternatives competed endlessly. For example, a person who complained of one of the fashionable conditions of the seventies—allergies to foods and pollens—could elect any number of proposed cures. He could rely on potentially harmful over-the-counter drugs or find an orthodox medical practitioner to administer a series of injections of small amounts of offending substances in a saline solution designed to relieve or eliminate symptoms. He could also elect chiropractic treatment, nutritional therapy, megavitamin therapy, metabolic body balancing, acupuncture, iridology, acupressure, uro-immunology (injections of the victim's own urine), thyroid therapy, biofeedback, faith healing, or an array of psychological regimens.

Since there was no way to assess the comparative efficacy of these increasingly popular modes other than through personal experience and hearsay, the seeker was free to approach them in one of two essential spirits: he could assume a sectarian attitude, selecting any one mode and regarding it as the only way. Or he could approach the smorgasbord of possibilities in an eclectic spirit, trying a bit of this and a pinch of that in hopes of discovering a workable recipe. In both approaches, truth was subjective, partial, and relative. As a consequence of both, authority was diffused: though orthodox treatments survived, their hegemony dissolved during the sixties and seventies. The temple of medical orthodoxy had been invaded though not yet overrun. In these circumstances, attitudes toward medical "science" grew more skeptical as responses to less epistemologically sophisticated modes of treatment became increasingly credulous.[65]

Most Americans, of course, rejected the sectarian spirit and refused to inhabit the extremes. A majority pursued physical and psychological aspects of fulfillment moderately and eclectically. They combined mortification (or indulgence) of mind and body with spiritual discipline or with some sociopolitical commitment. Or they pursued the project of fulfillment fitfully, dieting a bit, taking an exercise class, undergoing a few months of therapy, practicing meditation, or performing a few yoga stunts. They worked, often casually, at improving the unheroic aspects of life: marriage, family life, friendships, the conditions of their work. Most Americans, this is to say, heeded the ancient and sensible warning of St. Jerome: "Be on your guard when you begin to mortify your body by abstinence and fasting, lest you imagine yourself to be perfect and a saint; for perfection does not consist in this virtue. It is only a help, a disposition; a means, though a fitting one, for the attainment of true perfection."[66]

In his illuminating study of American culture in the sixties and seventies, *New Rules: Searching for Self-Fulfillment in a World Turned Upside Down* (1981), Daniel Yankelovich reaches similar conclusions concerning the temperate disposition of most Americans, though he does so from a perspective somewhat different from mine. Defining the therapeutic search as the central, energizing facet of the quest, Yankelovich imagines nearly all of American society as having become involved in therapeutics by the end of the seventies:

What is extraordinary about the search for self-fulfillment in contemporary America is that it is not confined to a few bold spirits or a privileged class. Cross-section studies of Americans show unmistakably that the search for self-fulfillment is instead an outpouring of popular sentiment and experimentation, an authentic grass-roots phenomenon involving, in one way or another, perhaps as many as 80 percent of all adult Americans. It is as if tens of millions of people had decided simultaneously to conduct risky experiments in living, using the only materials that lay at hand—their own lives.[67]

Yankelovich posits a category of fairly intense seekers (he calls them "strong formers") who spend much of their time on the trail of fulfillment, appraising and reappraising their personal lives, their jobs, their friends, their mates, their children from the perspective of the expressing and infinitely needy self. Members of this special minority—representing about 17 percent of the work force, according to Yankelovich—tend to be under thirty-five, college educated, white-collar professionals. They typically are liberal in their political views, whatever their party affiliation. Slightly more than one-half of this group is unmarried. Unchurched, and for the most part renters, they presumably can devote their weekends exclusively to therapeutic pursuits, having no lawns to mow or religious services to attend. Most other Americans have come to embrace the quest, too, Yankelovich maintains. But they go at it in a more moderate fashion, retaining many traditional norms and values, from the importance of having children to disapproval of extramarital affairs and of women who do not put husband and children ahead of career:

In the center of the continuum we find the majority of Americans struggling with the weak form of the self-fulfillment predicament. Most of them do not agonize over their inner needs and potentials. They do not fuss daily over existential life-decisions as if these were worry beads to be fingered at fretful moments. These people, especially if they are over thirty-five years of age, have mostly settled into stable commitments to family, work, friends, community, and leisure. These commitments, rather than creative forms of self-expression, fill their life space. Their inner lives are rarely subject to upheaval. The pressures that tear at the strong formers also tug at them but do not dominate their lives. The majority retain many traditional values, including a moderate commitment to the old self-denial rules, even as they struggle to achieve some measure of greater freedom, choice and flexibility in their lives.[68]

In Yankelovich's schema, what I have called the therapeutic search begins in the student movement of the sixties, breaks out of its quasi-political shell, and spreads unevenly, like cold peanut butter, over American society in the later sixties and seventies. In contrast to the active minority of strong formers, the rest of America is characterized as essentially passive, reactive, or at most, resistant to cultural novelty. Though plausible, and at least consistent with much of the evidence cited by Yankelovich, this approach appears to me to assign too great an influence to the strong formers. They are, it is true, the experimenters whose activities are prominently reported and re-created in the media. But it is the majority that watches, tests, and sifts through the models of behavior and modes of thought showcased by the fashionable cultural elites. It is the majority that was called upon at the end of the sixties, when elements of the cultural and political left threatened to run amok, to display sober if not altogether good sense, to exercise sound judgment, and to insist upon preserving large chunks of the American cultural past.

Yankelovich's perspective, which I think mistakenly assigns the therapeutic quest both a social locus *and* the place of honor in the definition of personal fulfillment, thus seems insufficiently pluralistic. Failing to posit a supple enough category of fulfillment, Yankelovich is disposed to assign insufficient weight to the Christian revival, to political elements of the Movement, and, in general, to the contributions of a multiplicity of groups whose more deliberate and more stubbornly skeptical responses to novelty strongly influenced the contours of American culture and society, and should continue to do so. As a consequence of his tendency to take strong formers too seriously and others rather too lightly—a tendency that he often follows only reluctantly because of his divided sympathies—Yankelovich comes to see American society of the seventies as more selfish and more narcissistic than I believe it was. If this is so, his hopeful forecast of an emerging ethic of commitment in the eighties probably will be confirmed (in its personal, if not in its political dimension). But the confirmation will depend upon a contrived contrast typical of decade history: namely, a too-harsh appraisal of the moral fitness of Americans in the seventies.

In any case, at the more moderate center—as well as at the extremes—the therapeutic search yielded a variety of salutary effects, despite its theoretical limitations, its empirical dubiety, and its tendency to enforce oscillating, antidemocratic styles of authoritarian and anarchistic inquiry. Citing the comparative study of Lester Luborsky, Barton Singer, and Lise Luborsky, Frederick Crews observes that "all therapies succeed, insofar as they do, for reasons other than the unique causal factors specified in their accompanying theories. It is easy to imagine such reasons—for instance, that patients who seek therapy have already decided to take themselves in hand, or that any explanation offered in tandem with a promise of symptom relief can be happily embraced, or simply that a hired friend is better than none."[69] Of course, there is no sure way to judge the overall success of the therapeutic quest. For one thing, the goal of the fulfilled self is hopelessly vague. For another, as in the case of the Christian revival, we are left with the fragmentary and contradictory evidence of subjective testimony.

One point, however, seems clear: the sheer growth of therapeutic alternatives testifies in yet another way to the cultural centrality of the quest for fulfillment within small, generally voluntary communities of significant others. Beyond this, the phenomenon is too diffuse to assess with much confidence. Still, the growth of personal expectations itself constitutes a remarkable phenomenon. It suggests the increasing concern for the dignity and well-being of individuals, as well as the democratization of this concern. Of course, no serious observer would applaud every embodiment of the search. The quest for salvation did display selfish and narcissistic sides; the search often brought out mean and petty tendencies in Americans. Many individuals failed to heed an old scriptural lesson, and instead of finding themselves while in the fields of therapeutic endeavor, they became lost. They stumbled into what Yankelovich calls the "fulfillment trap," wanting more than they could have and seeking it in "all the wrong places," as a popular lyric of the seventies put it. But selfishness and narcissism were not the main issues: they were, rather, side effects of the growing importance Americans of all backgrounds assigned to the self—to *their* selves.

Throughout the sixties and seventies, then—in the Movement, in the revival of expressly Christian experience, in the amorphous therapeutic quest—Americans pursued various modes of salvation as if these were crucially important facets of their quest for personal fulfillment. My intent here has not been to assess the extent to which evangelical forms of Christian salvation or their secular (often heretical) variants and analogues deliver on their promises, either to individuals or to the entire culture. It has been, rather, to suggest that even, or perhaps especially, when they do not deliver all the material and psychological goods—and this is apt to remain the most common case in American culture—they still define the outer limits of hope and desire. In fact, the Judeo-Christian exemplar sets these limits at a frustratingly high level: eternal (or vastly extended) life and more abundant physical, psychological, interpersonal, and spiritual life in the tangible present.

This is an elusive set of criteria for those who believe—or desire to believe—and probably as difficult a set of criteria of well-being for those who do not. Since the metaphors and rituals of remission of Christian vision are not universally accepted, the abstract criteria drawn from its dominant paradigm contributed not only to high, often inflated expectations, but also ensured continuing cultural and political division. During the sixties and seventies, the growth of dissent—personal, cultural, and political—was an enormously powerful and on the whole salutary development. As I shall suggest in the next chapters, dissent not only contributed importantly to political changes that have given significant numbers of Americans a fairer and fuller chance to pursue aspects of personal fulfillment. It cracked the hegemony of WASP culture, popularizing cultural patterns and possibilities that have enlarged, perhaps permanently, the boundaries of political discourse and political action in the United States.

During the quest for salvation, of course, personal frustrations proliferated. The deepest miseries, ranging from anxiety, inadequacy, and guilt to anger and rage, were brought into focus by the widest criteria of what salvation must feel like. But this should come as no surprise: greater freedom does not necessarily entail greater "happiness," defined as a slight disparity between aims and perceived achievements.[70] Increased freedom did, however, enable millions of Americans to experience life on a more intense scale, to lead fuller interior lives than their parents or grandparents had. What William James called "the sphere of the felicity"—the inner life of impulse and emotion—was expanded and enriched during these years. The quest for fulfillment, especially its salvific aspects, engaged millions who claimed complete or partial success. In such domains, subjective testimony must be taken seriously, despite its elusive character.

10

Social Justice
and the Logic of Dissent

In the spring of 1979, according to an Associated Press release, a young gay couple attended a dance at a Sioux Falls, South Dakota, high school. They were, the National Gay Task Force reported, the first "acknowledged homosexuals to attend a high school prom together in the United States." Randy Rohl, a seventeen-year-old student, and his date, Grady Quinn, age twenty, appeared "in matching light blue tuxedos, red rose boutonnieres and silver pierced earrings." Although the dance went on without incident, it was preceded by considerable public controversy in Sioux Falls, and, Rohl said, by several threats to "tar and chicken feather him," apparently from local high school boys. Nevertheless, Rohl observed at a post-prom brunch, "Many students came over and congratulated us. A lot of people were really glad we stuck to our guns and went."

This event was not sufficiently lurid to bring a Norman Mailer west in search of a sequel to *The Executioner's Song* (1979), his inquiry into the life of convicted slayer Gary Gilmore: there were no major acts of violence, no pathetic nymphomaniac to interview, no sulking murderer's story to chronicle. Still, the idea of a young gay couple breaking, or perhaps only broadening, a tradition observed by millions of gay young couples is arresting in its way. The incident compresses the main phases of dissent during these decades. At the onset of the sixties, no homosexual couple would have dared to appear at a high school dance, even in San Francisco or New York, not to mention Sioux Falls. By the end of that decade, when homosexuals had begun to come out of the closet, few apparently wished to pursue Rohl's intention, preferring instead life in what are alternately called gay communities or gay ghettos. At any rate, none did. At the end of the seventies, however, at least one couple preferred to have it both ways: they wanted to be openly gay, and to participate in a heterosexual ritual. And they were willing to press their case, to engage in a public act of dissent. What's more, they succeeded.

Beginning at the edges of American society in the late fifties and early sixties, dissent made its way to the respectable center and even to the right by the end of the seventies. A fugal pattern unfolded during these years, starting with the Beats and the civil-rights movement in the late fifties and continuing through the antinuclear movement and the so-called taxpayers' revolt of the late seventies. By the close of the seventies, dissent had become a generally accepted part of the repertoire of ordinary politics. No longer the more or less exclusive property of the left, various strategies of protest were employed by groups all across the spectrum of American ideology. Indeed, it has been estimated that in the final years of the seventies some sort of public demonstration occurred on the average of at least once a day.[1]

Dissent, then, had become ubiquitous, diffused throughout all the major social categories of ideology, region, sex, age, class, race, ethnicity, religion, and voluntary special interest groups.* Everything appeared to be an obstacle to fulfillment as material, social, psychological and spiritual hopes rose: old economic, political, and legal barriers, as well as relatively new cultural and psychological ones. Individuals within every part of the structure of disadvantage engaged increasingly in formal and informal acts of dissent, from personal dissatisfaction and withdrawal to public opposition, ordinary politics, protest politics, and even isolated moments of rebellion. Dissent, then, became the common denominator of the many-sided search for fulfillment, its most visible popular medium.

Although alienation and an unearned, automatic negativism were

---

* Whereas *dissent* is generally considered to be a state of mind, *protest* typically refers to a collective (or even a personal) action, often one with political intent. In the context of this study, dissent serves as the fundamental category and public protest as one of its many forms.

frequent outcomes of dissent, I wish to concentrate here on its positive role in the sixties and seventies. On balance, I believe, dissent was both a prime instrument in the quest for fulfillment and a major expression of the quest. Even the Women's Christian Temperance Union (WCTU) joined in, reviving the tradition of Carry Nation (sans hatchet). In August of 1979, members concluded their one-hundred-and-fifth annual convention by invading a Petaluma, California, saloon after having marched down Western Avenue waving placards and singing the songs of Zion. "There was a little difference of opinion over whether we should do it," Mrs. Marie L. Caylor, WCTU public relations counsel, reported. Although "some of the older members were a little disturbed," she said, "the others pointed out that these days everybody's rallying for something and we might as well do that too."[2] By this time, dissent had begun to encircle itself, having become the basis for acts of conformity.

The Essential Logic of Dissent

As the episode of Rohl and Quinn suggests, the essential logic of dissent in postwar America begins with expanded claims on behalf of the self. The fundamental question—the one most frequently asked, or perhaps most frequently answered without being posed—was this: "What measure of social justice (and cultural freedom) do I need to be fulfilled?" Answers varied widely, of course, if only because conceptions of fulfillment and salvation are so diverse. To pursue expanding images of the self, individuals required enactment of a minimal conception of social justice. Above all, they needed increased liberty—at the very least, freedom to participate in public life (or to withdraw from it) and equal protection under the law. The pursuit of fulfillment also (perhaps even primarily) entailed liberation from the main stereotypes of WASP culture—an enlargement of subjective space as well as a multiplication of cultural options. For without a sense of inner freedom a decisive majority of citizens would continue to lack the cultural resources to imagine themselves as more than typecast bit players in the American drama.

For the most part, individuals pursued images of fulfillment on their own or in small groups during both the sixties and the seventies: of all the activity in society, it should be remembered, only a fragment involved large-scale collective protest of the sort usually associated with "the sixties." At the same time, millions—in the end a clear majority—were moved to engage in some mode of dissent, having encountered social obstacles that limited their freedom and frequently violated their basic rights. Moreover, these forms of economic, social, political, and cultural injustice often resisted purely personal efforts at redress. Systematically disadvantaged to one degree or another, many individuals joined together in various forms of collective dissent: criticism, demonstrations, boycotts, single-issue electoral politics, and remedial action through the courts. The precondition to the advancement or preservation of their own freedom, this is to say, frequently turned out to be a group action (or an endorsement of group action). When advancement of individual liberty—the freedom to pursue fulfillment—seemed to entail collective dissent, people were compelled to seek some social rationale. In America, the most acceptable justification for collective dissent turns on vague and open-ended notions of equality and opportunity. For the claims to liberty in a nonascriptive society rest on assumptions of equality of condition. All citizens, it is generally supposed, ought to possess equally certain basic rights: rights to life, to personal liberty, to political liberty, to legal protection, to respect, and to the pursuit of happiness. At the very least, acts of collective dissent presuppose commitment to an actor's sense of his or her own equality and opportunity, and by extension, to that of the group that bears a certain recognized disadvantage.

The psychological routes through which an individual comes to profess a general idea of social justice can be complicated. But the essential logic of the process seems clear enough. If, for example, an individual gay man demands his own liberty and a measure of opportunity, he must be prepared to endorse the idea for the entire gay community, or at least for a decisive majority. Criminals, the mentally unsound, and the morally unfit may be excluded, although grounds for such judgments are often tenuous. Furthermore, to gain redress, he probably will be disposed to accept some extension of the idea of equality to some other similarly disadvantaged minorities. He may reach this conclusion out of purely or largely moral considerations, of course, especially if his conception of salvation and fulfillment incorporates a high degree of concern for others. Whatever the structure of his motives and beliefs, however, his situation gives the idea of equality a sustained—and potentially political—focus.

Although it often takes political detours, the logic of dissent thus begins and ends with expanded claims in behalf of the self. These claims range from securing the minimal terms of social justice to securing top positions in real or imaginary hierarchies. "My" liberty, then, might mean anything from the elemental right to a seat on a public conveyance to the cultural freedom to imagine myself as the most enlightened person in America. "My" equality might mean anything from equal protection under the law to the freedom to define myself as the equal—in brilliance, sensitivity, even accomplishment—of any other person. Since everyone was at a disadvantage in some facet of his or her life, anyone could fancy himself or herself a victim—deprived of minimal rights, substantial power, wide influence, or lavish recognition. Nearly everyone, this is to say, developed a set of reasons that would justify engaging in some personal or political form of dissent.

The logic of dissent, as I have sketched it, clearly does not guarantee enactment of general social justice. It makes at most a weak allowance for consideration of the good of others, especially when it conflicts with one's own. Indeed, most philosophers probably would regard what I call a "piece of social justice" as merely an obfuscating synonym for self-interest. To an extent, of course, it is. But given the circumstances of American society in the sixties and seventies—especially the structure of disadvantage—most individuals had some valid claim to an additional increment to their share of social power. To be sure, not every disadvantage—real or imagined—constitutes an injustice. Yet the inequities of opportunity, wealth, and power were sufficient to make plausible the claims of injustice registered by a plethora of groups, from blacks and women to old people and the handicapped. During these decades, the scope of injustice was reduced substantially, I shall argue, through various enactments of the logic of dissent, even though the idea of general social justice was neither commonly defined nor always approached in rational ways. But in a rough sense, individual claims to a larger slice of social justice often contributed indirectly to the haphazard advancement of general social justice.[3]

The logic of dissent was complicated endlessly by the range of meanings—often conflicting meanings—assigned to such key terms of American ideology as "liberty," "equality," "opportunity," and the related idea of "fairness" (the elusive optimum mix of advantage and disadvantage). It was complicated further by varying specifications of the notion of fulfillment—the ratios between "my" salvation and the slice of social justice "I" need (or believe I need). Such ratios in part reflected different situations people occupied within the conventional social categories of status, occupation, and wealth. Yet even if people had behaved like Marxist automatons and displayed attitudes wholly derivable from their class position, these intricate social and cultural differences would have produced considerable jostling in an affluent, pluralistic, multilayered society. And they would have strengthened tendencies toward fragmentation within various foci of protest. Both sorts of tension—among groups and within groups—were exacerbated by the scope of discretionary behavior, which expanded so rapidly that within fairly broad limits individuals, especially middle- and upper-middle-class individuals, could choose the terms of their own fulfillment and the terms of their dissent. The scope of choice widened largely by virtue of the rise in discretionary income, from 15 percent prior to World War II, to more than 25 percent following the war, and to 50 percent by the early seventies.[4] Although they were facilitated by economic gains, the resulting array of choices did not simply reflect affluence: the broad scope of elected choices expressed the rich possibilities and considerable diversity of cultures in the United States. Supplied with at least a minimal share of social justice, most people fashioned their own modes of salvation and hence of fulfillment. In these circumstances, attitudes and behavior became less and less a simple function of social class. Far from subverting the logic of dissent, however, this social diversity and relative lack of harmony clearly derives from it.

Two principal variants of this essential logic of dissent dominated the American scene in the sixties and seventies. The first was the logic of maximal cultural inclusion—the dissent of people wondering why they were not first. The second was the logic of minimal social inclusion—the dissent of people wondering why they were so often last. Although these variants mixed and merged, both in society and in the analytic frameworks of students of society, they displayed themselves in relatively clear prototypical forms from the outset of the explosion of dissent.

The Logic of Maximal Inclusion. Consider the scattered, essentially cultural protests of the so-called Beat generation. This loose network of poets, novelists, artists, and hangers-on came to public attention in the middle fifties. Such figures as Jack Kerouac, Allen Ginsberg,

Lawrence Ferlinghetti, William Burroughs, Gary Snyder, Neal Cassady, and Gregory Corso represented the beginnings of cultural dissent in postwar America, the first resurgence of avant garde protest since the twenties. They sounded themes that within a decade had become familiar parts of the counterculture and within two decades had affected every part of American life. Each of these figures had his own ax to grind, and some of them—Snyder and Ginsberg, for instance—ground them powerfully, often brilliantly. Taken together, however, the distinctive dreams of the Beats illuminate a collective logic—the logic of maximal cultural inclusion.

Allen Ginsberg's "America," a Whitmanesque poem published in 1956, articulates several of the main themes of postwar American cultural protest. Ginsberg's persona (through whom, I think it fair to say, he speaks) addresses the whole society: "America I've given you all and now I'm nothing./America two dollars and twentyseven cents January 17, 1956."[5] The persona casts himself as a victim yet emerges a defiant man, a dissenter who rejects the terms of conventional life. He refuses to conform in any way: to marriage, to work, to religion, to politics, to culture. "You should have seen me reading Marx," he boasts childishly. "I won't say the Lord's Prayer." He is a man who dissents not only because he feels left out but also because he feels unfairly discounted—not simply last, but rather not first.

Of course, there are moral, political, and ecological dimensions to Ginsberg's dissent: "Go fuck yourself with your atom bomb," he declares with inelegant simplicity. "America when will you send your eggs to India?" But these dimensions seem curiously pale in this poetic setting. The moral outbursts fit the larger autobiographical design of promoting the self—in this case, a stylized version of Ginsberg's self. At one level, Ginsberg demands a place on the American turf rather than inclusion in any of its several socially contrived hierarchies of wealth, power, influence, or authority. He seeks his own space: "I don't feel good don't bother me." He proclaims his freedom from responsibilities by posing as a man on the run, a slightly paranoid fugitive in total opposition to society and culture. The cover of *Time* "stares" at him every time he "slinks past the corner candystore."

But Ginsberg's dissent goes well beyond a search for the right to nonconformity. To establish himself, he must neutralize and denigrate others, reducing those in the middle echelons of society to a faceless crowd and ridiculing those with high visibility. Wanting to be left alone (or at least professing such a desire), he cannot let society be. Each week he pores over *Time,* a primer of middle-class conformity, in, of all places, "the basement of the Berkeley Public Library." "It's always telling me about responsibility. Businessmen are serious. Movie producers are serious. Everybody's serious but me." Rejecting people and places above the bottom of the social pyramid, Ginsberg nevertheless cherishes the idea of being somebody: "My ambition is to be President despite the fact that I'm a Catholic" (i.e., handicapped in the race for the most coveted position in society). He presents himself, this is to say, as a man with a right to personal freedom and a valid claim to be at least the equal of everyone who displays talent or registers achievement. His ambivalence suggests that he wants in at the top—or else he wants the entire structure annihilated.

In its extreme form, then, the dissenting logic of maximal inclusion frequently entails an alienated assault on culture and society, an attempt (often only rhetorical) to flatten and conflate the notions of privilege, power, excellence, and domination. Surely these elements were mixed ambiguously in the American compound of the middle fifties. Ginsberg, however, makes no attempt to analyze this compound or even to distinguish among the spheres of economy, polity, and culture. Although he reports that his "psychoanalyst" thinks he's "perfectly right," Ginsberg cannot afford to say why. He cannot commit political or social analysis because his protestation of equality (and superiority) rests on other than rational grounds. There are those other artists, businessmen, scientists, politicians—indeed, millions of people—above him, for whatever mixture of reasons. His dissent therefore must take the form of an impossibly general claim, a quasi-Hegelian conception of the world. It could as easily have been a facile celebration: "We love everything," Jack Kerouac once remarked, "Billy Graham, the Big Ten, rock 'n' roll, Zen, apple pie, Eisenhower—We dig it all." But it also fit the form that Ginsberg chooses: as long as distinctions are avoided, anything goes.

Ginsberg's attack on America (like Kerouac's celebration) exemplifies an essentially nihilistic epistemological conviction that Daniel Bell has called an affirmation of "the equality of all perception." In particular, Ginsberg's own vision, we are urged to believe, is at least as good as anyone else's, and probably superior by virtue of his talent. Feeling and sensitivity: these become the final criteria for judging selves. All forms of authority other than charismatic are dismissed. It is the territory beyond reason (and social structure) that counts, the place where all ambitions may be filled. "You made me want to be a saint," Ginsberg says at one point. And at another: "I have mystical visions and cosmic vibrations." A counterhierarchy that favors youth begins to emerge from this egalitarian rhetoric: the more you feel and the more intense the energy you pour into the environment, the higher you rank. Ginsberg's published work, and that of his circle of writers and savants, might leave ordinary mortals breathless. But their "unpublishable private literature," he boasts, "goes 1400 miles an hour and twentyfive-thousand mental institutions."

Having broken through conventional forms of knowledge, power, and morality, Ginsberg pushes his assault beyond the increasingly elastic boundaries of normality to celebrate his madness, his status as a holy fool. Though his imagined kingdom is not of this world, he must abide here, an underground man on the make. He is at once a self-proclaimed hero and a martyr—neglected by those who for no good reason continue to matter. In the end, Ginsberg seeks common cause with other disadvantaged groups, with those who in the middle fifties were beginning to move once again toward minimal inclusion in society. "Ugh. Him [America] make Indians learn read. Him need big black niggers. Hah. Her [Russia] make us all work sixteen hours a day, Help." In the concluding lines of the poem, this ambivalent man of many postures resolves to make a difference—on his own idiosyncratic terms, of course: "It's true that I don't want to join the Army or turn lathes in precision parts factories, I'm nearsighted and psychotic anyway. / America I'm putting my queer shoulder to the wheel." The irony gained by juxtaposing "queer" to a macho American cliché is striking. But the proposed alliance between the man of superior parts and disadvantaged groups is weak, just as his resolve is thoroughly unconvincing.

Here is a self-made victim, a debased romantic seeking to heal the wounds of social and cultural alienation through some blend of opposition and community. Rejecting, albeit ambivalently, the dominant assumptions and norms of society, he cultivates a dialogue among his own parts. And beyond this solipsistic community, he courts a symbolic community of outcasts. "I am America," he says at one point, only to realize immediately that he is "talking" to himself "again." His facile, fickle identification with blacks, Indians, and women may (and in the middle sixties did) lead him into a politics of sporadic protest. It even took him into an ill-fated encounter, as brief as it was comic, with members of the Hell's Angels motorcycle "club." But politics clearly is not his game: it is at most an occasional part of his quest. And sustained politics is beyond him: Ginsberg's poetic conceit may persuade him to seek fulfillment by participating in protest politics one day and smoking his way to the outskirts of Nirvana the next.[6] He remains above all an expressive dissenter, an individual who defines his freedom as liberation from the assumptions and responsibilities of citizenship, and his equality (if not superiority) on grounds of feeling and the equal value of all perception. He is a man not at the bottom of society but on its margins, an outsider who, though voluntarily last, feels himself entitled to be first.

"America" thus previews in surreal form certain popular modes of asserting personal liberty, equality, and superiority that emerged in the sixties and seventies. It is a celebration, often darkly ironic, of the affective, infinitely expanding self in search of some community, even a solipsistic one. An example of the dissident logic of maximal inclusion, "America" foreshadows most of the major themes and preoccupations of the counterculture. Ginsberg manages to name if not to explore the political themes of left dissent: discrimination, poverty, conscription, nuclear war, ecology. But he concentrates on the cultural and personal concerns of the quest. He emphasizes the "creative" self seeking small communities; the experiential self finding expression through drugs, high energy, and heightened sexuality; the mystical self garbling fragments of Eastern religions; the deviant, victimized self pursuing fashionable "madness," homosexuality, and sentimental identification with outcasts; and the superior self opposing existing forms of culture, material wealth, and most established patterns of success (except perhaps celebrity).

Though Ginsberg's dissident persona is unattractive—at any rate, I find him so—he does manage to register some of the claims for social justice and cultural space pressed by millions who sought personal fulfillment during the sixties and seventies: in the Movement, the Christian revival, and the expressly therapeutic quest. Ginsberg's dissenting persona explores the distant ends of paths that became increasingly open to ordinary people seeking a fuller sense of self: more personal freedom and flexibility, a sense of wholeness (salvation) within a small community of accepting equals, a feeling that no one is superior (especially for such arbitrary reasons as accidents of birth and unearned social advantages). Although some enthusiasts of the counterculture pursued Ginsberg's directions to their nihilistic dead ends, most Americans traveled only short distances along these paths. Instead of asking why they were not first—or in addition to such musings—most citizens wondered about their relative position in the structure of disadvantage: their economic and occupational station, their living arrangements, their political influence, their prestige, their cultural status. But many people moved far enough and stopped soon enough to contribute importantly to the democratization of personhood: their own, primarily, but that of others as well.

The Logic of Minimal Inclusion. The black civil-rights movement can be taken as a prototype of the second main variant of the logic of dissent in the sixties and seventies: the logic of minimal inclusion. "I Have a Dream," the Reverend Martin Luther King, Jr.'s, memorable address delivered on the steps of the nation's Capitol in August, 1963, outlines the shapes of dissent among the most obviously disadvantaged large group in America. Like Ginsberg, King addressed America—the more than 190,000 blacks and 60,000 whites gathered in Washington, as well as the rest of the nation through television and the press. The immediate background to King's speech was a mass politics of dissent that, though it stretched over more than a century and took every form from litigation to riots, gathered fresh momentum in the years following World War II.

King's speech conveys the affirmation of a man who, by ordinary standards, had sufficient reason to abandon his faith in the social order. Simply by virtue of his racial origins, he had experienced gratuitous pain and humiliation. Though he was relatively advantaged—the son of a prominent black minister—King nevertheless grew up in a semi-feudal atmosphere of Southern terror and systematic discrimination that circumscribed the opportunities of all black people. He served as a principal leader in a long and costly battle that, judging from promises set forth in the founding American documents, never should have had to occur. In the end, his premonition of assassination confirmed, he was martyred, but not before his experience on the mountain top, his vision of the promised land on the other side. The Washington speech was delivered midway through the battle, five years before King's untimely death at age thirty-nine.

The march on Washington was the culmination of this major phase of intensified dissent undertaken primarily by blacks, and assisted in various ways by a small number of whites. Individuals and small groups, mainly students, staged the early public protests: the sit-ins and freedom rides.[7] Larger numbers of black citizens supported boycotts and public demonstrations. By the spring of 1963, literally the entire black community in America had endorsed efforts to force the federal government to establish and guarantee civil rights and to break patterns of economic discrimination that had plagued black people from the days of slavery to the present. King's speech came at the end of a spring and summer of more than one thousand demonstrations that had spread from the South to parts of the entire nation. The speech followed long legal and political battles that had resulted in the important Supreme Court school desegregation decision of 1954. It followed the many protests in the South—some of them successful, others not—beginning in 1956 with the Montgomery bus boycott sparked by the refusal of Rosa Parks, a black seamstress, to give her bus seat to a white man. It came after the Greensboro sit-ins of 1960 and the Freedom Rides through the South a year later to desegregate public facilities. The address followed the first voter-registration campaigns and the 1963 Birmingham campaign to desegregate shops, restaurants, and the workplace, led by King and given national media attention largely as a consequence of the inhumane tactics of "Bull" Conner, the racist police commissioner. It followed, that is to say, a pattern of governmental sluggishness, white resistance, and white violence that had left more than a score dead, many injured, and even larger numbers of people jailed.

Four months after his own arrest and imprisonment in Birmingham, then, King delivered this minor masterpiece of American rhetoric. Paraphrasing the opening words of the Gettysburg Address ("five score years ago"), which Lincoln had spoken a century earlier, King also recalled the *Emancipation Proclamation.* He noted that Lincoln's "momentous decree came as a great beacon light of hope to millions of Negro slaves . . . One hundred years later," he continued, "we must face the tragic fact that the Negro is still not free."[8] The black person remains the victim of segregation, discrimination, and poverty —"an exile in his own land." Using a homely economic metaphor that Benjamin Franklin might have found congenial, King articulates the purpose of the demonstration: "In a sense we have come to our nation's Capitol to cash a check. When the architects of our republic wrote the magnificent words of the Constitution and the Declaration of Independence, they were signing a promissory note to which every American was to fall heir. This note was a promise that all men would be guaranteed the unalienable rights of life, liberty, and the pursuit of happiness."

But the nation clearly had defaulted. It had given the "Negro people a bad check; a check which has come back marked 'insufficient funds.'" The demand, then, was for minimal inclusion in the American enterprise: nothing less than full citizenship. And the demand was for this measure of justice *"now."* King issues a warning about the costs of delaying justice: "The whirlwinds of revolt will continue to shake the foundations of our nation until the bright day of justice emerges." He asks his own followers to avoid violence and to resist the temptation to distrust "all white people, for many of our white brothers, as evidenced by their presence here today, have come to realize that their destiny is tied up with our destiny and their freedom is inextricably bound to our freedom. We cannot walk alone." There were, however, to be no concessions to injustice. The pilgrimage, King vowed, would not end until "justice rolls down like waters and righteousness like a mighty stream." Here the speech modulates from a concern with redeeming the secular promises of justice to a vision of collective salvation. It sounds for a moment like Paul's letter to one of the early churches—at Corinth, say, or Antioch. Acknowledging the suffering of civil-rights activists, King counsels courage and urges them to press toward the mark: "Go back to Mississippi, go back to Alabama, go back to South Carolina, go back to Georgia, go back to Louisiana, go back to the slums and ghettos of our northern cities, knowing that somehow this situation can and will be changed. Let us not wallow in the valley of despair."

King is ready to outline his own dream, having earned the right to it as a man and as a speaker. He has announced his purpose, claimed the promissory note of minimal inclusion for black citizens, warned of the consequences of majority indifference and minority intransigence, urged restraint upon his followers, acknowledged their suffering, and consoled and challenged them to continue until the victory is won. "I say to you today, my friends, that in spite of the difficulties and frustrations of the moment, I still have a dream. It is a dream deeply rooted in the American dream." King's dream weaves together two themes: the minimal claims of social justice—full citizenship now—

and a larger utopian cultural vision of freedom, equality, and brotherhood later on. He dreams of an end to hatred and bitterness, a time when "on the red hills of Georgia the sons of former slaves and the sons of former slaveholders will be able to sit down together at the table of brotherhood." Here Christian visions of redemption and love in the spirit of Christ—a communion feast—merge with Judaic images of deliverance from immediate bondage and utopian visions of a harmonious future. "I have a dream," Kings says, echoing the sentiments of the prophet Micah, "that one day every valley shall be exalted, every hill and mountain shall be made low, the rough places will be made plain, and the crooked places will be made straight, and the glory of the Lord shall be revealed, and all flesh shall see it together."

King's dream, then, finally is compressed into a multifaceted, well-ordered vision of freedom—of secular freedom as the precondition and complement to widespread spiritual freedom: "When we let freedom ring," he concludes, "when we let it ring from every village and every hamlet, from every state and every city, we will be able to speed up that day when all of God's children, black men and white men, Jews and Gentiles, Protestants and Catholics, will be able to join hands and sing in the words of the old Negro spiritual, 'Free at last! free at last! thank God almighty, we are free at last!'" In the end this is only a hope. But it is firmly tied to a credible view of present suffering and present possibilities. King's hope was the energizing force of a powerful faith that he took home to the South to begin work again. Three weeks later, four young black girls were killed in the bombing of a Birmingham church by white racists. Three months later a president was assassinated. A year later several hundred black citizens died in urban riots in the north. But by early 1964 a comprehensive civil-rights bill had been signed by Lyndon Johnson, a white Southerner turned president. And in 1965 the landmark Voting Rights Act became law.

The significant differences between these two variants of the logic of dissent may be exaggerated by my choice of extreme examples. Though Ginsberg is a poet of some contemporary importance, King is an important historical figure. Ginsberg articulates the claims of the private self through his intensely autobiographical poem. King speaks for himself and for a large constituency of fellow sufferers in a public address. Ginsberg's persona manages to compromise the moral attractiveness of the already ethically difficult case for maximal inclusion by taking his dissent to the extremes of selfishness, narcissism, paranoia, and solipsism. King presents a morally compelling case for the logic of minimal inclusion. Ginsberg illustrates a primarily cultural process, King an essentially social and political one.

Differences between the two variants, however, should not obscure their important similarities. Ginsberg and King press claims for greater liberty of persons. Ginsberg wants cultural space for himself. King needs the guarantee of social space for a large minority if individual black people are to enjoy the rights of, say, a person like Ginsberg. Both demand an end to the main stereotypes of WASP culture. If he must try to conform to these cultural norms, Ginsberg—a Jew—can never be first or plausibly imagine himself to be so. Nor can King or any other black person. They cannot even exist confidently in the middle ranges of various hierarchies.

Most importantly, both variants of the logic of dissent stress the idea of personal fulfillment through community over the notion of ordinary politics. Ginsberg's character seeks his own ad hoc community—a community with a shifting population composed mainly of individuals on the outskirts of culture and society. King's long-term vision also emphasizes *gemeinschaft*—personal fulfillment in a land of liberty, equality, and fraternity. For Ginsberg's persona, politics is incidental, fitful, and often impossible, since his heterogeneous constituency is less able (and presumably less willing) to come together than King's. For King, politics is necessary to achieve full citizenship for himself. But in order to pursue his dream of a community of "brothers and sisters," and to permit others to pursue theirs, King also needs to combine his own dissent with that of an easily identifiable, publicly recognized category of others. Though King seems drawn into politics, his larger utopian dream nevertheless is post-political, perhaps anti-political in the ordinary sense of the term. Even the sense of immediate struggle he conveys departs somewhat from the norms of ordinary politics: he calls the civil-rights movement a moral and spiritual enterprise, an exercise in "creative dissent." Envisioning a politics of pressure and the pressures of politics as a pilgrimage—a quest—King led a movement whose members often prefigured bits of the future in the day-to-day course of their struggle.

Patterns of Dissent

In the sixties and seventies, the main limiting cases of the logic of dissent—maximal and minimal inclusion—were complexly related. The history of dissent during these years suggests that none of the foci of dissent conformed wholly to either early prototype. In fact, the two variants mixed and merged rather freely. If they could be measured, the differences in degree of preoccupation with self among Ginsberg (a poet), Huey Newton (a black radical), Tom Hayden (a white radical), and Abbie Hoffman (a countercultural megalomaniac) probably would turn out to be negligible. All pursued maximal inclusion, at least for themselves, even as some of them made their reputations as leaders of groups seeking minimal inclusion. In fact, the role of leader allows individuals to play out fantasies of maximal inclusion. Both variants—the essentially social one of minimal inclusion and the basically cultural one of maximal inclusion—follow from an overall logic of dissent governed largely by the increasingly diverse (and shifting) mixes of the aims of personal fulfillment: salvation and a piece of social justice.

By itself, of course, this logic cannot explain the history of dissidence in the sixties and seventies. But it does suggest several tentative hypotheses about the diachronic patterns of dissidence during these years. It appears that the logic of minimal inclusion is an essential process followed by groups plagued by high degrees of disadvantage. It is likely to assert itself when basic injustices persist and the group that suffers from them becomes willing and socially able to initiate remedial action. Expressing itself mainly through ordinary political processes, though with special emphasis on nonviolent protest, the logic of minimal inclusion intensifies pressures for a more equitable distribution of opportunity and reward. In the course of its public cycle, however, the logic of minimal inclusion reveals itself to be unstable, giving way sooner or later to the logic of maximal inclusion. Let me state these hypotheses more explicitly.

First, the logic of minimal inclusion becomes a live option when it must and can. As I have suggested, most black people, especially those living in the South during the fifties, confronted limited options. They could choose fantasies of maximal inclusion, and indeed, many black people claimed to have achieved eternal salvation and even a subjective sense of fulfillment under the most difficult social circumstances. Many were able to opt for minimal inclusion by migrating north, where their chances of social success were somewhat better. Nevertheless, every black American lived under a complex system of white domination— a system that denied each citizen elemental rights, often through outright terror and always through shifting mixtures of economic, political, social, and cultural oppression. Salvation in some theological sense may have been possible, but the slice of social justice accorded blacks was too small to permit most to experience what might reasonably be considered secular fulfillment. Pursuit of the social aspects of self-fulfillment presupposed achievement of basic civil rights and collective liberation from WASP cultural stereotypes about black people. Thus, the path to first-class citizenship entailed the logic of minimal inclusion.

Such a logic was not merely necessary in this conditional sense. By the middle fifties, the logic of minimal inclusion had become socially possible as well. As Frances Piven and Richard Cloward make clear in their intriguing analysis of twentieth-century American protest movements, a complex history of economic and political changes cleared the way for political victories. "The civil rights movement," they conclude, "was not the fundamental cause of this political transformation . . . Still, it took a long, arduous, and courageous struggle to force the political transformation which economic conditions had made ready."[9] Piven and Cloward trace the regional, national, and international changes that enabled the battle for civil rights in the late fifties and sixties. Among these were the development of industrial capitalism; the mass northward migration of blacks in the twenties; the greater degree of personal freedom and social anomie in northern ghettos; the emergence of a relatively independent black leadership of clergymen, business, and professionals in the South; the requirements of cold war foreign policy; and changes in the options of the national Democratic party. Since the sluggish political system consistently failed to deliver on its promises in the fifties, collective dissent became a dominant mode. The social stage was set. The spark was ignited in Montgomery, and largely private dissent took dramatic public shape once again, beginning at local levels, spreading through the South, and then, within a few years, to points across the nation.

Second, the variant of minimal inclusion usually expresses itself through ordinary politics, including public protest with limited aims. Although modes of dissent became worldwide phenomena in the late fifties and sixties, their collective manifestations in America were largely non-violent. In the civil-rights movement, as well as in other foci of protest, dissent almost always stopped short of rebellious demands to redirect the axes of the social system. There was, to be sure, some domestic political violence during these years—indeed, more than at any time since the Civil War. The state used excessive force against rioters and other demonstrators, inflicting by far the heaviest domestic casualties of the entire period in urban ghettos that had been the scene of more than a hundred major riots between 1964 and 1967. In these four years, "approximately 130 civilians, mainly Negroes, and 12 civil personnel, mainly Caucasian, were killed. Approximately 4,700 Negroes and civil personnel were injured. Over 20,000 persons were arrested during the melees . . ."[10] Several public figures were assassinated. And elements of the far left engaged in what their spokespersons defined loosely as "political" violence in the late sixties and early seventies.

Yet dissent in these years was overwhelmingly peaceful and directed at limited changes in the American system. As Ted Robert Gurr notes in his interesting comparative study of political protest and rebellion in the sixties, "civil rights demonstrators asked for integration and remedial public action to alleviate the consequences of discrimination; they did not agitate for class or racial warfare. Peace marchers vehemently opposed United States foreign policy and some of the men who conducted it; those who wanted to go beyond the reversal of policy and bring about violent revolution could muster so few followers that they had to go underground." Even a majority of the urban rioters who participated in the most violent domestic disturbances of the sixties were, according to their own testimony, "retaliating against the accumulated burden of specific grievances: inconsistent and abusive police control, economic privation, and social degradation." In nations characterized by relative affluence and more or less democratic political systems, Gurr concludes, dissent tends to be expressed as peaceful protest. But comparative wealth seems to be the principal factor. As opposed to poor nations and those governed by elitist or authoritarian regimes, "wealthy nations have the resources that can be used to help satisfy many kinds of demand." Moreover, "the leaders of democratic nations usually believe that they *should* make some kind of favorable response to popular protest, and fear losing their positions if they do not."[11]

Third, successful efforts to secure minimal inclusion create pressures for a more equitable distribution of opportunity and rewards throughout the structure of disadvantage. The meaning of "minimal" expands to include certain economic entitlements. When strategies of dissent embodying the logic of minimal inclusion worked tolerably well, as in the case of the black civil-rights movement, they were imitated (with important variations) by many other groups: other racial minorities, students, women, the old, the handicapped. In each of these instances, individuals had been denied some formal or substantive part of minimal access to the pursuit of fulfillment. They were barred for various reasons, but at the very least by virtue of some socially defined or socially reinforced shared disadvantage. Various foci of dissent employed different mixes of tactics. The battle against racial oppression in the South required, among other things, mass mobilization, whereas the women's movement has been largely though not exclusively a guerrilla war, a house-to-house, person-by-person effort to reconstruct the definition of female and male identity and possibility. The struggle for rights for the handicapped, a phenomenon primarily of the seventies, turned mainly on a series of legal skirmishes, the stage having been set by the black civil-rights movement in other arenas.[12] As the idea of personal fulfillment expanded, segments of other groups—also less disadvantaged than blacks—came together to express dissent through combinations of protest, political action, and litigation: consumers, environmentalists, working- and middle-class taxpayers, European ethnics, portions of the Jewish community. By the end of the sixties, then, the idea of dissent was in the air. Any collection of people could choose to try some combination of protest, ordinary politics, and litigation.

Fourth, since customized personal dissent constitutes the American norm and politically organized dissent the exception, the variant of minimal inclusion remains perpetually unstable. When it works (or fails badly), this variant tends to give way to that of maximal inclusion. After the middle sixties, for example, the degree of solidarity among members of various groups generally did not approach that of the early civil-rights movement or the early moments of the women's movement. For several reasons: above all, the objectives of various groups became less elemental. The search for minimal inclusion for all quickly gave way to a search for *full* social justice for some. This enlargement of the idea of minimal inclusion exerted pressure on the

social system. Extension of voting rights to blacks, for example, exerted less strain on the social system than efforts to compensate for
historical injustices that left blacks as a group in the lower reaches of
the structure of economic, political, social, and cultural disadvantage.
Once various groups asserted their rights to minimal inclusion, then,
the pursuit of general social justice immediately grew more difficult.
Though long-term efforts to ameliorate structural inequities persisted,
political leaders and followers emphasized immediate partial efforts to
redistribute opportunity and reward within the existing structure of
disadvantage. Real pieces, or even fragments of social justice generally
were preferred to a projected condition of general social justice that
many observers believed would obtain only when opportunity, responsibility, and reward came to be distributed roughly in proportion to the
percentages of various groups in the population (however sloppy, arbitrary, and ineffective such categorization often proves to be).

During the sixties and seventies, then, the common aims of minimal
inclusion persisted. But these common aims took on lesser degrees of
urgency within any single focus of dissent as they came to compete
with other goals of personal fulfillment: larger shares of social justice
and additional cultural space in which to imagine and enact scenarios
of the self. Success carried a considerable price. By the seventies, for
example, feminists could participate in the struggle for ERA, or day-
care centers, or shelters for battered women and, at the same time,
seek attractive work. Students in the anti-war movement of the sixties
could demonstrate while pursuing educational credentials that would
preserve their advantaged positions later on—at least as long as they
managed to stay out of the infantry. After 1965, many blacks could
divide their concerns more easily between measures to advance their
own personal fulfillment and group interests: between, say, the search
for an executive position and demands for an entry level job for every
urban black youth who desired one. Their aims frequently overlapped;
for example, as when a person became an executive in an organization
or agency charged with finding jobs for young black people. Often,
however, there was little or no overlap, and when interests diverged,
tensions grew. Successes and failures of strategies organized around
the logic of minimal inclusion, this is to say, gave way quickly to demands for larger, and not necessarily equitable, slices of social justice.
Here the specific and diverse recipes for personal fulfillment asserted
themselves with growing force, though hardly, I think, to the point

where most disadvantaged groups could be said to be promoting social injustice.

By the late sixties, then, small-group protest flourished, as did single-issue and single-group politics. These trends continued through the seventies. But the egalitarian thrust of the early movements gave way somewhat to a libertarian tendency to assert the equal right to expand the perimeters of one's own social and cultural freedom or the freedom of some special interest group. Partly as a consequence of the limited successes registered through group protest, individual dissent—a significant medium for cultivating personal authenticity and visions of maximal inclusion—grew even more popular than collective dissent during these years. Hence, for most Americans, politics and public protest remained a secondary and occasional aspect of their quest for fulfillment through some form of community, however limited. And for many citizens, protest itself was more a sporadic and communal experience than an exercise in sustained political activity.

Early on, the growth and diversity of personal expectations contributed to dissension within and among dissenting groups. The civil-rights movement experienced a measure of conflict before 1965—and indeed displayed conflicting interests even in the generally harmonious 1963 march on Washington. But it fragmented after helping to gain formal rights for black citizens.[13] Thereafter, divisions between poor blacks and a growing black middle class intensified, and divisions deepened among black leaders drawn mainly from the middle class. In spite of such divisions, coalitions did come into precarious existence when common interests were threatened, and groups such as the Urban League continued to attempt to view the American enterprise from the imagined perspective of the welfare of *all* black people. But there was no more than a pretense of black unity after the early sixties. Cultural issues, such as the choice of styles of life, became increasingly important among those who had achieved minimal rights and a measure of substantive opportunity in economic and political spheres. Multiple differences based on individual and small-group assessments of the requirements of salvation and social justice played a significant part in eroding the unity and dissipating the force of this movement. Other foci of dissent also experienced division based in part on proliferating economic, political, cultural, and personal aims of activists and their immediate constituencies: the anti-war movement, the women's movement, and the gay rights movement, for example.

The sheer growth of dissent further contributed to the erosion of solidarity, or rather to the failure of solidarity to bring about degrees of intensity and political results expected by many critics and activists. The spread of dissent placed more—and different—actors in the public arena. Nearly everyone took up the practice of making scenes at some point in the sixties and seventies, if only to register personal dissent. The wider dispersion and corresponding dilution of unambiguous moral appeal and available power among the many foci of dissent prevented any group from fully achieving its expanding political and cultural aims. This is an inescapable consequence of the democratization of personhood, one sign of its rapid advance. The growth of freedom projected by members of each group turns out to be limited by the major and minor successes of other groups of citizens. Without major structural changes, the social system could tolerate only moderate expansion in a number of directions. Moreover, the emergence of relative scarcity in the early seventies retarded the anticipated growth of the total pool of resources to be distributed. Economic, social, and political expectations grew more rapidly than did the resources to satisfy them. And since partial satisfaction served largely to intensify expectations, the perceived disparities between hopes and achievements did not diminish as quickly as millions of Americans had believed they would.

Throughout the sixties and seventies, then, the various foci of dissent were composed for the most part of people attempting to reduce a particular form (or combination of forms) of economic, social, political, or cultural inequality that curtailed *their* liberty. There were two overall effects of this dissent and protest, I shall argue in the next chapter. Dissent and protest contributed importantly to weakening the hegemony of WASP culture, thereby widening cultural options for tens of millions of citizens. And various modes of dissent advanced the idea and substance of general social justice, albeit intermittently and imperfectly. By hastening the democratization of personhood, both developments facilitated the quest for personal fulfillment.

Dissent and the Democratization
of Personhood

Commenting on the impact of dissent and protest in the 1930s and the 1960s, Eric Hobsbawm concludes that "it is not negligible, but it is not what we wanted . . . Capitalism inevitably reintegrated poor people's protest."[1] Hobsbawm's observation raises the central difficulty of assessing the impact of dissent and protest: the matter of interpretation. His chummy "we" obviously refers to a small group of socialist intellectuals who, as usual, did not get their political way (and hence probably lost another opportunity to discover how little they would have liked what they got). Socialist intellectuals were not alone in their disappointment. Few people, even those more closely in touch with American values and aspirations—not to mention American *people*— got precisely what they wanted during the sixties and seventies, much less what any social critic proposed for them.

At the end of the seventies, no major ideological tendency or focus of protest could reasonably report more than limited success, though some conservatives believed (naïvely, I think) that they might be on the verge of reshaping American politics and culture in their own image. Spokespersons for many groups regularly withheld a portion of their economic, political, and cultural income from public statements, thus not acknowledging all their gains. In his introduction to *The State of Black America 1980,* for example, Vernon Jordan, Jr., concluded that "for black Americans the decade of the 1970's was a time in which many of their hopes, raised by the civil rights victories of the 1960's withered away; a time in which they saw the loss of much of the momentum that seemed to be propelling the nation along the road to true equality for all its citizens. Within Black America in the 60s," Jordan continued, "there had been eager anticipation that racial wrongs might be set right, a feeling that perhaps the nation was at last serious about attacking racism and poverty. The 70's, however, brought forth in Black America a mood of disappointment, frustration and bitterness at promises made and promises unkept."[2]

William Raspberry supplies one of the very few exceptions to this rhetorical practice I have run across, observing that "it has become the new orthodoxy for black Americans—particularly those doing pretty well—to deny that anything has changed for the better." Denials of this sort, Raspberry speculates, protect individuals from seeming naïve when certain apparent advances turn out to be illusory or fleeting. Furthermore, admission of progress, some people assume, "will take white America off the hook," reduce guilt, and hence preclude further advances. In spite of these risks, Raspberry concludes, "it's time for blacks of accomplishment and influence to stop poor-mouthing in the name of black solidarity. It's silly, and worse, for black men and women, wearing designer suits, living in elegant homes, working at important and prestigious and lucrative careers to pretend that we are hardly better off than a sharecropper in the rural south. The sharecropper knows better, and so do we."[3] Rather than embodying Raspberry's suggestion, interpretations of the impact of dissent and protest in the sixties and seventies tend to be colored heavily by stark comparisons of hopes and perceptions of actual social change—perceptions unmediated by reasonable expectations. The overall effect of this critical practice of harboring unreasonable expectations, of course, has been to minimize actual achievements while classifying everything else—reversals, partial victories, unfilled hopes and unfulfillable hopes—as some species of failure.

My purpose here, however, is not to take issue with every alleged failure of dissent. It is rather to propose that the overall impact of dissent and protest on the quest for personal fulfillment in the sixties and seventies was impressive and, on the whole, salutary. During these decades, the quest deepened and widened; it was pursued with greater intensity by millions of individuals; and it was taken up with lesser degrees of enthusiasm by additional millions of Americans. There was, then, a rapid democratization of personhood during these years, a democratization evidenced by augmented personal and political rights, by rising economic rewards, and by enhanced cultural opportunities.

Such a judgment, I have suggested in earlier chapters on "Defining the Framework of Nostalgia," may be obscured from any particular ideological vantage point or from points of view within any focus of dissent. A fair estimate of the impact of dissent on the quest for fulfillment, however, requires that partisan criteria of success and failure be laid aside temporarily, or at least that they not be used as exclusive standards of judgment. Moreover, such an estimate requires that the phenomenon of dissent be imagined whole, in its political and economic dimensions, as well as in its cultural and personal dimensions. Thus, the political accomplishments partly attributable to dissent might have been fitful, incomplete, and to some extent reversible. Economic advances might have been less spectacular in the seventies than in the fifties and sixties, as many critics charge, and rather less affected by dissent than were the political and cultural spheres of American life. Yet when the political and economic gains of the sixties and seventies are taken together with the dramatic cultural and personal changes that occurred, the net result strikes me as remarkable. Let me illustrate.

The Political Impact

During the sixties and seventies, dissent and protest contributed importantly to a widening and deepening of the idea of citizenship, a crucial dimension of personhood. In unprecedented numbers, Americans within every disadvantaged category asserted their personal rights and claimed their political rights. Blacks, followed by Hispanics and other racial minority groups, sought to redeem old promises. In the first phase of the civil-rights movement, blacks claimed their rights to equal access to public facilities. As a crucial component of these claims, higher education was sought by ever larger numbers of black people. Between 1960 and 1977, their enrollment in the nation's colleges increased from 227,000 (about 6 percent) to 1.1 million (about 11 percent). In fact, black enrollment doubled within the decade between 1967 and 1977. According to a U.S. Bureau of the Census report issued in 1979, there was "already evidence that among young high-school graduates, blacks and whites" were "attending college at about the same rate [32 percent]."[4]

In these years, blacks strengthened their political clout dramatically. They won the right to vote in the South. They achieved a measure of political power in major cities throughout the country: in Washington, D.C., where Marion Barry, an activist of the sixties, served as mayor in the late seventies; in Oakland, Cleveland, Los Angeles, and Detroit. Even in Birmingham: in 1963 the police commissioner of that city turned dogs loose on a crowd of innocent black people, including children; in 1979 the mayor of Birmingham was a black man. Blacks also became a force in national politics. In the 1976 presidential election, more than 90 percent of the black vote went to Jimmy Carter, providing a central ingredient of his narrow electoral victory. By the end of the seventies, the black congressional caucus had become a political force to be reckoned with: there were 18 blacks in Congress in 1979 as opposed to 10 in 1969, 4 in 1959, and only 2 in 1949. Moreover, toward the end of the seventies when Andrew Young served as U.S. ambassador to the United Nations, black political leaders began to articulate their opinions on foreign policy, especially on American relations with the nations of Africa and the Middle East, much to the dismay of many of the political intellectuals gathered around such journals as *Commentary*. Shaping foreign policy—and playing quarterback professionally—apparently were considered in some circles to lie beyond the capacities of black people.

Summarizing black gains in political and personal rights since 1960, Elliot Zashin notes that "tangible results were achieved. The percentages of southern blacks registering and voting increased dramatically; black children began to enter previously all-white schools. Public and commercial facilities open to whites only, for example, restaurants, hotels, motels, parks, and libraries, were desegregated, although for poorer blacks equal access was often largely symbolic . . ." On balance, Zashin concludes, the gains of the sixties and seventies "have placed blacks in general much closer to equality—however defined—than ever before in our history. We cannot return to the conditions which prevailed before the 1960s; blacks are too conscious, civil rights legislation barring overt discrimination is too much a part of our practice, and blacks have achieved enough of a political foothold to prevent a return to a not terribly benign neglect."[5]

The re-emergence of the women's movement—its public resurfacing after several decades of a more or less subterranean existence—might have been the most far-reaching domestic manifestation of dissent in these two decades. Women registered significant progress in higher education, the chief public path of entry into positions of influence and responsibility. Although the rates of college attendance for women had risen steadily since 1950, women represented only 44 percent of those enrolled in higher education as late as 1974. By the end of the decade, however, women for the first time constituted a slight majority of the student population of American colleges and universities. Moreover, they were entering in ever larger numbers fields traditionally reserved for men. At the end of the seventies, nearly a quarter of all medical school graduates were women, as opposed to about 10 percent a decade earlier. And growing numbers of women were opting for business, law, medicine, the military, and engineering.

Women benefited from the Civil Rights Act of 1964, especially from Title VII, which prohibited discrimination in employment on various grounds, among them, sex. And as the feminist movement gathered force in the late sixties and seventies, women played a leading part in the struggle for equal rights in all public areas of American life. In 1972, following a period of intense political activity, Congress passed the Equal Rights Amendment (though only thirty-five of the necessary thirty-eight states had ratified it by the end of the seventies, and prospects for reaching the necessary thirty-eight were not bright).[6] Still, the Equal Rights Amendment had been ratified in the court of public opinion. In 1972, Congress also passed the Equal Employment Opportunity Act, which facilitated litigation in cases of employment discrimination. And Title IX of the Education Amendments, which prohibited sex discrimination in most federally assisted educational programs was enacted, opening a new era in women's participation in athletics.

Throughout the seventies, groups such as the National Organization for Women (NOW) brought women's issues to public attention— from employment and earnings discrimination to inequitable divisions of household responsibility. The political dimensions of women's lives, which previously had been buried under such other issues as child care, protection from assault, and abortion, were articulated and moved on to local and national agendas. More and more, women acted collectively on their own political behalf. And with growing success. The 1980 presidential election underscored the increasing political independence of women: 45 percent of women voters supported Mr. Carter, the loser, as opposed to only 37 percent of male voters.

But women did more than exercise their franchise more independently. The number of women holding public office doubled in the second half of the seventies, rising from 7,242 (or about 4.7 percent of officeholders) to 17,782 (or about 10.9 percent). The number of women elected to state legislatures more than doubled in this decade, rising from 334 (about 4 percent) in 1970 to 767 (about 10.3 percent) in 1979. In 1949, there were 10 women in Congress; in 1959 there were 17; by 1979 the number had grown to 21. In 1968, women comprised only 13 percent of the delegates to the Democratic national convention; by 1972, the figure had risen to about 40 percent, and by 1980, women made up about 50 percent of the delegates.

Moreover, women moved into political positions in the upper reaches of the judicial and bureaucratic pyramids. By 1979, for example, there were four women federal Court of Appeals judges (out of 97) and 14 women district court judges (out of 417)—more women than had served in such positions in all of American history. And in 1981, Sandra Day O'Connor was appointed to the United States Supreme Court, the first woman ever to serve there. In the Carter administration, two women—Juanita Kreps and Patricia Harris—held cabinet positions simultaneously (as secretary of commerce and secretary of housing and urban development). Prior to 1977, a *total* of three women had held cabinet positions in the entire history of the Republic. No woman had yet reached *the* top, though in 1978 Gallup reported that 80 percent of those polled said they would support a qualified woman for president, as opposed to about 55 percent in 1960 and only 34 percent in 1937.[7]

Advances in women's political fortunes in the seventies seem to have met with considerable public approval. Asked whether they "favor or oppose most of the efforts to strengthen and change women's status in society today," 64 percent of respondents answered affirmatively in 1978, as opposed to only 42 percent in 1970. And in the seventies, the number opposing such efforts declined from 41 percent to 25 percent.[8] Although the attitudinal and political battles for minimal inclusion were by no means completely won at the end of the seventies, substantial progress had been registered, and prospects for futher advances seemed reasonably bright. Taking the measure of this decade, Alice Rossi observed that "it is a hard fact of life that women live longer, are better educated and are less dependent economically on men. It is a fact that they are moving into more powerful positions in government and the economy, and in their private lives are showing more solidarity with other women, and more personal demands for equitable treatment by bosses and spouses."[9] Though full equality for women remained an elusive long-term goal, progress had been sufficient in the sixties and seventies to justify continuing the struggle—in political as well as personal terms. As Eleanor Smeal, president of NOW, put it: "I am 40 and I know I will never see full equality. But my daughter will have a better life because of my efforts, and that's what it's all about."

The sixties and seventies also witnessed what one astute critic of higher education has characterized as a "veritable revolution . . . in the degree of freedom of young people with respect to manners, mores, dress, general mode of life, and personal life decisions."[10] By the end of the seventies, the practice of *in loco parentis,* so adamantly opposed by radicals in the previous decade, had been abandoned by most campus administrations. Outside the classroom, students largely regulated their own behavior, with much the degree of freedom sought by many student activists in the early and middle sixties. But the emancipation of youth was not confined to campus life. In 1971, the Twenty-sixth Amendment, which lowered the age of majority, became law. Most of the rights and responsibilities of adults, including the right to vote, were extended to all eligible citizens age eighteen and over.

Race, sex, age, ethnicity: these social categories put people at a disadvantage in the exercise of political and personal rights. But they were not the only categories that were scrutinized during the sixties and seventies. Height, weight, physical appearance, and physical handicaps also came into play. During these years prevailing ideas of personhood changed, largely as a consequence of political and cultural dissent launched in the sixties. A neo-Romantic concept of the essential equality of persons spread through many regions of society. In one of its basic meanings, the idea of equality came to refer primarily to individuals, to the essential self stripped of such incidental characteristics as skin color, sex, height, age, weight, physical appearance, and social role.

Social and personal differences abounded, of course, in spite of the growing popularity of the idea of essential equality. And differences continued to matter, perhaps even more than ever as a consequence of heightened awareness of them. In the ideology of the quest, the origins and causes of disadvantage—genetic, environmental, social, individual— mattered less than their apparent effect on personal effort. Adoptive parents were rejected because of their age or weight; job applicants were turned down because they displayed too many freckles; cocktail waitresses pushing thirty were dismissed because their "figures drooped," according to their employers (themselves often fatter than Christmas geese). But the norm of essential equality, against which greater numbers of individuals measured themselves, assumed ever larger significance. Instead of being ignored or going unnoticed, discrimination on grounds of membership in every arbitrary social or cultural category was called to public attention. It was scrutinized, protested, and actively lobbied against in the political, bureaucratic, and judicial arenas. In many cases, individuals and groups, especially those representing the physically handicapped, turned dissent into effective political and legal action.

Even perceptions of beauty and ugliness became objects of dissent and protest. In 1973, Dan McCoy, then a twenty-nine-year-old Texan, founded Uglies Unlimited, one of many organizations devoted to publicizing discrimination on grounds of physical appearance. The concerns of fat liberation groups, which spun off from militant women's groups in the late sixties, also survived the seventies. After conducting a study based in part on interviews of 600 members of the National Association to Aid Fat Persons, David H. Tucker, a consultant to the Maryland State Human Relations Commission, concluded that fat people suffer nearly as much discrimination as blacks and other minorities. "Very few persons" who are obese, very tall, or very short, Tucker noted, "realize they are protected by law."[11]

The disadvantages of being short also were publicized. Randy Newman's song "Short People" typified widespread attitudes toward height: short people have such little legs, the lyric runs, you have to hoist them up merely "to say hello." Short people, he concludes hyperbolically, have no reason to live. In his study of "heightism," Ralph Keyes reached unsurprising conclusions. Businesses tend to discriminate in favor of moderately tall people: "high level" positions are filled more often than not by tall men (and women).[12] Short people are discounted, so much so that the pool of American clichés is well stocked with denigrating references to midgets, dwarfs, and half-pints. No one wishes to be caught "short-handed"; to be considered "short-sighted" or "short-tempered"; to come out on the "short end of an argument," or to get the "short end of the stick" in any transaction. The extension of struggles against discrimination to such categories of citizens as short people, fat people, and the physically different underlines the central thrust of dissent and protest in the sixties and seventies: the democratization of personhood animated by the many-sided quest for personal fulfillment.

Other social categories of disadvantage could be cited. Senior citizens and homosexuals, for example, asserted personal and political rights in the sixties and seventies with considerable success. In fact, when taken together, the various categories of dissenting minorities add up to a clear majority of Americans who worked to widen and deepen the rights of persons in these decades. In addition to measures to assist people in a variety of special categories, there were steady legislative, executive, and legal gains that improved the conditions of personhood for all Americans. For one thing, the chances of achieving personal security were enhanced considerably. A massive amount of federal, state, and local legislation designed to protect individuals against the vagaries of life—illness, accidents, occupational hazards, pollution, unemployment, old age, and premature death—was enacted in the sixties and seventies: amendments to the Social Security Act of 1935 and the Fair Labor Standards Act of 1938, the Occupational Safety and Health Act of 1970, the Employment Retirement Income Security Act of 1974, and a myriad of consumer protection laws. For another, a variety of legislative measures, executive orders, and legal decisions enhanced the rights of persons to due process, to access to decisions affecting them, and to personal privacy. Formal grievance and appeal procedures were adopted and strengthened in the growing state sector as well as in parts of the private sector.

The net effect of these changes is difficult to assess with any precision. Some of the attempted cures were inadequate to the increasing severity of the social diseases they were designed to treat. The federal Privacy Act (1974), for example, raised standards of protection for individuals, but it did so in the context of widening pools of data that represented a serious encroachment on the privacy of citizens. Moreover, new standards of individual rights often seemed incompatible: demands for privacy regularly came into conflict with pressures for full disclosure of activities of governmental bodies, universities, and business corporations. The requirements of planning, as well as those of increasing the fund of social knowledge, often collided with desires for personal privacy, as evidenced in 1980 by the reluctance of many citizens to supply detailed information requested in the long form of decennial census questionnaires. In general, two partially incompatible key terms gained force simultaneously: the idea of personal space and that of openness—open marriages, open government (sunshine laws), open communication, open classrooms. The paths toward the democratization of personhood thus were circuitous. Nor can all of the salutary changes in the area of personal and political rights be traced directly to dissent and protest. Doubtless some of them would have occurred in a more quiescent political atmosphere. But the political pressures, both direct and indirect, exerted by the proliferation of dissent surely accelerated the democratization of personhood in these decades.

The Economic Impact

As expectations of fulfillment rose and more and more citizens exercised their rights, personal and political demands took on increasingly economic dimensions. Though they were perhaps less obviously impressive than gains in other spheres and far less attributable to any politics of protest, economic advances during the sixties and seventies were more than simply "not negligible." The general level of economic well-being rose substantially over these decades, benefiting everyone, albeit unevenly. And there was some progress in reducing discrimination and other forms of unfair advantage in the contest for shares of wealth. During these years, Franklin Roosevelt's Economic Bill of Rights, set forth in 1944, moved closer to the center of the national agenda, though its various provisions were met only fitfully and incompletely. The bundle of civil rights and civil liberties was extended to encompass entitlements—social rights that included a series of complicated economic claims.[13] The social-justice dimension of personal fulfillment came to entail more than formal opportunity: it presupposed access to employment, a job for everyone wishing to work, and, beyond this, a challenging and useful job. The idea of fulfillment also came to include other guarantees prompted largely by dissent and enforced by the federal government: the right to a decent income, education to the limits of one's potential, adequate health care, and a habitable environment. During the sixties and seventies, the actual performance of the economy supplied the material basis for advances in the democratization of personhood. But ever higher expectations, including higher economic expectations and more exacting standards of economic performance, often clouded perceptions of these solid advances. Hence during these years the actual economic fortunes of Americans improved somewhat, even though they *seemed* to worsen.

During the sixties and seventies, the *general* level of economic well-being rose, despite recessions, international crises, frustrated expectations, faltering productivity, and high inflation. For one thing, there was a healthy increase in the number and kinds of available employment, especially during the seventies. Between 1960 and 1969, for example, the total employed labor force (including members of the armed forces) expanded from 68.3 million to 81.4 million, a gain of 13.1 million jobs. Between 1970 and 1979, the total employed labor force rose by 19 million, to 100.9 million. Within these two decades, then, 32.6 million new jobs were generated, far more than most critics and many supporters of advanced capitalism believed possible in the late fifties and early sixties.[14] As a point of comparison, it should be noted that between 1950 and 1960 7.7 million new jobs came into existence, a sizable increase, though considerably less in raw numbers than those of the subsequent two decades.[15]

Conditions of work improved, too (though disabilities from long-term exposure to new chemicals and other environmental hazards may weaken this trend in the eighties): between 1960 and 1977, deaths from industrial accidents dropped by a third, from twenty-one to fourteen per 100,000 workers, and injuries fell by 15 percent, from 2,594 to 2,541 per 100,000.[16] Reported job satisfaction increased in the sixties and seventies, with more than 80 percent of workers (male, female, black, white, grade school graduates, Ph.D.'s) professing to be "very satisfied," "somewhat satisfied," or "fairly satisfied" with their work.[17] Between 1960 and 1978, to cite a less mushy bit of evidence, there was an impressive increase in longevity, a benefit for workers and their dependents: life expectancy of all Americans at birth increased 4.1 years, from 69.7 to 73.8 years.[18]

By every measure, whether crude or sophisticated, the productivity and wealth of the nation increased considerably during the two decades under consideration. The gross national product (measured in constant 1972 dollars) doubled, rising from $737.2 billion in 1960 to $1,087.6 trillion in 1969, and from $1,085.6 trillion in 1970 to $1,483 trillion in 1979.[19] These figures do not include estimates of an extensive underground economy, which is composed of unreported income and bartering. Populated by cocaine dealers and immigrant busboys as well as by solid working- and middle-class citizens, the underground economy is impossible to measure. But it clearly is quite large: Peter Gutmann put it at $220 million in 1977; Edgar Feige proposed a larger figure of about $700 billion. The composition of the gross national product exhibited a continuation of a long-term trend away from the production of physical goods (agriculture, construction, and manufacturing) toward the production of services (government, trade, finance, entertainment, and the like). This is the sort of changing mix that defines a society of growing affluence. In this period, disposable personal income nearly doubled, rising from $489.7 billion in 1960 to slightly more than one trillion dollars in 1979.[20] Per capita disposable income climbed from $2709 in 1960 to $4493 in 1979 (it was just $1883 in 1929 (in 1972 dollars), when the American population totaled only slightly more than 120 million).[21]

Of course, per capita disposable income provides only a rough approximation of an individual's economic well-being. It does not include increased leisure time or augmented benefits such as pension funds and employer-paid medical insurance. Nor does it indicate the tangible wealth held by individuals. Between 1960 and 1977, there were significant increases in the tangible assets and items of domestic production held by Americans: autos and other vehicles; furniture; kitchen and other household appliances; china, glassware, tableware and utensils; other durable household furnishings; jewelry and watches; radios, television receivers, musical instruments, maps, and books. In 1960 the net stock of consumer durable goods was $421.5 billion. By 1977 it had risen to slightly more than one trillion dollars. Between 1940 and 1959, the stock of consumer durables had grown at a slightly slower rate, by a factor of about 2.3, from $171.1 billion to $391 billion.[22] The total increases in household wealth are all the more remarkable when broken down (roughly) between such passive assets as furniture and tableware, and productive tools such as motor vehicles, television sets, music, and books. Household production increased significantly, adding considerably to the wealth of Americans. Between 1925 and 1977, the percentage of productive household assets used to fashion new goods and services (such as tools), and of goods and services that previously had gone through the market (such as educational television), nearly doubled, from an estimated 32.3 percent to 66.3 percent. Between 1960 and 1980, this figure increased by about 12 percent.[23]

The performance of the economy in the sixties and seventies seems relatively unspectacular to some observers, in part because it only continued a spectacular long-term (albeit uneven) trend toward raising the material standard of living in the United States. Since 1900, as Stanley Lebergott has shown in his intriguing study, *The American Economy* (1976), astonishing gains have been registered in every measurable area. Taking an even longer view, Simon Kuznets concludes that "in 1960 population was about 10.5 times as large as in 1840; labor force almost 13 times; per capita product and, presumably, per capita real income, over 6 times; and product per worker, over 5 times."[24] Nor did these advances in income and wealth come about by greater exploitation of working people. They were achieved, rather, despite proliferating bureaucracies, rising tax rates, and growing nonmonetary benefits, such as a considerably reduced work week, a relaxation of work discipline, earlier retirement ages, additional years of schooling, and a solid increase in paid holidays, sick leave, and vacations. Without these varied forms of compensation, the gross national product (GNP) might have risen far more rapidly. "The average American today," Lebergott concludes, "works a third fewer hours than did his 1900 peer. Yet beyond food, rent, and clothing, his family spends ten times as much on all the other comforts and necessities of life as did the 1900 family (allowing for price change)."[25]

On balance, then, the stunning performance of the American economy during the first five decades of the twentieth century established the context for rapid advances in the democratization of personhood during the sixties and seventies. These advances, in turn, greatly facilitated the quest for personal fulfillment. It is true that gains in income, wealth, and productivity from the fifties through the middle sixties were more impressive than those registered in the sixties and seventies taken together. There is, this is to say, a factual basis in even the simplest economic data for the growing economic nostalgia for the fifties and sixties among economists and other sectors of the population in the seventies. Based on fifty years of remarkable if uneven progress in economic affairs, advances in the fifties were sufficient to enable the decades of the quest to take form. And the sixties clearly was a decade of solid economic growth. But in spite of the onset of relative scarcity in the seventies, high absolute levels of economic well-being permitted the search for fulfillment to continue, though increasing disparities between expectations and economic performance probably altered somewhat the shapes of the quest as this decade drew to a close. In the light of such expectations, the economic situation came to seem far worse than it was.

Advances in economic dimensions of the democratization of personhood in the sixties and seventies are evident not only in gains in total wealth and patterns of personal consumption. They are visible also in the patterns of collective consumption: amounts spent to raise the general standard of living, including billions allocated to protect the environment, to enhance the stock of human capital (through education), and to reduce such manifestations of economic and social injustice as insecurity, ignorance, disease, poverty, and discrimination. During these years, as many entitlements became law, a rising share of the national wealth was devoted to social purposes. Between 1960 and 1980, for example, federal outlays for all services rose from $93 to $602 billion (unadjusted dollars). These items included Social Security payments and Medicare and Medicaid, which covered large sectors of society, as well as an assortment of other important programs from food stamps and school lunches to military pensions and veterans' benefits. By the end of the seventies, about 40 percent of American households were receiving some form of transfer payment. Direct government transfer payments to persons rose from $21.6 billion in 1960 to $244.9 billion in 1980 (unadjusted dollars).[26] Between 1950 and 1960 the grand total of public (federal, state, local) and private expenditures for social welfare on health, education, welfare, and other services rose from $35.4 billion to $78.7 billion (unadjusted dollars), or from 13.4 percent to 15.8 percent of GNP. Between 1960 and 1978, the figures climbed far more rapidly, from $78.7 billion to $548.9

billion (unadjusted dollars), or from 15.8 percent to 26.9 percent of GNP.[27]

The growth of welfare, and especially of transfer payments, did not result in income equality, as some had feared, nor did it result in income equity, as others had hoped. But these mechanisms of redistribution did serve a powerful purpose as they grew from 4.1 percent to 10.7 percent of GNP between 1956 and 1978. Transfer payments benefited many groups within the lower reaches of the structure of disadvantage: poor blacks and Hispanics, unmarried mothers, and other low-income groups. During the sixties and seventies, for example, transfer payments brought the mean per capita income of the elderly nearly up to that of the rest of the population. Lester Thurow observes that "if social security were to disappear for the elderly, their incomes would fall by 50 percent. Half of the income going to the elderly comes from government transfer payments."[28] In these decades, the profusion of transfer payments served the cause of equity by preventing inequalities from becoming greater than they already were: transfer payments stabilized the distribution of income in America, and improved it in selected areas.

Furthermore, as the sum total of national wealth increased, more than keeping abreast of the rapid rise in the number of persons in employable age categories, the distribution of opportunity and responsibility altered perceptibly, largely as a consequence of the politics of dissent. Individuals within various disadvantaged and dissenting categories gained more—and more attractive—employment opportunities in government, the military, and the private sector. Affirmative action programs designed to compensate for historical injustices made considerable headway, though not without major opposition under the rubric of alleged discrimination against whites.

The much-publicized Allan Bakke case of the late seventies illustrated the complex and competing strategies of various constituencies seeking *their* piece of social justice.[29] Having been denied admission to the University of California medical school (Davis campus) in both 1973 and 1974, Bakke sued. He alleged that because he had been refused the opportunity to compete for one of sixteen of the one hundred available seats that had been set aside for minority applicants, he had been denied equal protection under the law guaranteed by the Fourteenth Amendment. In a five-to-four decision, the U.S. Supreme Court ruled in Bakke's favor in July 1978. Though the court declared the use of strict racial quotas illegal, it sanctioned the use of affirmative action programs (targets) to increase educational opportunities for minority groups. The court recognized complicated realities even as it finessed the problem: namely, that in this sort of zero-sum situation both sides could levy legitimate claims on the same scarce resources. Though quotas are not legal, the court ruled, resources no longer can be distributed in such a way that white males get all the plums. In the sixties and seventies, positions at the top, or near the top, of various occupational hierarchies were opened to women, racial minorities, European ethnics, Jews, and, in a few instances, the physically handicapped. And positions in the middle echelons were opened even more rapidly.

No serious observer of American affairs would deny the significant progress blacks registered during the sixties. As Robert B. Hill put it in his contribution to *The State of Black America 1980,* "blacks made major social and economic advances in employment, income, voter registration, home ownership, election to public office and in the reduction of blacks in poverty."[30] By the end of the sixties, average black family income had reached 61 percent of white family income, up from 48 percent in 1960. Not surprisingly, this rate of relative advance did not continue through the seventies. What is encouraging, however, is that the solid gains of the sixties very nearly held up through the economic difficulties of the seventies. Average black family income fell from 61 to 57 percent of white family income by 1977 but then rose to 59 percent in 1978, and the percentage received by black families headed by a full-time worker rose from 73 percent in 1970 to 77 percent of white income in 1978.[31]

The rises in the ratios of black–white income were limited by a number of factors beyond the decline of the black civil-rights movement, among them the persistently higher birth rates among poor blacks and the recessions of 1969–71, 1974–75, and 1979–80, which hit disadvantaged groups with particular intensity. Also, the entry of women into the labor force in massive numbers augmented the number of two-income white families, thereby increasing slightly disparities in black–white family income. Moreover, the distribution of income *within* the category of black Americans stayed grossly uneven and probably worsened.[32] Sectors of the black population remained in distressed circumstances: the black underclass, single-parent families, women, black youths. And overall black–white disparities remained a rough index of long-term economic inequality in America. Still, since black American families just about kept pace with the economic gains of the seventies and enjoyed relative advances during the prosperous sixties, they can be judged to have scored overall economic progress during these two decades. On balance, the absolute gains gave larger numbers of black citizens, especially younger, better-educated blacks, the material resources to pursue personal fulfillment.

Aggregate statistical portraits of the economic fortunes of women during the sixties and seventies present a similarly mixed though on the whole encouraging picture. Women moved into the labor force in unprecedented numbers during these decades, in part as a consequence of the women's movement. By 1979, 50.7 percent of the female adult population had entered the labor force, up from 42.6 percent in 1970, and 31.4 percent in 1950. Between 1950 and 1959, the percentage of women in the labor force increased from 29 to 33 percent (17,340,000 to 21,164,000). Between 1960 and 1979, the figure rose from 33 percent to 42 percent (21,874,000 to 40,446,000). And the proportion of women actively seeking work increased from 41.6 percent in 1968 to 50.1 percent in 1978. Women filled more than half of the nonagricultural jobs established between 1968 and 1978.[33] When estimates for unpaid household labor and volunteer work (about $18 billion per year) done by women are added to these employment figures, it is clear that women probably perform well more than their fair share of the useful labor in American society. On the other hand, certain studies suggest that "women's and men's time uses are converging." In 1965 married women allegedly worked 602 minutes per day compared to 548 minutes for married men. By 1975 married women appeared to be working slightly *less* than married men (515 minutes to 523). Of course, such studies lose a lot in the translation from time experienced to time recorded on time sheets: it may take Wanda only two minutes to fetch Harold, her time-and-motion-study wizard, his last cup of coffee in the middle of the evening, but it may be this final act in her hopelessly fragmented work day that tempts her to add a drop of arsenic. It may be that women are spending less time on housework while men are "pitching in" more.[34] At best, this is a clear gain for women. At worst, it leaves women with ultimate responsibility in the domestic sphere while diminishing the control many exercised under the old system.

In any case, one needn't be torn between intuition and soft data to

conclude that women's levels of compensation lagged far behind those
of men. In the late seventies, for example, women on the average
earned only fifty-nine cents for every dollar earned by men. In 1981,
women earned 64.7 percent of men's pay, a slightly higher percentage
than prevailed in the late seventies. Part of this disparity in aggregate
earnings is attributable to such factors as the recent influx of women
into the work force, the inertial effect of their traditional concentration
in lower-paying service and clerical sectors of the economy, the large
number of young and unskilled female workers, and the occasional
and part-time nature of many jobs women perform. But a major portion of the earnings disparity can be explained only by persistent discrimination in favor of men, for women regularly earn less than men
even when they occupy the same job category.

In the sixties and seventies, then, women altered the structure of
disadvantage significantly. They established their presence in the
economy. Many achieved positions of importance. Moreover, women
established the idea of equal pay for equal work so firmly in the
national consciousness that it became a legal and moral standard
against which to measure every woman's pay package.[35] Indeed, just
as the principle of equal pay began to be applied in some job categories, a new principle aimed at greater equity was announced: equal
pay for work of *comparable* worth. In the summer of 1981, municipal
workers in San Jose, California, won a settlement based on this
principle. Since it is difficult to assess the relative worth of such occupational categories as secretary, painter, librarian, and plumber, the
idea will be difficult to put into practice, as a brief piece in *The New
Republic* (or was it *Commentary?*) was quick to point out: it will
involve meddling bureaucrats and interfering judges. Probably so, just
as the long battle for equal pay has required executive and judicial
participation. Whatever the difficulties, however, the important if not
always consistent principles—of equal pay for equal work and of
equal pay for comparable work—are here to stay.

There were grounds on which to fault the performance of the American economy during these decades. Unemployment persisted at unreasonably high levels, though the overall problem was less serious
than most critics on the left insisted. In 1960, the official unemployment
rate was 5.5 percent (3.8 million); in 1979, it was 5.8 percent (5.9 mil-

lion). In the sixties, unemployment averaged only 4.8 percent; in the seventies, the figure rose to 6.1 percent. Unemployment among women twenty years old and older was only slightly higher than among men for both decades, averaging 5.1 percent in the sixties and 6.4 percent in the seventies. Minority unemployment (black and other) remained unacceptably high, averaging 8.9 percent in the sixties and climbing to an average of 11 percent in the seventies (the main increases being among black youths age sixteen to twenty-four).[36]

Aggregate unemployment figures may overestimate the problem or exaggerate the degree of deterioration in the employment picture in the seventies, a decade more notable for new employment than for unemployment. For one thing, unemployment among married men in both decades was considerably lower than aggregate unemployment: 2.7 percent in the sixties and 3.2 percent in the seventies. For another, a large percentage of those officially designated as unemployed were out of work for fourteen weeks or less: 75 percent in 1960 and 78 percent in 1979. On this criterion, the unemployment rate for those out of work more than fourteen weeks declined slightly during the sixties and seventies, from 1.4 percent in 1960 to 1.3 percent in 1979.[37] On the other hand, official figures underestimate the extent of unemployment insofar as they omit people who give up the search or never enter the job market. Under sunnier circumstances, Daniel Yankelovich imagines, many Americans would reenter the job market: according to a study of his, twenty-five million Americans were willing to take jobs as quickly as desirable work became available—nearly four times the number then included in government estimates of those actively seeking employment in 1978.[38] Between utopia and official versions of the present lies a gap that can and ought to be narrowed.

Moreover, official statistics also underestimate the degree of underemployment, which, along with unemployment, inhibits the quest for personal fulfillment. Indeed, the growing importance of the category of underemployment is itself an expression of the democratization of personhood. For the idea of underemployment gives quasi-official recognition to a new social value: namely, that the workplace ought to be an arena for developing and expressing a wide range of skills, talents, and emotions within a person's potential.

In spite of President Johnson's domestic war, poverty persisted during the sixties and seventies: women, children, minorities, and the elderly continued to suffer the consequences of poverty disproportionately. It is true, of course, that the official dimensions of poverty shrank somewhat. Between 1959 and 1978, the number of persons below the always too-low official poverty line dropped from 39.5 million to 24.7 million, a decline of about 50 percent, or from 22.4 to 11.6 percent of the population.[39] Though they are considerable, these gains do not excuse the misery that the majority of Americans permit millions of officially and unofficially defined poor people to endure, decreasing their chances to pursue such aspects of fulfillment as a decent job, a decent income, a pleasant place to live, a dignified retirement. A few skirmishes in the War on Poverty were won, such as the elimination of gross malnutrition, but the war did not accomplish what it could have: the eradication of *absolute* poverty among those who do not have enough to get by and give their children a decent start. Nor did the War on Poverty or any other combination of strategies do much to alleviate the gross inequalities of reward that sustain high degrees of relative poverty among those who fall behind their neighbors in the contest for ever larger amounts of income and wealth.

In all probability, however, the salutary decline of absolute poverty and the maintenance of a degree of relative poverty both contributed to the democratization of personhood, though in rather different ways. Minimum levels of economic inclusion rose during the sixties and seventies: floors of support were raised, mainly by virtue of general gains in the economy, but also by means of selective measures to redistribute wealth, largely in the form of transfer payments.[40] At the same time, new forms of occupational and income inequality created new forms of opportunity. General economic gains entailed a greater differentiation of function in the occupational structure, resulting in an increase in the number and compensation of professional and managerial personnel. The occupational structure grew more diverse, contributing to a slowdown in anticipated trends toward equality of reward.[41] Increases in the income and occupational responsibility in middle- and upper-middle-class ranges provided additional millions of Americans, including better-educated women and members of minority groups, with more of the material prerequisites to pursue fulfillment. Relative poverty within the context of generally rising levels of economic well-being, as Lebergott reminds us, is an unavoidable consequence of capitalist economy—one of its ambiguous blessings.

Unemployment, underemployment, poverty: these ills affected parts of the population. But stagflation—a historically unprecedented combination of sluggish economic growth and high rates of inflation—exerted generally negative effects on nearly everyone. These effects became progressively worse after 1973. Between 1960 and 1973, the average annual growth rate in real gross national product was 3.9 percent. Between 1974 and 1979, the figure fell to an average of 2.4 percent per year.[42] The historic rate of inflation—averaging 2 percent per year—persisted through the first half of the sixties; it then climbed to about 5 percent per year between 1965 and 1972; and, beginning in 1973, it grew to an average of 8 percent through the rest of the decade, depending on the mode of calculating the rate of inflation. (In 1979, for example, the consumer price index—one measure of inflation—rose 13.3 percent, whereas the GNP deflator, another measure, rose only 8.8 percent.[43]) By virtue of their differential impact, high rates of inflation—which brought disproportionate increases in the prices of such necessities as food, shelter, fuel, and health-care costs—hit the most disadvantaged groups hardest, psychologically if not always statistically: poor people, unorganized sectors of the working class, women, old people and others on small fixed incomes, racial minorities, children on welfare.

The sources of inflation are multiple: quasi-imperial designs, oligopolistic enterprises, inefficient public institutions, real estate speculators, government subsidies to ailing corporations—massive waste in various places. A portion of the high inflation rates, however, can be traced to less seedy practices: to social efforts to advance the democratization of personhood, including strategies to assist those in the lower economic reaches of the structure of disadvantage. As Howard R. Bowen observes, "in recent decades society has chosen to take an increasing share of the national product in the form of security, safety, health, participation, due process, equality, privacy, consumer protection, agreeable working conditions, environmental improvement, conservation of resources, information, etc. And it has chosen to take a smaller share in the form of conventional goods and services." Since there are no mechanisms in the conventional social accounting procedures to include these new goods, their cost is assigned "to the production of ordinary goods and services and shows up as reduced efficiency or impaired productivity in the production of these ordinary goods and services rather than as legitimate costs that yield distinctive and useful, albeit intangible, products."[44]

These new costs, Bowen suggests, amount to a form of taxation, a portion of which is shifted to consumers. Bowen speculates that "it is likely that some of the . . . relentless inflation we experience year after year is due to socially-imposed costs which are passed through to consumers in the form of higher prices or reduced quality of product, or to taxpayers and philanthropists through increased appropriations and more generous gifts." Though it is impossible to determine the extent to which "the price indexes have been biased upward," Bowen concludes, "it is certain that the effect has been substantial, and that the rate of inflation derived from monetary and fiscal factors has been substantially less than usually supposed." So is the rate derived from social programs. For all of the social programs of the late sixties and seventies would have exerted a more modest inflationary pull had they not been tied to outrageously large and wasteful military spending (approximately one trillion dollars in the seventies alone).

Surely then, substantial if uneven gains in the political and economic spheres were not sufficient to justify an uninhibited celebration of American performance in the sixties and seventies. Gains in both areas fell well below rapidly rising expectations. During the seventies, the economic future appeared increasingly uncertain, adding to the palpable anxiety of Americans: the problems seemed endless, ranging from foreign competition and high interest rates to inadequate savings and investment and sagging industries such as auto, steel, and housing. (Indeed, by the end of the seventies, the United States could be divided into several regional economies, some of them prosperous, others depressed.)

Moreover, economic gains were distributed unevenly, and measured in gross terms, they were distributed inequitably. In 1977, for example, the highest 5 percent of families received 15.7 percent of the money income, whereas the lowest 20 percent received only 5.2 percent, an income ratio of about twelve to one.[45] Although tolerable disparities are difficult to set with any precision, the more so because money income constitutes only an imperfect measure of total income, gaps of this magnitude should cause discomfort to everyone committed to social justice, and perhaps especially to those who participated in the Christian revival of the sixties and seventies: economically, the least of the brethren fared least well. The sisters did even worse.

Of course, fulfillment is not simply a function of rising economic fortunes. Nor is the significance of those gains that are statistically measurable altogether clear. A fair portion of increases (or decreases) in productivity figures may reflect dubious gains (or actual losses): additional paperwork in the form of medical insurance papers, bureaucratic divisions of labor that add to costs of production, work time not spent usefully, and so forth. Moreover, increasing the magnitude of social programs does not necessarily result in enhanced personal outcomes for individuals. Nor does a larger disposable income, though the benefits here are more immediate and less apt to be squandered, especially in overhead and delivery costs. Thus the relationship between economic well-being and "happiness" as reported by individuals in social surveys is both complicated and ambiguous. And it is complicated further by the fact that happiness is only a rough indicator of fulfillment. Some points nevertheless seem clear. It is obvious that people need minimal income levels to pursue what I have called the social-justice dimension of fulfillment. But the notion of a "minimal" level of support is itself historically relative. Minimal levels have tended to rise dramatically: it simply cost more to sustain a person in poverty in 1979 than it did in 1939. Hence, though gains in the floor of support were real, they were subverted by cultural and psychological factors, by the tendency of people to measure present levels of well-being mainly against rising present criteria rather than against past standards.

For a variety of reasons then, poor people always need more money, though precise amounts cannot be set. But the subject of equitable distribution becomes even murkier when optimal patterns for the whole society are sought. Doubtless there is a positive and fairly constant relationship between family income and reported levels of happiness: the higher the better. Between 1957 and 1978, for example, only 25 percent of the people in the lowest income quartile considered themselves "very happy," as opposed to 31 percent in the second quartile, 37 percent in the third, and 44 percent in the highest quartile. The average percentage claiming to be "very happy" was 34 percent throughout the sixties and seventies.[46] Surprisingly, general changes in the economy did not alter these percentages significantly, leading Richard Curtin to offer this rule of thumb: within limits, "general levels of happiness do not seem to respond to the ups and downs of the overall economy but do correspond very closely to one's own position relative to others on the economic ladder."[47]

This formulation leaves open the question of optimal distribution of that portion of social wealth devoted to consumption. A more equal distribution of income might advance the cause of general social justice, assuming such a distribution could be achieved without a great loss of efficiency. But a sharp move toward equal distribution might not greatly increase the sum of reported happiness or even that of fulfillment, since in American culture relative advantage represents a major source of personal satisfaction. Moreover, it should be remembered that the differences among those reporting themselves as "very happy" under present patterns of distribution are not staggering: after all, 25 percent of those in the lowest income quartile claimed to be quite happy, and the difference between the lowest and highest quartile amounted to only 19 percent. Despite these caveats on the necessity and insufficiency of wealth in the equation of fulfillment, it seems safe to conclude that improvements in the sum of economic resources probably facilitated the democratization of personhood during the sixties and seventies. And further, I think it reasonable to say that the distribution of opportunity and reward improved somewhat during these years, though it failed to reach the elusive optimal level.

No one, of course, could argue seriously that all forms of discrimination—or even those based on factors other than class—had come to an end. In fact, the registered gains made Americans far more sensitive to a wider range of disadvantages at the end of the seventies than they had been in the late fifties, from race and religion to age, height, and weight. The social agenda lengthened in the seventies, as environmental and resource concerns attracted growing attention. Even the measurable gains of disadvantaged groups tended to be obscured by shifting and in some ways increasingly exacting criteria of success in public spheres. It is true nevertheless that public-opinion polls showed a marked decrease in negative attitudes toward black Americans in the seventies. For example, between 1963 and 1978, according to a Harris poll, certain forms of racial prejudice declined substantially. Although minorities still reported experiencing considerable prejudice, "the readiness of the American people to make new strides forward in reducing and eliminating prejudice is far greater than is commonly assumed by the establishment today," Harris observed. "The assumption that we are mired in a long period of intense reaction against decisive steps in the area of reducing prejudice turns out to be patently false." In the fifteen years covered by the Harris survey, the number of whites who feared having black neighbors declined from 51 percent to 27 percent, and the number of whites who consider blacks "inferior" dropped from 31 percent to 15 percent. "What is more," Harris said, "when whites who have had contact with blacks are asked about this experience, over 90 percent say it has been 'easy and pleasant.'" Between 70 percent and 90 percent of blacks responded similarly, the difference in perception resulting no doubt largely from some mixture of condescension on the part of whites and defensiveness on the part of blacks.[48]

Yet as blacks entered higher education in ever larger numbers and gross exclusion ended, more subtle modes of discrimination became major issues: de facto segregation according to the prestige of institutions; intellectual segregation according to courses of study; and cultural segregation as a consequence of the exclusively WASP ambience of many campuses. Institutional racism persisted elsewhere, as successful blacks endured such forms of discrimination as highly personal old-boy (and new-girl) networks and impersonal seniority systems—arrangements for which no individual or group felt responsible. Similarly, as more and more women entered higher levels of business and government, modes of male chauvinism came to seem less tolerable than they had when bosses and secretaries inhabited an occupational world more neatly stratified by gender. But even here, new opportunities generated a fresh set of problems, or rather brought old problems into glaring new light. In 1980, for example, the matter of sexism in corporate boardrooms came to public attention when Mary Cunningham, a twenty-nine-year-old executive, was promoted to chief corporate planner (a vice-presidential position) after a mere fifteen months at Bendix, only to be forced to resign after having been accused of gaining her position on the basis of a sexual liaison with William M. Agee, chairman of the board. (The couple announced their engagement in the spring of 1982.)

This mixed though on the whole encouraging picture of political and economic advances in the sixties and seventies is rarely brought into clear focus by leftist critics. Indeed, matters seem far worse than they are when actual changes are set against the hopes of various critics. Their claims nevertheless deserve special attention, in part because of the sheer number of critics on the left—far and near—and in part because of the intense involvement of people on the left in every facet of dissent in the postwar period. My immediate point is not that leftists' expectations were based by and large on unrealistic hopes rather than on estimates fashioned out of the main facts and factors of American life: such a disparity energizes the left and in some significant sense defines it. It is rather that left assessments of the sixties and seventies depend too heavily upon unrealistic expectations, expectations that went largely unrevised in the light of important social and cultural changes during these decades.

The salutary political and economic changes to which dissent and protest contributed during these years seem to me to be well in line with reasonable expectations—expectations based on the fixed and fluid social conditions of the quest for fulfillment, as well as on its essential motives and criteria of success. As I have suggested, the logic of dissent was shaped in large measure by the terms of the quest for personal fulfillment. Even under the best social circumstances, the untidy outcomes of such a sprawling search would have been disappointing to those critics—left and right—who rejected its leading cultural terms: various forms of individualism, a plurality of values and aspirations, limited communities, and fitful participation in politics. It is possible, even desirable, for critics to quarrel with these assumptions. Despite shifting meanings, they nonetheless remained the most deeply and widely held assumptions of Americans. Any retrospective judgment about the reasonable prospects of dissent and protest during the sixties and seventies therefore must begin its speculative course here.

A fair assessment of the political and economic changes that advanced the democratization of personhood also must take account of other more or less fixed facts of American life, especially the persistence of democratic capitalism and the nature and limits of dissent and protest. For these factors shaped the social territory on which the quest unfolded. Neither leftist critics nor activists were able to evoke sizable demands to put an end to class society. Nor were their often able defenses of alternative systems—socialism, communism, anarchism—sufficiently attractive to persuade many people even to want to switch, much less to begin the arduous political task of doing so.[49] Although levels of confidence in business and business leaders declined rather sharply in the seventies, public faith in the American system survived both the radical assaults of the sixties and the unspectacular performance of the economy in the seventies. In response to a Harris survey taken in 1979, 78 percent of those interviewed agreed that "for all of its faults, the American economic system still provides our people with the highest living standards in the world." Nor did the ideology of socialism make much headway. A 1976 *Cambridge Reports* survey found that 62 percent of respondents opposed the introduction of socialism into the United States, 27 percent didn't know, and only 10 percent thought it a good idea. This last figure was down from the 25 percent reported by Roper in 1942.[50]

Leftist critics, especially Marxists, typically lamented the absence of a serious class politics or even a widespread perception of issues in terms of class. As Irving Louis Horowitz observed, the rise of ethnicity as a "separate factor in America" reflects a "cross-cutting culture"—a culture that "makes no particular effort to build a common identity among those who comprise the 80,000,000 members of the working class."[51] This absence of especially strong class ties in turn frustrates those who wish to influence, if not lead, the transformation of the working class from a "class-in-itself" (one on Marxist paper) to a "class-for-itself" (one pursuing socialist objectives). But as Horowitz and every serious Marxist knows, Americans tend to associate with one another on the basis of less abstract, more palpable categories than Marxist conceptions of class: the cross-cutting and overlapping categories of ethnicity, race, locale, gender, age, religion, education, work place, and common leisure-time interests. Occupational and income divisions count heavily, to be sure. Indeed, such class boundaries frequently seem more important than racial boundaries: middle-class blacks and whites share more values with each other than they do with lower-class members of their own races. But the abstract division between those few who own or control the dominant means of production and those who do not fails to ignite the political imagination of Americans—at least it failed to do so once again during the sixties and seventies.

Hence no working-class revolution occurred and no Marxist party of any consequence emerged. Nor should either of these turns have been expected. More interestingly, there was little popular pressure for a massive redistribution of income and wealth. In his ill-fated 1972 presidential campaign, for example, George McGovern proposed a 77 percent tax on all inheritances of more than $500,000. The idea attracted little support among voters, especially among middle Americans, leading McGovern to wonder whether they "think they're going to win a lottery."[52] In fact, McGovern was not far off the mark: few wished to eliminate the chance to strike it rich—a long-odds wager, to be sure, but one that provides a measure of psychic interest and consolation to the vast majority who never inherit much of anything, let alone sums in excess of half a million dollars.

A modest expansion and some redistribution of opportunity did occur as people from various dissenting groups entered into parts of economic, political, and social life previously closed to them. Moreover, economic and even political gains might have been greater were it not for a convergence of several new factors. First, there was a partial collapse of previous economic expectations of high sustained growth that moderated the anticipated rise of occupational opportunity after, say, 1973 and hence narrowed the anticipated distribution of occupational resources. Second, the entry of women into the labor force in unprecedented numbers restricted somewhat the opportunities that male members of other disadvantaged minority groups would have gained, largely as a consequence of dissent and protest.

Third, the passage of so many young people into the age of employability tended to diminish the opportunities of individuals. In his study *Birth and Fortune* (1980), Richard A. Easterlin puts forth a hypothesis to account for cycles of opportunity based on the notion of generational congestion. The sixties and seventies, especially the seventies, constituted a period of relative contraction of opportunity for young people. When the supply of young workers (age fifteen to twenty-nine) is small relative to the number of older workers (age thirty to sixty-four), Easterlin contends, the young workers' earnings are higher, their unemployment rates lower, and their rates of advancement more rapid. In such circumstances, more young couples decide to marry and more young marrieds elect to have more children, thus raising the birth rate. When the comparatively larger generation reaches work age, however, the situation is reversed, and the birth rate tends to fall. Counting both boom and bust phases, one cycle lasts about forty years. Thus low birth rates in the twenties and thirties resulted in comparatively greater economic opportunity for young workers in the forties and fifties. But relatively high birth rates in the forties and fifties contracted economic opportunities somewhat in the sixties and seventies. "When small birth cohorts are young adults," he concludes, "social and economic conditions seem relatively prosperous; when large cohorts are young adults, life generally seems afflicted with malaise."[53] Economic opportunities for young people, this is to say, probably were not as great in the sixties and seventies as they would have been in the absence of this complicating demographic factor. Reasonable assessments of economic and political advances, then, must take account of the class character of American society as well as of such apparently uncontrollable variables as the onset of relative scarcity, the zero-sum gains of various disadvantaged groups, and changing birth rates.

It was not only the powerful elites and powerful institutions of capitalist society that prevented the sorts of changes in class consciousness anticipated by leftist critics and activists (along with many other people). The operation of democratic features of the democratic system, faulty, fitful, and impure as it is, also contributed to the failure of socialist politics. Of course, the means of ideological and political influence were dispersed unevenly, as should be expected (especially by Marxists) in a society turning on a capitalist economic axis, even one tilted somewhat by the weak magnetic field of a rudimentary welfare state. But the more sweeping hypothesis of one-dimensionality—the notion that the operations of "the system" preclude the formation of "significant" opposition—breaks the limits of theoretical credulity and violates evidence of the senses. Advanced by critics from Herbert Marcuse to Christopher Lasch and Stuart Ewen, such hypotheses make sense only in terms of an exaggerated functionalism, only when every value, attitude, belief, theory, and perception (except perhaps those few that add up to socialist analyses) is judged to fit the design of monopoly capitalism.[54]

When theories fail and key historical actors (classes) refuse to play their assigned parts, radical thinkers tend to blame "the system" for confusing its citizens and preventing them from recognizing their own best interests. When all else fails, as it did in the late sixties and early seventies, certain sectarians of the left—the Weathermen, for example—resort to open condemnation of "the people." Blaming the people, of course, is not an exclusively left-wing sport. President Carter played a version of this rhetorical game when he descended from the mountaintop to deliver his energy sermon in the summer of 1979. As his popularity sagged, he began to question the moral mettle of Americans. The president doubtless had his own political reasons for taking such a stance. Leftist critics less rigid than the Weatherpeople (as they then called themselves) had their reasons, too. To the extent that democratic norms operated during the sixties and seventies—and it obviously was considerable—Americans chose to pursue self-fulfillment. A decisive majority elected to follow the main variants of the logic of dissent that I have described, and doing so they crossed ideological and political lines more freely than ever before. William James's magnificent notion of the "unconquerable subjectivity" of people might have been compromised somewhat by the growing material and ideological density of the technological society. But there remained a considerable latitude, a widening scope of political and personal choice during these years. In any case, these areas of choice proved too wide to suit most critics and activists on the left.

Many left-wing critics find the entire political system inhospitable to their aims. And many of them regard dissent and protest as tokens of dissatisfaction and utter powerlessness. As John Schaar and Sheldon Wolin put it, "The lack of clearly defined enemies is tacitly recognized in the vocabulary of the rebels: the use of words like 'dissent,' and of actions like 'protest,' 'resistance,' and 'demonstration' are an admission that they are reduced to seeking targets of opportunity within a generally benevolent system."[55] Schaar and Wolin press an important point too far. Compared to other modes of power—control of major economic decisions and dominance of ordinary political processes—dissent and protest surely are weak. They emerge as options of last resort among groups without great economic resources or political influence. When combined with ordinary politics, however, dissent and protest can and often do contribute to the sorts of limited results I have outlined. They become modes of temporary power that trigger some lasting redistribution of power.

Partial changes, of course, did not result in destruction of the dominant lines of power in democratic capitalism or in a massive redistribution of power. This, I believe, is what rubbed such critics as Schaar and Wolin the wrong way, prompting them to regard dissent and protest as evidence of "a universal sense of powerlessness."[56] Many less sophisticated political radicals clung to Marx's notion that disenchantment ought to initiate a process of criticism and radical action that provides the subjective energy for social change of the magnitude and kind they advocate. When disenchantment does not take predicted forms, or when, as in the sixties and especially in the seventies, additional participation assumes largely conservative or even reactionary shapes, certain critics characterize protest as weaker and politics in general as less democratic than they are. They define mere dissent as a waste of energies that ought to be expressed in *their* sort of politics. Indeed, dissent comes to be regarded as a perverse sublimation—a new sort of powerlessness, as Schaar and Wolin contend, enforced by the distracting contentments of high or even modest consumption.

Overestimating the prospects of dissent in the sixties, many radicals underrated its impact at the end of the seventies. Nor is the disposition to exaggerate the degree of powerlessness of disadvantaged people confined to ideologues. It is intensified in various ways by the working assumptions of academic social scientists who typically view America through certain whole social categories. As Robert Nisbet observes, "in sober social science, the individual has been replaced by the social group as the central unit of theoretical inquiry and ameliorative action" (and, he might have added, inaction).[57] The popular version of Christopher Jencks's valuable study of the determinants of success in America—*Who Gets Ahead?* (1979)—nicely illustrates the main dispositions of many social scientists, especially left-wing and left-liberal ones.[58] To determine the composition of factors contributing to "success," Jencks and his associates analyzed eleven major surveys taken between 1961 and 1973. What Jencks has to say about the relative importance of family background, scores on tests administered to sixth-grade students, years of schooling, and teen-age personality traits is interesting. But I shall not pause over his conclusions, since by his own admission between 25 and 65 percent of the equation of success falls outside the sphere of measurable variables. Moreover, limitations of available data confined the study to men, which slightly more than doubles the size of the statistical blank.

Although it is crude by any strict measure, Jencks's mosaic nevertheless is created out of numbers artfully and intelligently managed, and for this reason it carries a certain authority that mere social criticism lacks, usually for other good reasons.[59] Despite the indeterminate character of the numbers and a sophisticated use of multiple regressions, the portrait Jencks and his associates construct seems largely and deceptively deterministic. As Daniel Yankelovich notes in his thoughtful assessment of *Who Gets Ahead?*, "statistical norms" represent the "newest and most devious version" of an "ancient tyranny"—the idea of fate. "Mere averages are reified into the national norms against which many individuals measure themselves. Properly understood, these averages constitute useful bits of information, but

their meaning for any individual calls for exquisite qualification."
Yankelovich observes further that "It would be tragic . . . if Jencks's
findings were interpreted to mean that blacks should drop out of high
school, that people with low scores in the sixth grade should give up
trying, that people who don't finish college should assume they cannot achieve the kind of success they seek, that lack of leadership ability in school closes the door to future economic success, and that
credentials count more heavily than skill, character, knowledge, or
judgment."[60]

The average relative gains—or the projected chances—of individuals
in various groups may be significant long-term measures of egalitarian
change. But they do not constitute the only useful short-term or middle-range measures, especially when they are used to obscure absolute
gains or to minimize the advances of individuals and subcategories of
large groups. Such procedures, for example, may help to conceal the
prodigious growth of the black middle class during the sixties and
seventies. In *The Declining Significance of Race* (1978), William Julius Wilson estimates that by the middle seventies approximately 35
percent of black Americans belonged to a fairly stable middle class
composed of skilled blue- and white-collar workers (and another 30
percent belonged to a working class composed mainly of semiskilled
blue-collar employees).[61] Moreover, as Thomas Sowell observes, "Rapid
changes in the American racial scene are often concealed or omitted in
gross statistical comparisons which fail to separate out the younger generation reared under the new conditions." When such factors as age
and education are "simultaneously held constant," Sowell notes, the
"gross ethnic differences in income narrow but do not disappear."[62]
Of course, many social scientists who acknowledge the presence of a
black middle class do so only grudgingly, contemptuously, or fleetingly, as a necessary prelude to themes they find more congenial: their
portraits of the terrible plight of blacks considered as an aggregate
category in relation to whites.

Jencks's mosaic thus illustrates a common mode of allegedly neutral
scientific analysis that tends to preclude full consideration of the main
hypothesis I have been exploring throughout these chapters: that when
economic, political, *and* cultural gains are taken together, it is evident
that large numbers of Americans, including millions in several overlapping categories of disadvantage from race to blindness claimed a

fuller measure of personal freedom and psychological options during the sixties and seventies than seemed likely in the middle fifties.

The Cultural Impact

The work of social scientists further obscures progress in the quest for fulfillment by slighting or distorting the cultural and personal impact of dissidence. It does this in any number of ways—by overstressing cultural novelty, radical probes, or enlightened liberal values to the near exclusion of older norms, conservative responses, or the values held by groups lodged between the underclass and the upper middle class. Most frequently, social scientists in research universities, especially economists and political scientists, but also sociologists, simply neglect cultural factors or treat them amateurishly. They tend to hold stark views of ambition and success, often confusing variants of minimal and maximal inclusion. When, for example, the percentage of women enrolled in institutions of higher education reached a level of parity with men in the late seventies, it was claimed that too few women were full professors (a perfectly valid contention, though one that was beside this point). When a woman was named president of the University of Chicago in the seventies, however, the achievement was dismissed as another instance of tokenism.

The widespread disposition of social scientists to regard all forms of power and success below the top as modes of powerlessness and at least comparative failure derives, I think, as much from the peculiar social circumstances of their work as from their customary categories of analysis. Compared to the top echelons of power in society, which they often observe, social scientists live on the margins of somewhat lower levels. They may hope to get close to centers of public power and to exert influence. Though some do (mainly economists and political scientists), most of them do not. Almost powerful, these members of the intellectual elite characteristically think about themselves and others in hardball metaphors. They attempt to confine play on their own turf to big-league rules. Viewing the rest of academia as the minor and bush leagues, social scientists in prestigious universities are forever seeking the "top man" in every specialty to replace their fallen or fired comrades. Anyone not in the international majors doesn't count. This informal understanding of getting on, I believe, comes to influence definitions of power and success and to blur important distinctions of degree and kind.

Assuming this macho and essentially philistine view of society and culture, Jencks and his associates define success in other spheres as a function of financial achievement and upward occupational mobility. Although these measures remain important in American life, they no longer are supremely or exclusively important. Considered in isolation from other aims, the determinants of money and status lead to an incomplete definition and a badly skewed portrait of success and to an even more inadequate perspective on fulfillment. A rounded appreciation of the impact of dissent and protest in the sixties and seventies must go beyond these criteria to encompass the plurality of cultural values and issues associated with the quest for personal growth and fulfillment. During these years, the meanings of success expanded to include the diverse aims of the quest. Millions of Americans rejected a lockstep pattern of success: financial achievement and high status as preconditions to personal fulfillment. Within the equation of fulfillment, the borders between public and private life grew hazy, and the ratios of salvation and social justice shifted dramatically, subverting left-wing, liberal, and neoconservative sequences of desired change. Increasingly, dissent served not only as a vehicle for authentic personal expression, a way of saying "no" to the cultural norms that obstructed the search for fulfillment, but also as a vehicle for breaking the hold of dominant cultural stereotypes of power and success and establishing a range of alternative cultural and personal options. As a principal medium of the quest for fulfillment, dissent energized each of the main facets of the search outlined in Chapter 9: the Movement, the revival of evangelical and charismatic Christianity, and modes of the therapeutic.

The explosion of dissent spread beyond the vague borders of the Movement of the sixties and survived its formal demise in the early seventies. This is evident not only in the largely irreversible gains in civil rights and in the more precarious advances in economic, political, and social opportunity among minorities and women. The impact of dissent and its middle-range potential to initiate further change is perhaps most evident in the beginnings of a vast redefinition of the culture and politics of everyday life. In every sphere of activity, individuals began to conceive of themselves as possessing equal rights to self-fulfillment and to a greater measure of control over their inner and outer lives. This upsurge of the egalitarian and libertarian spirit has required a gradual redefinition and democratization of the cultural and social conceptions of persons and roles to match proliferating individual and group preferences. It signals the end of WASP male cultural domination in public spheres as well as in the minds and imaginations of citizens.

Despite public confusion generated by the proliferation of dissent, the social and cultural status quo of the late fifties and early sixties did introduce certain priorities that members of disadvantaged groups observed. The pragmatic logic of first things first—political and legal equality and a measure of economic opportunity—was influential in shaping the aims of much political and quasi-political dissent in the sixties. Many of the protests, after all, initially involved pursuit of civil rights and civil liberties. But this pragmatic logic of minimal inclusion was by no means decisive. For the issue of civil rights was tangled with the issue of cultural rights, which encompass among other things the right of persons to a measure of social space and a degree of social tolerance, even acceptance, of differences.

Many members of various disadvantaged groups sought full integration into the American enterprise by demanding that the abstract promises (and risks) of liberty and opportunity be extended to them. In exchange, they hoped, insofar as they could, to take on the cultural characteristics—the speech, manner, dress, even the cool sensibility—of the WASP. At the other extreme, representatives of varieties of cultural nationalism sought fulfillment of political and economic promises while rejecting the specific cultural forms of the WASP ideal altogether. Most minority citizens, it appears in retrospect, hoped to loosen the hold of the WASP ideal further, while at the same time claiming its political promises and perhaps contributing something of their own subculture to dominant fashions. And they did. Without the many contributions of disadvantaged groups—blacks, women, gays, lesbians, Pentecostals, Southerners, Jews, European ethnics—popular culture at the end of the seventies would have been far more impoverished than its harshest critics contend. An upward diffusion of styles—black, Southern, hillbilly, feminine, gay—expresses the loosening of WASP cultural hegemony and testifies to the cultural component of the democratization of personhood.

Blacks, for example, opposed dominant cultural stereotypes for obvious reasons: they were the most visibly excluded group. When black,
the most despised category in America, became beautiful in many circles, it was clear (liberal chic notwithstanding) that received standards
of beauty and popular images of attractiveness central to the WASP
ideal had begun to crumble. By the end of the sixties, more democratic, or at least more pluralistic, standards of beauty had established
themselves in America. Recalling the sixties, Diana Vreeland noted
that "the idea of beauty was changing. If you had a big nose it made
no difference, so long as you had a marvelous body and good carriage.
You held your head high, then you were a beauty."[63] Though this development favored the young and those with light frames, it did democratize the criteria of beauty somewhat: to win approval, one
merely had to learn good posture, diet, exercise, and disguise the marks
of age—all of which were leading pastimes of the seventies. By the
seventies, no single standard of beauty, dress, or appearance dominated
the American scene.

Though they may seem trivial, ideals of physical beauty are important cultural indexes of complex ratios of equality and excellence. To
perceive a racially different person as beautiful (or handsome) often
demands a greater degree of tolerance and genuine acceptance than is
required to accept that person as a political, moral, or spiritual equal.
The beginnings of this shift in standards of beauty indicate the far-
reaching, as yet unchartable consequences of the decline of authority
of the WASP cultural paradigm, a decline both enabled and intensified by dissent and protest during these years. One obvious and I think
salutary consequence of the democratized aesthetics of persons, however, is the significant growth in marriages across racial, ethnic, and
religious lines. Between 1970 and 1977 the number of marriages in
America increased by 7.6 percent. But the number of interracial marriages increased by 35.8 percent, from 310,000 to 421,000, and the number of black–white marriages nearly doubled in the same period, from
65,000 to 125,000.[64] About 50 percent of Japanese-Americans married
outside their race in the seventies, up sharply from the sixties and even
more dramatically from the fifties. Southern European ethnics continued to cross national lines in search of mates, though they tended to
stay within their common religious framework of Roman Catholicism
(albeit a changing Catholicism). And by the end of the seventies, Jews

were marrying people of other religious backgrounds at an astonishing rate of more than 40 percent.

Although the pace and ultimate outcome of this glacial shift in perception of persons and valuation of cultural hierarchies defies sensible prediction, a recurrent pattern seems to have surfaced: beginning with the black movement, dissent against social injustices has given way to dissent against cultural injustices. The pattern quickly becomes interactive, as cultural and political categories interpenetrate in the consciousness of citizens. Indeed, the pattern often was reversed—with cultural protest dominating—among such groups as the Beats in the fifties and adherents of the counterculture in the sixties. The cultural dimensions of these patterns, which permit a broader exercise of imagination, provide a basis for further egalitarian political and economic demands. The cultural dimensions also encourage the development of libertarian attitudes, as I suggested in Chapter 10. And they supply criteria for ongoing critiques of social and political gains. Although they frequently blind radical practitioners to short-term achievements, these critiques nevertheless have broadened the terms of subsequent political debate. In the fifties and early sixties, for example, gay men and lesbians were in the closet (perhaps I should say they were in separate closets); in the late sixties and seventies they took to the streets to protest legal and cultural discrimination. Even though a majority of Americans still resisted the idea of homosexual life as an acceptable equivalent to straight culture, and even though a sizable minority expressed reactionary sentiments, the civil rights of homosexuals were on the political agenda in the late seventies. Moreover, altered perceptions of the value of gay and lesbian styles of life were on the cultural agenda.

Of course, there is no reason to suppose that the center of gravity of cultural perception will shift to the extremes of the dissenting imagination. Nor should it, in my opinion, although women like Robin Morgan may lend a furious and florid eloquence to extreme options.

Women are the real Left. We are rising, powerful in our unclean bodies; bright glowing mad in our inferior brains; wild voices keening; undaunted by blood we who hemorrhage every twenty-eight days; laughing at our own beauty we who have lost our sense of humor; mourning for all each precious one of us might have been in this one living time-place had she not been born a woman; stuffing fingers into our mouths to stop the screams of fear and hate and pity for men we have loved and love still; tears in our eyes and bitterness in our mouths for children we couldn't have, or couldn't *not* have, or didn't want, or didn't want *yet,* or wanted and had in this place and this time of horror.

Women, she concludes, "are rising with a fury older and potentially greater than any force in history, and this time we will be free or no one will survive."[65] Although lesbianism does not threaten to become the American norm, its presence as an articulated possibility gradually loosens the hold of older, narrower visions of sex roles. It creates a number of frequently competing suboptions, from apolitical lesbianism to Marxist and cultural lesbianism. Making life at the widening edges of cultural respectability possible, if confusing, the dissent of lesbian and radical women also has enriched the possibilities for self-definition in and around the more moderate cultural center.

Throughout the sixties and seventies, millions of American women addressed Betty Friedan's "problem with no name." "Each suburban wife," Friedan wrote in *The Feminine Mystique* (1963), "struggled with it alone. As she made the beds, shopped for groceries, matched slipcover material, ate peanut butter sandwiches with her children, chauffeured Cub Scouts and Brownies, lay beside her husband at night—she was afraid to ask even of herself the silent question—'Is this *all?*' "[66] The question of fulfillment was articulated and answered in various ways, some new (or rather, previously marginal), and some used. The most politically and culturally radical feminists sought total separation—a conception of culture, sexuality, and self separate from a male-centered civilization. But a far larger percentage of American women—rich and poor, educated and illiterate, domestic and professional, lesbian and straight—sought entry into the industrial civilization on equal terms with men, along with renegotiation of the terms of family and personal life. And in response to the feminist protest movement of the late sixties and early seventies, a significant minority of women attempted to redefine the role of full-time housewife and mother, to reinvest the expanded role of "home manager" with dignity through an uneasy blend of traditional and contemporary values and strategies. Most of the answers suggested by women, even the incompatible and extreme ones, seem to me sensible: they are at least plausible ways to chart a life.

At the end of the seventies, the degree of progress in the democratization of cultural patterns was evident in the new issues and problems confronting women, especially women of the middle classes. Summarizing her impressions of the status of women's concerns at the outset of the eighties, Friedan observed that people in their twenties and thirties were wondering how to juggle their responsibilities as wives, workers, and mothers and whether they wanted to "be like men" in the occupational world. Others were asking why they could not stay home, "be a mother, and enjoy it." Surely life had grown more complex—in some respects even more difficult—for women by the end of the seventies. In the pursuit of equality—in the workplace, in the home, in personal relationships, and in sexual matters—many women gave up a measure of psychic and sexual protection that their mothers and grandmothers had used to advantage. Some women, especially younger women, were frustrated and paralyzed by an embarrassment of options. To complicate matters, few obvious models could be found for the new possibilities: young women had to invent their future. Not surprisingly, women in their twenties and thirties exhibited signs of stress. In spite of the profusion of difficult choices, however, American women of all ages apparently had attained parity with men in the important sphere of mental health. As Friedan notes, in 1960 "women's mental health in every age group over 20 was so much worse than men's that . . . Jessie Bernard . . . had concluded the marriage was good for men but was driving women crazy. Now, 20 years later, women's mental health seems to be as good as men's or even slightly better."[67] Though it is not without its costs, greater personal freedom seems quite within the range of psychic competence of American women.

Progress in democratizing cultural patterns was evident also in the rapid feminization of American culture. During the sixties and seventies values traditionally assigned to women—intimacy, warmth, nurturing, gentleness, touching, concreteness—gained ascendancy throughout American culture and much of American society, especially in its middle and upper socioeconomic echelons. So long associated with women and their domestic and cultural spheres, these notions met with resistance and mixed oddly with traditional male values of heroic aloofness, abstraction, and aggression. But the feminine values advanced just as women also began to experiment more freely with attitudes formerly reserved for men: anger, assertiveness, aggressiveness, ambition. Friendships among women flourished, much to the surprise of many men who in the course of predicting the impossibility of such relationships began to find genuine male friendships more and more difficult to establish and maintain: Huck and Jim no longer held exclusive American rights to the raft. "Feminine" values cropped up everywhere. Many radicals preached the importance of communities of affective selves, and some even made admirable attempts to practice such arrangements. The feminine touch of the Holy Spirit strongly influenced the Christian revival, which entailed a measure of opposition to ecclesiastical bureaucracies. Therapeutic seekers stressed fulfillment and the concrete, intimate character of personal relationships. Gender differences declined among straight people as well as among gay and lesbian citizens. Moreover, gender itself mattered less in many circles as values and attitudes came to be distributed more evenly between men and women. Finally, the traditional feminine values revealed themselves as central in a nuclear age and contributed powerfully, I believe, to the emergence of a strong antinuclear sentiment that was beginning to take visible form by the end of the seventies. The public world, especially the dimensions of war and peace, no longer could be run with assurance of survival by the likes of Henry Kissinger and Caspar Weinberger: their technology had outstripped their moral vision; in fact, it had outstripped plain sense.

In one sphere after another, then, the concept of normality was widened to encompass differences—racial and physical differences, differences in gender, mental and emotional differences, and differences in preferred ways of living. Once set in motion, the modulation from civil to cultural rights is hard to sustain but even harder to reverse. Its momentum may be uneven; the extreme visions of radicals may be ridiculed (even as they widen boundaries of public discourse). But the presence of a multiplicity of new and revitalized subcultures suggests that the status quo ante of American culture is unlikely to be restored. True, the uneven and partially overlapping currents of fiscal, moral, and social conservatism of the seventies appear to have slowed, even blunted, some of the force of radical dissent of the sixties. Unless the entire structure of economic, political, and cultural opportunity shrinks dramatically in the eighties and nineties, however, I do not see how these conservative currents can destroy the largely positive legacy of cultural dissent initiated by the various movements of the sixties. Indeed, it may be that further malfunctions of the late capitalist polity and economy will provide the catalyst for fresh radical probes between now and the end of the century—and perhaps well before. In any case, the radicalized sensibilities that dominated media versions of the ultra-left phases of the Movement figured importantly in evoking the conservative responses of the late sixties and seventies. This unintended legacy of conservative response, which was rather mild in the seventies in comparison with previous historical moments of reaction, seems to me salutary, at least to a point. It has provided a way of absorbing and tempering some—though by no means all—of the best insights of radicals into the American cultural repertoire.[68]

Still, the assertion of radical and conservative cultural values in the sixties and seventies has brought into the open serious divisions over moral questions. At the end of the seventies, liberals and conservatives disagreed less over such traditional political issues as foreign policy and the proper scope and degree of government power than over such issues as abortion, homosexuality, pornography, recreational drugs, and premarital sex. "At first glance," the framers of the *Connecticut Mutual Life Report on American Values in the '80s* conclude, "there seems to be a consensus on many of today's moral issues. Seventy-one percent (71%) of the American public, for example, feel that homosexuality is morally wrong, 68% feel this way about pornographic movies, and 65% about abortion. More than half of Americans (57%) feel that smoking marijuana is morally wrong."[69] In *New Rules,* Daniel Yankelovich also identifies a number of norms that have not changed: people still value their children sufficiently to claim they would have them again (90 percent); they favor disciplining children and want their offspring to be better off and more successful than they are (74 percent); they believe mate swapping to be morally wrong (81 percent); and they disapprove of married people having affairs (75+ percent).[70] But a closer analysis, the framers of the Connecticut report observe, reveals a "sharp division among many groups concerning moral issues. This divisiveness is demonstrated most clearly by the fact that there is a substantial difference between liberals and conservatives when [they are] asked to judge the morality of lesbianism (20% difference), sex between two single people (19% difference), pornography (18% difference), and the use of marijuana (18% difference)."[71]

Though they are genuine and can often be abrasive, these divisions do not threaten to destroy culture or to unravel the social fabric. The "cultural civil war," as some have gone so far as to call it, has been conducted more or less nonviolently, often casually. There are many injuries, of course, since everyone is armed, however lightly, but most wounds in cultural conflict turn out to be superficial, inflicted by bad rhetoric. Moreover, lurid scenarios of cultural civil war—Norman Lear's People for the American Way battling Jerry Falwell's Moral Majority—may obscure less dramatic though far more important implications of dissent: the survival of traditional American values as new, or, I should say, newly popular ones took root. Both phenomena occurred; both are important to an understanding of the shapes of American values in the sixties and seventies as well as in the future. At the end of the seventies, there were more cultural options than ever: clear old choices, clear new choices, and a fertile range of ambiguous syntheses of old and new. Yankelovich identifies twenty normative changes that occurred in America during these decades, among them a heightened desire for community, a growing distrust of politics, and, above all, greater tolerance for the liberty of persons. Yankelovich detects in the surveys solid support for greater freedom for women (and for men) to work, though not necessarily to be dominated by work; to remain single; to live together; to marry anyone, from a person of a different race to one of the same sex; to decide to have no children or fewer children or to choose an abortion.[72] His data, this is to say, document the chief cultural fact of the sixties and seventies: the largely apolitical quest for personal fulfillment within small communities of significant others.

In the sixties and seventies, then, dissent from all ideological perspectives and social directions challenged the hegemony of postwar liberal ideological and cultural norms. Thus far, however, neither extreme radical nor extreme conservative challenges have destroyed the framework of liberal vision of persons that permeates the responsible left and the responsible right. The values of individualism, political democracy, equality of opportunity, a degree of social concern for others, and cultural excellence survived, having been both tattered and embellished.[73] Public opinion polls covering the sixties and seventies not only confirm the widespread rejection of extremes but also trace the outlines of a slight overall shift to the left on cultural and political matters, as Yankelovich's data suggest. According to Ben Wattenberg, surveys "show that Americans accepted racial equality, but not reverse discrimination; they accepted environmental clean-up, but not the no-growth economy; they accepted women's demands for equal pay for equal work, but not the notion that roles for wife, mother or home-maker are demeaning; they accepted the notion that we ought to get out of Vietnam, but did not accept the idea that America was an im-perialist, immoral war-monger; they accepted the consumerist notion that big business might well be ripping us off, but did not accept the idea that the basic economic system was corrupt."[74]

In reviewing the gains initiated or facilitated by left-wing sectors of the Movement, one is led to wonder (as Walter Lippmann wondered of the Greenwich Village rebels of the late teens and early twenties) whether radical disappointment derived as much from success and the consequent burdens of enlarged freedom as from political and cultural "failure."[75] Of course, the radical challenge of the sixties quickly dis-covered the left ideological edges of popular social vision in America, but not before contributing to a leftward shift that was major in the sphere of culture, significant in the sphere of politics, and modest in the sphere of economics. These changes, which are in part the fruits of dissent and protest, seem likely to exert a continuing and largely positive impact on American life, though it is too early to tell whether the Reagan administration will undermine permanently many of the political and economic advances of the sixties and seventies. So too does the general idea and habit of dissent that began to emerge in the late fifties, interrupting the great "American celebration." The con-tinuing impact of dissent that the Movement evoked and others took up is evident in the proliferation of social criticism. It is evident also in the spread of the general idea of dissent and in the legitimation of social anger. These survivals constitute additional reasons for sup-posing that the interactive patterns of political and cultural dissent will persist, enlarging and perhaps even deepening the chances of Americans to pursue self-fulfillment in the eighties and nineties. Let me illustrate them.

First, consider the growth of social criticism. Since the aims of self-fulfillment were limitless, the obstacles seemed ubiquitous, and elements of the Movement pursued them one by one, initiating a national burst of social criticism and personal introspection perhaps as intense as in any period of American history. Elements of the Movement identified all facets of the main targets of dissent: industrial civilization and WASP culture. They questioned the distribution of income and wealth, the distribution of political power, the purposes of American foreign policy, the impersonality of large bureaucracies, the values and shapes of a consumer culture. They investigated the social and psychological functions of education. They challenged the scope and authority of scientific method. They examined the structure of work roles, family roles, community roles. And they called public attention to systematic prejudice against individuals by categories of race, sex, age, class, religion, education, sexual preference, marital status, and physical condition.

Other major critical revivals survived the explosion of dissent: doubts about the wisdom and feasibility of the industrial drive toward unlimited growth; reservations concerning the prevailing ethics of competition, consumption, and success; suspicion of anyone preoccupied with work to the virtual exclusion of other facets of life; uneasiness about exaggerated contrasts between so-called masculine and feminine traits. All of the issues raised (or resurrected) by intellectuals and activists remained live at the end of the seventies, though they had become subject to a broader range of analysis and interpretation. In the seventies, the emphasis of criticism shifted somewhat from political to social and psychological concerns and from left and left-liberal to conservative and New Right perspectives. Still, the left edge of criticism flourished, especially in the helping professions and in the academy. By the middle seventies, left-wing veterans of the Movement had found a permanent base in departments of literature, philosophy, history, economics, sociology, and anthropology from which to pursue a long-term, multifaceted critical inquiry into all the targets of dissent brought into preliminary focus during the sixties. A new generation of radical historians was beginning to publish respectable works, among them David Noble's *America By Design* (1979), Eugene Genovese's magisterial *Roll, Jordan, Roll* (1976), Linda Gordon's *Woman's Body, Woman's Right* (1976), Ann Douglas's *The Feminization of American Culture* (1977), and Christopher Lasch's *Haven in a Heartless World* (1977).

Second, the general *idea* of dissent survived the explosion of Movement social criticism and protest, even though it lost some of its dramatic potential and political persuasiveness through incessant use. In the sixties, particular targets of dissent were elusive: they were not defined uniformly, nor were they opposed universally, either by all elements of the Movement or by all sectors of society. As dissent generated further dissent, the idea of dissent spread. The Movement helped to popularize two related strategies of dissenting criticism that, though ideologically diffuse, are both radical in spirit. The Movement lent authority to a powerful populist vein of sentiment and a style of dissent characterized by an expressive psychology and an angry rhetoric of exposure. And radical intellectuals and activists pursued connections between personal troubles and public issues, stressing the interrelatedness of past and present and the connections among political, economic, social, and cultural/psychological dimensions of the quest for salvation and social justice.

Although radical elements in and around the Movement failed to inaugurate a sustained, coherent politics of the far left (an impossible dream under the circumstances), they did succeed brilliantly in bringing formerly private matters into the political arena: sex, feelings, handicaps, the family, children, leisure. Many left-wing critics have lamented the degree of interpenetration of personal, cultural, and political concerns promoted by various facets of the Movement, especially the counterculture and the women's movement.[76] Dissent did make everything political. It also made everything personal. Categories of analysis and modes of political action blurred, to be sure. But in the bargain, as the antinomian cultural spirit spilled over into political spheres, distinctions between public and private—real enough in some senses—were revealed in their phenomenological fullness. Rather than reinforcing the too-rigid boundaries drawn by critics and theorists, radicals in the Movement showed these distinctions to be part of a Gestalt, a fluid mode of vision.

At the end of the seventies expressions of dissent became habitual, even addictive, and as a consequence, authority in every sphere— political, cultural, social, religious, moral, parental—was subject to automatic challenge and deep skepticism. Even the authority of history withered. The opposition to authority so characteristic of contemporary dissent was projected onto the past, and history came to be viewed, as Jesse Lemisch put it, from the "bottom up"—or from any angle of entry an observer chose.[77] History's winners—the ideas, values, attitudes, heroes, and classes that prevailed—were subjected to intense scrutiny. And the losers—the defeated people and movements, as well as the discarded ideas, traditions, and values—became the subject of largely admiring inquiry. Social history came into high fashion. In the course of this reviewing of the past, a range of fresh possibilities presented itself: the entire past became potentially available. The late sixties and seventies witnessed a profusion of nostalgia for the American past: its customs, styles of dress, regional peculiarities, "antique" trinkets, and its neglected characters and overlooked ideas. In the burst of cultural energy released during later phases of the Movement, each focus of dissent—from blacks to women to homosexuals—searched out its neglected and frequently misinterpreted past.

In response to these currents, there was a new political and cultural emphasis on ethnicity. According to Michael Novak, a student of eastern and southeastern European Americans, the new ethnicity involves "a deliberate harnessing of ethnicity to politics." By creating a local space and investing it with sufficient cultural richness and texture, ethnics could hope to participate in the quest for fulfillment on less disadvantageous terms. The aim, in Novak's view, was to help individuals define themselves through their own ethnic heritage, to help them "find their own identity and pride from which they can meet others without anxiety."[78] And by analogy, as dissent became more customized and tailored to personal wishes, individuals searched out their family roots, reviving what had been an upper-class or at least a WASP sport. As a consequence of this democratization of the past, almost no one had any reason to be ashamed of his or her own origins by the end of the seventies. In the increasingly syncretic atmosphere of American culture, then, ethnic values were strengthened and weakened simultaneously during the sixties and seventies. Motion in both directions, however, conformed to the requirements of the quest for personal fulfillment. Although one person might attempt to deepen ties to an ethnic group while another might elect to marry outside the group, both are headed in the same direction of personal fulfillment. The democratization of personhood, this is to say, was evident both in the quickened patterns of assimilation and in the roots movement.

Third, the stress on dissent characteristic of the Movement helped to sanction public expression of anger about social matters. By the early seventies Americans of all persuasions could feel freer to say, in anticipation of Peter Finch's plea for a general expression of dissent in *Network* (1976), "I'm as mad as hell . . ." The willingness of citizens to make a scene, to speak and act out personal frustrations, cut across class and ideological lines, with mixed results. In the seventies, then, left-wing protest persisted, though on a less spectacular scale than in the sixties. Protests against the construction of nuclear power plants were staged around the country, a prelude to antinuclear arms demonstrations in the early eighties. The women's movement pressed for adoption of the Equal Rights Amendment and other measures aimed at gaining full equality. At the same time, however, lively opposition to the ERA took shape, initiated mainly by women. And groups of parents actively opposed to mandatory busing of schoolchildren designed to promote racial integration used techniques popularized by the integrationist civil-rights movement of the early sixties. In January 1979, an estimated sixty thousand advocates of laws against abortion marched on Washington, bearing signs reminiscent of the anti-war movement of the sixties: instead of "Give Peace a Chance," the signs of the pro-life advocates read "Give Life a Chance." Although many women's groups, especially left-wing groups, ridiculed all species of opposition to abortion—moral, theological, and political—a number of young radicals joined the anti-abortion or "pro-life" movement in the late seventies. As Valarie Evans, a twenty-year-old Berkeley student activist, put it, "Abortion, capital punishment, euthanasia, war—anything that takes people's lives and pretends there's some reason for it—it's really all the same . . . There's no reason at any time," she continues, "to take someone's life. Nobody can pretend to have a right to do that."[79]

Following the lead of tax protestors of the sixties who opposed large military appropriations, middle-income and working-class taxpayers protested what they considered excessive and inefficient state spending (especially in the area of welfare assistance). Demanding changes in government policy, about three thousand representatives of the American Agriculture Movement marched on Washington in February 1979, using tractors and other farm machinery to bring traffic on the main arteries to a standstill. The protest was followed by a series of intensive lobbying sessions on Capitol Hill. The idea of vigorous dissent thus survived the vagaries of Movement ideology, becoming available to constituencies outside the Movement and beyond the left. The anti-authoritarian dissenting spirit of the Movement, then, came to live a protean existence in the larger society.

Although the long-term impact of dissent remains a subject of lively speculation, a portion of its positive impact seems clear even at this brief distance: civil rights and civil liberties for all citizens, partial redistribution of inequality in the political economy, minimal material support for all citizens, significant democratization of cultural norms, and disintegration of demeaning cultural stereotypes. These advances, together with a continuing exploration of various dissenting patterns of personal and cultural definition, should widen the context of political debate and action in the eighties and nineties, though they will not necessarily drive it leftward. During the sixties and seventies these advances in the democratization of personhood gave millions of Americans the resources—cultural and personal, and, to a lesser extent, political and economic—to pursue self-fulfillment on a scale hitherto unknown. The chances of minimal inclusion in the American enterprise rose swiftly. And the chances of optimal inclusion—even for those bearing one or more social "disadvantages"—increased too, though as always they did so less rapidly and more fitfully than most people had come to hope.

III

Misreading the Signs

Of all evils the greatest is one which in the souls of most men is innate, and which a man is always excusing in himself and never correcting; I mean, what is expressed in the saying that "Every man by nature is and ought to be his own friend." Whereas the excessive love of self is in reality the source to each man of all offences; for the lover is blinded about the beloved, so that he judges wrongly of the just, the good, and the honourable, and thinks that he ought always to prefer himself to the truth. But he who would be a great man ought to regard, not himself or his interests, but what is just, whether the just act be his own or that of another.

PLATO
Laws, Book V

I do not think, on the whole, that there is more selfishness among us than in America; the only difference is that there it is enlightened, here it is not. Each American knows when to sacrifice some of his private interests to save the rest; we want to save everything, and often we lose it all . . . No power on earth can prevent the increasing equality of conditions from inclining the human mind to seek out what is useful or from leading every member of the community to be wrapped up in himself. It must therefore be expected that personal interest will become more than ever the principal if not the sole spring of men's actions; but it remains to be seen how each man will understand his personal interest. If the members of a community, as they become more equal, become more ignorant and coarse, it is difficult to foresee to what pitch of stupid excesses their selfishness may lead them; and no one can foretell into what disgrace and wretchedness they would plunge themselves lest they should have to sacrifice something of their own well-being to the prosperity of their fellow creatures.

TOCQUEVILLE
Democracy in America

12

The "Rise"
of Selfishness?

In the postwar years and especially during the sixties and seventies, I have argued, Americans engaged in a search for fulfillment, an open-ended quest for distinctive syntheses of personal salvation and shares of social justice. Tens of millions of citizens within overlapping social categories sought—and claimed to have discovered—paths to fuller definitions and expressions of themselves as individuals and as participants in one or more relatively small communities. This search seems to me easily the most striking fact about American civilization during these years, as well as the most hopeful. The growing involvement in the quest for fulfillment was evidenced, if only indirectly, in what I have called the democratization of personhood, whose social signs included an extension of economic benefits, an enlargement of political and civil rights, and an expansion of cultural and personal opportunities. Although they were uneven, gains in each of these interpenetrating spheres were on the whole impressive. Economic advances, as I have noted, did not keep pace with expectations: they were inequitably distributed, and they seemed precarious at the end of the seventies. Political gains were more solid: not only were the rights of citizens widened and extended to members of various groups previously less advantaged, but the personal and political rights of citizens were deepened as well. Important as these gains were, the most sweeping changes occurred within the sphere of culture. Equality, openness, flexibility, tolerance: these values came increasingly to characterize American culture.[1] During these decades, the ratios of salvation and social justice became more complicated than at any other moment in American history, permitting not only a greater diversity of conceptions of fulfillment but a far greater range of success, subjectively defined, in this endeavor.

I have dwelt on the achievements of the quest for personal fulfillment for two sets of reasons. First, I believe these advances to be of overriding importance. Second, I think that social and cultural critics have tended to overstress and frequently to exaggerate what strike me as side effects of the quest: an alleged rise of selfishness and a declining regard for various modes of authority. No doubt I have minimized costs in order to highlight gains. But as in medicine, side effects must be observed with care, for such effects have been known to disable or even to kill patients. These side effects of selfishness and a disorganization of authority reveal themselves most clearly in the light of disparities between rapid cultural advances and comparatively modest gains in the economic and political spheres. Cultural opportunities outstripped social opportunities: ideas of fulfillment grew more rapidly than opportunities for fulfillment. Consequently, myths of consolation proliferated, as did fantasies of omnipotence, or what I have termed fantasies of maximal inclusion. In such circumstances, assertions of supremacy of the self and the irrelevance of all modes of authority usually constituted unfulfilling versions of fulfillment.

Although they are fundamentally conservative, these concerns about selfishness and authority have been explored variously by critics and scholars of all ideological persuasions who inhabit the framework of nostalgia. This emphasis on the self—on its real and alleged pathologies—is not new: selfishness comprises a perennial theme of social and cultural commentary. By the end of the seventies, however, bipartisan groups of critics concluded that unseemly concern with self had become a blinding—and debilitating—preoccupation among American citizens. As a consequence, the idea of community seemed to have gone out of fashion. And critics of every ideological stripe concluded also that the quest threatened to make a shambles of politics and the idea of the public interest.

In critical inquiries into culture and society, three major questions recurred. Critics wondered whether a collection of what Philip Rieff called "therapeutic personalities" could sustain an authoritative culture.

They asked whether a culture composed of increasingly self-absorbed individuals could be an admirable one. Finally, critics puzzled over whether Americans could fashion a coherent politics capable of ensuring collective survival and advancing social justice, especially in an era of impending limits when the growing need for sacrifice seemed liable to collide with expanding desires for material and psychic fulfillment. Though many of these fears seem plausible *as* fears, I believe that much of what critics, theologians, and journalists characterized as selfishness, narcissism, and disregard for authority in the seventies was a predictable and largely inescapable byproduct of aims many of them had previously held: a genuine search for personal fulfillment made possible by decades, even centuries, of misery, hard work, and political struggle.

Whether these allegedly toxic byproducts of selfishness and declining authority turn out also to be socially tolerable in the coming years is a matter for speculation. The range of existing social and cultural issues confronting Americans surely is more complicated than ever; and these problems may turn out to be intractable, resistant to our best efforts. In exploring the important fears of critics in this chapter and the next, however, I want to stick to the less ambitious if scarcely less tidy line of speculation implied earlier on: that in spite of certain negative side effects the quest has left the present collection of American selves at least as well equipped—physically, intellectually, morally, spiritually, and perhaps even politically—to face both personal issues and the major public issues of the eighties and nineties as was its counterpart in the late fifties.

Even if it is correct, my hypothesis will not appeal to anyone who posits the need for some wrenching political or cultural transformation designed to ensure the emergence of "new" men and women, freed from an apparently petty, self-indulgent preoccupation with individual fulfillment. No such transformation occurred in the only circumstances we have: advanced capitalist society and present-day American culture. Nor, it now seems evident, could such a transformation have occurred, either in the sixties (when some radicals claimed to detect revolutionary stirrings) or, needless to say, in the seventies (when no one did). For serious critics and activists, the millennial edge, none too sharp even in the sixties, had lost its cutting power by the end of the seventies. A fascination with apocalypse, however, persisted and spread. Although I cannot rule out the possibility of such a dark turn, my speculation does not lead to the conclusion that moral imperfections and defects in modal personality have rendered Americans incapable of a decent effort to avert such an ending. In certain respects, which I shall specify in the next two chapters, the social, cultural, and personal costs of the quest have been high. But they have not been fatal. Nor, I think, do they threaten to become so in the near term.

In fact, I shall argue, selfishness and a partial decline of authority constitute *signs* of the quest. But I do not believe that selfishness was dangerously on the rise or that authority was in perilous decline during the sixties and seventies, even though such assessments have become conventional features of American social and cultural criticism. Though they were evident at the margins of society and in extreme cases, these characteristics, when stressed too heavily, can lead to a serious misreading of the ambiguous signs. These negative side effects were overshadowed by rather more hopeful signs. There was a rise in concern with the self, a development that constitutes one expression of the quest and suggests the increasing disposition of individuals from all social categories to assert themselves, to feel entitled to seek fulfillment. And there was a largely salutary evolution of authority, a decline of certain modes that interfered with the quest and precluded progress in the democratization of personhood, and a simultaneous rise of other, more internal modes of authority that facilitated the search.

Postdeprivational Man: Philip Rieff and Daniel Bell

Let me begin with the most speculative issue, the fear that, following the triumph of Rieff's "therapeutic personality," culture would disintegrate. In *The Triumph of the Therapeutic* (1966), a seminal postwar American critique of culture and personality, Rieff goes beyond the problem of whether a civilized human being can "believe" to ask whether "unbelieving man" can remain "civilized." According to Rieff, the twentieth century marks a potentially unique cultural revolution. It is similar to others in that a past set of controls and remissions is breaking down. But no new symbolic of control seems possible under modern conditions of affluence and cultural and religious pluralism. There is, this is to say, no longer any externally imposed need for culture—no need for individuals to adopt a "design of motives directing the self outward, toward those communal purposes in which alone the self can be realized and satisfied."[2] Rather, a growing collection of therapeutic personalities embraces "the gospel of self-fulfillment." Bound to an expressive ethic, they pursue this "cultural revolution," Rieff declares, "for no other purpose than greater amplitude and richness of living itself."

In the course of their quest, therapeutic men and women run the high risk of becoming permanently unable to establish a new system of controls. Without these, according to Rieff, genuine individual salvation becomes impossible. The idea of culture as we have known it dissolves. And the future of a social order held together only by force, affluence, routine, and a measure of inertia becomes problematic. Rieff, of course, is too able a critic to predict flatly the dissolution of society, though his study clearly announces the possibility of such a turn. He rather offers this conditional projection: should "psychological man" become the norm, he will lack the resources of character and will to establish and sustain a culture in any previously held sense of the term. "The next culture," Rieff speculates, "may be viable without being valid; on the other hand, the old faiths could be judged valid even by those who consider them now no longer viable." The next culture, this is to say, will be an "anticulture."

Rieff may be correct. But neither he nor any other cultural critic, whether conservative or radical, has shown that the pure form of the therapeutic personality—the totally remissive self—has triumphed or is on the verge of doing so. Critics have held back from such demonstrations, I suspect, because no convincing cultural or social evidence exists. Surely there are significant, probably growing, numbers of people who embody the therapeutic ideal to one degree or another. And they are to be found mainly, though by no means exclusively, where Rieff proposes we look: among the educated middle classes and among the young. But the notion that American culture is becoming thoroughly remissive and anomic under the impact of therapeutic urges seems to be at least a serious exaggeration. Rieff's speculation depended upon several dubious assumptions. He predicted, for example, that affluence would persist and spread along a more or less uninterrupted path toward abundance, a forgivable expectation considering that his work was published in the middle sixties. And he assumed, unforgivably, that "affluence" corrupts the moral faculties of ordinary people.

Furthermore, Rieff airily dismissed what seem to me to be three of the most visible cultural vehicles of the quest for fulfillment in the sixties and seventies: the Movement, the Christian revival, and the human-potential movement. In his view, the "revolutionary," the "clergyman," and the "therapist" all have ceased to be effective spokespersons for culture. Regardless of whether they primarily speak the language of politics, theology, or psychology, Rieff suggests, those few figures who propose renunciation of the self for the ends of a larger community are by now ignored. And the rest—the phony revolutionaries, the therapeutic preachers, the pop psychologists—have become part of a problem with no salutary solution. For Rieff, then, the Christian idea of salvation ceased to be authentic or even possible when it lost its ascetic dimension, or rather when hedonistic variations supplemented this dimension. The idea of community gave way to a cold, impersonal welfare state, and isolated individuals, thinking themselves saved, were lost. Similarly, the chances of sustaining civilized existence decreased when Freudian mechanisms of repression and sublimation allegedly lost their hold on individuals. Everything in this culture threatens to collapse into the black—or rather pastel—hole of the therapeutic.

Only through such a rigorous imposition of selected past standards on present realities, I think, could contemporary American culture present such a cheerless visage. Even so, there is a considerable difference—a disjunction, in fact—between what may appear to Rieff and others as a selfish, narcissistic, mean, petty, unauthoritative culture and one unable to survive. Rieff offers a glum projection of a future devoid of heroism, character, responsibility, spiritual discipline—a time when human excellence will have passed forever from the scene. He conveys his disapproval of this future in an elegantly controlled ironic mode that nevertheless implies a sense of disappointment, even bitterness, and perhaps a hint of moral arrogance as well.

Like Marcuse's images of comfortable slavery in the affluent welfare state, however, Rieff's middle-sixties intimation of the future is in some respects benign. But even here, Rieff cannot escape his ironic mode of vision. "The wisdom of the next social order, as I imagine it, would not reside in right doctrine, administered by the right men . . . but rather in doctrines amounting to permission for each man to live an experimental life. Thus, once again, culture will give back what it has taken away. All governments will be just, so long as they secure that consoling plenitude of option in which modern satisfaction really consists." What "apocalypse," Rieff asks, "has ever been so kindly? What culture has ever attempted to see to it that no ego is hurt?"

By the middle seventies, as the assumption of relative scarcity began to dominate American social thought, easy projections of comfortable slavery had grown quaint. Yet critics continued to explore Rieff's concern over the character of American culture. They wondered whether the emerging personality type—which they took to be selfish, narcissistic, and hedonistic—was in any sense commendable and whether men and women with such personalities could sustain an esteemable culture and a viable politics.

In his work of the middle and late seventies, *The Cultural Contradictions of Capitalism* (1976) and *The Winding Passage* (1980), Daniel Bell explored much the same territory that Rieff had covered in the middle sixties. Like Rieff, Bell concentrates on what he takes to be a long-term trend toward preoccupation with the self. His essays—at least those centered on cultural themes—turn on an opposition between the growth of the unbounded self and disciplined countertypes that have flourished mainly in material milieus characterized by relative scarcity and cultural and religious configurations informed by restraint: Judaic, Christian, bourgeois. But Rieff and Bell differ somewhat in their assessments of the character of what might be called postdeprivational man. And they differ sharply over his prospects.

A celebrant of the discipline made possible by history and tradition, Bell nevertheless seems moved to stress the peculiarities of his individual talent, to press—within limits, of course—the claims of the self. In *The Winding Passage,* he seeks to construct a mature, distinctive self out of the materials of his past. And he endeavors to understand that past, both its parochial Hebraic center and its larger Western (and non-Western) circumference. From this tense interplay of autobiographical and historical ambitions Bell's work derives much of its range and power— its reflective and unfinished character, its lucidity and its energy, its steadily contemporary focus. "These are the essays of a prodigal son," Bell announces in the preface to *The Winding Passage.* "They are essays written in my middle years, midway in the journey of our life, in that dark wood, seeking a return to the straight way of my ancestors. I know that the world I live in is vastly different from theirs, yet the duplex nature of man remains largely the same, now as then.[3]

The Winding Passage, then, does not portray another callow and submissive youth returning to his father superficially wiser about the ways of the world yet merely grateful to be home. Bell's attempted return is more tentative, more complicated, and perhaps less immediately satisfying. For these reasons it also holds greater interest for an audience of his contemporaries. In this re-creation of an ancient parable, the accent does not fall on the wayward son, the envious brother, or the forgiving father, but rather on the ironies of the son returning as father. At once more at ease in the larger world than his biblical analogue and more uneasy at the prospect of coming into a space resembling home again, Bell is alive not simply to the unresolvable character of tensions between parochial and universal themes. At his best, he also insists that such claims be bent though not wrenched into coherence: the essays are explorations of *a* prodigal son, not *the* prodigal son.

Bell, then, is something of a modernist in spite of himself. At least, he resorts to the rhetorical techniques of modernism in order to reconcile himself to a past that he no longer wishes to evade yet cannot fully accept. Self-conscious (though perhaps not unreasonably so) about his own disposition to the sin of intellectual pride, Bell seeks the discipline of Mosaic Law and the clarity of orthodoxy: "When heresy becomes *a la mode,* orthodoxy, paradoxically, is the stronger standpoint for criticism of society." He underlines this notion with a concluding parable, a Zen story: "Two monks have been circling in the desert for a long time. Finally they sit down. Neither says a word. Sometime later, one speaks: 'My brother is lost.' The other is silent. After a long meditation, he says: 'No, I am not lost. I am here. The Way is lost.'" But for one making his way through the winding passage—the Dantesque transition from "the netherworld to the fires of redemption"—the Law is the indispensable compass: "if The Way [i.e., the Law] is lost," Bell observes, "all is lost."

Although Bell insists too modestly that he does not explore a single thesis, the essays in *The Winding Passage* do display an overriding concern. They amount to a series of meditations on the wages of selfish excess—explorations of the economic, political, social, cultural, and personal consequences of ignoring the Law. Throughout these pieces, the dramatic opposition turns on the disciplined, knowing self in conflict with its unrestrained, antinomian, and thoroughly subversive underside. "The uniqueness of man lies in his capacity, for self-consciousness and self-transcendence, to stand continually 'outside' himself and to judge himself. This is the foundation of human freedom. It is this radical freedom which defines the glory and the plight of man." But the "modern view of man takes over only the aspect of freedom, not man's . . . finitude," Bell observes in an impressive piece on technology, nature, and society: "it sees man as a creature of infinite power able to bend the world to his own will . . ." Thus, "modern culture," especially in its utopian versions, obscures "the biblical idea of sin . . . which derives from the fact that man as a limited and finite creature denies his finiteness and seeks to reach beyond it—beyond culture, beyond nature, beyond history."

Without a sense of justice, righteousness, and proportion—a commitment to limits imposed by the Law—human beings become their own enemies. The Law can be tyrannical, Bell admits. Yet when authority is neglected, there can be no freedom, no mature self, no civilization. In such circumstances the cord of religious memory snaps, and the antinomian self, which haunts Bell's imagination, spreads like a plague as individuals consider themselves unbounded by tradition and the authority of institutions. This theme animates Bell's vision, guiding his circuitous return to his Jewish roots and informing his reflections on the brief historical period through which he has lived, beginning in 1920. It structures his criticisms of the millennial character of utopian Marxism (a passing condition of his own youth). It shapes his critique of the nihilistic implications of modernist and postmodernist culture, which in his view subordinate moral to aesthetic considerations and in the end subsume both under unrestrained sensuality. And it girds up his critique of the "hedonistic" imperatives of late capitalism, its stress on the pleasures of consumption and its subversion of the Protestant ethic of work.

Whereas Rieff's psychological man tends to be remissive, withdrawn into private concerns, Bell's unrestrained self may be active or passive, bent on some mixture of power and pleasure. Bell too laments what he takes to be the dominance of the unrestrained self: appetitive, absorbed in its own usually petty concerns. Such selves lack the intellectual, moral, and spiritual resources—and will—to fashion a mature, well-crafted identity. And they are unfit to participate in caring communities. Moreover, Bell resembles Rieff in his frequent representations of the present as counterfeit, lacking even the dramatic power of those subversive impulses that haunted earlier moments of Western culture. "American capitalism," Bell concludes in *The Cultural Contradictions of Capitalism,* "has lost its traditional legitimacy, which was based on a moral system of reward rooted in the Protestant sanctification of work. It has substituted a hedonism which promises material ease and luxury, yet shies away from all the historic implications of a 'voluptuary system,' with all its social permissiveness and libertinism."[4]

Like Rieff, then, Bell often shows little regard for the cultural surfaces of the recent American past. He dismisses most of the Movement and the therapeutic quest as cheap, lifeless imitations of Romantic and modernist themes, illustrations of the social, cultural, and personal consequences of the boundaryless self in pursuit of unlimited experience. He exaggerates the difficulty people encounter in managing demanding work *and* strenuous leisure. And if he does not quite write off the Christian revival, Bell treats it as only another eruption of "Fundamentalism," born of status anxiety and carried out by people without claims to intellectual respectability. In spite of this gift for caricature, Bell strikes me as a more interesting figure than Rieff. Rieff's work may be more polished, his display of erudition more restrained, and his views more settled (even in *Fellow Teachers,* a rambling follow-up to *The Triumph of the Therapeutic* published in 1973). But Rieff sets himself a far easier task, inasmuch as he does not consider his principal subject in significant motion.

Whereas Bell wrestles with the dynamo of history, Rieff polishes a static, dystopian myth. Bell remains a major figure in American intellectual life—an engaging prophet who warns of the wages of self-centeredness and examines cultural patterns and institutional structures patiently, as if culture and history have not ceased to matter. Behind his rhetorical pose of detachment and irony, Rieff comments retrospectively on the end of serious things. His "kindly" apocalypse does not even contain the power to annihilate the future. The human spectacle may drag on, in Rieff's view, but since it can go nowhere—achieve no peaks of excellence, offer no widespread religious consolation worth having—it ceases to hold more than, shall we say, academic interest. Rieff expects no surprises—in culture, people, or politics. And he discovers none.

Bell does not share Rieff's apparent contempt for politics in general and liberalism and the welfare state in particular. He considers the cultural ascendance of unrestrained man neither complete nor permanent. The ascendance of the endlessly selfish self is incomplete, Bell maintains, because the antinomian thrust of culture occurs within the context of other norms, institutions, and historical forces. Society, he believes, is divided into several realms: economy, polity, culture. An "axial principle" presides over each realm: functional rationality and efficiency govern the economy; equality—of opportunity, of rights, of legal status—regulates the polity; fulfillment of the self constitutes the leading norm of culture (at least of the culture of advanced industrial society).

Although they are complexly related (in ways Bell has yet to delineate fully), these realms obey different rhythms of change. The economy follows a linear path toward ever higher productivity. The polity moves within a grid of known organizational and moral alternatives set out by the earliest political philosophers. And culture displays either "the continuity of tradition" (in stable societies) or the principle of "syncretism," which Bell describes as an "indiscriminate mingling or borrowing of diverse cultural styles." Moreover, Bell observes, "it is the tensions between the norms of these three realms—efficiency and bureaucracy, equality and rights, self-fulfillment and the desire for novelty—that form the contradictions of the modern world, contradictions that are enhanced under capitalism, since the techno-economic realm is geared to promote not economic necessities but the cultural wants of a hedonistic world." The project of self-realization may dominate our culture, though I believe that Bell exaggerates the extent of hedonism. But in a society composed of disjunctive realms, Bell maintains, self-fulfillment does not lead an uninhibited existence: the contradictions he posits create space and ensure a measure of indeterminacy. Preventing a complete victory of the unrestrained self, Bell insists, the spheres of economy and politics influence individual attitudes and behavior.

Nor is the apparent triumph of the unrestrained self necessarily permanent. The present, Bell speculates, is a moment of cultural exhaustion, a time in which the "ground impulses" of modernity have largely played themselves out. "These were the impulses to abolish God and assume that Man could take over the powers he had ascribed to God and now sought to claim for himself. This is the common bond between Marx and Nietzsche and the link between the aesthetic and political movements of modernity." Bell's diagnosis of exhaustion constitutes a thread of hope, a small opening onto a decent future. Endings make room for fresh beginnings, since culture, Bell asserts in an operatic figure, is always a *"ricorso."* People have returned again and again to a core group of questions concerning the human predicament: the character of love, the significance of tragedy, the conduct of life, and above all, the conduct of death. These questions, Bell observes, are codified in religion: in "institutions, rites, creed or answers." And because they recur, he suggests, the Enlightenment conviction that religious impulses would die out as scientific knowledge replaced superstition and ignorance is naïve. It violates all we know about the processes of culture. And after more than two centuries during which knowledge has grown along exponential curves, it seems to have been refuted by history.

Preoccupation with self, Bell conjectures, has been significantly responsible for the historical rise and present exhaustion of certain irreligious (or perhaps only heretical) cultural themes: rationalism, aestheticism, existentialism, civil religions, and political religions (in particular, utopian Marxism). Each of these perspectives sanctioned the growth of unrestrained selves. None served to temper the unbounded self, because each steadily ignored the existential ground of religion: its capacity to acquaint people with their "finiteness" and their "limited powers." None of these alternatives helped people discover coherent paths toward reconciliation with the intractable features of the human predicament. For these reasons, Bell anticipates a return of the sacred, though he does not pretend to know the shapes or outcomes of this fresh religious encounter. "Whether that new vision will be genuine, that is, fully responsive to the deepest feelings of people, I do not know; and whether such new threads can be woven into meanings that will extend over generational time and become embodied in new institutions is something even further beyond my purview."

Before his vision of the future turns cloudy, as anyone's must, Bell manages to rescue conservative cultural discourse from its modern extremes of dystopian myth and apocalyptic vision. He offers a powerful sermon on the excesses of self-regard that are promoted by the quest for fulfillment, both in its long historical arc and in its most recent manifestations during the sixties and seventies. He calls attention to the continuing (even increasing) importance of ordinary politics, a theme in partial disfavor among many literary intellectuals. And he insists on the centrality of religious questions, a theme thoroughly out of fashion in such circles. Bell's conservative strictures, then, are both perennial and important. But they are also partial: they blur parts of the past, they mute hopeful aspects of the present, and they may obscure salutary prospects for the future. His familiar characterization of cultural conservatism thus calls for a familiar critique. That critique is nevertheless worth proposing once again, even in brief outline. For all its refinements and attention to technological and economic progress, Bell's vision seems to me inadequate as a basis for describing, analyzing, and evaluating the entry of ordinary persons into the workings of modern history.

Bell's cultural conservatism encourages a certain condescension toward democratic politics, especially its harsh edges. This is not to say that Bell has discarded his liberal political philosophy. At best, he observes in an interesting piece, "Liberalism in the Postindustrial Society," politics "can be the conscious art of bargaining, of tradeoffs, of what, in game theory, is called non-zero-sum games." At worst, Bell declares in an essay on "Ethnicity and Social Change," politics becomes more than an "arena of interests or of social transformations": it turns into an arena of passions. "The 'risk' of such inflamed political competition is that issues may not be negotiable (as they are when tied to interests alone), but become 'causes' that invite violent conflict and even civil war."

It is not enough, however, to regret the intrusions of passion—even crude, quasi-religious passion—as a force in politics. Nor is it sufficient to point to the logical extremes of protest politics. The dangers are real and the risks are often high. But the stakes, at least in recent American political history, have been even higher: in the black civil-rights movement, in the anti-war movement, in the women's movement. How could these causes have succeeded so far as they have without passionate expressions of social anger, without a willingness to violate rules and disrupt routines? As Bell himself admits, a reasonable politics requires unusual circumstances. All sides must accept the rules, he observes. "But this is itself possible not only where there is a high degree of legitimacy to a society, but where there is a conscious effort to reduce inequalities and expand opportunities, and where there is a sense of fairness for all individuals in the society." Progress toward a democratic polity and the even more elusive goal of a fair distribution of wealth has required a more spirited approach to politics than Bell's vision easily condones. Cultural conservatives may applaud the results of democratic movements. Often as not, however, they do so post facto, once the political dust has settled.

Similarly, I find Bell's vision of culture and religion cramped. Repulsed by extremes, he nevertheless seems fascinated by them. His account of the profanation of modern society, for example, weaves together several thematic strands: the gradual realization of the antinomian self following the Reformation; the emergence and spread of modernist and postmodernist culture; the diffusion of hedonistic values throughout the culture of consumption. Bell gravitates toward the most outrageous extensions and distensions of modern experiments in self-definition and self-expression. "What modernity has done—in its drive to enhance experience, in its repudiation of tradition and the past, in its sanction for the new and the idea that the individual could remake his self in accordance solely with desire—is to disrupt" the coherence that marks the well-crafted self "in the name of an unbounded self." Examples of the dispositions that Bell names may be found in the work of everyone from André Gide to R. D. Laing. But Bell's Wagnerian orchestration of these dispositions, I think, depends too heavily on the assumption that extremes haunt the subcultures of art and intellect and, through a combination of diffusion and coincidence, eventually characterize the wider culture.

One indirect test of such a reading of culture turns on how well it accounts for the textures of American life in the sixties and seventies. Here, I believe, Bell's cautionary tale becomes misleading. I at least fail to find American society overpopulated by atheists, nihilists, hedonists, narcissists, slackers, and connoisseurs of the unbounded self. Bell may fail to do so as well, since he carefully distinguishes culture from social structure. In fact, his useful though strained analytic separation of culture from social structure allows him a certain indulgence. For in the course of maintaining the importance of this distinction against the claims of holistic thinkers, Bell is able to delay a more difficult task. He has not yet gotten around to offering convincing characterizations of the interplay between innovators of culture and its recipients—between artists and intellectuals on the one side, and ordinary citizens in various social categories on the other. Both contribute importantly to the changing mixes of cultural values and social practices, since innovators cannot create culture wholly out of novel materials.

Even in his exploration of the sphere of culture, I think, Bell minimizes the salvific aspects of the democratization of the quest for self-fulfillment.

Bell's observations on religion are incisive, though here too he strikes me as insufficiently sympathetic to various manifestations of the search for salvation already evident in the sixties and seventies.[5] A presumption of widespread selfishness precludes a rounded perception and appreciation of current varieties of the sacred. Consider his speculations on the prospects for a religious revival: "Unlike romanticism," he writes, "it will not be a turn to nature, and unlike modernity, it will not be the involuted self; it will be the resurrection of Memory." Bell imagines this revival in three forms: moralizing, redemptive, and mythic/mystical.

The moralizing form closely approximates the evangelical and neo-Pentecostal movements, which Bell subsumes under the heading of "fundamentalist." It is, he believes, perhaps "the strongest element" at the moment, but since its traditional social sources are to be found among such declining groups as "farmers, lower middle class, small town artisans," this thrust may be short-lived. Bell foresees the redemptive variant emerging among the intellectual and professional classes. It will represent in some sense a reaction to the excesses of modernity and the impersonality of bureaucratic institutions. A retreat from the heresy of the search for an infinite self, this redemptive mode will include attempts to rediscover the traditional sources of a responsible self mindful of its rights and aware of its obligations to observe moral imperatives of the community. Through a revitalization of mediating institutions—family, church, neighborhood, voluntary associations— these responsible selves will resurrect the idea of *caritas,* "a form of love that has been crushed between rationalized *eros* and profaned *agape* and superseded by the welfare state." The third form, Bell suggests, will be more diffuse, bound neither to declining nor ascending social groups. It will represent a return to "some mythic and mystical modes of thought" and an incorporation of Eastern themes: the emblem of the Tao, for example. "Its purpose," Bell observes, "is not to discover sequences but to uncover solidarities, not cause and effect but the common root of phenomena in which pictorial images can be substituted for one another as symbolic images that unite the event and the world."

Bell's speculations on the future of religion are interesting. Once the current scene is recalled, however, his prediction of a *return* of the

sacred seems less bold, for the three modes he sketches bring into at
least partial focus the many-sided quest for salvation that formed a
major thrust of American culture in the sixties and seventies. Bell's
hunch about the future seems to have been confirmed in the recent
past.

Consider the description of what he calls moralizing religion—a
category clearly intended to stand for strains of evangelical and neo-
Pentecostal Christianity. Bell does not ignore its numerical strength
in the seventies, nor does he fail to note that this movement may
rather quickly lose some of its momentum. Observing the historical
and social sources of born again Christianity, he stresses the antimodernist cultural and political biases that a majority of its adherents
doubtless share. But he fails utterly to take account of the rich
religious character of the experience of salvation as reported by participants in countless formal and informal sources. Unwilling to attempt
a description of this pattern of faith, Bell virtually ignores it, concentrating instead on the fundamentalist cross-stitch. The admittedly
venal aspects that do come under his purview must stand for the
entire range of spiritual expression. Hence, what are at least arguably
the most spiritually vital religious stirrings of the present get dismissed
as merely the strongest: the largest, the fastest-growing, the best publicized. Denying or at least slighting the religious character of the
Christian revival, Bell is able to locate his projected religious awakening in the future—his redemptive and mythic/mystic modes. To do
otherwise might threaten the clarity of his glum portrayal of the cultural present and recent past.

Bell locates the second form—redemptive religion—almost wholly
in the future. Yet it too was in evidence at least by 1977, when "The
Return of the Sacred?" first appeared. Though it is less spectacular
than the revival of evangelical and neo-Pentecostal Christianity, the
search for a responsible self in communities of caring people roughly
describes the main program of liberal Jewish and Protestant groups in
the sixties and seventies. During these years, reform and conservative
Jews, Methodists, Episcopalians, Congregationalists, and Presbyterians,
for example, might have belonged to organizations less vital than
they once had been or might have become had certain other hopes
been realized. But within these bodies there were decent efforts to
enact versions of Bell's redemptive model. For many members of these
organizations, the quest for salvation was already complicated by an

awareness of the inadequacy of received doctrine and the insufficiencies of present religious institutions. Yet people continued to confront the perennial religious questions, to fashion responsible selves and communities of concern, often without the comforting presence of an anthropomorphic God or even the consolation of an abstract conception of a divine creator with perhaps only restricted capabilities. Moreover, the quest for salvation spilled beyond denominational confines, whose declining significance Bell notes. Many Christians concluded that the distinction between confessing believers and unbelievers had become hollow. They dared to live through Bonhoefferian paradoxes: "The God who lets us live in the world without the working hypothesis of God is the God before whom we stand continually. Before God and with God we live without God. God lets himself be pushed out of the world on to the cross. He is weak and powerless in the world, and that is precisely the way, the only way, in which he is with us and helps us." Christ ministers to us, Bonhoeffer writes, "not by virtue of his omnipotence, but by virtue of his weakness and suffering."[6]

Bell's third religious mode—the mythic/mystic—also has been present in a variety of imported Eastern disciplines, from Zen to Vedanta. Explored on the fringes of American culture from the 1850s on, it enjoyed its widest influence and most attentive press from the middle sixties through the seventies. Yet Bell apparently regards contemporary manifestations of these practices as phony and superficial, at least when they are compared with his elegant projections of what might count as a revival of genuine mythic modes. Throughout his discussion of the future of religion, then, Bell seems determined to deny either the existence or the spiritual validity of the present range of Judeo-Christian and Eastern forms. Working within the framework of nostalgia, he considers the present to be both a pale imitation of the religious past and a moment of spiritual exhaustion that may yet turn out to be a prelude to the sort of religious renewal he imagines. Hence, although it is sentenced to a finite existence, the uninhibited self—selfish, narcissistic, appetitive, morally irresponsible—is given full space in Bell's imagination of American culture in the sixties and seventies.

What Bell obscures through this management of perspectives on the past and future is a sympathetic and rounded version of the present, a steady view of the salvific aspects of the quest for fulfillment as they unfolded in the sixties and seventies. Were he to bring his categories back into the present and allow them greater flexibility and overlap, especially between the spheres of culture and social structure, Bell probably would focus on a mingling of tradition and innovation, old theological premises and newer therapeutic nostrums, plain sense and nonsense. In a word, he would encounter a syncretic mixture (to borrow his own formulation) at once splendid, sordid, and consolingly ordinary. He would see millions of citizens going about ancient tasks, at once sacred and mundane, self-regarding and altruistic: earning a living, caring for children, comforting aging parents, cultivating friendships, exploring the large issues of the human predicament, and even enduring the frequent disappointments of political involvement. The Law may restrain antinomian impulses. But what of the redemptive possibilities of grace? These have no clear place in Bell's conceptions of a culture populated by "unrestrained selves."

The Narcissistic Self:
Christopher Lasch

If Tom Wolfe publicly articulated the theme of selfishness in the seventies with his metaphor of the "me decade," Christopher Lasch, more than any other serious critic on the left, refined the idea in the latter part of the decade. *The Culture of Narcissism: American Life in an Age of Diminishing Expectations* (1978) was the premier work of American social criticism in the late seventies, a time in which cloning, the ultimate form of narcissism, emerged from laboratories into public view. Lasch's book not only received serious and sustained attention in intellectual circles but also attracted considerable attention in the media, having been the focus of several symposia.[7] Lasch was photographed for *People* magazine and interviewed on several national television talk shows. Having become a minor celebrity—a category he professes to detest—Lasch was invited in the summer of 1979 to a dinner at the White House given in honor of several American critics who had diagnosed the cultural malaise of the late seventies to the apparent satisfaction of President Carter and a group of his top aides. Although he claimed that it was all a misunderstanding—that he really is a radical intent on transforming the system rather than tending its sores—Lasch nevertheless accepted the invitation, joining with others such as Bell and Robert Bellah.

This decision to dine with a celebrated adversary would be unremarkable—a pardonable vanity—were it not for Lasch's preoccupation with the idea of cooptation. Every idea, every institution, every person in America, he contends, plays some role in the only show in town: the drama of monopoly capitalism. On this dubious (or at least hopelessly inclusive) assumption, I suppose, such an invitation might as well have been accepted. In any case, Lasch might have felt somewhat at ease, since his own list of enemies matches—indeed exceeds in length—the one circulated during the Nixon years. Lasch has little use for corporate managers, capitalists, bureaucrats, administrators, politicians, entertainers, new Left students, gay men, counterculture types, feminists, lesbians, Christians, psychotherapists, humanistic psychologists, educational radicals, and so forth.

Like *The Triumph of the Therapeutic, The Culture of Narcissism* is essentially a work of the dystopian imagination. It reminds one of Herbert Marcuse's *One-Dimensional Man* in its dominant rhetorical perspective: the material is formed around the idea of a progressive flattening of personality by the hegemonic operations of a ubiquitous, evil system.[8] And it illuminates many of the conservative insights of Rieff through Lasch's own blend of classical Freudian and Marxian assumptions. Attempting to explain the descent into the present and to offer, however fleetingly, a socialist alternative, Lasch produces a sweeping indictment of American culture, politics, and people in the seventies. He highlights what is usually apprehended on the left as "reactionary" and "oppressive"; he also unmasks what many critics on the left interpret as "progressive" and "liberatory" tendencies. Everything fits his mold: freedom is being progressively diminished and psychological gratification only apparently enhanced.

If his method recalls Marcuse's, Lasch's moral tone is reminiscent of a much earlier figure, Swift's Gulliver, who on returning from his extensive travels expresses his disenchantment by retreating to the stables, preferring the company of horses to that of his fellow citizens. Here, I think, is part of the appeal of *The Culture of Narcissism.* The book not only displays Lasch's genuine gifts: his large canvas, his control of historical material, his intriguing insights into cultural phenomena, his frequently elegant style. It also provides a delicious exercise in social criticism, an exercise that confirms the presumed moral superiority of author and reader while providing an occasion to practice the very vices they condemn. Existing as it does within a closed Marcusean circle, Lasch's work almost seems calculated to outrage the unconvinced, but it also should persuade sympathetic readers of the futility of any collective action short of an unlikely socialist revolution. Implicitly endorsing political quiescence, Lasch struck a responsive chord, giving many readers the grim news they apparently wished to hear, if not about themselves (though perhaps this too), then about their fellow citizens. The enhanced value of grim news seems to me as much a function of increased freedom as of real (or fancied) powerlessness. In a pluralistic culture marked by rising and diverse personal expectations, negative judgments about large sectors of society serve some of the stabilizing, consoling purposes formerly assigned to positive images of unity and progress.

Lasch's reading of American civilization at the end of the seventies is refracted through a double optic of an idealized past and an unlikely future. Through these lenses, the present comes to seem the worst of all possible worlds, a manifestation of the broken promises of the bourgeois (and even prebourgeois) past and of the unredeemed promise of socialism. For Lasch, contemporary America represents a culmination of the worst features of the past, a realization of its least salutary potentialities. America continues the pattern of exploitative relations in the centralized work place, mixing brutal features with more subtle, even pleasant therapeutic modes of control. And it all but completes the pattern of domination of formerly decentralized spheres beyond work: the family, leisure, education, personal relationships, and, in the end, persons. In the course of the transition from competitive to monopoly capitalism that began about a century ago, a growing institutional apparatus has deprived individuals of any enclave in which authentic, admirable traits of character can be formed. There are, Lasch insists, no more havens in the heartless capitalist world. Even the family has been virtually destroyed, in large part by well-intentioned reformers, and its functions have been progressively taken over by schools, peer groups, advertisers, therapists, and a bevy of human-relations experts. As a consequence, individuals have become playthings of the larger forces of the system.

Invading the regions of personality, monopoly capitalism produces powerless, dependent individuals who lack the strength of character to oppose their own often quite subtle enslavement. Lasch's vision of America at the end of the seventies is thoroughly Hobbesian. It is a nation whose communitarian impulses remain unrealized and whose once largely admirable tradition of individualism has degenerated into sheer narcissism. Lasch sets out to describe "a way of life that is dying—the culture of competitive individualism, which in its decadence has carried the logic of individualism to the extreme of a war of all against all, the pursuit of happiness to the dead end of a narcissistic preoccupation with the self."[9] Genuine fulfillment is impossible in such a jungle: the aims of life are reduced to a narcissistic preoccupation with survival. "People no longer dream of overcoming difficulties, but merely of surviving them," Lasch declares, as if the idea of survival were a recent or unworthy historical invention. The ideals of self-discipline and disinterested love of others did not work their way from the bourgeois family through lower spheres of the social order, as genteel reformers had hoped. Instead, according to Lasch, the anarchic jumble of the interior and exterior ways of life in the lower classes has spread upward to the now defenseless regions of the middle and upper middle classes (the old rich have ceased to matter).

Despite a reservation here and there, Lasch apparently believes that his Hobbesian metaphor conveys the essential truth about American culture and American life in the late seventies. He skillfully weaves the many conspicuous examples of narcissistic personalities into his narrative: professional athletes, corporate executives, celebrities, politicians, certain new Left megalomaniacs, and counterculture gurus. Although they might exert greater cultural influence than their numbers suggest, these representative figures, as Lasch recognizes, can do no more than embroider his ambitious hypothesis. He rather locates the key to his judgment of America in the clinical evidence of rising narcissistic disorders.

The most illuminating chapter of *The Culture of Narcissism,* "The Narcissistic Personality of Our Time," gives a central variant of the morally vague and multivalent idea of selfishness a precise etiology and a specific historical location. Narcissism, Lasch suggests, is the dominant personality type of advanced capitalist society. Relying on the work of Melanie Klein, Otto Kernberg, and Heinz Kohut, as well as on a growing body of clinical literature, Lasch provides an interesting summary of a shift in dominant pathologies—a modulation from Freudian symptom neuroses to the more recent profusion of character disorders that typify victims of secondary or pathological narcissism.[10] Vacillating between grandiose conceptions of his or her talents and self-contempt, the narcissistic personality cannot find genuine fulfillment. Salvation eludes narcissists, for they suffer from a syndrome in which "love rejected turns back to the self as hatred." "Plagued not by guilt but by anxiety," the new narcissist "seeks not to inflict his own certainties on others but to find a meaning in life."

Taking note of the growing number of cases of such personality disorders over the past several decades, Lasch goes on to assert that the "character traits associated with pathological narcissism" appear in less extreme form "in the everyday life of our age: dependence on the vicarious warmth provided by others combined with a fear of dependence, a sense of inner emptiness, boundless repressed rage, and unsatisfied oral cravings." Critics, he suggests, have been reluctant to pursue the social implications of the main marks of this personality type or to explore its secondary characteristics: "pseudo self-insight, calculating seductiveness, nervous, self-deprecating humor." Lasch sets out to remedy this apparent failure. "Every age," he asserts, "develops its own peculiar forms of pathology, which express in exaggerated form its underlying character structure." There is, then, "a continuum between pathology and normality." Having established the growth, if not the dominance, of pathological narcissism, Lasch proceeds to illuminate all (or nearly all) of American culture as more or less narcissistic. This key opens all doors: it permits Lasch privileged insight into American minds and offers a way to explain without recourse to mere evidence why *they* routinely neglect *his* form of salvation.

In his assessment of American culture during the sixties and seventies, Lasch summarily dismisses the primary manifestations of the quest for salvation: most of the Movement, all of what passes for religion, and all of the expressly therapeutic modes of self-fulfillment. Lasch believes that the new Left made some important contributions to political understanding in the middle sixties, in particular by clarifying the ways in which bureaucratic society marginalizes and trivializes political conflict. But he concludes that this small, theoretically savvy, and politically vital facet of the Movement was overwhelmed by the therapeutic sensibility that pervaded the counterculture and ultimately invaded the new Left itself. Moreover, because Lasch assumes that reforms usually make things worse, he remains unmoved by the political victories facilitated in part by the various foci of protest, from civil rights to gay rights. The Movement, then, turns out to have been a misguided search for self-fulfillment, since the quest for salvation degenerated into narcissism and the pursuit of social justice yielded mere reform.

Lasch dismisses the religious facets of the search for fulfillment during the sixties and seventies on grounds similar to those used by Rieff. The persistence and revival of evangelical Christianity is, for Lasch, apparently beneath sustained discussion. Only certain classical, essentially ascetic conceptions of salvation qualify as genuinely religious. And since Lasch finds scant evidence of a willingness to subordinate the self to the purposes and disciplines of a larger community either among Christians or among adherents of the human-potential movement, he judges them all as areligious or irreligious. Whether focused on life after death or upon a future utopian community, ascetic patterns of Christian salvation are the only ones that count—or rather the only ones that used to count. The sole alternative to this moribund model is, for Lasch, its opposite: intense preoccupation with the self, indifference to the past, despair over the future, and desire for survival rather than transcendence. In Lasch's mode of caricature, one is either a Cotton Mather or a revolutionary Anabaptist—or one cannot be counted as seriously religious at all. None of the possibilities between these extremes matters. None of the syntheses of hope for the future and expectations of more abundant life in the present qualifies as a legitimate pattern of salvation.

Lasch's surreal presentation of American culture makes everything fit the dimensions of the therapeutic sensibility. Therapy, not religion, becomes the opiate of the people in this jeremiad. But therapy, according to Lasch, is an "anti-religion," the narcotic of a society "which has no future and therefore gives no thought to anything beyond its immediate needs." The therapeutic outlook displaces religion "as the organizing framework of American culture" and "threatens to displace politics as well, the last refuge of ideology." Recommended in the twenties and thirties by psychologists, educational reformers, and marriage counselors as a means of liberating personality, and adopted by many new-Leftists and an ever larger number of counterculture enthusiasts as a mode of liberatory opposition in the sixties and seventies, the therapeutic sensibility is finally a deceptive illusion. "The ideology of personal growth, superficially optimistic, radiates a profound despair and resignation. It is the faith of those without faith."

Although Lasch distorts parts of American culture and ignores much of the rest, he is not simply out of touch. Indeed, *The Culture of Narcissism* presents powerful if nearly always exaggerated characterizations of the worst features of contemporary culture. Who has not encountered too many walking examples of the " 'liberated' personality of our time, with his charm, his pseudo-awareness of his own condition, his promiscuous pansexuality, his fascination with oral sex, his fear of the castrating mother (Mrs. Portnoy), his hypochondria, his protective shallowness, his avoidance of dependence, his inability to mourn, his dread of old age and death"? Who, in fact, does not catch unnerving glimpses of this figure (or its female variant) in his or her own mirror? Still, Lasch has badly confused the vices of the times with the virtues, the peculiar excesses with the norms. Using his logic, one would be compelled to judge the Victorian era of American capitalism by its Freudian excesses: hysteria and obsessional neuroses, "acquisitiveness," "fanatical devotion to work," "repression of sexuality." These excesses were there, of course, but they constituted distortions of a personality type whose moderate incarnations were, as Lasch himself insists, admirable in many respects.

Lasch seems to have mistaken an important part for the whole. Pathological narcissism may be on the rise. But therapists, I am told, still encounter a fair share of patients plagued by old-fashioned guilt. Both extremes persist, though, as Lasch argues, pathological narcissism seems to be the recently fashionable vice. What Lasch refuses to see, or at least fails to report, however, are the endless combinations between these polarities, the variegated patterns of normality that still continue to define American life. No one, for example, could infer from Lasch's characterization of contemporary American culture the persistence and even growth of the idea of service. Between 1960 and 1980, for example, Americans increased their voluntary contributions to religious, educational, civic, cultural, and charitable causes from $9.4 to $43.3 billion annually, far more by any measurable standard than comparable Western European nations. By 1974, despite the growing numbers of women in the work force, the number of individuals who participated in volunteer work had reached nearly thirty-seven million, more than one-fifth of the population over age fourteen. By 1981, more than forty million adults volunteered for some charitable or social-service activity. And more than sixty-five million people (or 50 percent of Americans over age fourteen) volunteered at least occasionally.[11] Nor could a reader infer from Lasch's text the sacrifices (often heroic ones) that millions of people still make in behalf of their children, their mates, their friends, and, as they approach middle age, their own aging parents.

Nearly every hopeful facet of American culture and politics succumbs to Lasch's dialectical logic. Highlighting the ugly features, he exposes everything else as illusion, a subtle appearance concealing evil. For example, even though the increasingly voluntary conditions surrounding marriage in the sixties and seventies may strike some observers as welcome in many respects, Lasch remains undeceived: "This appearance," he warns, "is an illusion," for "the cult of intimacy conceals a growing despair of finding it." Or consider this *ex cathedra* pronouncement: "Americans have not really become more sociable and cooperative, as the theorists of other-direction and conformity would like us to believe; they have merely become more adept at exploiting the conventions of interpersonal relations for their own benefit." How does Lasch know all this? He simply assumes (correctly) that pathological narcissists are incapable of genuine love, and then, in a leap of faith that should impress even the most gullible evangelical, infers the motives, feelings, and beliefs of others by invoking the notion of a continuum of pathology and normality.

This dubious pattern of psychological inference and cultural projection unfolds under Lasch's theoretical umbrella—his functional Marxism, which is mentioned only fleetingly, perhaps in deference to his larger audience. Still, he does make Marxian noises at certain points in the text, presumably to account for the illusory character of all contemporary forms of progress. Discussing the apparently fruitful interplay between individuals and various institutions of modern American society, Lasch concludes that "what appears to social scientists as a seamless web of 'interdependence' represents in fact the dependence of the individual on the organization, the citizen on the state, the worker on the manager, and the parent on the 'helping professions.'" Thus, whatever reforms have been sought and implemented in this century—even those apparently at odds with the class interests of capitalists—become, for Lasch, part of the design of the whole system. "The therapeutic ethic," Lasch observes, "does not serve the class interest of professionals alone, as Daniel P. Moynihan and others have argued: it serves the interests of monopoly capitalism as a whole."

There is only one way out, one path to salvation: Lasch's shadowy socialism. "After the political turmoil of the sixties," he asserts, "Americans have retreated to purely personal preoccupations. Having no hope of improving their lives in any of the ways that matter, people have convinced themselves that what matters is psychic self-improvement." Lasch, of course, professes to know what counts: his own curiously concealed alternative of socialism. "The will to build a better society," he concedes, "survives, along with traditions of localism, self-help, and community action that only need the vision of a new society, a decent society, to give them new vigor." This condescending view of Americans, including those on the left, to which Lasch claims some allegiance, allows him to profess a modicum of hope. But his pale vision of the future—at least as it is embodied in *The Culture of Narcissism*—seems little more than a rhetorical ploy, a means of dismissing all current efforts to achieve salvation and social justice.

Lasch repeatedly declares that Americans live in a culture without a future. It is rather his own essentially dystopian vision that lacks this dimension. Condemning every expression of the quest for self-fulfillment, Lasch leaves no space for a cultural or social future, no space even for his socialist values to ripen into a majoritarian vision. Positing a virtual blockage of history, he focuses primarily on the interplay between an idealized past and the fallen present. Thus even Lasch's radical pretensions serve to place him in the dominant critical framework of the late seventies: the essentially conservative framework of nostalgia. Lasch exhibits an admirable respect for the past, regarding it "as a political and psychological treasury from which we draw the reserves (not necessarily in the form of 'lessons') that we need to cope with the future." Surely there can be no quarrel with this sentiment. Moreover, like other critics who lament the decline of one orthodoxy or another—Christian, Marxist, Freudian, bourgeois-democratic— Lasch indicts his version of present American realities in terms of past hopes and values.

He takes a further step, asserting that "the belief that in some ways the past was a happier time by no means rests on a sentimental illusion; nor does it lead to a backward-looking, reactionary paralysis of the political will." It probably is true that "the past was a happier time" in a variety of ways. It surely was for certain elite groups. As Fred Hirsch has shown in his excellent study *Social Limits to Growth* (1976), the present marks a decline of a range of possibilities once reserved for small groups of well-to-do citizens. The sheer number of people and the complexity of large institutions undermines nineteenth-century notions of personal freedom, which was defined negatively as ample physical and mental space. Our lives now are more crowded—physically and psychically—than they were even twenty years ago. They are more interrelated, more affected by public issues and large institutions. We live at a much faster pace. Ironically, the culture of consumption has robbed even time of its rich, subjective dimensions: consumers do not have time to take time. Even when they buy time, it comes in discrete particles made ever smaller by the felt need to get on with something else—to produce and consume more. In a word, the bourgeois ideal of leisurely, gracious living has neither survived well among the very privileged nor spread throughout society.

Many people have had to seek smaller living quarters, for example, and the costs of home ownership had grown burdensome even to those fortunate enough to have raised a down payment before mortgage rates ascended to double-digit levels in the late seventies. (Even so, the proportion of housing units that were owner occupied reached 65.2 percent in 1978, up from 62.9 percent in 1970 and 61.9 percent in 1960.[12]) Real food was becoming a luxury—a memory for some, an unimagined possibility for others. At the end of the seventies, millions of Americans had never savored a vine-ripened fruit or vegetable, never tasted a slice of whole-grain bread (with crumbs), never enjoyed butter churned from raw cream, never eaten meat, fish, or fowl not made hazardous and often tasteless by pollutants, hormones, and chemical preservatives. Even citizens lucky enough to have escaped the plagues of foul air, urban congestion, grating noise, and street crime in their larger environments encountered new problems in the household. For everyone, it seemed, claimed to need a "wife," someone to perform a smorgasbord of chores from caring for children, cooking, washing, cleaning, and gardening to managing the mounting administrative and logistical trivia of personal life: shopping, paying bills, arranging insurance, confirming and cancelling appointments.

In the sixties and seventies, as the very rich continued to trim their household staffs, the servant problem also extended to middle- and working-class households: fewer people were willing to play the part of housewife with even contrived cheerfulness.[13] Women entered the work force in unprecedented numbers, leaving less time for work in the home. And though they continued to perform more than their share of useful labor (paid and unpaid), many women did so with justifiable and growing resentment. It is true that as earlier sources of paid domestic labor—principally performed by black women—diminished, new pools of immigrant labor became available, mainly on the coasts and along the southern rim of the country. Yet the drawbacks to hired help remained formidable. Domestic laborers, though poorly paid, were expensive, beyond the fiscal reach even of most two-income families. The presence of some two million such workers at the end of the seventies evoked guilt in some and embarrassment in others reared to accept certain services only from mothers and wives.

This list of lamentable changes that have occurred over the past century could be extended and its causes debated. Much of the decline in the quality of life that has impeded cultivation of fulfilled selves seems to be an inescapable social consequence of growth. "Beyond some point that has long ago been surpassed in crowded industrial societies," Hirsch observes, "conditions of use tend to deteriorate as use becomes more widespread." Hence "what each of us can achieve, all cannot."[14] Part of the decline, as Lasch contends, can be traced to the present shapes of the specific institutions of capitalist society, though in the absence of a popular alternative mode of social organization such lamentations lose a good deal of their appeal. But much of the so-called decline is only apparent, an expression of nostalgia that results in part from egalitarian pressures: imaginative recreations of the past are abundant, available to everyone. It should be apparent, however, that the past was on the whole *not* a more fulfilling time—and certainly not a more just time—for most Americans: for members of racial and ethnic minorities, for women, for children, for working people, for all but the upper layers of the middle class—indeed, for a decisive majority of citizens. Many of the regrettable changes, therefore, are side effects of the democratization of personhood, consequences of rising expectations and rising satisfactions among a growing number of citizens in all social categories.

Unlike some philosophical conservatives, Lasch does not seem to wish for a restoration of past social arrangements. He manifests a more subtle disappointment, a regret that the democratization of personhood has not resulted in sufficient cultivation of the kind of self he admires: the morally responsible, rational, well-educated, post-Christian man who fronts the world stoically, with Freudian courage and radical derring-do. (Lasch's position on women seems less clear: "Women today," he claims, in one of those defective sentences any writer should want to recall, "ask for two things in their relations with men: sexual satisfaction and tenderness.") What Lasch, along with many other critics and academics actually laments is the failure of the liberally educated man to become the norm. In a chapter on education, he declares that "the democratization of education has accomplished little . . . It has neither improved popular understanding of modern society, raised the quality of popular culture, nor reduced the gap between wealth and poverty, which remains as wide as ever." Failing to redeem its liberal promise, education "has contributed to the decline of critical thought and the erosion of intellectual standards, forcing us to consider the possibility that mass education, as conservatives have argued all along, is intrinsically incompatible with the maintenance of educational quality."

Lasch's critique of education, especially his treatment of educational radicals, is plausible and frequently trenchant, though each of the assertions I have quoted seems at least debatable. What he cannot acknowledge without subverting his main assumptions is this: during the sixties and seventies the sort of education that was designed to cultivate his implied model of the realized self did survive. There surely was an increase in the absolute numbers of such people in American colleges and universities, in spite of their relative decline as a percentage of campus populations. Moreover, the professoriat grew dramatically, and despite a certain narrowness graduate training improved. The rapid growth of the professoriat and the even more rapid growth in the number of students may help to explain why so many people found teaching—especially the teaching of undergraduates—a particularly burdensome activity in the sixties and an odious chore in the seventies. The supply of highly trained faculty members exceeded by far the number of able—and willing—students, particularly in the humanities and the social sciences.

As a consequence of improved training, research of all kinds registered impressive gains. Although the vast explosion predictably yielded an unprecedented amount of trivia, it also contained a body of research, scholarship, and criticism unequaled anywhere in size, variety, and sophistication. (Lasch's own field, history, constitutes a prime example.) All of this, of course, occurred in a context that served to disguise the persistence of excellence: a system of higher education that grew at an unprecedented rate—from 3.2 million students in 1960 to 7.1 million by 1970 and to more than 11 million by the end of the seventies (an increase of 35 percent for the decade). Significant increases in enrollment testified to the democratization of personhood: they included a substantial number of members of minority groups, working-class people, students beyond the eighteen-to-twenty-four age range, and women (who by the end of the seventies comprised slightly more than half the total number of students in American colleges and universities). Although many of the new arrivals pursued traditional modes of liberal study, a larger number of all students sought a variety of ends outside the customary boundaries of liberal learning: preparation for work, retraining for second careers, a transition to adulthood, self-discovery, and so on.[15]

At the end of the seventies, higher education (not to mention elementary and secondary education, where matters were considerably worse) received criticism from all quarters, much of it richly deserved. Lasch's assumptions, however, require him to condemn the whole enterprise on the basis of selected criteria appropriate to the one important part whose persistence he fails to acknowledge. Unable to view newer developments in postsecondary education with critical balance, he can only satirize them. Taking Donald Barthelme's parody *Snow White* (1967) as a closing text, Lasch concludes that the heroine is "a typical victim of mass culture, the culture of commodities and consumerism with its suggestive message that experiences formerly reserved for those of high birth, deep understanding, or much practical acquaintance of life can be enjoyed by all without effort, on purchase of the appropriate commodity" (in this case, a smorgasbord of unrelated courses at "Beaver College"). This example seals the case for Lasch. In a typically humorless aside, he notes that "Barthelme's parody of higher learning in *Snow White*—like all parody in an age of absurdities—so closely resembles reality as to become unrecognizable as parody."

Easy acquisition of the traits of character and presumed satisfactions once reserved for those of superior birth, high intelligence, and *savoir faire:* these, Lasch correctly observes, cannot simply be had for the asking. Although advertisers and purveyors of popular culture do play on these desires and often cheapen them, as Lasch suggests, the wishes themselves ought not be dismissed so cavalierly. The wish for fulfillment—along with many other, more purposeful modes of pursuing it—is one important expression of the popularization and democratization of the quest. Like so many other social critics, however, Lasch regrets the cultural implications of the quest. Too few people have chosen the only sort of fulfillment that matters to him: cultivation of a disciplined self and pursuit of his version of a decent society. Lasch's functional Marxist assumptions permit him to dismiss the democratic temper of the quest, since most of what ordinary people hope (and have achieved) only reinforces a rotten social order. Whereas a Tory radical like Lasch finds such a social theory necessary, a thoroughly conservative critic like Rieff does not: tensions between elitist and democratic values present no special difficulties for him. Americans, he simply concludes, have made a cultural revolution merely for "greater amplitude and richness of living itself," an un-heroic and apparently unworthy aim. It is, for Rieff, a predictably corrupt response of the lower orders and the ignorant middle echelons to their enhanced freedom.

Painful tensions between elitist cultural values and the results of democratic participation admit no easy resolution. One of the main tasks of social and cultural critics is to insist on the importance of values, customs, and traditions that are frequently at odds with the drift of a consumer society. Critics, moreover, ought to convey a sense of this difficulty. Otherwise they run the high risk of misperceiving the search for self-fulfillment and judging it too narrowly on criteria suitable perhaps for some facets of the quest but not for others, and certainly not for the whole of it. Thus conservative critics as well as those on the left tended to slight the salvific aspects of the search for fulfillment in the sixties and seventies. Most critics on the left treated the Movement more generously than Lasch manages to do (though often not as shrewdly). A few conservatives, such as Robert Nisbet, were rather less harsh on the Christian revival than most. And nearly everyone who discussed therapeutic facets of the quest came to bleak conclusions.

In the end, most critics were dissatisfied with the state of American civilization at the end of the seventies, often with good reason. Measured by past criteria—which might have fit certain privileged groups—the present did appear to be increasingly selfish and narcissistic, even anarchic. The lower orders increasingly refused to accept their place. They no longer, as Lasch puts it with characteristic recklessness, experience "oppression as guilt. Instead, they internalize a grandiose idea of the opportunities open to all, together with an inflated opinion of their own capacities." Lamenting a decline of authority, a large percentage of serious critics refused to endorse the mixed cultural consequences of the democratization of personhood during the sixties and seventies. But it was not simply, or even primarily, a cultural decline that critics were witnessing. It was rather a failure of certain expectations amid a series of changes that, while they were by no means wholly admirable, did express the relatively free choices of millions of citizens formerly denied such luxuries.

On Selfishness as a Metaphor of Culture

Why was the perennial theme of selfishness (and narcissism) so eagerly advanced and so widely accepted as the central metaphor for American culture and society in the seventies? Why did so many critics conclude that the venerable American practice of making and remaking the self had grown beyond acceptable moral limits during these years? In retrospect, the notion of selfishness seems almost uniquely suited to American circumstances in the sixties and seventies: a fluid, syncretic culture marked by individualism, affluence, and pluralism. A more or less open-ended idea, selfishness can serve as a convenient way of interpreting the attitudes and behavior of others. It works neatly as what Richard Weaver terms a "'tyrannizing' image or vision," though in the seventies it did so ironically, in ways perhaps not intended by Weaver.[16] Rather than lending unity to American culture, the metaphor of selfishness only served to unify *perceptions* of American culture at a high (and not very useful) level of abstraction. It offered a coherent way of representing what by earlier standards could only be judged a fragmented culture and a divided society.

A household word—and a useful one at that—"selfishness" came to stand for vague suspicions about oneself and certain knowledge of the motives, attitudes, and behavior of other individuals and other groups. Of course, the traditional project of understanding selfishness was well advanced by the sixties. Its meanings, causes, extent, social effects, and cultural significance had been explored pretty thoroughly by theologians, ethicists, and social theorists in the Western tradition, beginning with Plato and Aristotle. As the concept of selfishness gathered metaphorical energy in the sixties and seventies, however, it evoked a variety of new critiques, many of them able ones in spite of the narrowing possibilities for originality. Although the tyrannizing cultural vision of selfishness gained ground, extensive discussions of this phenomenon produced little agreement on particulars. In what follows, I shall explore the metaphor of selfishness and suggest why it finally fails to fit American society and culture of the sixties and seventies.

To begin, let me propose several reasons why so many critics—historians, theologians, journalists—promoted or at least endorsed some version or other of the inapt metaphor of the "me decade." First, selfishness is one obvious expression of the quest for fulfillment: it is its typical excess and characteristic vice. In fact, a rise in the incidence of selfishness, actual and alleged, can be deduced from a description of the principal terms of the quest—the many-sided search for individual salvation and a piece of social justice. In a syncretic and pluralistic culture, the search for fulfillment lacks firm moral and social boundaries. The lines between assertive and aggressive behavior blur. And the rush of claims in behalf of selves for autonomy, for space, for power, and for privilege strikes others as unseemly. Moreover, in the absence of authoritative standards and well-defined social roles, certain individuals can and do push their search to extremes. At these extremes, their behavior appears selfish in any definition of this term. Here the glare of publicity is most intense. In these circumstances the idea of selfishness as a cultural metaphor gathers momentum and comes to serve as a shorthand way of indicting the entire quest.

Second, the idea of selfishness fits the framework of nostalgia. It is a way of characterizing a present that fails to conform in any obvious way to standards and expectations fashioned in the past. When once-vital ideological perspectives show signs of wear, a culture may seem to be governed by unacceptable patterns of moral behavior or to be characterized by a sort of moral anarchy. The idea of selfishness covers both possibilities. The culture of selfishness or a society composed of selfish individuals may appear to be the result of a withering away of bourgeois ideology: a perverted liberalism, a failed socialism, a violated conservatism. Or it may appear to be largely the consequence of a lapsed Christianity: "What the culture critic calls 'narcissism' and 'desacralization,'" a group of Roman Catholic and Protestant scholars concluded at the end of the seventies, "we see as a fist shaken in the face of God."[17] Hence the Hobbesian metaphor, which gained currency among critics in the seventies, was not, I think, merely a response to the onset of relative economic scarcity and a growing confusion of social roles. It was also a response—often angry, usually disappointed—to the apparent decline of bourgeois standards, the diffusion of the best energy of the Movement, and the decreasing authority of left-liberal cultural and political perspectives. In a larger sense, the metaphor of selfishness was a shorthand indictment of the project of the Enlightenment and its aftermath.

In the seventies, I have argued, the quest shifted direction somewhat, or rather added new cultural and political thrusts. It began to affect sectors of society and ideological configurations to which intellectuals, especially those on the left, were either largely indifferent or openly hostile. At the same time, the main personal terms of the quest became increasingly detached from ideological contexts that stressed social and communal dimensions acceptable to critics on the left (and to some philosophical conservatives as well). In these circumstances, the essentially individualistic thread of the quest was displayed more prominently, often without benefit of social embroidery. And individuals who in massive numbers refused to participate in one or another ideological project were judged selfish by everyone from the Weatherpeople to President Jimmy Carter.

The argument over the alleged rise of selfishness in the seventies resists any settlement satisfactory to all parties, if only because we do not know the extent of this phenomenon or its effects on politics and culture. Though they are subject to crude empirical treatment, these matters do not submit to empirical resolution, for both the extent and consequences of so-called selfishness are largely functions of perceptions of its meanings. What counts as selfish thought and behavior? In what circumstances is it legitimate or salutary for individuals or communities? A definition of "selfishness" thus seems a necessary place to begin. This notion, after all, is a rather straightforward element of ordinary discourse. Selfish persons tend to exhibit an excessive concern—often a pathological preoccupation—with their own perceived interests: their material well-being, their comfort and safety, their status, reputation, or image, their activities, their inner lives. And they display a systematic disregard for the expressed concerns and interests of others.

To recall an outmoded concept, selfish people are unable to overcome original sin. Their preoccupation with the claims of the self cannot withstand an objective appraisal of their worth in any sphere—economic, political, social, psychological and personal, cultural and spiritual. Nor can their attitudes and behavior withstand the scrutiny of others. Moreover, selfish people are in the strictest sense unbalanced, unable as a rule to gauge even their own interests. As Walter Lippmann observed, self-interest "is precisely what no man is certain to know, and what few men can possibly know if they consult only their own impulses."[18] In their internal makeup, selfish people tend to stress one part—frequently the appetitive—to the virtual exclusion of others. In their stance toward the world, they may be similarly disoriented, concerned only with the self and its immediate environment. But they need not confine themselves to such narrow scopes: many public and even public-spirited people exhibit the marks of selfishness and narcissism. Selfish people often show a contempt for authority, custom, and tradition. They also may cling to these when it suits their individualistic purposes. Selfishness thus can be displayed by all types of people in all echelons of society.

We all know in a general way what "selfishness" means. And we usually feel able to identify selfish individuals. Yet it is obvious that formal definitions quickly break down. For in the course of explaining judgments of selfish persons and, even more, of selfish cultures, a network of social ideas, attitudes, and perspectives comes into play. For one thing, specifications of the concept rest upon social definitions of the self. Rieff's psychological man, for example, is thoroughly selfish when compared to the spare, disciplined self that serves as his implied ideal in *The Triumph of the Therapeutic*. For another, the concept of selfishness raises the issue of social justice. Judgments of selfishness frequently turn on whether a citizen ignores a just balance between rights and duties, privileges and responsibilities, entitlements and obligations. Similarly, judgments of a culture of selfishness may rest on perceptions of a social system that enforces unjust cultural definitions or subverts just conceptions of social justice in subtle ways. In such circumstances, selfish behavior on the part of certain persons

and groups may be encouraged, merely tolerated, or even unnoticed—
screened out by prevailing categories of discourse.

It is not only in their role as private citizens that Americans were
counted as selfish in the seventies. The "me decade" referred above
all to the sphere of culture and personality, where the measure of
generosity, of caring for others, required for an individual (and a
culture) to be judged not selfish acquired a seemingly endless set
of complications. In the context of the quest for personal fulfillment,
as greater attention was paid to the claims of an increasing number of
selves, the issue of selfishness became central. When, for example, the
rights and privileges of everyone in a nuclear family expanded, their
corresponding obligations passed into a state of flux. Every member
was liable to the charge of selfishness: the father who wished to change
careers in his forties, or simply to maintain household arrangements as
they were; the mother who wished to resume an interrupted education;
the parents who wished to spend more of their young lives as free persons; the children who wished to be seen, heard, and loved. In such circumstances, the grounds of selfishness multiplied, though their validity
and application became ever more problematic.

Although everyone managed to orchestrate a defense, it was apt to
be dismissed as insufficient by its intended audience. Everyone felt
free to speak, but no one had compelling reasons to listen. For there
was no authoritative way, or what amounts to the same thing, there
were too many plausible ways, to tell what a family member (or a
worker or a friend) needed to do in order to gain immunity from
frequent charges of selfishness. Nor was there an accepted way to
determine how many instances of selfishness of what sort justified
saddling a person with a reputation for self-centeredness. Immunity
from the judgment of selfishness was about the best one could hope
for, since the notion of "unselfishness" proved even more elusive in a
culture increasingly tinged with cynicism about the motives and
behavior of others. Unselfish acts were common enough. But few people gained a solid reputation for unselfishness. Heroes, saints, fools,
martyrs (or wealthy professional athletes prone to granting postgame
interviews): the unselfish occupied small niches in the pantheon of
American culture. And they remained suspect, especially the athletes.
The unselfish were people who gave up too much or who had so
much that their giving seemed not to count as sacrifice. Or, like
Mother Theresa, who may after all conceal boundless pride behind

that chiseled, impassive Yugoslavian face, they lived by rules that contravened ordinary notions of giving and receiving.

Thus conceptions of personal and cultural selfishness are elastic. Their significance and their relevance to particular situations presuppose an understanding of the nature and limits of the self, the demands of social justice, the requirements of civil society (family, friendship, service), and the imperatives of culture (moral temper and religious conviction). Because these understandings vary, the concept of personal and cultural selfishness, as I shall suggest in the next chapter, raised the issue of authority, or rather suggested a convenient way to illuminate its decline: the absence, in this case, of a clear and widely accepted ethic of selfishness and unselfishness. Whatever other causes might have been responsible for this phenomenon, the decline of authority was at least intensified both by the selfishness and the self-assertiveness of all but the most privileged individuals. And in the sixties and seventies even the most privileged often showed little concern for authority.

This brief tour of the complications of the idea of selfishness cannot settle the question of whether American civilization in the seventies was so extraordinarily self-absorbed as to merit the designation the "me decade." But it does permit me to proceed with a sense of the difficulties and implications of the notion of selfishness. One thing at least seems clear: the idea of America as a culture of selfishness constitutes an alternative way of apprehending what I have described as the quest for fulfillment. But the idea of selfishness and the idea of the quest are not equally accurate or equally useful generalizations. The period of the sixties and seventies, I have argued, was a time of transition marked by a diffusion of enlarged desires for fulfillment, by significant advances in the democratization of personhood, and by subjective claims of success reported by millions of Americans. In considering this quest, it is hardly surprising to discover that individuals tend to lavish attention on their selves. Nor does it seem odd that extreme manifestations of selfishness and narcissism arise, or at least receive prominent notice, and that ever larger numbers of citizens exhibit a growing indifference to various modes of authority. Though they are plausible to a degree, characterizations of America as a selfish culture typically confuse excesses with norms, byproducts with central and on the whole salutary outcomes of the quest. When the quest is viewed unsympathetically and, in comparative historical terms, unfairly, judgments of selfishness are apt to be applied indiscriminately to the entire search: to its aims, its successes, and its excesses.

Let me illustrate this tendency by comparing the ideal and representative selves advanced by Rieff, Bell, and Lasch. If the exemplary personae fashioned by these critics could gather for an evening, they probably would recognize one another easily—if not as comrades in intellectual arms, at least as serious figures with roughly similar interests who speak mutually comprehensible dialects of the same ethical language. And doubtless they would bear more than a passing resemblance to their creators. Still, their evening together might easily turn into a social disaster. Differences of temperament would soon become apparent: Rieff's persona is haughty; Bell's is more congenial, mixing amiable and judgmental dispositions; Lasch's is dour, doggedly humorless. All three, however, propose as a norm a middle-aged, white male who is highly educated, mature, realistic, sexually restrained, and morally sensitive. Although their composite self realizes its own possibilities largely through a careful crafting of character, it cannot thrive on its own. The admirable self must submit to the discipline of authoritative standards as well as to the purposes of some community or other.

Were it considered possible in contemporary circumstances, Rieff's implied self might be Christian in some high Anglican sense, Bell's might find its way back to some mode of Jewish orthodoxy, and Lasch's post-Judeo-Christian self might embrace the secular faith of socialism. To survive honorably in a venal culture, however, all three personae might be willing to funnel the religious yearnings of their implied selves through a Freudian moral prism. As Rieff puts it, "a tolerance of ambiguities is the key to what Freud considered the most difficult of all personal accomplishments: a genuinely stable character in an unstable time."

But Rieff, Lasch, and even Bell express reservations about the sufficiency of bourgeois character. They endorse it with varying degrees of reluctance, allowing their religious (or quasi-religious) convictions to persist in the only way they believe possible: in ironic counterpoint to a stoic world of more restricted possibilities. Though each of them proposes that the self be bound to a higher authority to achieve fulfillment, none goes so far as to recommend losing oneself in order to find it. None of them, this is to say, celebrates anxiety as the preferred medium for understanding and enacting the self. According to Kierkegaard, Ernest Becker writes, "the school of anxiety leads to possibility *only by destroying* the vital lie of character. It seems like the ultimate self-defeat, the one thing that one should not do, because then one will have truly nothing left. But rest assured, says Kierkegaard, 'the direction is quite normal . . . the self must be broken in order to become a self . . .'"[19]

However much they might disagree over ways of binding the self to moral and religious norms, these personae probably would close ranks as they compared their versions of more typical selves of American culture in the sixties and seventies. If they differed over proper degrees of *losing* the self in process of fulfillment, they would come together on the dangers of *loosing* the self. Rieff, Bell, and Lasch surely would not represent their ideal selves as immune to charges of systematic selfishness. Such selves are capable of selfishness. But they possess sufficient moral resources to resist succumbing to selfishness as a typical response and sufficient taste to refrain from celebrating it. The ideal self, then, is a foil for the critics' "selfish" types: Rieff's therapeutic personality, Bell's boundaryless self, Lasch's narcissistic personality. All of these allegedly representative types are by their very nature selfish, congenitally unable to define or observe received moral imperatives. Ignorant despite years of schooling, immature, nihilistic, hedonistic, appetitive, sexually unrestrained, incapable of commitment to others or to causes beyond the self, the antinomian self is unable to find salvation and uninterested in advancing social justice.

Rieff, Bell, and Lasch thus deal in binary oppositions between a vanishing breed of moral selves and the allegedly deficient selves of contemporary American life. In fact, the remissive types portrayed in their work constitute crude caricatures of abstractions advanced by advocates of the human-potential movement. In this penumbra of views, the self is considered "the essential being of the individual, substantial as itself yet constantly emerging through actualization of potentials."[20] The language of this conception of the emerging self surely is unsettling: terms like "self-actualization" and "self-gratification" are dropped with no apparent embarrassment. Yet contemporary adaptations of romantic images of the open-ended self, from Rousseau and Johann Herder to Carl Rogers and Abraham Maslow, need not be caricatured as sinful, morally disordered, and mentally unsound.

Though experience serves as the main source of authority for the realized self, it does not necessarily yield a culture of unrestrained creatures given over to nihilistic moods and sensual displays. As Carl Rogers declares in his autobiographical essay "This is Me," "The touchstone of validity is my own experience. No other person's ideas, and none of my own ideas, are as authoritative as my experience. It is to experience that I must return again and again, to discover a closer approximation to truth as it is in the process of becoming in me."[21]

Moreover, representatives of the human-potential movement frequently attempt to construct ideal selves capable of defining and avoiding what such critics as Rieff regard as selfish behavior. Consider Maslow's notion of the self-actualized person. In his schema, fulfillment is a precondition and a constituent of actualization, but it is not identical to it: both depend upon satisfaction of elemental material needs. "Self-actualizing people," Maslow observes, "are gratified in all their basic or fulfillment needs (of belongingness, affection, respect, and self-esteem)." They are not alienated, since they do not chronically "feel anxiety-ridden, insecure, unsafe . . . alone, ostracized, rootless, or isolated . . ."[22] In the process of seeking and expressing the needs associated with fulfillment, self-actualizing people experience a subtle shift of perception and goals. Regarding work and play, duty and desire, as interpenetrating categories of experience, self-actualizing individuals begin to devote their energies to tasks "outside themselves"— a cause, a vocation, a profession.[23] In the process of self-actualization, however, customary distinctions between the self and the nonself lose much of their force. For self-actualizing people, the idea of the self becomes enlarged "to include aspects of the world": they are interested primarily in "seeing justice done, doing a more perfect job, advancing the truth, rewarding virtue and punishing evil" rather than in personal payoffs, material or psychological. They are, this is to say, interested mainly in "intrinsic values" and in "transpersonal, beyond-the-selfish, altruistic satisfactions."[24]

The contemporary debate over selfishness and self-concern recapitulates and often caricatures a significant chapter in the intellectual history of the modern period: the broad transition from orthodox notions of human nature in Western religious and political thought— that of *homo homini lupus*—to more genial Enlightenment views, a transition brilliantly delineated by Arthur O. Lovejoy in *Reflections on Human Nature*. Rieff and his fellow critics generally favor the pre-Enlightenment view of individuals as creatures of passions checked, in part, by reason and virtue. Maslow defends the cause of sentiment, arguing that self-esteem and the desire for approval constitute the healthy springs of self-concern and self-actualization. Were he compelled to choose sides, Maslow might find himself in such odd company as Adam Smith and John Adams. In his delineation of the modes of the master "passion for distinction," for example, Adams foreshadows some of Maslow's concerns. Some people, Adams maintains, search for distinction merely by attracting attention: the celebrity of the star or the notoriety of the flashy criminal. "The greater number, however, search for distinction . . . by the means which common sense and every day's experience show, are most likely to obtain it; by riches, by family records, by play, and other frivolous personal accomplishments. But there are a few, and God knows, but a few, who aim at something more. They aim at approbation as well as attention; at esteem as well as consideration; and at admiration and gratitude, as well as congratulation. Admiration is, indeed, the complete idea of approbation, congratulation, and wonder, united."[25] Noting that the desire for self-fulfillment is also a desire to win the recognition of others, Adams, unlike Maslow, observes that the passion for distinction remains a passion and therefore is in need of restraint. In many respects, then, the seventeenth- and eighteenth-century debate over the character and consequences of selfishness and self-concern had lost much of its dialectical edge by the time it was taken up by such figures as Maslow, Rieff, Bell and Lasch. Needless to say, it also remained unresolved.

Maslow's postscarcity model of fulfillment and actualization may be morally impractical and politically indeterminate, altogether less elegant than Adams's reflections. And it may lack the clear resolution of the ideal selves implied by Rieff, Bell, and Lasch. Yet Maslow conceptualizes fulfilled and actualized selves as not simply selfish or beyond the bounds of reasonable moral discourse. By offering only caricatures of the vices of the human-potential model of the self, however, Rieff, Bell, and Lasch perpetuate a false dichotomy of personality types: their own ideal selves versus a corruption of the idea of the self as an open-ended project, which they take to be representative of contemporary American culture—pure classic versus corrupt romantic. Throughout these chapters I have assumed the ascendance (though not the complete triumph) of the human-potential model of a free, gratified, unalienated self with sufficient energy and resources, both personal and cultural, to explore a range of possibilities. Since the implied admirable self of the critics and the human-potential image of the self both fit this broad definition, the conception of fulfillment I have assumed does not rule out the potential for moral excellence in either type. But it does suggest that pure representatives of the Rieff, Bell, and Lasch model are in decline both as a dominant ideal type and as an estimated percentage of a growing American population.

If they exist, these developments may be interpreted as evidence of a rise in selfishness. But they need not, and I believe ought not be taken as conclusive or wholly damning evidence. For by concentrating the possibilities for moral excellence in one type, critics distort a valuable prism through which American life in the sixties and seventies can be glimpsed. A fair characterization of both types might clarify a prevailing confusion between two limiting cases of self-fulfillment and hence two styles of selfishness. Unless it is carefully qualified, however, even a fair characterization of both types obscures the probably mixed distribution of these virtues and their corresponding selfish modes of behavior in individuals as well as throughout American society. Let me explain.

For the ideal self imagined by Rieff, Bell, and Lasch, the criteria of selfish behavior are pretty well established. Indeed, such selfish selves typically are governed by bourgeois norms of self-interest in the economic and occupational spheres. They profess an ethic of service and duty in public life, and they adhere to norms of generosity, even personal sacrifice, in their well-defined roles in families and among friends. Self-interest and generosity, of course, come into play in each of these spheres, but each lays out a special emphasis, a different set of partial remissions. A businessman, for example, need not express the same generosity toward competitors as toward his children. A laborer need not display as much altruism on the job as he does in his role as volunteer soccer coach, and so on. Moreover, all of these norms are grounded in unequal and overlapping regions of relative scarcity: of goods, of reputation, of love. Most of them were refined in the several stages of capitalist evolution and in Enlightenment and post-Enlightenment cultures. The selfish bourgeois, then, is a man whose sense of reality—and possibility—turns on gratification of elemental needs, or, after these are met, on hedonistic, obsessive repetitions of these activities: the endless accumulation of money, power, goods, food, sexual conquests, space, fame, or some combination of these.

In the case of the human-potential model, however, criteria of selfishness are less well defined. The classic forms of self-concern remain possible, of course. But they persist and mingle with newer concerns with the self that often violate received codes. Apart from the remote ideal of self-actualization, the idea of the enlarged or "growing" self carries with it no lucid ethic of selfishness and responsibility, no ethic of reasonable service. Even the ideal of self-actualization is optional. Hence, when personal fulfillment is accepted as a worthy aim and individuals pursue more or less open-ended syntheses of salvation and social justice, the criteria of selfishness blur and the occasions of potentially selfish behavior multiply.

This growing density of potential occasions of individual selfishness is compounded by another development: the democratization of personhood, which brings millions of actors into the quest for fulfillment whose claims formerly were denied or accorded only formal or marginal status. Hence, in the seventies, as the Movement disintegrated and left-liberal politics faltered, American society seemed to many to be a complex field of selfishness—of individuals, interest groups, and classes governed by the old selfishness and variants of Maslow's higher selfishness. To some, the working class appeared selfish in the old-fashioned sense of the term. To others, blacks appeared to be consumed by vulgar motives: corrupted by the "successful revolution of the rich," Rieff observed in the middle sixties, "the poor Negro believes that he too can live by bread alone. What the Negro asks, essentially, is a place at the American trough." Still other critics focused on middle- and upper-middle-class individuals (and their children) who in ever larger numbers embraced venal forms of the higher selfishness. Since both varieties mingled in American life, the entire culture came to appear selfish, narcissistic, hedonistic.

Despite appearances, the metaphor of America as a culture and society of selfishness cannot withstand much probing. Selfishness no doubt persisted in the sixties and seventies. And by any reasonable definition it probably was on the rise during these years. But the phenomenon came to seem ubiquitous—the defining mark of American culture—

only in the absence of authoritative ways of separating excesses of self-concern from ideas that were in the process of becoming new norms of concern for the self. As the quest for fulfillment deepened and widened, the criteria of much allegedly selfish behavior became problematic. In such circumstances, the practice of lumping examples of purely selfish behavior together with emerging patterns of concern for self and of referring to the entire culture as selfish, hedonistic, or narcissistic prejudges the quest and deflects attention from its main thrust and salutary effects. To gauge American culture by means of a rising index of selfishness (and a presumed one, at that) seems to me as unprofitable as assessing progress made in cardiac surgery during the sixties and seventies by counting the number of patients who died in operating rooms. The procedure may not be incorrect: it is rather incomplete and beside the point. Insofar as it can be defined and authenticated, the rise of selfishness may serve as a crude index of the quest for fulfillment, of the vast profusion of possibilities for self-definition and self-fulfillment that tens of millions of Americans gained in these decades.

The accent, then, should be placed where it belongs: on the vast expansion of possibilities for personal fulfillment. The central problem is not how to rate individuals and subcultures on scales of selfishness and narcissism. It is rather how to formulate criteria of self-concern and responsibility that recognize new, more democratic social and psychic realities, and help to govern and even shape them in morally sound and socially just ways: how, that is, to resolve burgeoning conflicts of interest in a world of expanding rights, privileges, and entitlements. This task of distinguishing morally unacceptable kinds and degrees of self-regard from growing concerns for the self is not eased by critics who exaggerate contemporary modes of selfishness and fail to give proper weight to mitigating and countervailing factors.

Exaggerations of contemporary manifestations of selfishness typically turn on inappropriate comparisons between past criteria and present circumstances. It is not only the multiplication of claims on the part of a growing number of individuals that accounts for the real and apparent rise of selfishness. It is the changing distributions of selfishness that are often ignored, misfiled, or minimized. The implied self recommended by Rieff, Bell, and Lasch often required a cast of thousands to enact itself. And it frequently required the full "cooperation" of intimates. The morally tuned, well-crafted self, this is to say, needed a privileged place in a structure of advantage. His selfishness was largely concealed in settled social scripts. Consider, for example, the sorts of acknowledgments scholars and critics offered (until recently without embarrassment) in prefaces to their works. Wives typically were thanked for their lovingness, their willingness to attend to the details of life, their cleverness in keeping children and pets at bay, and, less usually, their ability to criticize the manuscript and to handle editorial and typing chores. Praise of this sort flowed freely, usually, no doubt, from a grateful heart, though perhaps occasionally also from a reserve of unspoken guilt. Acknowledgments of a higher order were reserved for colleagues: for men of equivalent intellectual and moral resources.

I do not wish to propose that modes of praise be homogenized, still less that they be made so dishonest as to represent every spouse or intimate other as a genius. Nor do I wish to deny that much of the work of intellectuals has social utility that may offset the selfish behavior of authors. I simply am illustrating ways of concealing selfishness—or self-concern—and distributing it inequitably that until recently escaped sustained criticism. Once supportive family structures began to weaken under pressures intensified by the quest, they turned into arenas of enlarged demands on the part of all members. The dutiful wife developed other interests—in some cases a public identity separate from her husband and her husband's work. Each person appeared to be more selfish when in fact two related developments were unfolding. As everyone fashioned a lengthening agenda of claims in behalf of the self, the monopoly of selfishness, previously held by Father, became problematic and subject to reconsideration, negotiation, and redistribution. (It probably is no accident that by and large men took the part of critical Cassandras in the seventies.)

Or consider a theological example of alleged selfishness in the sixties and seventies. In one way or another, Rieff, Bell, and Lasch find evidence of selfishness in altered conceptions of death. Bell regards the refusal to accept death gracefully as a sign of "self-infinitization." Lasch considers the therapeutic slogan popularized by advertisers, "You only go around once in life," to be a sign of excessive self-regard. Why, they imply, are people who no longer believe in an afterlife that balances moral accounts and eases the sting of death so preoccupied with extending their own lives? "Why not?" strikes me as a proper reply. Although fewer people than the critics allow have adopted this set of beliefs, most of those who have do not seem to me pathologically or even inappropriately concerned with their own welfare. "Self-infinitization" may be more widespread than it was a half-century or a century ago, but it is hardly a novelty. It represents rather a reasonable response to weakened traditional structures of spiritual consolation, reassurance, and promise.

Multiplied millions of times over, such examples of self-regard may add up to a perception of America as a culture of selfishness, a Hobbesian field dominated by selfish persons and selfish groups. But America at the end of the seventies may be more plausibly seen, I think, as a culture in the midst of a redistribution of an enlarged bundle of privileges, rights, entitlements, responsibilities, and obligations. This vision is obscured further by the critics' failure to give adequate weight to the relative novelty of the quest for fulfillment. In the sixties and seventies, millions of individuals from all social categories who had previously been excluded by law and by custom concentrated on the search for fulfillment. Psychological me-ism spread, and in the course of this diffusion it became the psychic equivalent of new wealth. Judged by settled standards, novices in the search often went to extremes or failed to display their concerns with the self skillfully or tastefully. There is some validity to this charge, of course, though less than many critics allow. Since the novelty of unrestrained selves can be expected to wear off rather quickly, dire projections of cultural nihilism seem at least premature, if not silly.

The course of self-concern was roughly similar to that of running in the seventies. Although the activity of running is on the whole commendable (Pascal's reservations about exercise notwithstanding), the results were uneven, predictably so. In time, the initial enthusiasm wore off. Yet the culture of running improved, as personal experiences were shared, articles and books written, and classes and clinics offered. Some sedentary people learned to walk short distances, others practiced fitfully, if at all, and still others acquired shin splints and pulled hamstrings. A few suffered fatal heart seizures. Of those who did not quit, however, a significant number became competent runners and a minority attained admirable speed and distance. A sophisticated subculture of marathon participants took shape. This new elite did not meet the higher and more settled standards shared by participants in traditional track-and-field clubs and organizations. But as the activity was democratized and patterns of stratification grew more complex, the varied health benefits of running became more widely available. Of course, older standards of running survived along with the new, and Olympic times even improved steadily. Still, it would be unfair to judge the entire activity solely by Olympic standards, for multiple standards of judgment are required.

There is no guarantee that the initial displays of self-concern in the quest for fulfillment will follow the course of my analogy. Yet this seems at least as plausible a scenario as those advanced by critics who traffic in Hobbesian metaphors. By the end of the seventies, there already was some evidence for it. In the opening phases of the women's movement (or in the initial phases of a women's awareness), for example, tentative expressions of dissent may be registered. Thereafter, anger frequently emerges as the dominant emotion in the private sphere and in spheres of collective protest as well. This may be followed by an extreme display of "selfishness," of consideration only of the claims of her self. But these do not usually remain the most prominent responses, as the course of the women's movement and the biographies and autobiographies of countless women in the sixties and seventies suggest. What seems to be—and in part may be—irresponsible and self-destructive behavior more often than not evolves into reasonable and nurturing behavior. Individuals within the structure of disadvantage meet others on uncertain social and moral terrain. Novices become apprentices in the quest for fulfillment. And apprentices become journeywomen and then craftswomen of selves able to attend to a new agenda of personal and interpersonal needs, desires, and responsibilities.

Such patterns of evolution, as I have argued, fit many manifestations of the quest in the sixties and seventies: they were apparent in sectors of the Movement, in the Christian revival, and in the therapeutic search. But since they occur most frequently in individuals (and relatively small groups) who take up the search at different times and in different circumstances and define it variously, overall social changes are less evident. Still, in a general way, the idea of personal authenticity and the need for cultural and psychic space serve as foci for personal demands in initial (or fresh) assaults on the structure of advantage. Those who succeed, if only partially, then proceed to organize the space gained and to set about establishing connections with others. Such a pattern, which serves to mark different moments of the sprawling quest, may not be efficient when assessed in political terms. But it vaguely defines the important cultural transition from the sixties to the seventies.

Finally, critics intent on perceiving America as a culture of selfishness and hedonism tend to underplay or simply lament the survival of restraints and constraints on the self. Such critics on the left as Russell Jacoby did find in narcissism an element of "protest in the name of individual health and happiness against irrational sacrifice" and hence judged it condescendingly as not wholly regressive.[26] But most advocates of the metaphor of the culture of selfishness—conservative and Tory radical alike—usually failed to give a fair account of the cultural and social forces that held American civilization together in the sixties and seventies. These forces range from economic self-interest, bureaucracy, law, and raw power to intermediate institutions: families, churches, schools, and other voluntary associations. And they include moral and spiritual convictions.

The actual mixtures of power and authority, I shall suggest, proved more than sufficient to hold American society together in these years. They added up to a tolerable contemporary equivalent of the checks and balances that the founding fathers considered a necessary restraint on the passions, including the largely salutary passion for self-esteem and self-fulfillment. In spite of gains in the democratization of personhood and a corresponding rise of selfishness, real and fancied, most American selves remained quite bounded by economic needs, occupational requirements, social position, and personal obligations. One might go so far as to suggest that there was not enough selfishness and not nearly enough genuine concern with the self in the sixties and seventies. In any case, the rise of this phenomenon surely did not justify the metaphor of America as a culture of selfishness in these years.

13

The Evolution
of Authority

Critics who deplore the apparent rise of selfishness are often among the first to lament what they take to be a precipitate decline of authority in postwar America. These phenomena seem to reinforce one another: a loosening of authority creates space for self-regarding behavior, which in turn subverts structures of authority. For individuals concerned primarily with the exfoliation of the self, then, respect for authority may appear at best a temporary expedient rather than a genuine article of faith or canon of reason. The self-conscious flight from authority toward autonomy is a thoroughly modern theme, though not a uniquely modern one. Scenarios of decline stretch back at least to the Middle Ages, when Henry Adams's Virgin lost her aura of mystery and neither Aquinas nor any subsequent philosopher could discover a lasting, universally accepted principle of authority capable of governing the cosmos.[1] Differences in scale and intensity presumably set the sixties and seventies apart from earlier American evasions of authority: disenchantment with authority of every sort was supposed to have been deeper and more widespread than in the early postwar period and perhaps more pervasive than at any extended moment in the history of the Republic.

As recently as the early fifties, it will be recalled, many critics worried about excesses of authority, not its imminent collapse. Disturbed by the apparent willingness of "other-directed" citizens to submit to the authority of their peers, David Riesman registered the hope that a renewed interest in the neglected self might offset a growing conformity among Americans. "If the other-directed people should discover how much needless work they do, discover that their own thoughts and their own lives are quite as interesting as other people's, that, indeed, they no more assuage their loneliness in a crowd of peers than one can assuage one's thirst by drinking sea water, then we might expect them to become more attentive to their own feelings and aspirations."[2] Less than two decades later, at the end of the sixties, the search for distinctive selves had quickened probably well beyond Riesman's expectations. And the idea of authority itself (including Riesman's unheroic, other-directed subtype) had come to seem obsolete to such observers of American civilization as Margaret Mead, who calmly announced the advent of a "prefigurative" culture. In such a culture, Mead concluded, "there are no more knowledgeable others to whom parents can commit the children they themselves cannot teach . . ."[3] The dynamo of history had inverted the oldest claim of authority—"that of fathers and mothers . . . [and] of progenitors to rule over their offspring," as Cleinias puts it in Plato's *Laws*. In the absence of alternatives, Mead was driven to conclude, children would have to take charge of initiating their hapless elders into worlds neither had made.

It may be uncharitable to hold anyone strictly accountable for lines written between, say, 1967 and 1973. Even then, however, in that time of wild hyperbole, few critics were persuaded that authority had crumbled as badly as Mead suggested. Fewer still were prepared to take a sanguine view of the "prefigurative" future she foresaw. Yet by the end of the sixties authority in every sphere, from parental to theological, did seem to be losing ground, albeit at different rates. During the seventies, "the twilight of authority," to recall Robert Nisbet's phrase, served as a central theme for sophisticated neoconservatives and unvarnished right wingers. In their different idioms, Irving Kristol and Jerry Falwell chronicled the erosion of authority in one sphere after another, blaming "adversary intellectuals," humanists, liberals, and other leftists for demystifying the idea of authority. Although it comes most easily to conservatives, this tune of waning authority was not confined to choruses of the fractious American right. On the left, for example, Christopher Lasch located the origins of narcissism in the passing of firm patriarchal authority.

And Eugene Genovese traced the feebleness of the American left in part to an unwillingness of individuals to submit to the authority of a revolutionary party.

Nor were perceptions of decline limited to the intelligentsia: large numbers of less ideologically self-conscious citizens—parents, teachers, ministers, physicians, bosses, foremen, husbands, generals, politicians, intellectuals, and law-enforcement officials—complained about the unravelling bonds of authority. Subordinates refused to acknowledge any need to submit themselves to legitimate authority. And authorities failed to behave authoritatively. In these circumstances, the idea of a missing authority, variously defined, came to serve as a partial explanation for the ills of American civilization. The failure of authority was considered a major source of personality disorientation and impoverishment. It was held to be significantly responsible for the balkanization of ordinary culture and the trivialization of high culture. And it was cited as a principal cause of entropy and stalemate in the political economy. More than a key to negative diagnoses of our condition, the idea of authority also came to serve once again as a prescription. Larger doses promised to bring the quest under control and to restore a measure of individual and social health, assuming that such a serum could be devised, manufactured, properly administered, and willingly consumed.

At first glance, the idea of authority does not seem to figure prominently in the quest for fulfillment. It is true that in most specifications of the quest authority was taken for granted as a constituent of social order, a component of democratic politics, and an element of personal identity. More often than not, however, the idea of authority occupied a subordinate and inarticulate place in schemes of fulfillment. Frequently it loomed as an obstacle. In most cases, a person searching for fulfillment sought initially to push back various incarnations of authority—to get institutions and imperious others off his back and to drive certain ideas out of mind. As I have shown in earlier chapters, varieties of dissent against the authority of the structure of advantage were common to elements of the Movement, the Christian revival, and the therapeutic search. During the sixties and seventies authority went on the defensive in nearly every region of American civilization: it was regularly questioned, doubted, tested, and in some instances al-

together rejected. In large numbers, gay men and lesbians rejected the
authority of straight culture. Women denied the authority of men.
Children abandoned parental authority. Blacks and other minorities
rejected the authority of whites. Libertarians on the right opposed
most forms of institutional authority. Catholics in ever larger numbers
dismissed the authority of the Pope. Evangelicals and neo-Pentecostals
ignored the authority of mainline Protestant denominations. Therapeutic seekers dismissed the authority of orthodox medical practitioners, traditional psychiatrists, and each other. Radicals spurned the
authority of bourgeois ideas and institutions.

The list of principled and capricious rejections of authority is exceeded only by the number of reasons submitted for such rejections.
But rhetorical and behavioral assaults on the idea of authority typically
turned on the supposition that less of it—at least less of certain kinds—
constituted a precondition to attaining more immediate and highly
valued social ends: liberty, equality, democracy, cultural pluralism.
This supposition similarly informed many strategies employed to attain the personal ends of fulfillment: individual salvation and a slice
of social justice. Of course, authority in these years did not slide
directly toward dissolution and anarchy. Individuals and groups engaged in a search for autonomy rejected certain sorts of authority only to embrace others. Elements of the Movement accepted the
authority of Marx or of their own fitful readings of the classic texts.
Other people submitted themselves to contemporary idols, from Che
to John Lennon and from Mao to Janis Joplin. Dissident Christians sought authority in literal readings of Scripture, in a pastor or
teacher, and most of all, in the idea of "Jesus as Lord." Therapeutic
seekers attached themselves to such gurus as Arthur Janov, Werner
Erherd, and Swami Muktananda. In popular culture, the simple, direct, and overwhelming authority of a Vince Lombardi or even a Don
Corleone in *The Godfather* (1972) came to seem an attractive relief
from actual complexities. And toward the end of the decade, the Reverend Jim Jones came to exert a charisma that was fatal to nearly one
thousand people and grimly fascinating to millions of others.

The quest, then, cut two ways. It involved multiple rejections of unearned authority, even occasional rebellions against all authority. At the
same time, it quickened the search for authority. Some people sought fulfillment through a progressive enlargement of options. Others wished
to narrow—and clarify—their options by submitting themselves to one

authority or another. Many did both. Most Americans, of course, did not embrace the extremes of rejection or submission but rather sought and accepted intermediate modes of authority: authority sprang from external sources and from internal resources. Thus the transformations of authority in the sixties and seventies cannot be understood simply through a metaphor of decline, of twilight preceding a dark night of chaos. The multiple ways in which the quest unfolded suggest that different modes of authority were in the process of being broken down and built up, rejected and recast, demystified and remystified, subdivided and multiplied. On balance, as I have implied throughout these chapters, these transformations of authority facilitated the quest for fulfillment without significantly damaging American people, culture, or politics. Not only did American civilization survive multiple assaults on authority in the sixties and seventies: it even weathered a proliferation of new centers of competing charismatic authority.

The Idea of Authority

Jeremiads about the decline of authority obviously fit the framework of nostalgia, but they do not focus exclusively on the recent past, on comparisons between the seventies and the sixties. Some critics remember the fifties and early sixties as a rather orderly time, a period in which various species of authority commanded respect. But people who worry about this theme usually scan the prewar American past—even the distant Western past—for images and incarnations of "genuine" (or what might be called "original") authority. An arch-conservative such as Philip Rieff might hold that "authority is never lost," yet he clearly believes that genuine authority has succumbed to the pressures of modernity. "Authority," Rieff observes, "is the achievement of a rank order of possibilities so slow to change that they appear as commands and obediences—the form of every living teaching by which, until modernity, self has contained its own artfulness . . ."[4] On this view, genuine authority is impossible under conditions of modern life. Acknowledging the immense difficulty of maintaining authority in modern societies, more moderate conservatives like Irving Kristol stop short of denying the chances of rough approximations. Yet they too consider the American twentieth century, as Kristol has it, to be a time of progressive depletion of the "accumulated moral capital of traditional religion and traditional moral philosophy."

Although they are far less nervous about this matter, critics on the left nevertheless propose their own distinctions between modernity and lost ideological and historical regions where genuine authority may have flourished. "Wherever it has got the upper hand," Marx and Engels declare in the *Communist Manifesto,* the bourgeoisie "has put an end to all feudal, patriarchal, idyllic relations. It has pitilessly torn asunder the motley feudal ties that bound man to his 'natural superiors,' and has left remaining no other nexus between man and man than naked self-interest, than callous 'cash payment.' " What masquerades as authority in capitalist society is illegitimate—"ideological," or false, in the strict Marxian sense of the term. Marx's rhetorical strategy turns on a set of comparisons designed to condemn bourgeois society in the light of both the projected communist future and the actual past—and to do so without denying the overall progressive character of history (including its capitalist phases).

Less ambivalent rejections of existing modes of authority mark the most radical facets of the broad tradition of the left since Marx. In the sixties, elements of the Movement claimed to have prefigured a free future by abandoning all present sources and varieties of authority. In the more reflective seventies, however, such critics on the left as Richard Sennett developed second thoughts about the possibility of a utopian future.[5] As a consequence, many aging new Leftists revised their views of the status of authority in the present—any present. Although authority may be disbelieved consciously and openly in American society, Sennett admits, it cannot be done away with—now, or in any reasonable projection of the future. According to Sennett, then, authority might have enjoyed a more authentic existence at certain moments of history, and it may yet have a somewhat brighter future, though he displays less confidence in this possibility than many of his predecessors and some contemporaries on the left. Whatever its prospects, however, the current status of authority is counterfeit. Needs and desires for authority persist, yet they remain, in Sennett's view, frustrated, perverted, not satisfied in humane ways. "The dilemma of authority in our time," he writes, "the peculiar fear it inspires, is that *we feel attracted to strong figures we do not believe to be legitimate.*"[6]

Proceeding with quite different conceptions of authority in mind, then, critics on opposite ends of the ideological spectrum argue variously that contemporary modes are phony, oppressive, or ineffective. But critics converge on this essential point: that the idea and perhaps the social practice of genuine authority lies in an irrecoverable past (or in an impossible future). Differing over which elements, if any, of this complex idea ought to be recovered, critics typically subscribe to one version or another of what might be termed the "big bang" theory of authority. Although ordinary varieties of authority might be a historical constant, present in different amounts everywhere, genuine authority moves inexorably toward extinction. Such authority may dim and brighten in different historical skies, but it cannot thrive in the atmosphere of modernist and postmodernist culture.

Let me be fanciful for a moment. In some distant past—perhaps as early as the neolithic era—chieftains exercised the purest sort of authority, the sort based on natural ability. The original authority of *mumis* ("big men"), and later of early kings, displayed most of the characteristics of the genuine article, albeit in crude approximations.[7] Authority was sacred—indivisible, omnipotent, universal, and timeless. At least it was (and is) represented in this way to those in and under it. The source of authority was visible, embodied in a man or a god. Or, later on, it was legible, embodied in law, institutions, and tradition. Authority was lodged primarily in the father, the mother, or the elders: tensions among household, state, civil, and ecclesiastical authorities were either unknown or held to a minimum. Superordinates and subordinates (to borrow Simmel's pairing) perceived authority as true, as good, and as in some sense beautiful, or at least whole: aesthetically pleasing and psychologically satisfying, if usually fearful. Authority might have been challenged from time to time, but it was not regularly questioned or demystified through incessant questioning. It rather was at once inescapable, desired, and voluntarily observed.

Of course, we don't know, for example, precisely why slaves usually obeyed their masters' commands, though it seems safe to assume that raw power figured as importantly in the equation of obedience as did dazzling displays of authority. My caricature has no pretensions of anthropological or historical accuracy. It is meant rather to call attention to contemporary intuitions of original authority and to the general ways in which critics recall the career of this concept: its circuitous paths from unity to division, from sacred to profane, from limitlessness to partiality, from timelessness to transcience, from legibility to obscurity, from potency to various degrees of impotence, from mask to self-conscious masquerade. As early as the beginnings of the Judeo-Christian era, divisions were evident, even in legend. The Israelites

might have centralized the authority of divinity through their mono-
theism, but in the course of their history one authority became two
and two became many. Nor did the emergence of Christianity simplify matters, centered as it was on a charismatic figure who placed
himself both within and above the law. The authority of Caesar and
that of God, whose boundaries Jesus shrewdly advised others to specify, unfold on perpetually contested ground. It is true that the authority of the church and that of the crown struck uneasy compromises
during the Middle Ages, when popes often dominated the European
ecclesiastical and political landscape. Thereafter, until the emergence
of modern society, the sovereign exercised dominant authority. From
Machiavelli and Luther to Hobbes and Locke, the idea of authority
was translated into a set of problems: how and to what extent fragmenting forms ought to be preserved against the proliferating claims
to freedom registered by ever larger numbers of people (and social
classes). Protestantism and capitalism, Weber observed, altered the vis-
ages of authority and forever complicated its character and exercise.[8]

From the outset, the American experiment was a self-conscious attempt to reduce the scope of authority, to establish a society with as
little public authority as possible—certainly less than obtained in the
Old World. Prevailing notions of what was minimal authority changed
swiftly, of course: recommended amounts and kinds of authority required for different areas of life have varied over three centuries of
American experience. Yet from the beginning of the Republic, ecclesiastical authority was at least dispersed, if not altogether destroyed, and
the authority of the crown wholly rejected. Following Hobbes and
Locke, the founders based sovereign authority and state power in the
consent of the governed—a consent formalized by the Constitution,
periodically ratified through the electoral process, and executed by representative government. The history of authority in nonpublic spheres
complicates matters, though not hopelessly. Historians of the family,
such as Lawrence Stone, maintain that the ascendance of the modern
nuclear family, which began in the early seventeenth century, resulted
in the concentration of authority in the father. If this is so, then private authority was strengthened, multiplied, and dispersed all at once.

My intent here is not to suggest that American practice has conformed fully with American theory. Nor do I propose that the idea of
authority has yielded wholly to the claims of autonomous selves. What
does seem incontestable, however, is that Americans by and large have

resisted the temptation to endorse a strong version of genuine authority in the public sphere. And in this century they have increasingly resisted strong modes of authority in private spheres as well. Even so, radical and conservative critics seem to proceed in part on an intuition of what genuine authority must be like, and then, registering differing degrees of nostalgia over its passing, confront present modes as if they were largely counterfeit. In one sense, of course, they are. Critics in the tradition of Henry Adams know that they cannot give an authoritative account of their intuitive sense of genuine authority—an account demonstrably true, right, and compelling. Moreover, most of those who regret the passing of authority seem unwilling to accept or unable to foresee social conditions in which the genuine article might thrive: aristocracy or the rule of a big man (or woman). And most claim to favor preservation or creation of some measure of democracy, at least in certain spheres. Self-conscious about all this, nostalgic conservatives concentrate on exploring varieties of the counterfeit, the present fallout from the original big bang.

Useful working definitions of authority, then, must take account of intuitions of the properties of original authority, if only to note their relative absence. Such definitions also must illuminate the currently fragmented forms of authority. Harry Eckstein, a close student of the subject, offers a neutral definition that provides a point of entry. "An *authority pattern*," Eckstein explains, "is a set of asymmetric relations among hierarchically ordered members of a social unit that involves the direction or governance of the unit."[9] Some command, others obey. Inequality based on a variety of criteria—from talent, experience, knowledge, expertise, position, and election to sheer power—constitutes the most significant prerequisite to a relationship that it makes sense to describe as characterized by a flow of authority. But authority entails more than the power to control. As Max Weber remarked, it requires an ability to justify, or legitimate, the use of strength. Weber's three main types—traditional, rational-legal (bureaucratic), and charismatic—all include modes of potential legitimation: through endless reiteration, through reference to abstract sets of rules, or simply through the force of personality.

For Weber, real authority can be gauged by the amount of willing compliance it exacts. There is a problem here, however, as every student of Weber quickly notes. Although observed compliance can indicate the operation of authority, as Weber suggests, it can also reveal no more than simple acquiescence to power. Hence even voluntary compliance does not automatically demonstrate legitimacy. Though it is far from useless, the Weberian typology has other limitations. It does not get at a central facet of original authority—the phenomenological interior, what it feels like to be in and under authority. Concentrating more on the private sphere—the self and the family—Weber's contemporary, Freud, consolidated an approach to authority as a collection of images of parental, especially paternal, strength formed out of the unequal status everyone enjoys and endures as a child. Drawing on both Weber and Freud, Sennett fashioned a definition that emphasizes the affective dimensions of authority. Authority, he suggests, is a "bond between people who are unequal." Figures of authority possess such recognizable qualities as "assurance, superior judgment, the ability to impose discipline, the capacity to inspire fear." The bond of authority, therefore, is "built of images of strength and weakness; it is the emotional expression of power."[10]

Roughly complementing one another, and synthesizing Enlightenment and pre-Enlightenment views of authority, these two definitions of the term as legitimate power and as an image of strength represent valuable approaches to observable and subjectively reported relations of authority. Yet these definitions fail to capture more than pieces of the idea of original authority. And they do not account satisfactorily for a modern form: the democratic variety that frequently permits people who are morally and intellectually inferior to many other citizens to occupy superordinate positions in government, education, religion, and business. Attempts to generalize about authority, even at the level of definition, thus encounter a familiar paradox: the larger the sphere or collection of spheres, the less specific and useful the definition. Dividing the issue into a number of smaller problems has been a precondition to a measure of intellectual progress, but it has not permitted anyone to conquer the subject. Even the Weberian types mix, merge, and cut across social spheres. Traditional authority endures in all spheres of society, though it does so only tenuously. Rational-legal authority thrives, mainly in the public realm—in bureaucracies and in democratic politics—but also in private spheres, including the family. Charismatic authority persists in some religious communities, in families, and to some extent in politics. From the point of view of critics who regret the passing of genuine authority, these difficulties represent the wages of too-willing concessions to contemporary social and cultural realities. Even the definitional difficulties themselves seem to count as evidence of a decline of genuine authority in America.

No one has invented culturewide definitions of authority of any great descriptive or interpretive value. No one could have. For authority in America is divided, limited, and transient. Ecclesiastical, state, civil, and familial sources and modes of authority are incongruent, and the epistemological, ethical, aesthetic, and psychological dimensions of authority lack coherence. This situation assuredly is untidy, but it is not hopeless. For I see no need to choose between a definition (or criteria for a definition) that incorporates all the features of original authority and a bland definition such as Eckstein's. The fact is, that for American civilization as a whole, authority is fragmentary but not absent, despite a probable postwar decline in citizen participation in any single culturewide concept of authority—even democratic authority.[11] During the sixties and seventies, all previous modes of authority flourished in the parts of society. Indeed, the extent to which most individuals and groups were in and under authority of one or many kinds and sources seems to me at least sufficient, and probably more than sufficient, to have met personal and social needs for this commodity. Of the many problems confronting America in these years, the alleged decline of authority and the implied need to strengthen it strike me as among the least pressing.

It should be clear by now that I am no great admirer of authority. I would not go so far as Oscar Wilde, who considered all authority degrading both to "those who exercise it, and . . . to those over whom it is exercised." Nor would I invert the argument of Dostoevsky's Grand Inquisitor, who irritates the modern temper by defending rather than attacking every effort to mystify authority. Still, I should not be inclined to endorse any version of authority that entails significant compromise of a single major value promoted by the quest: personal freedom, autonomy, equality, democracy, cultural pluralism. Such choices between authority and autonomy may not be the most intellectually intriguing ones, yet over the past four centuries the most significant options individuals and social classes have faced can be understood roughly along the lines of such a dichotomy. Thus the fragmentation of genuine authority (and, to a point, the growth of venal varieties) has served the salutary end of enlarging the scope of personal and social freedom in America.

Still, authority, like fire, fosters ambivalence. It can assume forms that cause great harm, but it is undeniably useful. At best, the various species of authority strike me as instrumental values. A measure of democratic authority, for example, is necessary to ensure political freedom, without which personal freedom is either impossible or impossibly fragile. A measure of authority in private spheres can help meet elemental needs for security, nurture, identity, and religious faith. Beyond such minimal requirements, however, authority loses whatever charm it may possess. My unenthusiastic view of authority, then, does not proceed from a contempt for its limited uses nor, I should add, from any concern over its impending disappearance. In spite of assaults on it—salutary, phony, destructive—authority seems always more than able to take care of itself. Lodged as it is in psychic structures, the need for authority is enforced by the perennially dependent situation of early childhood. And the idea never lacks public defenders—revolutionaries and reactionaries, intellectuals and philistines—if only because it is such a convenience to people in charge of every sort of social unit and such an attractive fantasy to many who long to be in charge. Even in infrequent and temporary moments of social collapse, authority finds new enforcers.

Overuse and plain abuse represent the likely negative potentials of authority, at least the ones most often enacted. The overriding question about authority, then, is not how much of what sorts we need in various spheres or how much it is convenient for people in positions of command to possess. The question rather is how *little* we can get by on. Especially in the public spheres of culture and politics, I believe, the bonds of authority ought to be minimal in order to facilitate the quest for fulfillment: for salvation and a piece of social justice. Similarly, I assume a more or less laissez faire attitude toward authority in the more fluid private and quasi-private spheres, including individual consciousness, family, work, and religion.

Of course, those who are unable to choose must have their rights protected, and those who elect other than democratic modes must stay within the law. Within these vague limits, however, I believe that choice should prevail. Any version of authority can be useful insofar as it promotes individual versions of salvation. Some people choose the extremes of submission or full independence, but most do not. In the sixties and seventies, at least, Americans typically avoided extremes in most areas and at most stages of their lives. Although the bonds of public and private authority shifted during these years, they held, often too securely, I think. In any case, they held firmly enough (often as a consequence of their suppleness) to permit a significant measure of progress in the quest for fulfillment. In the process, America avoided the dire consequences of the predicted decline of authority. Most selves resisted anomie. And American culture survived, despite fragmenting, syncretic trends. So did the political economy and the essential constituents of American ideology.

Self, Culture, and Authority

Proper doses of authority are supposed to promote certain minimal results: coherence in the personal sphere, hierarchy in the cultural sphere, and order in the social sphere. Untreated deficiencies culminate in such distressing symptoms as personality disorganization, cultural discontinuity, social injustice, or even social chaos. Critics disagreed over how disordered American society had grown in the sixties and seventies and on how far its culture had slipped. They differed too in their estimates of the role that neglected authority played in this decline. And they wrote many prescriptions: prescriptions for common varieties of authority as well as for such rare compounds as "authority without domination," to borrow one of Sennett's formulations. In spite of their differences, critics of many persuasions condemned what they took to be the typical way of resisting deficiencies of authority in the larger society: a "retreat" into private life. A cliché of social and cultural criticism in these years, "privatization" was considered to be self-defeating, inasmuch as efforts to find fulfillment along personal alleys allegedly led to dead ends: thin, impoverished, alienated, confused, disconnected selves. Moreover, privatization was judged immoral—a selfish neglect of social duty and often an abrogation of expressly political duty.

These serious charges challenge the most elemental assumption of the quest—that personal fulfillment is widely available even in the absence of a high degree of general social justice and a unified, influential high culture. Throughout these chapters, I have maintained that salvation can be managed even on thin, uneven slices of social justice, that fulfillment can indeed be gained by individuals who venture into public life as well as by those who prefer private life. Let us delay consideration of alleged breaches of political obligation in order to concentrate on the charge that privatization subverts the aims of fulfillment by depriving individuals of materials requisite to a coherent self, a secure identity.

Laments about the privatization of American life litter social and cultural criticism of the sixties and seventies. In his widely noticed study *The Fall of Public Man* (1977), for example, Sennett argues, often quite persuasively, that the therapeutic surge has contributed to the destruction of what he calls "public man." In the eighteenth century, Sennett maintains, impersonal conventions regulated behavior, creating a cosmopolitan public sphere distinct from the private. People were civilized by enacting a set of roles that facilitated a politics of enlightened self-interest. By contrast, the present moment represents a further corruption of nineteenth-century Romanticism, which itself precipitated the alleged fall of public man. Impersonal disguises fell away, leaving a collection of private selves that were no longer able to conduct an admirable or even an effective public life. The privatized self, Sennett argues, became the measure—the distorting measure—of all things. By gauging society wholly in psychological terms, individuals cease to be politically serious, and, ironically, they also fail to realize even personal ends: "The closer people come, the less sociable, the more painful, the more fratricidal their relations."[12] Privatized man thus loses the capacity to distance himself from himself and from others: he becomes unable to recognize even his own interests. His interest in politics diminishes, his capacity for serious thought about public matters atrophies, his concern for general social justice pales.

Sennett neatly illustrates one prevailing view of the effects of privatization on the self: privation. In this oldest sense of "private," the self suffers loss of coherence and ultimately of identity through separation from all things public: public affairs, public culture, public spaces. In extreme cases, no bond of authority can reach the privatized self, the individual cut off from the community. Doomed to dependence on social forces beyond its influence—and possibly to madness as well—the privatized self continually threatens to come apart at its psychic seams. Or it shrivels up and ceases to matter: in certain higher circles of criticism during the sixties and seventies the self as subject was reduced to a pronoun, a fiction of merely lexical significance. There is, of course, a complementary view that plays on such later senses of "private" as "privileged," or separated from and above the common. In this view, the privatized self may be coherent, even psychically prosperous, but its professed contentment usually is diagnosed as morally shallow and fragile—a patina of self-deception that encases a psychic hollowness. Reporting preliminary impressions in his long-term investigation of white middle-class Americans in the late seventies and early eighties, Robert Bellah observes, with maddening condescension, that "what is striking is that we are discovering a private world of great intensity and no content whatever. There is a vehement insistence on selfhood but it is an absolutely empty self; except for the sheer quantity of excitation there is nothing there at all."[13] In such views, a preference for private life may facilitate the work of securing personal identity, but it does so at the high cost of reducing levels of amplitude: there is coherence without resonance, self-proclaimed fulfillment on the part of people blind to the thinness of their own personalities.

Whether apprehended as a form of deprivation or as a self-defeating privilege, the retreat into private life generally draws critical fire, much of it well aimed. For on nearly every set of reasonable criteria, many American lives must be judged unspeakably trivial. But triviality, thinness, incoherence—or even personal intensity without apparent purpose—are not caused primarily by the so-called flight into private spheres that critics assumed to be an accomplished fact of American life in the seventies. Diminished selves are more a consequence of increased personal freedom than of any failure to participate in public, or, God knows, political life. They represent casualties of the quest, probably unavoidable ones. Such casualties, however, should not divert attention from the main thrust: the emergence and development of the private self, which is one of the most admirable fruits of freedom. Exaggerated interpretations and dire projections of the side effects of the quest often turn on archaic conceptions of public and private—on typically nostalgic recollections of historical moments when these spheres might have been sharply distinguished, more easily located in separate social spaces. It may be that in pre-Socratic Athens, for example, the rich possibilities of citizenship, from political debate to intelligent conversation, were identified largely with the public realm—with physical as well as mental space. And the realm of the household might have been far more restricted, so much so that by analogy private mental space came to be considered empty and the sequestered self diminished.

Clearly such clean divisions did not characterize American culture and society in the sixties and seventies. It is true, no doubt, that the balance of American life in the twentieth century has shifted in the direction of private space: the movement from cities to suburbs provides an obvious metaphor. But such demographic changes do not constitute prima facie evidence of the evils of privatization. They rather underscore changes in the character and significance of public and private space. By the end of the seventies, these boundaries ranged from fuzzy or indistinguishable. Of course, some clear differences persisted: certain public spaces—inner cities, for example—became less frequented because of urban deterioration, including high rates of violent crime. Elsewhere, people might have met less regularly on village greens. But these physical spaces no longer were the only—or even the primary—common spaces in American culture. Technological advances, especially television and the further development of computers, brought public events into private (usually household) spaces. Though they were criticized regularly as invasions of privacy, such changes nevertheless reduced the importance of older boundaries that separated public and private spheres; in fact, the "information society" threatened to obliterate such borders. Still, the terms remain useful, however much they resist precise definition.

Public life might have appeared to be in relative decline when measured against the ascendance of the private sphere. And it might have seemed to be in decline when set against the expectations of critics who consider man in his proper state not simply a political animal but one who belongs in *their* ideological cages. In fact, however, since "public" life was transacted increasingly in private spaces, private life took on a quasi-public character. Hence the case for decline no longer could be made convincingly on the basis of mutually exclusive definitions of public and private. Individuals had access to far more information (and even more misinformation) than ever before about growing communities, regions, nations, and empires. They had more contacts with others—at work, on extended trips, in neighborhoods, in voluntary associations, in their homes. The dense, increasingly rich textures and complications of private life made more psychic demands than before and provided more opportunities. Individuals could be more intensely involved in public life than their parents or grand-parents had been without leaving home as frequently. Moreover, the enrichment of private life probably led increasing numbers of people who had formerly been moderately to severely disadvantaged into public service of one sort of another. Many people whose private lives were deepened chose to exercise themselves in public service—in politics, in large bureaucracies, in business, in nonprofit religious and service organizations, in universities and colleges. Thus it was not so much a decline of public life that marked the sixties and seventies as it was a significant expansion, thickening, and enrichment of private life, which I have discussed under the rubric of the quest for fulfill-ment and the democratization of personhood.

Of course, the term "privatization," as it is employed by critics, often refers to more than public and private *spaces*. It often means a trivial, local cast of mind, a disposition to look only at issues of immediate concern: the fate of one's job rather than problems of structural unem-ployment, personal auto safety rather than the issue of speed limits, and so on. Similarly, "privatization" can mean an informed selfish-ness, a willingness to conceive of issues in structural terms, but only as a prelude to illuminating private interests. Hence the idea of privatiza-tion can be used to identify individuals who refuse to take part in public life as well as those who participate only from the most venal motives. Privatization thus becomes largely a measure of anarchic inner space, a region where authority easily breaks down. Large numbers of Americans must have fit these conceptions of privatization in the sixties and seventies, though I doubt that such moral construc-tions mean very much. For one thing, any rise in the number of self-consciously "privatized" citizens that occurred during these years may constitute indirect evidence of progress in the quest for fulfillment. Most of the privatized citizens whom critics usually have in mind belong to various social categories previously excluded from significant public participation *and* from participation in rich private lives. For another, the notion of privatization frequently serves as an expression of the unalloyed resentment of critics who are almost wholly insensi-tive to the vitality and the variety of American life. "Where there is no common world between working life and private life the in-dividual's public life is reduced to shopping expeditions, church at-tendance, and movie-going, all homogenized to suit family-tastes, which are, of course, presensitized to the appeal of the 'goods life.' "[14]

Anyone who counts such clumsy passages as descriptive of American
life in the sixties or seventies rather than as symptomatic of a writer's
personal preoccupations may find value in these loose moral condemnations of privatization.

On balance, I think it fair to say that the privatization of American
life has not fit the classical model of progressive deterioration ending
in cultural impoverishment and psychic dislocation. Privatization
rather has contributed to an embarrassment of psychic riches, a thickening of individuality. More often than not, incoherence—the threat of
personality disorganization—stems from too many psychic options
rather than too few, from privilege rather than from privation. The
problem of identity—of getting one's act together, to borrow a revealing vaudevillian cliché popular in the sixties—surely was complicated
by the privatization of American life: the move away from cities, the
spread of the automobile culture, the explosion of the media, the profusion of computer technology, the increasing importance assigned to
interior living spaces. But the complications themselves testify to a
significant enlargement of individual options. Indeed, this task of
exploring possibilities of the self, of pushing in many directions at
once and then seeking a semblance of shapeliness, becomes endlessly
time consuming. Idleness finds no room in this utopia. The project of
fulfillment of the self ensures the seeker steady if not always engross-
ing work. "For us," Sennett observes, "discipline means organizing
and orchestrating this panoply of inner resources so that it *coheres.*
The task for us is not to repress part of the psyche, but to give the
whole a shape."[15]

Sennett exaggerates, perhaps deliberately, in order to underline the
growing accent on personal expression. But there can be no doubt
that the private space of the self has been enlarged, creating potentially
anarchic zones that require some form of authority as a condition of
personal identity (or coherence). More of everything had to be brought
into focus—more information, more desires swirling along the surfaces
of consciousness, more potential directions in which to take the self.
And there was less potent culturewide authority, fewer internalized
commands shared by large sectors of the population. Hence the
authority of self-discipline assumed growing importance in the seventies. But since self-discipline is difficult to come by and even more
difficult to sustain, many citizens failed to give the self a decent
shape, sinking instead into incoherence or seeking predigested forms of

order: the authority of some guru or other, the authority of Jesus, the authority of a political figure or doctrine. Critics found most of these responses to the decline of culturewide authority woefully inadequate. At best, many observers maintained, the anarchic areas of private space yielded thin selves—surface coherence without amplitude. At worst, these anarchic zones remained incoherent, anomic. Individuals might have been able to patch themselves together with doses of self-discipline or with patent medicines such as *est* or *lifespring*. Moreover, such attempts at personal survival might have yielded a relatively high rate of subjectively experienced success, as I have insisted throughout these chapters. Still, even the scope of potential success (not to mention to rate of perceived failure) was far too narrow to satisfy critics who, like Bellah, located the white middle class in a zone between psychic incoherence and some spiritual equivalent of bleached flour.

Though most individuals survived the sixties and seventies, critics conceded, too few flourished: the custom-designed, well-crafted self became rarer, ceasing even to serve as a widely shared cultural ideal. As I have suggested in earlier chapters, however, the admirable self posited by critics as diverse as Daniel Bell and Christopher Lasch did not disappear during these decades. In fact, the absolute number of well-crafted selves grew rather than dwindled, though such persons may have become a smaller percentage of the total population and certainly a smaller percentage than critics had hoped. Moreover, I have maintained that the well-crafted or narrative self is not the only variant of the realized self—that a more romantic, open-ended, fluid conception dominated the Movement, the therapeutic search, and even segments of the Christian revival in the sixties and seventies.

What of these more fluid selves, many of whom lived within the nonelite range of society? Can they be said to have sought (and found) admirable modes of fulfillment, or must they be judged failures—victims of self-indulgence or of a depleted culture beyond authority? There is no obvious way to mediate this dispute within the schema of fulfillment I have used through this book. Choosing to be as inclusive as possible, I doubtless have forgone the chance to be neutral, or even to be as discriminating as I ought. In presenting yet another variation of what Richard Hofstadter calls the unresolvable conflict between the elite character of the intellectual's own class and democratic aspirations, I might have been too inclusive, too willing to credit nearly every claimant to salvation with the achievement of some worthy version of fulfillment. Often I have seemed to prefer coherence to incoherence without insisting firmly enough on amplitude (a mark of both the well-crafted and the fully realized self). Hence, I have had to take seriously the subjective claims to fulfillment of many who pursue coherence without much regard for amplitude (a fail-safe formula for rigidity and narrowness): devotees of Hare Krishna who chant one formula more than 1,700 times each day as well as black Muslims, followers of Swami Muktananda as well as fundamentalist followers of Jesus.

Needless to say, no serious person can regard all forms of the quest as equally valuable, either to individuals or to society. I have concluded rather that any variant that does not involve gross violations of the law may be preferred equally by any citizen in the quest; and further, that during the sixties and seventies the usual range of cultural options offered far more variety, a far greater scope of choice, and significantly more potential for self-fulfillment than social and cultural critics regularly allowed. I have insisted, then, not simply on the increasingly democratic character of the quest—its historically unprecedented scope, the chance (often the first chance) afforded to individuals within all social categories to participate, to take one path and then, if necessary, a second or a third. I have exhibited also a naïve article of democratic faith by supposing that the results, while perhaps not up to the standards of any particular intellectual elite, have been excellent on the whole—not ideal by any means, but far better than they seem when viewed through the customary lenses of social and cultural criticism.

Even though the dispute over the quality of American selves resists full resolution, let me proceed a bit further to consider the contention that American culture grew progressively unable to sustain a society of selves that were both ample and coherent. Here the decline of authority was supposed to be central, a contributing cause of the loss of unity and the demise of excellence, which in turn diminished the possibilities of life beyond the narrow boundaries of the self. The boundaryless self, lamented by such critics as Bell and Rieff, had nowhere to go—or rather, it could go nearly anywhere in an expanding cultural space without experiencing much change in atmospheric pressure, especially as what passed for public culture itself became ever more privatized, more filled with local, personal concerns.

Writing in the late seventies, Kevin Phillips concluded that "for the past several years the symptoms of decomposition have appeared throughout the body politic—in the economic, geographic, ethnic, religious, cultural, biological sectors of society. Small loyalties are replacing larger ones. Small outlooks are also replacing larger ones." Phillips gathers under the umbrella of "balkanization" all the major sources of conflict in American society, from regional chauvinists to socially divisive women who demand full personhood. Though such phenomena as "regionalism, separatism, fragmentation, and rampant ethnicity" are as old as the American experience, Phillips concedes, they took on new, ominous meanings in the sixties and seventies. "From George Washington's day through the Trajan-like imperial high-water mark of the early 1960s, Americans retrospectively can see ethnicity, regionalism, and states' rights yield before growing concepts of global optimism, the melting pot, equality, homogeneity, and centralization of (benign federal) power."[16]

Casting his reflections in the framework of nostalgia, Phillips concludes that present tendencies toward reparochialization portend more than the reappearance of a familiar bend in the cultural road. They suggest that we have reached what Andrew Hacker has termed "the end of the American era": cultural decline bound up with decline in every area of American life, from international presence and military superiority to such domestic concerns as inflation and the instability of the nuclear family. American culture survives, but it does so precariously, in what Robert Nisbet terms the "twilight of authority." In the view of such critics as Phillips and Nisbet, America has lost its "sense of authority and common purpose." Unity has given way to division, national purpose to local drift.

Laments about the balkanization of American culture usually include fading hopes of national greatness: loss of unequalled military prowess, international clout, economic superiority, domestic unity. Indeed, such nostalgic laments, which typically are voiced by critics on the right and echoed during the late seventies in public-opinion polls, seem animated more by these concerns than by worries over the alleged demise of cultural excellence. Though often articulated in cultural terms, this theme of disunity is fundamentally social and political. The unalloyed notion of cultural excellence and its steep decline, on the other hand, is advanced regularly by high humanists—radical as well as conservative. Marxists and other radicals infer the alienation of men and women from lurid examinations of the tawdry artifacts of mass culture. And cultural conservatives claim that the intellectual elite—those few who produce and uphold the intellectual and aesthetic tradition—has been disoriented by the growth of kitsch.

Faced with claims made on behalf of an embattled intellectual elite, few serious critics defend mass or even middlebrow culture. For one thing, little in these realms stirs critics to more than guarded celebration. In fact, defenses are usually defensive, focusing more often than not on the rhetorical excesses of arrogant apologists for high culture than on the intrinsic qualities of such cultural artifacts as popular fiction or commercial television. For another, most critics like to think of themselves as part of a cultural elite—a modest aim, easily enough indulged. In the late fifties, for example, William Phillips, a founding editor of *Partisan Review,* took stock of the perennial argument over the decline of cultural excellence. Phillips conceded that "both individual talent and serious culture go on, but under constant threat of seduction and disorganization . . . they are often forced, out of the instinct for self-preservation, into greater isolation, alienation from the rest of the community, and lately, into academicism." Mass and middle culture, Phillips continues, are largely responsible for "the breakdown of traditional authority and standards, in all areas, including that of education itself . . ." Yet according to Phillips it is not simply a case of Gresham's law applied to culture, of meretricious products driving out superior merchandise, but also, even primarily, the emergence of a new intellectual "establishment" dominated by "middlebrow writers and thinkers, academic experts who are ignorant in most areas, cultural custodians who are dedicated to the classics but uncertain in their relation to new works, and that amorphous body of professional people who inhale and exhale the prevailing cultural modes."[17]

Phillips's rhetorical strategy is transparent. Inferiors of various sorts populate his vision of the "American establishment": lower-status intellectuals who write for *Harper's* and *The Atlantic;* narrow academic specialists, pedants, and trivial followers of changing cultural hemlines. This new "establishment" of intellectuals, academics, journalists, and bureaucrats threatens to overwhelm the few serious minds who publish their work in, well, let us be candid, such journals as

Partisan Review. Two decades later, at the end of the seventies, such neoconservative critics as Norman Podhoretz were holding a similarly vague new stratum of adversary intellectuals, mostly left-wingers, responsible for the alleged destruction of cultural authority.[18] Indeed, the second-string players in these games are always easy to identify: they include everyone but the arbiter and a select circle of designated superstars.

No amount of ordinary evidence could persuade Phillips that the various segments of American culture flourished in the sixties and seventies. The proliferation of cultural options—of ways to symbolize and enact scenarios of fulfillment—probably would be dismissed as dull variations on a mediocre theme, politically welcome perhaps, but not culturally hopeful. Nor would Phillips be impressed by statistical evidence of the growing consumption of cultural offerings. Though they must be taken cautiously, such figures as are available do suggest a certain vitality and democratization of American culture in these decades. For example, between 1960 and 1978 the number of radio stations increased from 3,688 to 5,748; the number of television stations grew from 530 to 714 (with PBS stations climbing from 56 to 272); and the number of cable television systems grew spectacularly, from 640 to 4,150.[19] Although the number of newspapers declined from 11,315 in 1960 to 9,620 in 1980, the number of periodicals rose from 8,422 to 10,236. Federal aid to the arts and humanities rose from zero in 1960 to more than $300 million in 1979 as a consequence of the establishment of the National Endowment for the Arts and the National Endowment for the Humanities.[20] Attendance at operas and concerts doubled during the seventies. The annual rate of new books and new editions published increased from 15,000 in 1960 to more than 45,000 in 1979. The number of telephones per 1,000 population jumped from 408 in 1960 to 793 in 1979. And postal service, measured in pieces of first-class mail, rose from 33 billion in 1960 to 58 billion in 1979.[21]

Phillips airily dismisses such evidence in advance, declaring in 1959 that "the quantitative approach is just a tautology: all it proves is that a given number of people read a given number of books, or listen to a given number of classical symphonies, and generally such data belong to the department of adult education." His parochial concerns surface when he wonders why "the audience for the kind of work—in poetry and criticism, for example—that has not been glamorized remains so small, despite all the sales figures . . ."[22] Of course, Phillips has a point: the statistics I have cited do not constitute conclusive evidence of anything, not even, as he implies, of the number of books actually read, let alone of a cultural renaissance or the unlikely political triumph of an intellectual elite. They prove less than Phillips supposes, but they suggest more: that the elite he has in mind survived decently through the sixties and seventies, a period of challenge to all forms of authority, even the authority of intellectuals. In fact, members of this elite—first its left and left-liberal representatives, and more recently its conservative members (some of them former leftists)—have exerted considerable influence on the shapes of middlebrow culture during these years.

The regions of mass and middlebrow culture grew more varied and more sophisticated, as a comparison of the periodical, radio, or even television offerings available in 1960 and in 1980 reveals. Such changes are apparent not only in the proliferation of special-interest radio stations, CB channels, television channels, cable networks, and specialized periodicals, from *Working Mother* to *Vegetarian Times.* Improvements are evident too in the maturation of middlebrow culture, in the growing syntactical complexity and stylistic range of a middlebrow magazine like *Time,* for example, or in the development of television situation comedy, from *Life with Luigi* in the fifties to *All in the Family* in the seventies, or in crime drama, from *Richard Diamond, Private Eye* to *Kojak* and *Harry O.* The thickening textures of middlebrow culture, so obviously influenced by an intellectual establishment whose members mostly taught college for a living, provided the details, if not the outlines, of the principal modes of fulfillment, from the styles of Movement culture and the therapeutic search even to selected parts of the Christian revival.

Thus I think it fair to speculate that the alleged decline of cultural excellence in the sixties and seventies was more apparent than real. It is obvious even at this brief distance that intellectual activity flourished during these decades—in social criticism, in the social sciences and the humanities, and in the hard sciences. But it is too soon to tell whether developments in science or the arts approached the highest levels of previous American achievement. We cannot know, for example, whether key scientific discoveries in, say, genetic engineering, astronomy, or the earth sciences equal or surpass those of earlier decades of American history, though the sixties and seventies should hold up rather well, inasmuch as the volume of scientific knowledge continued along its exponential curve. Nor can we know, for example, whether the fiction of the sixties equalled that, say, of the twenties— whether Bellow, Malamud, and Doctorow will match Hemingway, Faulkner, and Fitzgerald in the judgment of later generations. Because they are subject to periodic revisions, such aesthetic evaluations cannot proceed very far until the facile ideological biases in favor of the glittering sixties and opposed to the dull seventies lose their grip. It may turn out even then that, for example, the visual art of the sixties—the work of Jasper Johns, Roy Lichtenstein, Frank Stella, and Andy Warhol—will be judged superior to comparable work of the seventies, or, on the other hand, that film in the seventies —from *M*A*S*H* (1970) to *Apocalypse Now* (1979) and *The Deer Hunter* (1978)—may seem superior to the fare of the sixties. Still, I think it safe to say that high culture survived and that cultures in the middle range thrived and probably even improved somewhat during the sixties *and* the seventies. The charge of declining excellence, especially in the seventies, represents yet another failure of unrealistic and not altogether innocent expectations held by certain members of the American intelligentsia.[23]

But the charge of runaway mediocrity (and vulgarity) is not without substance. In certain circumstances, of course, a deliberate cultivation of mediocrity—even of vulgarity—can advance democratic ends, as anyone acquainted with adolescents quickly comes to learn: a suspension of manners, an all-around lowering of taste, a corruption of language can serve to include larger numbers of people in widening circles of social acceptability. Democratic possibilities notwithstanding, relaxation of certain modes of authority, even the fundamentally repressive political and cultural modes that composed much of WASP culture, produced a number of untoward side effects, including an outbreak of thoughtless conformity. Though serious intellectual and artistic activity might have survived and even flourished during the sixties and seventies, it did so within the context of an explosion of flashy mass- and middle-cultural products: in all areas of culture, food tended to be replaced by groceries. High culture lost its central position in the hierarchy of cultural excellence in part because it became a rapidly diminishing fraction of the total cultural output. To complicate matters, authoritative standards of judgment that sustain hierarchies of value were increasingly difficult to discover, or at least ever harder to elicit agreement on.

Of course, this was not a new condition, but it no longer confined itself to avant garde artists and critics. Hence high culture suffered a far greater loss: it was deprived of much of its social authority, its capacity to elicit the respect that accompanies informed appreciation or even to command deference from large numbers of people unable (or unwilling) to produce or appreciate serious art, music, literature, scholarship, and criticism. This demise of deference is evident in the indifferent successes and large failures of liberal education from the middle sixties through the end of the seventies. It is evident also in the growing willingness of citizens and students to speak out against the authority of high culture and its academic and intellectual guardians, a habit cultivated by left-wing students in the sixties and acquired by others in the seventies. Students who wondered aloud about the "relevance" of the study of serious literature or philosophy in the sixties were joined by other students and parents who demanded a direct vocational payoff for dollars invested in higher education in the seventies. A college major came to be measured strictly in terms of its applicability to employment, as if a sociology student ought to intend to practice that dull trade or else seek another course of study.[24] It is impossible to tell how many people valued the production, dissemination, and cultivation of serious cultural artifacts in the postwar decades, or to plot the changes across these decades: what obviously did change was the willingness of individuals to *speak* their cultural prejudices in the sixties and seventies.

A rising inclination to register opinions appears to be a clear expression of the quest for fulfillment, and a salutary one at that. Yet the growth of such a disposition under democratic circumstances also results in a disproportionate rise of ignorant and prejudiced opinion, since informed opinion, being more difficult to acquire, can expand only at a comparatively slow rate. Opinions are increasingly celebrated in public rhetoric as free expressions of ordinary selves, important primarily as expressive acts rather than as reasoned judgments or as counters in a serious inquiry. Hence the status of opinion itself declined, in part as a consequence of its burgeoning volume. There are other reasons as well. Since opinion cannot measure up to the authoritative claims of science, all opinion may be construed as mere opinion, interesting perhaps but inconsequential. Nor need opinion any longer conform to intrinsic standards of reason and good taste. Citizens bound for work pause to give their views on foreign-policy questions to television interviewers in a tossed-off sentence or two: "No, I don't think we should build the MX missile"; "I believe that all weapons should be destroyed"; "We should go ahead with it if the Russians invade Poland"; "What's an MX?" Others chat casually about the death or survival of God, creationism, and astrology on radio talk shows or in informal conversation.

And why not? As deference to cultural authority wanes, talk becomes cheap. Authoritative standards of cultural excellence sag. And the ever receding limits of bad taste become the object of an intense, often richly comic and uniquely American search through the regions of culture. Just when these limits appear in sight, as for example in such television situation comedies as *Maude* (1972), someone else manages to push the frontiers back even further. Chuck Barris develops the *Gong Show* in 1976, a campy parody of the old Major Bowes variety show (and later, *Ted Mack's Original Amateur Hour*) featuring talking bears, obese violinists playing "Dark Eyes" while riding unicycles or standing on their heads, and Italian accordionists from Trenton in breathless pursuit of the "Lady of Spain." When high culture begins to lose its social function as an object of deference, it cannot easily impose standards of excellence on the wider culture or even set limits on what is not to be done.[25] Mediocrity is not simply tolerated; it is celebrated. Middle and lowbrow modes of cultural expression are promoted aggressively. And amateurs of all sorts proliferate, as in the seventies when the number of American "musicians" grew from an estimated 16 percent to 25 percent of the population, or about thirty-five million citizens.

When consensus on what is not done dissolves, bad taste abounds. Standards of civility decline in the public realm and indeed everywhere. Aesthetic and moral categories overlap. Name calling becomes an increasingly popular sport: *Fuck You!*, the title of Ed Sanders's little magazine, so shocking in the middle sixties, springs effortlessly from the lips of automobile drivers of both sexes and all ages. Next to "fuck you"—the crudest way of dismissing other persons—"bullshit" emerged as the coarsest way of dismissing new information or unfamiliar beliefs. The "crap detector" that Ernest Hemingway sensibly advised each person to cultivate as a prudent strategy of self-

defense was transformed into an offensive weapon to be used indiscriminately by many citizens.

A cheapening of opinion, a lowering of taste, lapses of civility: disregard for authority contributes to a variety of such untoward effects.
Social divisions obviously were intensified by a growing spirit of
negation, which nearly everyone observed in American culture of the
sixties and seventies. Each person was entitled to an opinion on every
conceivable topic with no strings attached: even grade-school children
were asked for their ideas on how to secure world peace in contests
sponsored by such civic organizations as the Lions' Club. In such
banal circumstances, there was little pressure to make opinions conform to any culturewide standard and even less pressure to make them
informed: the only task was to deliver them. Tolerance and intolerance
flourished in tandem. Part of the increased tolerance for a diversity of
cultural perspectives that opinion polls displayed surely derived less
from liberal convictions than from a weary sense of resignation, a
willingness to allow others to pursue their own images of culture,
however simple-minded and ignorant, in exchange for being left
alone—ideological pollution be damned. Whatever its subjective
sources, however, a negative consensus on cultural matters, amounting
to an agreement to disagree, represents perhaps the most salutary
outcome in an increasingly syncretic culture. A negative consensus,
the price exacted by pluralism, represents a bearable cultural cost,
surely preferable to current alternatives: Jerry Falwell's rigid Moral
Majority or the triumph of unopposed laissez faire.

   In the sixties and seventies, intolerance represented the counterpoint
to growing tolerance of diversity. When culturewide authority is
routinely questioned, doubted, and judged insufficient to sanction and
order the growing diversity of standards and taste, charismatic authority multiplies. In the extreme, the isolated self fancies itself the primary
or even the sole authority over the entire sphere of art, letters, science,
and morals. Everyone else becomes an occasion for an exercise of
intolerance. Alienation, as Lionel Trilling remarked, seems no longer
"a deprivation or deficiency but a potency." Such chic poses permit
individuals who are beyond the discipline of authority to cast themselves in exalted cultural roles without bearing or even having to
comprehend the costs of such achievements. "The falsities of an alien-

ated social reality," Trilling goes on to say, "are rejected in favour of an upward psychopathic mobility to the point of divinity, each one of us a Christ—but with none of the inconveniences of undertaking to intercede, of being a sacrifice, of reasoning with rabbis, of making sermons, of having disciples, of going to weddings and to funerals, of beginning something and at a certain point remarking that it is finished."[26] Though most Americans avoided such extremes of attitude and behavior, there was an ample supply of willing authorities freshly anointed by their own hands and a sufficient number of followers to guarantee a disturbing rise in charismatic modes of authority during the sixties and seventies.

Such authority flourished in elements of the Movement—in the black civil-rights campaigns led by Martin Luther King, Jr.; in SDS under a variety of leaders, some of them disingenuously reluctant, we are now asked to believe. It flourished in the Christian revival, both in certain evangelical christologies and in a widespread willingness to submit to authoritative pastors and prophets. Charismatic authorities were prominent, too, in the therapeutic quest: individuals differing as widely in intellect and charm as Arthur Janov and Fritz Perls attracted followers, appealing to them largely through the force of personality.

"Trust me," "listen to me," "follow me," "lean on me": the appeal of charismatic authority—strong and seductive in any case—was augmented in an atmosphere of cultural pluralism. It was augmented too by a world of growing scientific complexity that multiplies an individual's ignorance of most matters relentlessly, year by year. Under such circumstances, charismatic authority registers gains by default: even though suspicion rises as sellers of cultural nostrums multiply and buyers become more wary, the search for reliable narrators intensifies and indeed spills over from cultural to political spheres. After the political demise of Richard Nixon, arguably the least plausible narrator in postwar American politics, presidential searches during the remainder of the seventies centered first on character and integrity, which assisted Jimmy Carter in his 1976 campaign; then, when mere honesty failed to satisfy or perhaps even to display itself fully, the search moved on to qualities of leadership: "don't lie to us" gave way to "lead us" (but not in undesired or uncomfortable directions). If only by virtue of the right of succession, Edward Kennedy hoped to convey such attributes of leadership in the seventies. But, at least in 1980, Kennedy failed to satisfy the prior criterion of character in the opinion of a decisive number of voters. Of all the participants in presidential politics, Ronald Reagan managed most ably to project the qualities of an honest leader through the television screen, at least during the campaign and the opening phases of his administration: the politically unmanageable part of president called for an actor, and this time one who did not come from New York, Boston, or Georgia.

In a syncretic culture and heterogeneous society such as the United States of the sixties and seventies, charismatic authority was the only sort that elicited much popular enthusiasm. Other forms of authority survived and exerted great influence, though bureaucratic authority, the authority of science, and even the authority of such conventional professionals as doctors and lawyers all lost a measure of public confidence. Whereas these modes advanced here and retreated there, charismatic authority registered clear gains in the sixties and seventies. Charismatic authority obviously is the fundamental mode of authority in the quest for personal fulfillment. It dominated the increasingly important private spheres of friendship and the family, where authority roles often are reversed voluntarily and always reverse themselves slowly in the dance of generations. Charismatic authority also gained force on the larger cultural landscape—in religion, in therapeutic circles, and even in politics. The apparent growth and the certain legitimation of charismatic authority probably yielded a series of unpleasant outcomes, from the studied promotion of theological, cultural, and political ignorance to the prolongation of needless psychological dependence in families and among friends. Moreover, as cultural authority fragmented and gathered around charismatic figures or in ordinary selves, images of apocalypse more terrifying though less realistic than plausible fears of nuclear destruction stalked the imaginations of many citizens: some revolutionaries of the sixties, many born again Christians hoping for the rapture, and not a few therapeutics seeking refuge in a present moment, wishing to erase memory and block anticipation.

Anxiety about the future obviously animates the apocalyptic theme; so too do anger and revenge, which figure importantly in evangelical views of *your* destruction following *their* rapture, and in revolutionaries' fantasies of *your* blood flowing in *their* (newly acquired) streets. An eye for an eye; even an eye just for the hell of it: this motif also runs through popular culture of the seventies. It dominates *Death Wish* (1974), an enormously popular film starring Charles Bronson as a middle-class New Yorker who practices architecture by day and bloody vengeance by night. After discovering his wife dead and his daughter in a catatonic state, Bronson sets out on a shooting spree. Not taking the trouble to track down the rapists who attacked his family, Bronson simply murders shady-looking characters at random, dispensing a rough form of class, or rather caste justice. Instead of leaving the destruction of the wicked to God, to a revolutionary committee, or even to the slow processes of the bourgeois judicial system, Bronson does the job himself, reviving a dimension of rugged individualism and adapting it to the urban landscape. Though eventually arrested in the film, Bronson is not booked but rather set loose to continue his exploits elsewhere (in *Death Wish II,* 1981).

Though they were far from negligible, abuses of charismatic authority in the sixties and seventies nevertheless strike me as minor compared to the pleasures and salutary effects of such authority: its uses as the glue of small communities, its importance in friendship and in family life, its theological potentialities—even, in moderate doses, its political utility. The abuses of charismatic authority seem small, this is to say, when compared to the benefits of the quest for fulfillment. It should also be noted that with the exception of cults, which remained on the fringes of society despite their steady growth, charismatic authority within the family and beyond frequently was taken lightly—suffered for a season and then easily abandoned, as one guru was exchanged for another or for no other. The widespread assertion of the self that fueled the growth of charismatic authority also nourished a skepticism and detachment. Widely practiced, these same dispositions finally protected American society from charismatic authorities who thoroughly subjected followers to their whims: People's Temple leader Jim Jones was a terrible exception, not the norm, and he managed to act out his scheme of death only by thoroughly isolating his followers, culturally and geographically. Fierce competition prevented the formation of monopolies on charisma, putting off the emergence of the Antichrist once again. Thus I think it fair to say that the proliferation of charismatic authority probably was an unavoidable side effect of the larger, more important, and far more salutary set of phenomena that I have discussed under the rubric of the quest for personal fulfillment. What remains to be observed, however, is the effect of slackening authority on American political culture.

Authority and Political Culture

American culture seems able to endure without much centralized authority: it can bear considerable disorder, even disunity, without falling apart. Indeed, the increasingly syncretic nature of postwar culture represents the price of pluralism, the cost of preserving, enlarging, and democratizing personal options. What is more, serious culture survived an epidemic of mediocrity, which, like disorder, is an inescapable side effect of the quest for fulfillment practiced on an ever wider social scale. The quest for fulfillment, this is to say, has flourished in what it partly created: a disordered, multicentered culture. But can the same be said of the sphere of politics, or, more broadly, of the sphere of American political culture? Are the consequences of a general decline of authority as pronounced—and as tolerable—in this sphere of social affairs as they are in the larger culture? Certainly the bulk of critical opinion in the late seventies stressed the dangers of what might be seen as negative political manifestations of the quest for fulfillment: entropy rather than energy, fragmentation rather than wholeness, disintegration rather than integration, breaking apart rather than coming together, atomization rather than structure, drift rather than direction. The decline of authority revealed its influence variously, according to critics: criticism had lost much of its power; ideology had lost much of its coherence; and politics had lost much of its capacity to direct public affairs.

Criticism. Authority cannot bear endless criticism; sooner or later relentless unmasking of venal figures and unjust social arrangements subverts authority, robbing it of elements of mystery. In the sixties and seventies talk not only was cheap and loose. It was also, according to any number of critics, altogether too critical in the worst sense of the term: quarrelsome and often simply stupid. Phillip Rieff went so far as to suggest that "this culture is being levelled, and therefore destroyed, by a remissive teaching elite that makes a piety of endless criticism."[27] More temperate critics such as Andrew Hacker lamented certain negative effects of the expanding universe of discourse: "An atmosphere pervaded by conversation is bound to undermine agencies of control. Silence, particularly one that is self-imposed, implies acquiescence to symbols of existing authority."[28] In his interpretation of the Kennedy–Johnson era, Samuel P. Huntington assigns a prominent place to what he calls a "democratic distemper," a political disease of the sixties that brought on the ubiquitous decline of governmental authority in the seventies. According to Huntington, intense participation in public discourse and politics on the part of previously silent or quiescent minorities overloaded the democratic circuits of the American political system.[29] Even on the left, which thrives on a diet rich in criticism, critics confessed reservations. Irving Howe, for example, observed that the culture of modernism makes a fetish of perpetual criticism, turning it into yet another form of novelty.

There are, these commentators seem to agree, limits beyond which criticism loses its edge: when there is too much of it, when there is too much of an inferior sort, or (for some) when it is overtaken by precipitate action. Concerns over the amount, quality, and timing of criticism in the sixties and seventies came easily to critics. Of course, they did not reach a consensus on just where the limits of their activity ought to be set or how they ought to be enforced; serious people, especially critics, would not even attempt such a project. Still, the widespread conviction that criticism in the sixties and seventies might have pushed beyond its fruitful limits, thereby sacrificing a degree of its potential effectiveness, seems to me well founded. Certainly this proliferation of criticism was a predictable outgrowth of the larger cultural design of these decades. As I have argued throughout these pages, dissent served as a crucial and on the whole salutary vehicle of the quest for fulfillment and the democratization of personhood. Criticism became far more widely practiced in American political culture—left, right, and center—by journalists, critics, and academics, to be sure, but by other citizens as well. In the course of this expanded practice, criticism was democratized. Yet while high standards of criticism survived and even improved in certain quarters, the overall quality of criticism inevitably dropped, as everyone, it seemed, felt qualified to criticize everything from other people to social systems and competing cosmologies. Demystification without understanding: this aptly characterizes much of what passed for social criticism in the sixties and the seventies. One exposure after another might have left the emperor unclothed, but such exposures also stripped critics and deprived them of an element of freshness.

Of the many effects of the constant criticism of every facet of society and culture that took place during the sixties and seventies, none was more important to political culture than the spirit of automatic negativism that pervaded criticism, reached all levels of media journalism, and, judging from casual conversation, penetrated ordinary consciousness as well. When the "critical" element in criticism receives incessant stress, an imbalance of perception and judgment can be expected to occur. Like a hypoglycemic patient whose metabolism is disabled permanently from repeated dietary abuses, a person living on a diet too high in criticism, especially junk criticism, can easily lose a good portion of his or her critical sense. In the sixties and seventies, skepticism, doubt, cynicism, pessimism—those healthy elements of mature critical consciousness—threatened to take over, to control the mood, tone, and even the presuppositions of ordinary perceptions of public issues. Commenting on the attempted assassination of Pope John Paul II in May of 1981, an unidentified New York woman told NBC: "It's just disgusting what this world is coming to. Just disgusting. Nobody's safe anymore. It's terrible."[30] One Mediterannean madman, a part of what is after all a comparatively small wave of international terrorism, managed to provoke this global sigh, a typical lament from the chorus of ordinary citizens.

Even pieces of good news were likely to get strained through negative categories that became habitual, almost second nature, in the press and in informal conversation. Here is a news item on income and inflation in the seventies published in the spring of 1981: "A family of four must earn a pretax income of more than $22,000 today [1981] to equal the purchasing power of a $10,000 income in 1970, according to a report by the Conference Board. Inflation has cut the purchasing power of a dollar approximately in half over the past decade, just as rising incomes have pushed Americans into higher tax brackets, requiring much larger federal income and Social Security tax payments."[31] Two paragraphs of gloomy developments with no hint of the major point of the story until the next-to-last paragraph, when the modestly good news finally appears: "Median family income has more than kept pace since 1970, with the typical family expected to have an income of $24,035 this year, compared to $9,867 in 1970, the board said. The median family was left with $8,528 to spend in 1970, while today's family is slightly better off, having $9,184 (in terms of 1970 dollars) to spend after taxes."

An inversion of the optimism that characterized American discourse in the late fifties and early sixties, the hypercritical knee-jerk pessimism of the seventies served some of the same ends. It provided a shared framework accessible to nearly everyone. Especially with the aid of proliferating analytic and predictive devices of the social sciences, it is far easier to pronounce any experiment, program, policy, activity, institution, or leader a failure, to sigh wisely about the "mess in Washington," than it is to arrive at a balanced, informed, truly critical judgment. In a pluralistic culture in which differences of all kinds abound, the surest and perhaps the last public bond seems to be a self-indulgent critical attitude. Meet a stranger and you are far less apt to find common beliefs (at any level of specificity) than shared convictions about things that don't work: marriages, appliances, children, governments, middle and old age. What the new Left of the sixties and the New Right of the seventies agreed upon was this: nothing currently in public operation functions very well. By the end of the seventies, continuous criticism had ceased to be the province of the left and the right, having become common American property, the blest tie that binds citizens. This tie of negativity about public matters strongly influences the ethos in which ideology and politics unfold and make their way.

Ideology. Uncritically critical attitudes toward everything public spread so rapidly in the sixties and seventies that they came to seem the only basis for an American consensus: a largely anti-ideological public philosophy of negations. One thing was certain: the public philosophy that prevailed throughout most of the sixties no longer controlled ideological and political play. From the middle thirties through the middle sixties, the New Deal had served as a dominant "state of mind, an outlook on politics and government, a public philosophy."[32] The New Deal shaped the American political consensus during these decades and even gave political conflict a certain coherence: "liberal" and "conservative" took on the peculiarly American meanings they were to retain for more than four decades. In the sixties and seventies, however, the American ideological landscape—opaque in the simplest of times—grew considerably more dense, and as it did so it became harder to predict where self-described "liberals" and "conservatives" might position themselves on important public matters.

The ideological field was increasingly complicated and divided in

these decades for many reasons, not least the rising capacity—and disposition—of Americans to express the rudiments of ideological consciousness, as Norman Nie, Sidney Verba, and John Petrocik argue in
their study *The Changing American Voter* (1976). From the middle
Eisenhower years, when ideological issues were buried in the great
American consensus, through the middle seventies, ever larger numbers of citizens—perhaps as many as 50 percent, Nie and his associates
generously estimate—cultivated at least a faint appreciation of ideological terminology. At the same time, constituencies grew more
diverse and more vocal, with the entry of various minorities into the
political process. To complicate matters even further, the issues grew
more varied, more complex, and more bewildering in these years: gains
in coherence of political thinking were threatened by the burgeoning
volume of information that needed to be digested. In addition to the
dense thicket of usual policy questions, from poverty to transportation
and from education to health care, people were moved to take positions on everything from nuclear arsenals to life-styles. The scope of
political concerns expanded dramatically. Ever larger numbers of
advocates and opponents of uncommon personal styles, from dress and
length of hair to drugs and cohabitation, brought previously less controversial private matters into the public sphere. And what formerly
had been a largely theological question acquired an ominous political
dimension when the capacity to stage a nuclear apocalypse became part
of the human repertoire.

More people thinking ideologically about a greater range of increasingly complex issues: this is one part of a formula for ideological
complexity, division, and confusion. Another part, of course, is the
rising perception of collective failure in the battle against public
problems—in particular, the breakdown of the left-liberal conviction
that virtually every social problem can be ameliorated through democratic politics and a strong central government. By the end of the
seventies Americans had lost a good measure of their faith in the
federal government and national political action, a faith nurtured
from the New Deal through the Great Society. Since the middle
sixties, when opinion divided over a number of issues from the war
in Vietnam to the rights of minorities, public confidence in government dropped, as did confidence in such other institutions as medicine, organized religion, organized labor, and business. Despite some
fluctuations, the proportion of respondents to Harris surveys expressing

a "great deal of confidence" in the national government fell from 41 percent in 1966 to 17 percent in 1979.

Confidence declined, as every poll on the subject reported, feeding a growing pessimism. But it did not disappear. Under these circumstances, ideological divisions—among groups and within selves—grew more intense. In the late seventies, according to various surveys, a majority of citizens identified rising government spending as a significant cause of inflation, which had come to be perceived as America's chief domestic ill. Hence popular support multiplied for what might be construed as anti–New Deal measures—schemes to cut taxes, to legislate balanced governmental budgets, or to limit growth of public (especially social) spending to a certain percentage of the gross national product. But divisions between "liberal" spenders and "conservative" budget cutters, though still clear in some circles, were too neat to capture the complexity and vagaries of public opinion on questions of the size and scope of government. To the extent that opinion polls can be trusted, it is fair to conclude that Americans expressed considerable ambivalence toward the public sector by the late seventies. "Even as they endorse measures to restrict the growth of government spending and taxation," Everett Carll Ladd Jr. and Seymour Martin Lipset observe, "Americans remain extraordinarily supportive of a high level of government services in virtually all sectors."[33] At the end of the seventies, according to a composite of polls, majorities ranging from 51 percent to 72 percent registered the opinion that America spends *too little* on crime prevention, health care, defense, education, drug addiction, and the environment. Even larger majorities claimed that amounts spent on big cities, blacks, and space exploration were not excessive, but rather just "about right." A majority favored cuts on only two items: "Foreign Aid" and "Welfare."[34]

Surely this ambivalence about the role of the state derives in part from tensions between the egalitarian and libertarian impulses that traditionally comprise the chief materials of American ideology. But it derives more directly, I think, from reasonable, if arguable, readings of recent experience: the alleged failure of many antipoverty measures of the sixties; the runaway costs of government; and bureaucratic arrogance, waste, and inefficiency on one side balanced by economic and social benefits flowing from government programs such as Social Security on the other. As Ladd and Lipset put it, "Americans appear to want a society in which each individual is self-supporting and is able, through competition on an equal basis with others, to improve his situation without outside assistance." But ordinary citizens recognize certain realities at least as competently as do members of more ideologically sophisticated elite groups. Because Americans "are aware that such equal opportunity does not exist," Ladd and Lipset continue, "they also endorse remedial programs by the state. As a result, in spite of their continued adherence on an ideological level to individualistic anti-state values, when asked to approve various proposed federal programs, their commitment to equal rights and opportunities leads them to support such proposals by sizable majorities."[35]

The ideological confusion of the sixties and seventies, then, reflects the added complexity of social problems and the difficulty of arranging solutions, as well as the obvious pressures exerted by new and newly aroused constituencies, from minorities to women and from environmentalists to the handicapped. It reflects further the rising political sophistication of a better-educated citizenry. Ideological confusion, this is to say, is partly a function of the quest for fulfillment and the democratization of personhood. Of course, the quest exerted powerful anti-ideological and antipolitical biases, which we have observed in such predictable quarters as the human-potential movement and in such unlikely domains as the new Left. But the multifaceted search for a piece of social justice sufficient to permit salvation and thereby promote personal fulfillment exerted important ideological effects as well. The quest augmented the role of ideology, multiplied ideological options, and intensified ideological cleavages. The same individuals assumed different positions on a variety of issues, and it was not uncommon for a person to be liberal on economics, moderate on foreign policy, and conservative on civil liberties. An individual's position frequently was subdivided even further, as for example when a supporter of gay rights opposed liberalization of marijuana laws, or a born again Christian opposed rights of such unpopular minorities as members of the Hare Krishna sect.

Thus, although political beliefs were apt to be more "constrained," to borrow Phillip Converse's term—more coherently related to a central core of values—political vision became more individuated, more personalized and customized in the sixties and seventies. In such circumstances, the controlling vision of individuals often had to be welded together through irony and paradox: the diversity and complexity of issues, as well as a proliferation of subcultural groups and an intensification of the democratization of personhood, militated against simple and politically useful consistency.[36] Hence nothing in the realm of political behavior could be taken for granted. As Nie and Verba put it, "membership in a population group no longer predicts political behavior very well; region, class, religion are still associated with party affiliation and the vote, but not as closely as they once were . . . The individual voter evaluates candidates on the basis of information and impressions conveyed by the mass media, and then votes on that basis. He or she acts as an individual, not as a member of a collectivity."[37]

It is true, of course, that such ideological confusion as was evident among masses and elite groups in the sixties and seventies took place mainly within conventional American limits. The dominant impulses of American ideology toward personal liberty and equality of opportunity persisted, informing the main ideological thrusts of the period. Every ideological episode of any sustained consequence was fashioned from these elements of liberty and equality. Indeed, each thrust seems reasonably derivable from the terms of the quest for fulfillment: the rise and rapid demise of marginal radical political perspectives; the growth, diffusion, and dilution of radical cultural perspectives; the ascendance and partial eclipse of left-liberal outlooks from the early sixties through the late seventies; and the swift growth of neoconservative and New Right perspectives in the late sixties and seventies. The reliable American center held pretty well through all this, though the public did tilt somewhat to the left on social issues such as civil rights and civil liberties for various minority groups in the structure of disadvantage. As usual, the actual course of ideological tides disappointed people with exaggerated expectations—those who hoped their ideology would become a wave of substantial social and cultural change and those who feared the ideological power of their opponents.

Yet in spite of the appearance of ideological normalcy, which by definition has come to include radical disappointment at the left and right edges of the spectrum, the growth of customized perspectives within the usual limits of American political thought worried many observers. Under the implosive force of the quest, it has been suggested, ideology might be subverted by uncompromised personal preferences too idiosyncratic and too capricious to provide coherence, continuity, and direction to political affairs. Thus, even as it flourished in America during the sixties and seventies, ideology in its political dimensions became problematic as it threatened to pass from baroque to rococo, from a mode of public rhetoric that unified people, or at least clarified their major differences, to a mode of individual expression.

Politics. A decisive majority of Americans demonstrated far higher levels of ideological constraint in the late seventies than they could manage in the middle fifties, although, as I have suggested, gains in sophistication might have been offset largely by a loss of coherence: a disposition to bend ideological categories out of political shape and into complex, modernist modes of personal expression. In any case, the political system survived both moments: it seems to run well enough either on a mixture of low-grade coherence or on a higher-octane fuel of more idiosyncratic thought. The fact is that political ideology, understood even in the broadest sense of constrained beliefs, never has been the supreme force in American politics. It does not elicit unrestrained enthusiasm even among elite groups, whose members exhibit relatively high degrees of constraint and self-conscious use of ideological categories.

Philosophical conservatives distrust the *idea* of ideology, considering it an arrogant invention of the left, a weak instrument of arid rationality designed to affect history without proper regard for its rich textures, its slow rhythms, its surprising variety. Because they are less patient with historical process, indigenous American conservatives appear more at ease with ideology than do philosophical conservatives such as Michael Oakeshott: at least the natives cherish their own compounds of laissez faire, blaming the citizenry for wandering far from the proper political path, or more recently, in a flush of electoral success, daring to hope that the nation might be coming round once again to the old faith. Radicals on the left have traditionally placed enormous confidence in their own ideology, so much so that ideological conversion served as a central goal among old Left groups. Elements of the new Left, however, were aggressively anti-ideological, uninterested in highly charged warfare conducted with political symbols. Moreover, the left of the sixties and seventies experienced, without much enjoying, what would have been counted a smashing success in earlier decades: the dominant ideology crumbled at many crucial points under a new burst of cultural and ideological pluralism, including a profusion of social criticism. Despite apparent success, a conviction of failure haunted the left of the seventies, a sense that ideology might no longer comprise a crucial political target. "Bourgeois ideology" did fragment, but the political system and the economy managed to survive the changes. In these circumstances, many critics on the left concluded that they had been victims of a capitalist game of mirrors: other modes of authority and power had taken up the ideological slack. As Christopher Lasch observed, echoing critics from Weber on, "the ruling class in advanced countries has largely outgrown its earlier dependence on general culture and a unified world view and relies instead on an instrumental culture resting its claims to legitimacy not on the elaboration of a world view that purports to explain the meaning of life, but purely on its capacity to solve technological problems and thereby to enlarge the supply of material goods."[38]

If conservatives were diffident or nostalgic about ideology and radicals increasingly cynical about it, liberals, who dominated the postwar American intellectual and political scene through most of the sixties, were steadily restrained. Small amounts of ideology lubricated the engines of politics, it was supposed, whereas greater amounts gummed them up. The "genius of American politics," to borrow Daniel Boorstin's phrase, derived in large measure from a broad consensus on basic values and a low incidence of destructive ideological infighting. Ideology in America was imagined as essentially "feminine": its soft edges and indistinct curves permitted compromise and consensus in a political process dominated by interest groups exercising "masculine" muscle. These groups provided concentrations of power stable enough to avert chaos yet sufficiently dispersed to preclude a monopoly by any group—corporations, farmers, labor. The interplay of interest groups within a political field controlled by loose common ideological assumptions concerning liberty, equality, and due process ensured a relatively productive, orderly, and just political life.

Though not without some critical opposition, including a few reservations of their own, liberal thinkers confidently articulated variations of this dominant vision of American political democracy in the fifties. The idea of a ruling class was dead, liberals maintained, frequently in implicit opposition to Marxian themes. So too was the era of small, competitive, capitalist enterprise. The old lobbies, David Riesman argues in *The Lonely Crowd* (1953), had given way to "veto groups," each of which "has struggled for and finally attained a power to stop things conceivably inimical to its interests and, within far narrower limits, to start things."[39] Riesman's maze of veto groups—business, movie-censoring organizations, farmers, labor, professional associations, major ethnic and regional groups—held varying degrees of power. Because they were able to initiate programs but unable to impose their will at will, these groups specialized in defensive power, in strategies to protect their rights, privileges, status, and power.

In *American Capitalism* (1952), John Kenneth Galbraith developed the idea of "countervailing power," which is similar to Riesman's "veto groups" but applied mainly to the economic sphere. In an effort to account for the decline of competition and the rise of economic concentration without describing the historical present as an era of corporate or monopolistic capitalism, Galbraith argued that "private economic power is held in check by the countervailing power of those who are subject to it."[40] Although "in principle the American is controlled, livelihood and soul, by the large corporation," Galbraith admits, "in practice he seems not to be completely enslaved."[41] Concentrated economic power evoked its own countervailing force. In Galbraith's characterization, business, labor, and farm groups constituted the main repositories of countervailing power—modes that facilitated the practice of democracy in postwar America. Even Reinhold Niebuhr, whose neo-orthodox pessimism about political life prevented him from joining wholeheartedly in what C. Wright Mills termed the "Great American Celebration," conceded that "such justice as we have achieved in a technical age has been due to a tolerable equilibrium between various power structures."[42]

Countervailing power, then, was seen by many liberal critics as a facilitator of social justice. At the very least, such power protected us from one another, ensuring that particular interests did not deteriorate while the general level of well-being rose as a consequence of a steadily rising output of goods and services. And the dispersed power of veto groups was judged to be the basis of a reliable if fluid political order. Though they were reluctant to identify justice as an attribute of the system, even radical critics of the fifties and early sixties reluctantly conceded resilience and relative stability. In *One-Dimensional Man*, for example, Herbert Marcuse envisioned "advanced industrial society" as a "system of countervailing powers" that thwarted socialist revolution: "these forces cancel each other out in a higher unification," Marcuse complained, "in the common interest to defend and extend the established position, to combat the historical alternatives, to contain qualitative change. The countervailing powers do not include those which counter the whole."[43] There is, this is to say, no power capable of delivering a knockout punch either within the system, or, from a revolutionary angle, beyond it. Nor is there a single power within the political economy capable of subjugating the other powers. The system of countervailing power works against revolution and tyranny, an arrangement that, however dismaying it might have been to Marcuse, gave liberal thinkers cause for modest celebration.

I rehearse these familiar celebrations of countervailing power because they form elements of a stunning irony, a reversal of perspective that unfolded over the past quarter-century. What struck so many observers as the genius of American politics in the fifties and sixties had come to seem a major obstacle, perhaps even a fatal flaw, by the late seventies. Dispersed power had provided structural protection against concentrated antidemocratic authority. Now it threatened to bring about political paralysis, a blockage of concerted action against mounting economic ills.

Lester C. Thurow's widely noticed *The Zero-Sum Society* (1980) forcefully summarizes the escalating difficulties encountered and engendered by the liberal vision of countervailing power. Abandoning earlier liberal projections of endlessly rising curves of prosperity, Thurow emphasizes the possibility of relative scarcity. Americans, he declares, now live in a zero-sum society: policies adopted to meet domestic problems involve a proverbial theft of Peter to pay Paul; they create winners and losers and hence supporters and opponents. But Thurow considers even the largest economic problems technically solvable: inflation, slow growth, energy, environmental pollution, inequitable distribution of income. Indeed, he asserts that "for most of our problems there are *several* solutions."[44] The principal difficulties are political—even, he might have added, cultural: "all these solutions have the characteristic that someone must suffer large economic losses. No one wants to volunteer for this role, and we have a political process that is incapable of forcing anyone to shoulder this burden.

Everyone wants someone else to suffer the necessary economic losses, and as a consequence none of the possible solutions can be adopted." Every proposed solution to economic problems involves massive distributional consequences, but the political system cannot deal with these consequences by virtue of its inability to allocate losses effectively. As Thurow observes, "we veto the other's initiatives, but none of us has the ability to create successful initiatives ourselves."[45]

The portraits of dispersed power drawn by liberals in the fifties—portraits of veto groups and countervailing powers—are elegantly simple when seen against the growing complexities of the late seventies. Public problems multiplied, and the material resources to solve them no longer seemed limitless or even sufficient. Moreover, the demands that individuals made of the political economy had grown, not only in the upper reaches but throughout society: each group imagined defeat more readily, and no group could be counted on to endure defeat graciously, as was the case in the fifties. "In the past," Thurow notes, "political and economic power was distributed in such a way that substantial economic losses could be imposed on parts of the population if the establishment decided that it was in the general interest. Economic losses were allocated to particular powerless groups rather than spread across the population. These groups are no longer willing to accept losses and are able to raise substantially the costs for those who wish to impose losses on them.[46]

During the sixties and seventies, "veto groups" within the structure of disadvantage had gained in size and power: from blacks, Hispanics, Asian-Americans, and native Americans to Jews and other white ethnics, women, senior citizens, consumers, and workers. But the proliferation of such groups, each interested in protecting gains and preventing losses, reduced the power of any one of them to initiate political solutions to pressing economic problems. And it weakened any propensity to enter into long-term coalitions. Nearly everyone claims to favor economic security *and* economic growth, for example, but no group possesses the power to initiate successfully policies capable of reconciling these frequently incompatible aims. Security is usually defined as maintaining things as they are—guaranteeing present jobs or subsidizing outmoded plants and equipment. Defenders of such arrangements enjoy a high degree of short-term success: they can veto changes in policy, including generous compensation to losers, that might yield long-term economic gains. The result is one standoff after another, with political paralysis engendering economic paralysis.

Cultural pressures did contribute to significant changes in the shapes of politics and economics during the sixties and seventies. Next to international developments such as the OPEC cartel, or long-term domestic trends toward further concentration of capital, or the growth of the state, such changes in attitude may seem of relatively modest importance. Though their impact cannot be determined with precision, new and newly diffused attitudes concerning the self did affect the conduct of politics and economics in these decades, powerfully so in my opinion. Indeed, most of the familiar assessments that critics made of the American political system in the late sixties and seventies rested on diverse though usually pessimistic readings of changing attitudes. In particular, the decline of authority and the corresponding rise of selfishness were cited repeatedly as significant sources of political instability and paralysis. The erosion of party loyalty and affiliation; the rise of single-issue and single-group politics; an ever more dense network of lobbyists and policy professionals in Washingtion and state capitals; the escalating dissatisfaction of voters with the entire political process, evidenced by waning participation in elections and growing reliance on referenda: all of these developments and their frequently negative effects on the operation of political parties as well as on legislative, executive, and even judicial processes are traced regularly to individual and group selfishness, coupled with spreading disrespect for authority. Too many people acting in their own "narrow" interests (the adjective has become inevitable) thwart the public interest.

This strikes me as a mean-spirited reading of American culture and political economy. I have maintained rather that the declining regard for authority and the growth of self-concern constitute essentially salutary developments in American civilization during the sixties and seventies. They are important facets of the primary cultural thrust—a many-sided quest for personal fulfillment whose main social effects are evident in what I have called the democratization of personhood, the substantial extension of the many facilitating conditions for self-fulfillment: enhanced cultural opportunities, rising standards of living, augmented civil rights and civil liberties. The scope of my inquiry does not permit anything like a full assessment of American politics after 1960. Clearly, however, political attempts to enact the quest laid major strains on the relatively stable political economy of the fifties, as Thurow suggests. Whether the American political system can bear up under accumulated pressures generated by the quest and the democratization of personhood in the eighties and nineties is hard, if not impossible, to say. Surely the ideological terms of the quest, with the stress on individual fulfillment (salvation and a piece of social justice), are sufficiently constricted to arouse the fear that no one will be left to imagine, let alone enact, large and difficult solutions to problems of national and international scope.

Fragmentary and mixed as it is, the evidence of the sixties and seventies nevertheless suggests that the political system and the economy held up quite well. Electoral participation in presidential contests did fall after 1960, though not below the levels of the twenties and early thirties. On the other hand, participation in political organizations rose as more and more citizens joined in local causes, helped shape the political agendas of the major parties, and took up single issues such as abortion, nuclear power, hand guns, rent control, school busing, the equal rights amendment, and capital punishment.[47] In spite of dissatisfaction (resulting in part from increased participation and heightened expectations), there was no lack of able people seeking even the most minor party posts or the more than one-half million elective public offices. The evidence, then, points not merely to survival, which would have been notable in itself considering the new circumstances of political life, but to considerable achievement as well: augmented civil rights and civil liberties, partial redistribution of the inequalities of wealth and power in the political economy, minimal material support for all citizens, significant democratization of cultural norms, and disintegration of denigrating cultural stereotypes. In a word, the chances of individuals within most of the various subcategories of disadvantage to pursue fulfillment expanded dramatically in the sixties and seventies, in part as a consequence of activity in the political sphere. In the course of this major cultural thrust toward fulfillment, the political structure and the economy were challenged, stretched, even battered. The political system was reformed in minor ways, and by the end of the seventies many of the reforms themselves stood in need of reform (the system of presidential primaries, for example). But the American political economy was hardly brought to the edge of paralysis.

Critics such as Thurow tend to engage in odd rationalist illusions. Whatever their intentions, they manage to make the actual course of events appear far worse than it is in the light of alternative scenarios that, despite a certain elegance, lack plausibility. To assert as Thurow does that economic problems are technically solvable may be accurate, however strongly those of us who are not professional economists may be disposed to perhaps pardonable skepticism. In any case, Thurow's dubious assertion about the capacity of economists to provide solutions leads him to a too-strenuous condemnation of the self-interested attitudes of actors in the political sphere, as if adopting properly "distinterested" perspectives would clear the way for technical solutions to every economic ill from inflation to maldistribution of wealth. Such alternatives are implausible given the cultural assumptions of the quest: a vastly expanded search for personal fulfillment in small groups.

In fact, such alternatives are nearly as implausible as left-wing complaints about the real—and alleged—lack of citizen participation in politics. After a lengthy indictment of American politics, Sheldon Wolin concludes somewhat rambunctiously that "the end of the state raises the question of our state or condition. The answer is simple and impossible, or so it must seem; it is to reclaim our politicalness. This means not only finding new democratic forms but . . . recovering an old idea, the idea of Everyman as a morally autonomous agent."[48] Whereas Thurow appears to wish to remove the crassly "political" element from politics, Wolin seems to wish that Americans were more political than they are or are likely to become. Thurow's vision is affected by his passion for economics, Wolin's is distorted by his passion for politics of a certain sort. Neither critic is very convincing, though Thurow strikes me as the more interesting student of contemporary problems. In the end both may be antipolitical. Thurow wants to sanitize politics, to purge it of its venal elements of self-interest and ugly struggles over power; Wolin claims to want to expand the present company of political actors and deepen their involvement—on his own terms, needless to say. One critic apparently wishes to make politics safe for economists; the other hopes to make it safe for all right-thinking citizens (who turn out to be right-thinking intellectuals).

By claiming the existence of a privileged category beyond scrutiny—Thurow's economic solutions, Wolin's politicized Everyman—critics permit themselves indulgent indictments of actual processes. Though they are often telling in their particulars, such indictments finally distort the overwhelming fact about American politics in the sixties and seventies: the capacity of the system to survive and to serve as an important vehicle of the quest for fulfillment and the democratization of personhood. As Michael Novak put it, "the system as a whole"—its cultural, political and economic spheres—"is better than any theory we have of it."[49] The rise of selfishness and the waning of various modes of authority, then, are important, though finally comparatively minor side effects of a quest for personal fulfillment that dominated American civilization in the sixties and the seventies, animating culture and powerfully affecting the sphere of politics.

14

Epilogue

1980 would be a tempting point to end this study and encase the sixties and seventies as decades of quest: these were, after all, years of stunning progress in the search for personal fulfillment, for what I have called some synthesis of salvation and a piece of social justice. Although too little time has elapsed to make speculation about the eighties very compelling, the endpoint of 1980 is too convenient, for it has the effect of finessing a set of questions that have come to haunt my text ever since the election of Ronald Reagan. As early as 1981, the framework of nostalgia was given a new focus by critics who only months before had judged the seventies a hopelessly bleak time and Jimmy Carter as not significantly better than Republican alternatives. Some commentators on the liberal left were beginning to reassess these years less harshly against their grim intimations of the Reagan reign. Suddenly they began to lay greater stress on economic, political, and cultural gains, now apparently ensconced safely in the past, that a conservative administration seemed determined to reverse. Commentators on the right also were given to rhetorical excess, often seriously comparing the Republican electoral victory in 1980 to the major political realignments of 1896 and 1932. This constellation of fears and expectations raises the question of whether, and in what forms, the quest can survive what many observers believe might become a lingering conservative political moment.

I have paid considerable attention to economic and political advances registered in the sixties and seventies, arguing that the cause of general social justice was advanced largely though by no means exclusively through a leftward drift of politics and culture. The democratization of personhood, perhaps the most accessible indicator of social progress in the quest, depended not simply on economic expansion but also on a growing welfare state that was animated, if not always directed, by left-liberal and left-wing advocates of reform. Although sheer growth was central to this progress, redistribution of income and privilege (or, more precisely, prevention of further maldistribution) mattered also. Money, legislation, regulation, and judicial decisions aimed at providing ever larger numbers of citizens with the essential material and legal requisites for pursuing full, or at least fuller, personhood: these were some of the main political fruits of complex social and cultural moments. Although they were often meager, redistributive efforts of the welfare state nevertheless were crucial in expanding opportunities for people in many disadvantaged categories. At the most elemental levels, the working poor, the desperately poor, senior citizens, children, the unemployed, and the unemployable benefited from transfer payments; many people literally survived on such payments. A significant number of women, along with members of racial and ethnic minority groups, found employment in government; others received federal encouragement and protection in the private sector through affirmative action programs. Throughout the structure of disadvantage, a large number of Americans within each social category, from homosexuals to the physically handicapped, used the political system to articulate, expand, and protect their rights as citizens.

Although they were important, a vast postwar economic expansion coupled with a politics energized by the broad left in the early and middle sixties were only structural analogues to the most visible and most astonishing changes of the sixties and seventies—changes in the sphere of culture and subjectivity. During this period, I have argued, options for cultural development and self-expression widened and deepened in ways simply not comprehended by the political economy. This is not to say, however, that cultural changes were unrelated to the political and economic spheres or that they do not require certain structural arrangements to be sustained. Hence, we must wonder what may happen to the quest for personal fulfillment when economic expansion slows, or fails to match earlier expectations, and a leftward, quasi-egalitarian drift of politics yields ground to a conservative mood and a politics of the New Right.

The Conservative Mood

There was nothing surprising or even novel about the conservative mood that received more—and more sympathetic—attention from intellectuals and journalists as the seventies wore on. In fact, native conservative responses to economic, political, and cultural issues were in evidence throughout the sixties and the seventies. The left-liberal coalition composed of organized labor, intellectuals, public-sector professionals, and various disadvantaged constituencies fractured after the election of Lyndon Johnson in 1964, and, despite the persistence of Democratic majorities in Congress, presidential politics clearly revealed the popularity of vaguely conservative sentiments from 1968 through the time of the election of Ronald Reagan. That Richard Nixon should have won two presidential contests in spite of his visibly shady character suggests the vitality of the conservative mood. Nor was Jimmy Carter a great exception: having run for office at an opportune moment, he was himself something of a fiscal and cultural conservative.

In its dominant articulations, American conservatism, I have suggeted, is primarily a matter of personal attitude, mood, perspective, and, especially, feeling in a setting marked increasingly by therapeutic concerns. The prevailing conservative mood of the early eighties was more coherent than an impulse and less definite than any diverse doctrines or ideologies claimed by neoconservatives and champions of the New Right. Both impulse and principle figure importantly, but neither takes us to the vague center of the matter. Although it contains varying compounds of sensibility, the conservative mood arises when significant numbers of people begin to focus on the idea of limits. Evoking caution and restraint in some and in others a sort of populist anger directed toward the very rich and the very poor, this mood disposes individuals to recognize, and where necessary establish, limits and limitations—on ideas, feelings, values, resources, institutions, other people, and even themselves. The perception and discovery of limits—limits to American leadership abroad, limits to economic growth, limits on the capacity of institutions, especially the state, limits on the moral generosity of individuals—was a gradual, even haphazard affair during the sixties and seventies. It was a collective response to an accumulation of events and trends that had been in evidence since the middle sixties, from new experiments in unrestrained sexuality to the war in Vietnam and the OPEC cartel. There is, of course, fierce disagreement over just where unavoidable limits lie—over, say, the maximum feasible size of the economy or the role of the federal government in providing economic security for all citizens. A similarly wide divergence of opinion marks controversies over where social limits ought to be set—in child rearing and education, for example. By the end of the seventies, however, there was broad agreement that the concepts of limits and limitations had become controlling ideas, if not *the* controlling ideas, of a large body of American political, social, and cultural thought as it sought to comprehend a world of relative scarcity and continued high expectations.

Whereas the most highly publicized articulations of the quest in the sixties turned on the idea of transcending limits of all sorts, the diffuse mood of conservatism revolved around a growing awareness of limitations and a recognition of the need for limits. Both impulses, however, were present throughout the sixties and the seventies. And both impulses formed the emotional bases of authentic expressions of the ideology of the quest for personal fulfillment, expressions that at least were consistent with its dominant presuppositions. The conservative mood, I have maintained, did not subvert the search for fulfillment, but rather allowed people to explore other facets implicit in the ideology of the quest. Many people pursued salvation along more conventional lines, as the revival of evangelical Christianity suggests. The idea of social justice also took on familiar dimensions, having been assigned a more libertarian or laissez faire construction by many citizens.

In its less rigorous articulations among groups on the New Right, however, the ideas of limits and limitations were applied selectively and not altogether consistently. Individuals were held responsible for their own success or failure in the world. And government, especially at its remote federal level, was credited with few successes and a multitude of failures: it had caused staggering problems by exceeding its scope and by promising entitlements to various groups that it could deliver only at the high price of wrecking the economy. According to this logic, those in charge of government could ease problems by prophylactic measures—cutting spending, reducing taxes, contracting the scope of state activities, trimming regulations, and allowing the free market to bring prosperity to everyone. The cinematic metaphor of undoing real and apparent social mischief by running the government film in reverse broke down on some social issues, principally abortion, prayer in public schools, illicit drugs, and pornography. On such matters, many proponents of economic laissez faire called for more governmental intervention, regulation, and control. Even the supply-side economic proposals advanced by many representatives of the New Right required governmental intervention, though of somewhat different sorts than had been practiced from the New Deal through the Carter administration: large American businesses became more than ever the recipients of governmental aid in the form of investment tax credits and lavish depreciation allowances. Although these inconsistencies may simply testify to a healthy diversity of views within the New Right, they also compromise its moral appeal.

Whatever one thinks of such views, however, they surely constitute plausible expressions of the quest. In fact, as I argued in Chapter 10, essentially libertarian moments of the quest tend to follow egalitarian ones: a politics of equality often provokes a counterpolitics of individual achievement. As segments of social groups succeed in securing their own rights and opportunities, they do not need to rely as heavily on politics, especially on a politics of minimal inclusion, to pursue the pleasures and rewards of fulfillment. Hence relative success in seeking the material prerequisites of the quest may dispose people to the conservative mood. Failure, or relative failure, combined with a perception of unfair advantages conferred on other groups, also serves as an incentive to take up conservative themes. Once in this mood, individuals may seek a politics of the right aimed at reducing the scope of government, enlarging their private sphere of consumption, and expanding social spaces in which communities can take form. Many citizens may grow less and less interested in politics or become concerned only about certain single issues or isolated causes, while relying on past material gains as an adequate basis for seeking their own fulfillment in small groups.

During the seventies this conservative mood nurtured varieties of ideological and political conservatism, from the neoconservatism (or, if you will, neoliberalism) of Irving Kristol to the New Right philosophy of Richard A. Viguerie and the Reverend Jerry Falwell. The election of Ronald Reagan in 1980 and the conservative dominance of both houses of the Ninety-seventh Congress were in some sense expressions of the emerging conservative mood. But conservative enthusiasts who detected a seismic shift in American ideology and politics as a consequence of the 1980 elections were premature, at the very least. According to opinion polls, the ideological preferences of Americans changed very little between 1976 and 1980. The number of individuals identifying themselves as either "conservative" or "liberal" stayed about the same. Moreover, the *combined* percentage of those calling themselves liberal (18 percent) and those calling themselves conservative (31 percent) in 1980 just about equalled the number identifying themselves as moderate (51 percent).[1]

Of course, this is a floating ideological crap game populated by many unqualified, uninterested, and labile players. Through it all, however, the center held, even though since 1960 it perhaps had become less moderate, moving leftward on many issues and rightward on some. In spite of the relativity of the ideological game, it did yield some fairly stable positions: American voters, for example, consistently defined themselves as less conservative than their new president, who was perceived as a strong leader in contrast to the ineffectual Carter, a man plagued by his own failures as well as by such events as the Iranian hostage crisis and growing stagflation in the domestic economy. More than ideology, trust constituted a dominant issue in 1976, whereas leadership emerged as the central issue of presidential character in 1980. Above all, perhaps, leadership in a single sphere: American voters gave Ronald Reagan an unambiguous mandate to improve the economy. In less clear terms, however, the electoral triumph in 1980 also may reflect other facets of the conservative mood—political, social, and cultural concerns of the New Right and of tens of millions of more moderate citizens as well. But the election did not, I think, signal a major ideological shift to an American variety of conservatism. In the early eighties, ideological diversity remained vital in America, as did a measure of ideological tension and confusion.

The Political Consequences

Although the ideological shifts of recent years have not been decisive, as some commentators on the right have claimed, the possibility remains that conservative power will dominate the American political scene in the eighties. Such a turn, however, strikes me as improbable, at least insofar as it presupposes the workability of Reaganomics. Still, should the Reagan administration begin to implement its grand strategy and achieve decent economic results by 1984, conservatives may become sufficiently entrenched in government to reverse many of the political gains registered by ordinary citizens over the past half century. And they may be in a better position to begin to enact items on the social and cultural agenda of the New Right, from prayer in public schools to legislation aimed at effectively denying abortions to poor citizens. Should Mr. Reagan's economic policies fail, or should the economy flounder for other reasons, the political and social damage, though rather more extensive, probably will be confined to a single Republican term. Either way, in my judgment, the president and his associates promise to inflict a measure of harm—from moderate to serious—on the quest, especially on the dimension of social justice, though the net effect is impossible to estimate with any confidence.

Put simply, the Reagan program chips away at certain economic and political facets of the democratization of personhood. As James Tobin observes, the program is designed to bring about "a conservative counterrevolution in the theory, ideology, and practice of economic policy. The aim of the counterrevolution is" to repeal aspects of the New Deal, "to shrink the economic influence of government, especially central government, relative to that of private enterprise and free markets."[2] Reflecting a range of conflicting opinion among conservative economists, from advocates of supply-side theory to monetarists, Mr. Reagan pushed in several conservative directions at once during his first year in office, hoping by the force of his charismatic presence, it seemed, to convey an impression of coherence. In an effort to cure the problems of inadequate capital formation, low productivity, high interest rates, inflation, and unemployment, the Reagan people advocated selective tax cuts, lower government spending on social programs, a reduced role for government in the area of human services, fewer regulations on the private sector, a restrictive monetary policy, and increased military outlays. Once in motion, its defenders predicted, this scenario promised to revive the American economy quickly: federal deficits would melt away as a consequence of smaller allocations and rising tax receipts; interest rates would fall; private investment would soar; the wheels of economic progress would turn, and as they did, inflation and unemployment would drop to acceptable levels. Everyone was scheduled to benefit: the rich, the middle class, working people, and even the poor. Moreover, all of these economic measures were supposed to exert a salutary effect on political, social, and cultural life, enabling citizens to pursue their visions of the quest more freely. The capitalist equivalent of grace—economic growth in the free market-place—would ease all pain, but only after a brief period of more or less intense economic suffering (a fitting component of an essentially theological formula).

From the election through August of 1981 such prescriptions were pursued with impressive political skill. In 1981, following his sizable electoral victory and his narrow escape from death by assassination, Mr. Reagan managed to guide the first phase of his program through Congress. Hefty cuts in 1982 domestic programs amounting to $35 billion were passed, along with large tax cuts of up to $750 billion through 1984. A massive program was launched to modernize the armed forces at a staggering projected cost of more than $1.5 trillion over five years, a figure that some administration insiders say could swell to more than $2 trillion once cost overruns are tabulated. Significant cuts were made in social programs to aid students, poor people, children, and old people. The size of the *Federal Register,* the president noted in his first State of the Union address, shrunk by 23,000 pages, representing a significant reduction of federal regulations on enterprise in the private sector. Many journalists applauded these bold strokes during the post-election honeymoon months. Judicious opponents recommended, often cynically, that the plan be given a chance. After all, it had not been tried (at least not recently). And the economic game plan did address an issue nearly everyone thought important, an issue that Democrats had proved politically unable to address: the need to control spending at all levels of government.

Yet by early autumn of 1981, several weeks before the economic plan took effect officially, the president began to seem vulnerable, his charismatic mask not quite in place. His scheme was attacked by journalists, critics, labor leaders, and the Democratic opposition, and his capacity to enact it was thrown in doubt. Fearing a far larger federal deficit than administration planners had predicted or had been willing to announce, and consequently rising interest rates, Wall Street investors registered an important vote of no confidence that prompted Mr. Reagan's "Chicken Little" remarks in mid-September: "Now I have listened to those Chicken Littles who proclaim the sky is falling and those others who recklessly play on high interest rates for their own narrow political purposes," Reagan declared. "But this concern about a plan not even in effect yet is nothing more than false labor." The president said that his scheme was a sure thing, that you could bet the "rent money" on its success.[3]

Not everyone proved willing to place such a bet. The next day (September 19), was proclaimed "Solidarity Day" by the AFL-CIO and more than 200 smaller organizations: over 260,000 people marched on Washington to protest the selective effects of Reaganomics on working people, poor people, minorities, women, the handicapped—in short, on all disadvantaged people. By the end of November Congress had grown reluctant, refusing to endorse all of another requested 12 percent reduction in federal spending beyond the $35 billion already cut from such programs as higher education loans, job training and retraining, Medicaid payments to the poor, food stamps, and nutrition benefits for expectant mothers. The cuts in social spending apparently had approached their politically tolerable limits: only politically sensitive programs such as Social Security remained—along with a swollen defense budget that already had cost roughly one thousand billion dollars during the seventies.

Economists advanced critiques of the political and ideological inconsistencies of Mr. Reagan's actions.[4] The large tax cuts and tax advantages, which benefited corporations and wealthy taxpayers first, were seen as inflationary and not necessarily productive of useful investment. The generous check made out to the Pentagon was viewed increasingly as a wasteful diversion of funds needed to invigorate the economy—the work of fiscally inept minds unable to think lucidly about military needs and nuclear consequences. Investors doubted the political capacity and willingness of the administration to make cuts in spending sufficient to lower interest rates, stimulate investment, and revive such depressed industries as housing. Such fears were compounded by the Federal Reserve Board's insistence on tight money policies that helped to slow inflation temporarily at the high cost of dampening investment and contributing to rising unemployment. By the end of 1981 it was evident that something had to give. Mr. Reagan could not have all of the wishes that he had turned into campaign promises: astronomical defense budgets, a relatively high (if inadequate) social budget, reduced taxes, lower interest rates, and a balanced federal ledger.

Criticism was not confined to pointing out inconsistencies. There was growing concern also over the apparent moral insensitivity of the president's priorities: an overstuffed military budget and a needlessly thin social sector, a denuded federal government and overworked state and local governments (the promise of Mr. Reagan's "new federalism"). Instead of substantially reducing government inefficiency, streamlining the war machine, investing wisely in people, and husbanding the environment, the Reagan visionaries seemed bent on subverting humane priorities and economic ones as well, since long-term growth depends upon sufficient resources, including healthy human resources.

By mid-autumn of 1981, in the president's moment of triumph over Congress, it appeared that Reaganomics was being botched by ideological surgeons unable to distinguish between scalpels and bludgeons. Economic recovery was postponed by the onset of the most painful recession since the Great Depression. National unemployment, which reached 8 percent in October, threatened to climb into the double-digit range. The federal deficit, originally estimated at $42 billion by administration economists, was put at about $100 billion in 1982 (the sort of practice that threatened to place economists somewhat below psychiatrists on a reliability index). And the bright image of the Reagan administration began to tarnish in the media. A counterimage took form of a group of uncaring, cold-hearted men setting about the task of transferring wealth from less-well-off citizens to the affluent and the very rich, and doing so using the dreaded machinery of government.

Mr. Reagan's handling of the air traffic controllers' strike in the summer of 1981, when he summarily dismissed more than ten thousand workers and then refused to negotiate with them, was one of the first public signs of this image—one made worse by the president's subsequent clumsy decision to woo organized labor by giving the fired workers preferential consideration for other jobs in government. Nancy Reagan's decision to spend a quarter of a million dollars on a set of china for the White House irritated many citizens, even though the money had been gathered from private sources (tax deductible ones, no doubt). The president apparently managed to maintain a high degree of personal popularity through all this, but by Thanksgiving the polls had begun to reveal a mild slip in public confidence, especially in his capacity to mend the economy.

To make matters worse, the administration's budget director, David Stockman, granted an interview to William Greider that ran in the December 1981 issue of *The Atlantic*. In an apparent bid to become the John Dean of the Reagan years, Stockman confessed to ineptitude and dishonesty and revealed the shabby philosophical premises and seedy moral tone of the Reagan team. According to Greider, Stockman conceded that supply-side economics amounted to a rhetorical device to make palatable the old Republican gambit of granting tax concessions to the rich. " 'It's kind of hard to sell "trickle down," ' he explained, 'so the supply-side formula was the only way to get a tax policy that was "trickle-down." Supply-side is "trickle-down" theory.' "[5]

Much of the Reagan economic program, then, did not mesh well with the president's expressed moral aims of restoring America's global leadership, returning government to the people, correcting injustices of the welfare state, and providing positive incentives to its victims. In the early months of 1982, even many of the faithful were given to bouts of disbelief. The pace of inflation, as measured by the consumer price index, did moderate, dropping from 13.3 percent in the twelve months ending in December 1979 to 12.4 percent in 1980 and 8.9 percent in 1981. And the administration was able to curtail a number of nonessential federal programs, thereby reducing the impact of government on the lives of citizens. But the rest of the short-term economic news, on which the decline of inflation rates seemed to depend, was bleak, a worsening of developments already visible in the preceding year. The recession deepened. Interest rates remained distressingly high, with the prime rate fluctuating at or above 15 percent. Investors were nervous. Unemployment was on the rise, having reached 9.4 percent in April 1982, when more than ten million Americans were out of work, a disproportionate number of them blue-collar workers, women, and members of minority groups. Even officials in the administration, who originally foresaw a balanced budget by the end of Mr. Reagan's first term, projected deficits approaching $100 billion per year through 1984 ($273 billion from 1982 through 1984, according to the *Economic Report of the President* for 1982). With the 1982 elections approaching, many Republicans feared a disaster. Though members of Congress appeared restive, Reagan himself gave every sign of trying to stay on his course, adding in his January State of the Union message only a largely cosmetic plan (ironically dubbed the "new federalism") to hand over federal responsibility for a number of social programs to the states.

In fact, Mr. Reagan displays himself as a man pretty well satisfied with his one essential answer to nearly every problem: free men in a free market. Although he seems to be an ideologue with few ideas, Mr. Reagan used his first eighteen months in office to articulate cogent questions concerning the direction of the economy and the future of American political and cultural life. But his programmatic answers for the most part betrayed his inaugural pledge to seek "equitable" solutions "with no group singled out to pay a higher price." As Tobin observes, "The Reagan economic program is advertised to cure inflation and unemployment, to revive productivity, investment, hard work, and thrift. It probably cannot achieve those wonderful results. What it is sure to do is to redistribute wealth, power, and opportunity to the wealthy and powerful and their heirs."[6] Stockman, along with a number of other Reagan advisers, knew that the economic program advanced by the president did not have a chance of working unless the administration could go beyond cuts in so-called discretionary social spending such as housing assistance and aid to higher education. Sooner or later, deeper cuts would have to be made in anticipated increases in such essential and politically sensitive benefits as Social Security and Medicaid, or else even larger slices would have to be taken from projected increases in defense. Mr. Reagan found the idea of cutting human services attractive but politically perilous; the option of slashing defense spending was personally odious and perhaps also somewhat risky, considering the widespread public enthusiasm for a stronger military. Nor did the idea of delaying or canceling tax cuts hold much appeal. While the president's critics focused on inconsistencies, inequities, and narrowing options that could ultimately cramp his political style, Mr. Reagan continued to display considerable political acumen in his dealings with lawmakers. In the spring of 1982, following sustained partisan debate, the president managed to push what he considered a minimally acceptable budget through a reluctant Congress. And in August, Mr. Reagan, having abandoned for the moment his opposition to levying new taxes, threw his support behind a $98.3 billion tax increase that narrowly cleared Congress.

Insofar as Reaganomics succeeds in increasing inequality through further cuts in federal social spending, it will subvert the quest for personal fulfillment among less-well-off citizens, a sector in which economic survival often precedes a coherent concern with salvation and almost always precedes fulfillment. The cause of general social justice will be harmed. But the quest should continue, for a measure of success in this venture, I have argued, does not depend upon achievement of *general* social justice any more than it depends upon ever higher levels of personal consumption. The quest normally proceeds fitfully, as individuals seek salvation and a piece of social justice for themselves or a measure of justice for themselves by way of some category to which they belong. In the sixties and seventies, I have contended, the cause of general social justice was advanced somewhat, though mainly as a byproduct of the open-ended quest for personal fulfillment, and in particular of left and left-liberal versions of this search. It might be argued that Reaganomics will enhance the material bases of fulfillment in other ways, such as by catering to a sizable minority of well-off citizens. But this promises to be an inefficient and unjust reallocation of wealth, since the principal beneficiaries of the differential changes do not need such subsidies. Nor can the range of entitlements be sustained at present levels in the absence of a general economic recovery, on which the moral appeal of the Reagan program hangs.

It is true, of course, that Mr. Reagan's economic initiatives may enhance the chances of an even larger number of citizens should the economy recover and move on to higher levels (by design or by accident) before the 1984 elections. Whether it achieves a vigorous economy along with, or even as a consequence of, making the wealthy wealthier, the Reagan administration in any case will probably continue to chip away at the democratization of personhood in lower reaches of the structure of disadvantage. My guess, however, is that the Reagan visionaries will not be able to carry to ideological fruition their political program of a lively, prosperous, free-market economy supporting an indefensible doomsday military machine, both existing at the probable price of growing inequalities in income, wealth, privilege, power, and status. Political forces must intervene: they may not overwhelm the new conservatives in the early eighties, but they constitute a lively opposition that promises to shrink Mr. Reagan's options.

In fact, political forces limited Mr. Reagan's maneuverability from the outset of his administration. Although his celebrated counterrevolution did produce a number of victories in the first year of his term, this burst of success, which many commentators have compared to the opening days of Franklin Roosevelt's New Deal and the first months of Lyndon Johnson's Great Society, may come to seem modest in time. In the area of social spending, for example, Mr. Reagan's major first-year accomplishment was to prevent an increase of $40 billion rather than to effect huge cutbacks. Consider this comparison. In 1964, the first full year of Johnson's presidency, 28.8 percent of the federal budget (or $34 billion) went to "human services," including health, education, welfare, veterans, social security, nutrition, and the like. In 1981, 53.3 percent (or $349 billion) of a far larger budget was devoted to human services. Rather than cut back to previous levels, Mr. Reagan managed to reduce social spending only slightly; moreover, in projected budgets through 1986 he proposes to trim this sector by a mere 1.5 percent, to 51.8 percent of the federal budget.[7]

Of course, such gross comparisons do not highlight those disproportionate cuts that the poor and the working poor must bear. Nor do they suggest such other modes of reallocating income and wealth to more affluent citizens as tax reductions and eased regulations on business and the environment. There have been a few clear winners and many losers in this game that was supposed to benefit everyone. And the probable outcomes for the most part will not contribute to the cause of general social justice in America. But it should also be recalled that a relatively disorganized political opposition and a wonderfully byzantine stabilizing bureaucracy probably will prevent enactment of more than a few pieces of the New Right's dream in the eighties. By the middle of 1982 it was politics as usual again in Washington: Mr. Reagan had enjoyed his dramatic moment, but he could not turn the nation around.

Although Nancy Reagan's china may retain its polish, her husband's vision will shatter: it has all the characteristics of a one-act play without much prospect of an extended run. Mr. Reagan's design amounts to a rejection of previous governmental scripts; it gives the momentary illusion of being a durable scenario of its own, when in fact it is little more than a transparent design to let social problems take care of themselves—a vision of malign neglect. We may grant the need to control inflation and to retard the growth of government, as well as the need to think carefully about its scope and efficiency. We may grant, too, the need to reconsider the human effects of a welfare state that, although meager by relevant Western European standards, is often morally unjust to its tax supporters and its presumed beneficiaries. These are old yet important themes that our most humane conservatives can reiterate with a measure of moral dignity. But in its first eighteen months the Reagan administration pursued its ends unfairly and perhaps foolishly. In the end, we may hope, adherents of the New Right will cultivate the political arts required of a party in office as well as they mastered the art of oppositional rhetoric earlier on. Those on the right who do not may suffer the largest political disappointments, although many citizens doubtless will retain their faith, taking the Reagan administration's failure to enact its vision with sufficient fervor and skill as a sign of their own purity and rectitude. But ideological faith without political works is dead, or at least difficult. Although ideological temperatures on the right may rise as a consequence of Mr. Reagan's shortcomings, fevered participants nevertheless must play on restricted courts, and these are still situated on the contested middle ground of American politics.

The Cultural Consequences

The cultural consequences of the conservative mood do not strike me as dire. Of course, the venality of President Reagan and his top appointees is painful. They set a subdued moral tone for American political culture, promoting as they do a mean-spirited embodiment of conservative readings of the nation's public philosophy. The people who have been closest to the president are middle-aged white males, many of them first-generation financial successes living on the rough edges of a decent moral vision. A few of them may be certifiable white-collar criminals. They occupy dominant positions of power that permit them to attempt to shape the near-term domestic economy and to make decisions on nuclear issues well beyond their moral range. In one sense, it is as if nothing much happened in American culture and society between the end of the Eisenhower era and the beginning of President Reagan's first term: aging white males still fill the upper reaches of the structure of advantage, although the breed of Californian that Mr. Reagan cultivates exhibits perhaps less character than, say, a John Foster Dulles. The Reagan coterie, from the "kitchen cabinet" down, reminds one of shallow male presences at a USC alumni get-together.

This cast of characters fits nicely with its mentor. When the president was shot early in his term, newspeople made much of his alertness in the hospital, his series of one-liners, presumably unrehearsed. The next morning, however, an aide was asked by a reporter whether Mr. Reagan had yet inquired about the welfare of others, whether he had wondered about their fate in the melee. No, he had not, was the reply, and the aide stuck to this response even after repeated questioning from surprised representatives of the media. This and the president's quips seem to be parts of the same thin if rather genial character. The president's approach to philanthropy provides a similar insight from another angle. Invoking the biblical story of the good Samaritan, Mr. Reagan regularly advised individuals and representatives of religious organizations to help distressed citizens "rather than leaving it up to the bureaucracy." It is impossible to analyze the relative strengths of sincerity, ignorance, and cynicism in such rhetorical compounds. Judging from his recent tax returns, which display minuscule gifts to religious and charitable groups, I think it fair to say that Mr. Reagan has yet to set a stirring philanthropic example for other Americans. In fact, charitable deductions on the Reagans' 1981 return amounted to only 1.4 percent of their adjusted gross income in 1980— a bit more than one-tenth of the biblically suggested tithe.

The view *at* the top might have been similar to 1960 vistas, but the view *from* the top, I have argued, was enormously different. American culture had changed dramatically as a consequence of the quest in ways that neither the president nor his associates could understand, appreciate, or change. Whatever real cultural damage the Reagan administration may inflict will come about as a consequence of too much political success of the wrong sort: its operatives will manage to deprive some individuals of their piece of social justice and cut the slice of others, thereby subverting their quest for personal fulfillment. But this number will be comparatively small, I think—sufficient to justify moral anguish and a renewed commitment to combat social injustice, though not large enough to provide compelling grounds for condemning the whole civilization.

In its early stages, the Reagan administration did not display much interest in the moral convictions of its New Right supporters, a refusal that no doubt will be seen as salutary by people on the liberal left in retrospect, when their initial rhetorical blasts against conservatives cease to be persuasive or even cathartic. With the possible exception of the campaign to permit voluntary prayer in public schools once again, I do not think that the so-called social issues pursued by the New Right, from pro-life positions (which are shared by many others) to censorship of offensive books and films, have much chance of being enacted or observed. These are issues on which Americans remain divided, or perhaps I should say, issues on which they have become deeply divided; as a consequence, such matters resist sharp political resolution.

These issues may be the stuff of political small change, and for this reason manage at least to reach the councils of government. Such issues, however, do not constitute stable political capital: people who really count in the administration have avoided them as much as they have dared. Through 1981, the only social matter Reagan himself took on forcefully, though only in a rhetorical flourish, was the relatively undivisive issue of crime. In spring of 1982, however, when his culturally conservative constituencies grew restive, he did mount a weak defense of prayer in schools, a controversial issue of symbolic importance to many of his New Right supporters. Meanwhile, the administration avoided engaging Americans in a debate over important moral issues, hoping, it seemed, that the economic program would confer social and cultural benefits on the nation.

In spite of my disappointment at the Reagan administration's failure to test the best ideas of American conservatism fairly, I do not find the conservative mood itself a subversion of the idea of the quest, having insisted all along that the cultural (or even the political) future of American civilization does not rest exclusively with the left or with advocates of cultural novelty. The search has both radical and conservative sources and expressions, elements of novelty and important elements of tradition. Different specifications of the quest contain novel and traditional materials in various, often contradictory, proportions and combinations. On balance, the substantial growth of cultural opportunities for expression and the consequent enrichment of subjectivity, remains the most impressive achievement of the sixties and seventies, and perhaps the most durable one as well. The cultural transformation of these years was neither exclusively left, liberal, nor right in impulse, but rather a syncretic and serendipitous mixture of many elements. It was more vital than ideology, larger than the conservative mood, and more durable than political changes of the sort we have witnessed, say, from the middle fifties on. In the end, these changes in culture and the sphere of subjectivity left a powerful legacy of independence, dissent, and innovation—an enlargement of human capital unimagined by most of us in the late fifties and not comprehended in any facet of American ideology: left, right, or center.

The ascendance of a conservative mood and a vigorous politics of the right surely is one consequence of the quest as I have characterized it.

This ascendance may turn out to be more salutary than I have been able to imagine. Still, the health of American politics requires a lively opposition that at least one serious observer believes may be imperiled by successes registered in the quest during the sixties and seventies. Dennis Wrong puts the question nicely: "What if there is a progressive increase in the number of people who are *relatively satisfied* with the positions they have achieved in the prevailing distribution of power, privilege, and prestige, and are therefore less responsive to appeals for further egalitarian reforms, although considerable social inequality remains." In this case, Wrong continues, "one would have to conclude that the leftward drift of the rhythm of democratic politics is counterbalanced over time by a rightward tendency in which each era of left ascendancy reduces the social base remaining available for a future turn to the left."[8] The energy of democratic politics would be depleted well before the achievement of a condition even approximating general social justice.

But I have not claimed that the quest has—or will—lead to full social justice or that entire disadvantaged groups have been (or could have been) set free during the sixties and seventies. Nor have I insisted that fulfillment for a vast majority of Americans awaits a new social order. I have contended rather that advances in the quest by millions of citizens comprise the most useful short-term test of American civilization, even if the quest should entail a decline of the left and an ascendance of the New Right. Both the decline and the ascendance promise to be temporary phases: they do not add up to a demise of the left or a long-term political reign of the right. Such decisive turns would compromise the conduct of the quest, perhaps hopelessly, but neither development seems to me likely. Wrong makes an interesting point about the relative satisfaction of people and their consequent reluctance to participate in an egalitarian politics. But I do not find it finally a persuasive point, for two sets of reasons.[9]

First, consider the conventional egalitarian bread-and-butter politics of the left that Wrong has in mind. The political activities of the New Right and their economic consequences should lead shortly to a revival of political action on the part of constituencies whose financial and occupational situation is worsening (either absolutely or relative to their earlier expectations). Whether this collection of groups, including organized labor, can formulate appealing positions and form a coalition capable of winning national power are open questions, ones that cannot be assessed confidently at this point. But at least they are live questions once again. The characteristics of the quest permit a reasonable speculation concerning the sources of such a politics. The politics of poor people, of women, of the aged, and of relatively powerless segments of minority groups probably will not proceed on a program of advancing Great Society promises very much further. The liberal left, I believe, must propose new programs that preserve its dominant vision and concern for the less advantaged while incorporating certain lessons inelegantly conveyed by conservatives, from the need to limit government spending equitably to the need to reduce the untoward impact of large institutions on personal freedom, initiative, and dignity. Otherwise, working people will reject initiatives of the liberal left and a lively politics of the left will prove impossible.

Nor will new political thrusts quite fit the old social-gospel model of wealthy people bent on helping less fortunate brethren. Such people may participate actively and contribute financially. But individuals within the disadvantaged groups, from blacks and women to senior citizens and the handicapped, now exercise a measure of leadership on their own behalf: this is a ripening political fruit of the democratization of personhood in the sixties and seventies. As a consequence, however, broad political coalitions involving organized labor, sectors of the middle class, and the severely disadvantaged may be more difficult than ever to establish and maintain. Still, it seems fair to say that the stuff of coalitions—special-interest groups, single-issue groups, local groups—will persist and grow in the eighties. And further, we may be certain that the Reagan team, along with other elements of the New Right, will continue to provide powerful incentives to groups of people to coalesce.

Second, the economic, political, and cultural legacy of the quest in the sixties and seventies should activate people to pursue an "egalitarian" politics of collective survival. The therapeutic cast of the quest disposes people to be involved more than ever in the immediate, the local. Indeed, electoral participation in local affairs was on the rise in the seventies, whereas participation in national politics declined somewhat. Certain issues, however, such as the nuclear arms race, misuse of the environment, and waste of resources, including human resources, involve people in a democracy of danger: failure to take action against these dangers threatens grave harm to everyone. Under certain circumstances, large issues may come to seem personal, even local.

The case of nuclear arms constitutes an obvious instance. The Western European experience of a lively antinuclear movement has set an example for an American movement that promises to become sizable in the next few years. Europeans possess the dubious advantage of living in the shadow of the proposed medium-range weapons and of providing the theater for some future nuclear battle. But we have growing advantages of our own: nuclear plants and projected nuclear plants, as well as the prospect of deployed MX missiles. Here too Mr. Reagan and his associates have enlivened the opposition by heating up the cold war and speaking as if a "limited" nuclear war might be winnable, with acceptable numbers of casualties (in the tens of millions). In the early eighties opposition to an endless nuclear arms race grew in various quarters. It encompassed a broad spectrum of religious figures, from Jewish leaders and Catholic bishops to Billy Graham. It attracted important political personages such as Edward Kennedy. It roused scientists, physicians, and other professionals. It reached ordinary citizens troubled by the apocalyptic image of even a "limited nuclear exchange." By late 1981, according to an NBC News/Associated Press Poll, the American public favored "a new agreement between the United States and Russia which would limit nuclear weapons" by a dazzling margin of more than 3 to 1 (70 percent to 21 percent). And grass-roots support grew rapidly for a freeze on the "testing, production, and further deployment of all nuclear weapons." By the spring of 1982, eight state legislatures, along with the governing bodies of several hundred cities and counties, had approved the idea of a freeze on nuclear weapons. And on June 12, the largest public demonstration in American history was staged in New York, where an estimated 750,000 people gathered to declare their support for a freeze.

Considered naïve by some and hopeless by others, the antinuclear movement and the nuclear freeze movement in particular promised at least to exert some welcome pressure on the shapers of defense policy, perhaps considerable pressure. The movement (both in Europe and the United States) seemed partially responsible for persuading President Reagan to attempt public proposals to limit nuclear arsenals and to begin the process of negotiating a substantial arms limitation agreement with the Soviets in the spring of 1982. It clearly is difficult, some say potentially dangerous, to attempt a translation of simple public feeling into the theological complexities of nuclear strategy. So it may be, since the effects of any political act in this uncertain and risky sphere cannot be foreseen. But this, I believe, remains the most sensible form that mass protest can take. Many of us not versed in the subtle ways of nuclear strategy at least can distinguish plans for an adequate, essentially defensive military force from designs to fatten an already bloated nuclear monster.

Moreover, there are encouraging precedents for protest that conform to the logic of the quest. Widespread anxiety about radioactive fallout contributed to the limited test-ban treaty in the early sixties. Later on, citizens in larger cities scheduled to be defended by ABM systems mounted protests that subsequently affected the shape of SALT I. And more recently, Mormons and other local citizens effectively lobbied against locating the MX system in Utah and Nevada (local ground that, according to church officials, happened also to be sacred ground). It is true, of course, that thus far the arms race has been slowed only momentarily by such dissenting pressures, whereas the military machine grinds on relentlessly.[10] But in the eighties the staggering economic and political costs of continuing the nuclear arms game between the United States and the Soviet Union may persuade both sides to enter into a serious long-term agreement to reduce nuclear stockpiles drastically and perhaps even to limit conventional arms. In any case, the depth and extent of public sentiment against the endless stockpiling of nuclear weapons, and against their possible eventual use, suggests that it should become increasingly difficult to make nuclear policy in the eighties behind the backs of Americans—or even under public cover of battered clichés.

In both areas, then, on traditional bread-and-butter issues and on newer bread-or-(radioactive)-stone issues, Americans will take up protest and politics as a facet of fulfillment. They will do so as authentic individuals pursuing fulfillment who find politics, including at times a politics of protest and opposition, a necessary detour once again. How large or how effective these movements may become, what ideological colorations they may assume, what measure of influence and power they may attain will depend upon an arrangement of social factors that no one can pretend to know in advance. But I should be surprised if new energies that are now barely beneath the surface of public and media attention do not emerge in the eighties. And I should be even more surprised if these movements do not conform to the psychological terms of the quest. If the quest is as widespread as I think it is, there should be fresh probes to enlarge the scope of personal fulfillment within small communities. There also should be new political and social efforts to enrich and deepen the quality of lived experience in America—to redeem the promise of a more abundant life.[11]

In the sixties and seventies, I have insisted, changes in the sphere of culture and subjectivity outpaced advances in the social, political, and economic spheres—an uneven pattern of development that entailed mixed consequences: partial fulfillment for many people on a painfully thin slice of social justice and frustration of another sort for many others living on a diet too rich in unreasonable, or simply fruitless, expectations. On balance, however, the American standard of life improved dramatically during these years. And, barring a nuclear apocalypse, I believe that many of the most important gains will be preserved and extended, albeit fitfully, in the eighties and nineties. Measured against the criterion of a more abundant life for all, we come up painfully short, appearing as perpetrators of needless inequalities as well as of material and spiritual waste on a lavish scale. And so we have been. But we need not sell ourselves short in spite of our deceptions and self-deceptions. During the sixties and seventies, Americans came a long if haphazard way toward discovering the terms of a decent, full life—far enough, in fact, to persuade most of us to continue the quest.

Notes

Chapter 1: Prologue

1. *In These Times,* May 18–24, 1977, p. 23. See also Michael Andrew Scully, "Would 'Mother' Jones Buy *Mother Jones?" The Public Interest* 53 (Fall 1978):100–108.

   Parts of the prologue are adapted from my "Culture and Politics in the Sixties," *Dissent* 24 (Fall 1977):439–43. An earlier version of this essay was presented at the California Conference on American Studies, Annenberg Center, The University of Southern California, April 1, 1978. For this occasion, Betty Chmaj and Frances M. Rademacher compiled a useful, generously annotated bibliography of books and articles on the sixties and seventies, *The Sixties and the Seventies: A Bibliography and Soundings* (Department of Humanities, California State University, Sacramento, California 95819).

2. The concept of generations is at best arbitrary. At the end of the seventies, five contemporary generations were distinguished by the National Opinion Research Center in Chicago: (1) the prewar generation (composed of those who became 20 years old before or during 1945), (2) the forties generation (those who became 20 years old from 1946 to 1953), (3) the fifties generation (those who became 20 years old from 1954 to 1963), (4) the sixties generation (those who became 20 years old from 1964 to 1972), and (5) the seventies generation (those who became 20 years old from 1973 to 1978). (Source: *Public Opinion* 3 (February–March 1980):38.)

3. Bathed in generational conceit, the sentimental version of this metaphor of recent American history is largely an oral tradition fashioned by survivors of "the sixties." But it crops up increasingly in written accounts of the sixties and seventies. Sara Davidson's *Loose Change: Three Women of the Sixties* (Garden City, N.Y.: Doubleday, 1977); Ann Beattie's *Chilly Scenes of Winter* (Garden City, N.Y.: Doubleday, 1977); and Marge Piercy's *Vida* (New York: Summit Books, 1979) present fictional variations. The speeches and tracts of Tom Hayden

supply countless political examples of the new revisionism. Morris Dickstein's *Gates of Eden: American Culture in the Sixties* (New York: Basic Books, 1977) is the most coherent cultural formulation of this position that I know of. Robin Brooks's interesting paper, "Antithesis: Radical Culture and Politics in the 1960s," presented at the meeting of the Organization of American Historians, April 11, 1978, contains most of the assumptions of what might be termed "the new revisionism." See also Kirkpatrick Sale, *SDS* (New York: Random House, 1973); and, Howard Zinn, *Postwar America: 1945–1971* (Indianapolis and New York: Bobbs-Merrill, 1973). *Mother Jones* offers examples of the new revisionism in every issue.

4. Tom Wolfe, "The 'Me' Decade and the Third Great Awakening," *New West* (August 30, 1976):27–48; Christopher Lasch, *The Culture of Narcissism: American Life in an Age of Diminishing Expectations* (New York: W. W. Norton, 1978); Jim Hougan, *Decadence: Radical Nostalgia, Narcissism, and Decline in the Seventies* (New York: William Morrow, 1975); Henry Fairlie, "A Decade of Reaction," *The New Republic* 180 (January 6, 1979):15–19 and (January 13, 1979):15–18.

5. Irving Louis Horowitz, *Ideology and Utopia in the United States, 1956–1976* (London and New York: Oxford University Press, 1977), pp. 6–7.

6. See, for example, Morris Dickstein, "Winding Down the '60s," *The Nation* 224 (May 21, 1977):632–33.

7. Howard Junker, "Who Erased the Seventies?" *Esquire* 88 (December 1977):152–55 ff.

8. Charlie Haas, "Goodbye to the '70s," *New West* (January 29, 1979): 29, 33.

9. See Angus Campbell, *The Sense of Well-Being in America: Recent Patterns and Trends* (New York: McGraw-Hill, 1980).

Chapter 2: The Argument

1. See Daniel Yankelovich, *New Rules: Searching for Self-Fulfillment in a World Turned Upside Down* (New York: Random House, 1981), Chapter 5, "The Strong Form of the Self-Fulfillment Predicament," pp. 49–71. "Because this analysis was conducted among Americans who work for pay, it excludes several large groups: housewives, full-time students, retired people, and the unemployed. The proportion of strong formers among these groups is not known since data are lacking, but [except among college students] it is almost surely smaller than among those who work for pay . . ." (p. 60).

For an extended discussion of modes of self-fulfillment, gleaned from readings of historical and contemporary sources, see Richard W. Coan, *Hero, Artist, Sage, or Saint? A Survey of Views on What Is Variously Called Mental Health, Normality, Maturity, Self-Actualization, and Human Fulfillment* (New York: Columbia University Press, 1977).

2. U.S. Bureau of the Census, *Historical Statistics of the United States: Colonial Times to 1970* (Washington, D.C.: Government Printing Office, 1975), p. 243.

3. Throughout, I follow, although very loosely, Daniel Bell's analytic distinctions among "economy," "polity," and "culture." See Bell, *The Coming of Post-Industrial Society: A Venture in Social Forecasting* (New York: Basic Books, 1973).

4. See Peter Schrag, *The Decline of the WASP* (New York: Simon and Schuster, 1973), p. 13.

5. It should be remembered that despite the large impact of dissent and protest, the explosion was detonated by a small percentage of the population. Ashby and Stave note a 1970 report issued by the Education Commission of the United States: "only 12 percent of the adults queried had ever attempted to get any law changed, whether by signing a petition, joining an organization, writing letters to officials, or actively demonstrating. In fact, the study showed that less than half (49 percent) of the adults surveyed could point to any specific law that was unfair or unjust." LeRoy Ashby and Bruce M. Stave, *The Discontented Society. Interpretations of Twentieth Century American Protest* (Chicago: Rand McNally, 1972), p. 3.

6. H. L. Nieberg, *Culture Storm: Politics and the Ritual Order* (New York: St. Martin's Press, 1973).

7. There is, of course, considerable overlap among these categories.

8. Material for this paragraph is drawn from Yankelovich, *New Rules,* Chapter 8, "New Norms: Being Obliged To Do What You Want To Do," pp. 85–105.

9. In thinking about socialism, liberalism, and conservatism as facets of the bourgeois spirit, I have found John Lukacs's perceptive study, *The Passing of the Modern Age* (New York: Harper & Row, 1970), particularly helpful.

10. Joseph Veroff, Elizabeth Douvan, and Richard A. Kulka, *The Inner American: A Self-Portrait from 1957 to 1976* (New York: Basic Books, 1981), p. 529.

11. Marge Piercy, "Through the Cracks," *Partisan Review* 41 (1974):215, 216.

12. On this, see Warren I. Susman, "The Thirties," in Stanley Coben and Lorman Ratner, eds., *The Development of an American Culture* (Englewood Cliffs, N.J.: Prentice-Hall, 1970), pp. 179–218.

Chapter 3: The Seventies versus the Sixties

1. Harvey Gross, "The Problem of Style and the Poetry of the Sixties," *The Iowa Review* 5 (Winter 1974):69.
2. "To Set the Economy Right," *Time* (cover story) 114 (August 27, 1979):24. A more balanced, though still largely negative assessment of the seventies may be found in *Newsweek,* "Ten Years That Shook America . . . Now, The '80s" (November 19, 1979):84–176.
3. Meg Greenfield, "How To Think About the '60s," *Newsweek* (April 10, 1978):108.
4. Arnold A. Rogow, *The Dying of the Light* (New York: Putnam, 1975), p. 11.
5. Michael Harrington, *Decade of Decision: The Crisis of the American System* (New York: Simon and Schuster, 1980), p. 287.
6. Michael Novak, *The American Vision: An Essay on the Future of Democratic Capitalism* (Washington, D.C.: The American Enterprise Institute, 1978), p. 23.
7. See Henry F. May, *The End of American Innocence: A Study of the First Years of Our Own Time, 1912–1917* (1959; reprinted New York: Oxford University Press, 1979), part 4, pp. 333 ff.
8. Optimism was, of course, strained even in the 1890s. Bellamy's utopian fiction, *Looking Backward,* mirrored middle-class fears of anarchy and revolution.
9. Allan Nevins, "American Civilization: 1922–1938," *Saturday Review* 23 (October 22, 1938):15. Review essay on Harold E. Stearns, *America Now: An Inquiry into Civilization in the United States. By Thirty-six Americans* (New York: Charles Scribner's Sons, 1938). Nevins contrasts the optimistic tone of this volume to the pessimism of its predecessor, *Civilization in the United States,* which Stearns edited in 1922.
10. Thomas L. Hartshorne, *The Distorted Image: Changing Conceptions of the American Character since Turner* (Cleveland: Case-Western Reserve University Press, 1968), p. 186.
11. I have discussed the effects and challenges of the advent of relative scarcity on various ideological traditions in *Crooked Paths: Reflections on Socialism, Conservatism, and the Welfare State* (New York: Harper & Row, 1977).
12. Robert L. Heilbroner, *An Inquiry into the Human Prospect* (New York: W. W. Norton, 1974), p. 13.

Chapter 4: The Radical Left

1. Marcuse's *One-Dimensional Man* (Boston: Beacon Press, 1964) is in many ways a rewrite of the major themes of Aldous Huxley's *Brave*

New World. "A really efficient totalitarian state," Huxley notes in his 1946 foreword to the Modern Library edition of *Brave New World,* "would be one in which the all-powerful executive of political bosses and their army of managers control a population of slaves who do not have to be coerced, because they love their servitude" (p. x).

2. Both themes of this all-weather, quasi-theological critique—alienation and exploitation—are by now perennial. Rooted in varieties of Marxism, both themes always manage to attract at least a core of defenders, since the choice of emphasis corresponds loosely to the class preferences, if not the class backgrounds, of radicals. Alienation remains the special province of middle-class radicals, whereas exploitation is emphasized often by those who wish to appeal to the immediate financial and political concerns of working-class people and members of the underclass.

3. During the seventies the most interesting Marxist theoretical account by an American of the difficulties that the modern capitalist state encounters in meeting conflicting fiscal and political demands was James O'Connor's *The Fiscal Crisis of the State* (New York: St. Martin's Press, 1973).

4. In the late sixties, as revolutionary rhetoric intensified, there appeared a number of serious pieces arguing against the possibility of such fantasies. See, for example, the essays in Roderick Aya and Norman Miller, eds., *The New American Revolution* (New York: The Free Press, 1971).

5. Greg Calvert and Carol Nieman, *A Disrupted History: The New Left and the New Capitalism* (New York: Random House, 1971), p. 10. For a more sympathetic estimate, see Kirkpatrick Sale, *SDS* (New York: Random House, 1973), especially pp. 656–57.

6. See, for example, Martin J. Sklar and James Weinstein, "Socialism and the New Left," *Studies on the Left* 6 (March–April 1966). "The first step is for new leftists to examine the content of their radicalism and determine if they are committed to a transformation of American capitalism into that higher form of society envisaged by Marx. If they are, then all of their activities should be consciously determined by an intention to build a revolutionary movement and then a party that has the perspective of gaining power in the United States" (p. 70).

7. Norman Birnbaum and Christopher Lasch, "America Today: An Exchange," *Partisan Review* 42 (1975):361.

8. The Editors, "Introduction: American Politics in the 70's and 80's," *Socialist Review* 50–51 (March–June 1980):5.

9. Peter Dreier, "Socialism and Cynicism: An Essay on Politics, Scholarship, and Teaching," *Socialist Review* 10 (September–October 1980): 128.

10. Tom Hayden, "America and the Populist Impulse: The New Left's Legacy," *Los Angeles Times,* September 17, 1978, part 7, p. 1.

11. Cleaver then proceeded to unsettle his evangelical colleagues by declaring his admiration for the Reverend Sun Myung Moon, the South Korean businessman who considers himself the contemporary reincarnation of Christ. In the sixties, the media conferred a sort of public importance on many activists in their late teens and twenties that otherwise would have taken at least another decade or two of study, work, and a measure of luck to come by. For an interesting if somewhat one-sided account of the negative influence of the media on the development of the Movement, see Tod Gitlin, *The Whole World Is Watching: Mass Media in the Making and Unmaking of the New Left* (Berkeley and London: University of California Press, 1980).

12. Irving Howe, "Socialism and Liberalism: Articles of Conciliation?" *Dissent* 24 (Winter 1977):22–35.

13. See Robert Paul Wolff, Barrington Moore, Jr., and Herbert Marcuse, *A Critique of Pure Tolerance* (Boston: Beacon Press, 1965).

14. See Eugene D. Genovese, "Reflections on the 1960s: Preface to the Italian Edition of *In Red and Black*," *Socialist Review* 8 (March–April 1978):59–71. Aronowitz's proposal was made at the 1979 convention of the New American Movement and reported in *In These Times* 3 (August 22, 1979): 2.

15. See Peter Clecak, *Radical Paradoxes: Dilemmas of the American Left, 1945–1970* (New York: Harper & Row, 1973), especially chapters 1 and 2.

16. For an interesting and balanced assessment of twentieth-century American radicalism, see Milton Cantor, *The Divided Left: American Radicalism, 1900–1975* (New York: Hill and Wang, 1978).

17. Some of the most lively discussions of American radical problems in the seventies and radical prospects for the eighties are to be found in *Socialist Review* (formerly *Socialist Revolution,* a significant change of name). See Harry C. Boyte, "Building the Democratic Movement: Prospects for a Socialist Renaissance," *Socialist Review* 8 (July–October 1978):18, and the depressing responses by his colleagues in this and subsequent issues. See also Harry C. Boyte, *The Backyard Revolution: Understanding the New Citizen Movement* (Philadelphia: Temple University Press, 1980). See also Lawrence Goodwyn, "The Cooperative Commonwealth and Other Abstractions: In Search of a Democratic Premise," *Marxist Perspectives* 10 (Summer 1980):8–42. "One reason we are so innocent about structures of democracy and how to build them is that we are unaware of many democratic moments in human history, for we do not know how to find them in any systematic way or to explore them when we do stumble upon them" (p. 32).

18. Quoted admiringly in Tom Christoffel, "Thinking About the Unthink-

able: Socialist Revolution *versus* Pessimism," in Tom Christoffel et al., *Up Against the American Myth: A Radical Critique of Corporate Capitalism* (New York: Holt, Rinehart & Winston, 1970), p. 458.

19. Mark Rudd, "Columbia: Notes on the Spring Rebellion," in Carl Oglesby, ed., *The New Left Reader* (New York: Grove Press, 1969), p. 301.

20. Nadine Miller, "Letter to Her Psychiatrist," in Phil Brown, ed., *Radical Psychology* (New York: Harper & Row, 1973), p. 488.

21. John Judis, "NAM and the Revolutionary Hernia," *In These Times* 3 (August 22, 1979):2.

22. For a guide to the sects, see Jim O'Brien, *American Leninism in the 1970's,* New England Free Press pamphlet (reprint of an article that appeared originally in the November 1977–February 1978 issue of *Radical America*).

Chapter 5: The Liberal Left

1. William Lee Miller, "The New Anti-Americanism of the 1960's," reprinted in LeRoy Ashby and Bruce M. Stave, eds., *The Discontented Society: Interpretations of Twentieth Century American Protest* (Chicago: Rand-McNally, 1972), p. 294.

2. For a middle sixties example of left-liberal economic theory, see Gardner Ackley, "Expansionary Fiscal Policy Does Work," in Marvin E. Gettleman and David Mermelstein, eds., *The Great Society Reader: The Failure of American Liberalism* (New York: Vintage Books, 1967), pp. 59–67.

3. Lyndon B. Johnson, June 26, 1964. Reprinted in Gettleman and Mermelstein, eds., *The Great Society Reader,* p. 22.

4. David Riesman and Michael Maccoby, "The American Crisis," in James Roosevelt, ed., *The Liberal Papers* (Garden City, N.Y.: Doubleday, 1962), pp. 46–47.

5. Arthur M. Schlesinger, Jr., *The Vital Center* (1949; reprinted Boston: Houghton Mifflin, 1962), p. xii.

6. C. Wright Mills, "The New Left," in Irving Louis Horowitz, ed., *Power, Politics and People* (New York: Ballantine Books, 1963), p. 248.

7. See Sar A. Levitan and Benjamin H. Johnston, *The Job Corps: A Social Experiment That Works* (Baltimore: Johns Hopkins Press, 1975).

8. See Herbert J. Gans, *More Equality* (New York: Vintage Books, 1974), especially pp. 235–39.

9. Seymour Martin Lipset, "Coalition Politics—Causes and Consequences," in Seymour Martin Lipset, ed., *Emerging Coalitions in American*

Politics (New Brunswick, N.J.: Transaction Books, 1978), pp. 445–46.

10. Benjamin C. Bradlee, "The 22nd of November," in Lynda Rosen Obst, ed., *The Sixties: The Decade Remembered Now by the People Who Lived It Then* (New York: Random House/Rolling Stone Press, 1977), p. 102. See also Tom Wicker, "Kennedy without Tears." in Edward Quinn and Paul J. Dolan, eds., *The Sense of the 60's* (New York: Oxford University Press, 1968), pp. 68–86.

11. See John Kenneth Galbraith's review of Kristol's *Two Cheers for Capitalism,* "A Hard Case," *The New York Review of Books* (April 20, 1979):6–9.

12. Richard Locke, "Novelists as Preachers," *New York Times Book Review,* April 17, 1977, p. 3.

13. Robert Coles, *The Middle Americans: Proud and Uncertain* (Boston: Atlantic Monthly Press, 1971), p. 45.

14. Morris Dickstein, *Gates of Eden: American Culture in the Sixties* (New York: Basic Books, 1977), pp. x, 26.

15. The Editors, "Get Serious About Inflation," *The New Republic,* 180 (January 20, 1979):13. For a rehearsal of the tragic option in liberalism, see Glenn Tinder, "Liberals and Revolution," *The New Republic* 180 (January 27, 1979):21–23.

Chapter 6: The Neoconservatives

1. Quoted in Geoffrey Norman, "The Godfather of Neoconservatism (and His Family)," *Esquire* 91 (February 13, 1979):42.

2. Peter Steinfels, "The Reasonable Right," *Esquire* 91 (February 13, 1979):24. See also Peter Steinfels, *The Neoconservatives: The Men Who Are Changing America's Politics* (New York: Simon and Schuster, 1979). As Irving Kristol suggests, "neoconservatism" is more an intellectual "persuasion" than a movement. It is, he claims, "an intellectual current full of all sorts of little knotty whirlpools, each being agitated by some problem in political, social, or economic theory that needs further exploration, further thought." Though it is not a movement, neoconservatism does represent a powerful intellectual network, many of whose members, whatever Kristol may say, work cooperatively to exert political influence. Irving Kristol, "Confessions of a True, Self-Confessed—Perhaps the Only—'Neoconservative,'" *Public Opinion* 2 (October–November 1979):51, 52.

3. Daniel Bell, "Modernism and Capitalism," *Partisan Review* 45 (1978): 206.

4. Norman Podhoretz, *Breaking Ranks: A Political Memoir* (New York: Harper Colophon Books, 1980), pp. 305–306.

5. See Samuel P. Huntington, "The Democratic Distemper," *The Public*

Interest 41 (Fall 1975):9–38. For a fuller account, see his *American Politics: The Promise of Disharmony* (Cambridge, Mass.: Harvard University Press, 1981).

6. This and subsequent quotations from Kristol are from *Two Cheers for Capitalism* (New York: Basic Books, 1978).

7. Daniel Bell, "The New Class: A Muddled Concept," in B. Bruce-Briggs, ed., *The New Class?* (New Brunswick, N.J.: Transaction Books, 1979), p. 189. See also Daniel Bell, *The Cultural Contradictions of Capitalism* (New York: Basic Books, 1976).

8. Norman Podhoretz, *The Present Danger: "Do We Have the Will To Reverse the Decline of American Power?"* (New York: Simon and Schuster, 1980), p. 76.

9. Ibid., p. 94.

10. Ibid., pp. 77–78.

11. Seymour Martin Lipset, in "Human Rights and American Foreign Policy" (A Symposium), *Commentary* 72 (November 1981):49.

12. This point is developed nicely by Michael Walzer in "Totalitarianism vs. Authoritarianism: The Theory of Tyranny, the Tyranny of Theory," *Dissent* 28 (Fall 1981):400–402.

13. Richard A. Viguerie, *The New Right: We're Ready To Lead* (Falls Church, Va.: The Viguerie Company, 1981), p. 122.

14. See Daniel Bell, "The Return of the Sacred?" in his *The Winding Passage: Essays and Sociological Journeys 1960–1980* (Cambridge, Mass.: Abt Books, 1980), pp. 324–54. See also Robert Nisbet, *History of the Idea of Progress* (New York: Basic Books, 1980).

15. See Ben J. Wattenberg, *The Real America,* revised ed. (New York: Capricorn Books, 1976), for an optimistic neoconservative perspective on the seventies written in the early part of the decade. Wattenberg seems less interested in cultural conservatism and more concerned with imagining successful political strategies than are many neoconservative critics. As a rule, the closer to the action of politics a critic moves, the less play he or she allows to cultural pessimism.

16. See, for example, Ben J. Wattenberg, "Needed: Two Coalitions," in Seymour Martin Lipset, ed., *Emerging Coalitions in American Politics* (New Brunswick, N.J.: Transaction Books, 1978), pp. 389–93.

17. See Alan Crawford, *Thunder on the Right: The "New Right" and the Politics of Resentment* (New York: Pantheon Books, 1980), especially pp. 176 ff.

Chapter 7: The Ascendance of Nostalgia

1. For an interesting account of the persistence of vital family life through a series of major social changes, see Theodore Caplow et al., *Middle-*

town Families: Fifty Years of Change and Continuity (Minneapolis: University of Minnesota Press, 1982).

2. See Everett Carll Ladd, Jr. and Seymour Martin Lipset, *The Divided Academy: Professors and Politics.* (New York: W. W. Norton, 1975).

3. Jim Hougan, *Decadence: Radical Nostalgia, Narcissism, and Decline in the Seventies.* (New York: William Morrow, 1975), preface.

Chapter 8: Conditions of the Quest

1. The secularization and profanation of American society, so often assumed to be complete, is only partial. See Peter L. Berger, *A Rumor of Angels: Modern Society and the Rediscovery of the Supernatural* (Garden City, N.Y.: Doubleday, 1970). For a view of the religious diversity in America at the end of the seventeenth century, see Sydney E. Ahlstrom, *A Religious History of the American People* (New Haven and London: Yale University Press, 1972). "A traveler in 1700 making his way from Boston to the Carolinas would encounter Congregationalists of varying intensity, Baptists of several varieties, Presbyterians, Quakers, and several other forms of Puritan radicalism: Dutch, German, and French Reformed; Swedish, Finnish, and German Lutherans; Mennonites and radical pietists, Anglicans, Roman Catholics; here and there a Jewish congregation, a few Rosicrucians; and, of course, a vast number of the unchurched—some of them powerfully alienated from any form of institutional religion" (p. 4).

2. See Elaine Pagels, *The Gnostic Gospels* (New York: Random House, 1979).

3. See Daniel Bell's influential study *The End of Ideology: On the Exhaustion of Political Ideas in the Fifties* (Garden City, N.Y.: Doubleday, 1964). The apparently endless "end of ideology" controversy is itself a complex and highly ideological one. In a largely convincing defense of Bell's thesis, which hostile critics caricatured tirelessly, Seymour Martin Lipset demonstrates that a variety of critics—pluralist and Marxist, radical and conservative—posited one variant or another of this thesis, beginning in the late twenties with Karl Mannheim's *Ideology and Utopia.* See Lipset, "The End of Ideology and the Ideology of the Intellectuals" (mimeographed typescript). An earlier version was published as "Ideology and No End," *Encounter* 39 (December 1972): 17–22.

4. See David Riesman, *Abundance for What? and Other Essays* (Garden City, N.Y.: Doubleday, 1964), pp. 300–308.

5. See Paul A. Baran and Paul M. Sweezy, *Monopoly Capital: An Essay on the American Economic and Social Order* (New York and London: Monthly Review Press, 1966).

6. The minimal conditions of individual liberty and equal opportunity are hard to define in any generally acceptable fashion and even harder to enact. They nevertheless form a continuing problematic of American ideology and politics.

7. In an interesting study of continuity and change in American values, based on a review of the descriptive literature beginning with Crève-coeur and ending with a comparative analysis of twentieth-century opinion polls in the United States and several Western European nations, Alex Inkeles demonstrates the continuity of such values as individualism, self-fulfillment, pluralism, personal liberty, and the fundamental equality of all citizens (rooted in the sentiment of the intrinsic worth of every person). See Alex Inkeles, "Continuity and Change in the American National Character," in Seymour Martin Lipset, ed., *The Third Century: America as a Post-Industrial Society* (Stanford, Calif.: Hoover Institution Press, 1979), pp. 390–416.

8. For a survey of the complicated career of the concept of individualism, from which my list of characteristics is drawn, see Steven Lukes, *Individualism* (Oxford: Basil Blackwell, 1973). See also David M. Potter, "American Individualism in the Twentieth Century," in Don E. Fehrenbacher, ed., *History and American Society* (New York: Oxford University Press, 1973), pp. 257–76; and T. George Harris, "From Rugged-Individualism to Helpless-Individualism," in John G. Kirk, ed., *America Now* (New York: Atheneum, 1968), pp. 315–24. An important discussion of the notion of individualism and the related idea of individuality in America may be found in Yehoshua Arieli, *Individualism and Nationalism in American Ideology* (Cambridge, Mass.: Harvard University Press, 1964).

9. Charles Reich, *The Greening of America* (New York: Random House, 1970), p. 225.

10. For an elaboration of the tensions between charismatic and routine modes of authority, see Reinhard Bendix, *Max Weber: An Intellectual Portrait* (Garden City, N.Y.: Doubleday, 1960). See also Spencer C. Olin's interesting paper, "The Oneida Community and the Instability of Charismatic Authority," *Journal of American History* 67 (September 1980):285–300.

11. Irving Kristol, *Two Cheers for Capitalism* (New York: Basic Books, 1978), p. x.

Chapter 9: The Shapes of Salvation

1. Paul Goodman, "The New Reformation," in Irving Howe, ed., *Beyond the New Left* (New York: McCall Publishing Company, 1970), pp. 85, 89, 95.

2. Charles Perry, "The Gathering of the Tribes," in Lynda Rosen Obst, ed., *The Sixties: The Decade Remembered Now, by the People Who Lived It Then* (New York: Random House/Rolling Stone, 1977), p. 190.

3. Gloria Steinem, "Up from Powerlessness," in Obst, *The Sixties,* p. 285.

4. See Sara Evans, *Personal Politics: The Roots of Women's Liberation in the Civil Rights Movement and the New Left* (New York: Alfred A. Knopf, 1979). Discussing the role of Southern white women in the Southern black movement of the sixties, Evans notes the importance of the church, both as a source and subverter of vision. Recounting the experiences of two young activists, Dorothy Burlage and Jane Stembridge, Evans observes that "religious conviction had nourished their own rebellion and provided the vocabulary to describe their mission and their vision. They understood its centrality in southern life and the paradoxical reality it presented, offering them the possibility of transcending the barriers of race and sex while formally exercising an opposite role in the society as a whole" (p. 58).

5. For an extended discussion of the legacy of the Movement in the seventies, see Peter Clecak, "The Movement of the 1960's and Its Cultural and Political Legacy," in Stanley Coben and Lorman Ratner, eds., *The Development of an American Culture,* 2nd edition (New York: St. Martin's Press, 1983).

6. Estimates of the size of the principal new Left organizations are vague at best. From the outset, SDS was a decentralized collection of local groups. Since many people identified themselves with SDS without ever joining, the notion of membership is hazy. According to official membership statistics, SDS grew from 250 members in eight chapters in 1960 to between 30,000 and 100,000 members in 350 to 400 chapters in 1968–69. See Kirkpatrick Sale, *SDS* (New York: Random House, 1973), pp. 663–664.

   SNCC was a smaller, more tightly structured organization than SDS. It mobilized large numbers of people for voter-registration drives in the South and exerted an influence on SDS and on the nation far in excess of its numbers. SNCC grew from an organization with only fifteen full-time field workers in 1961 to about 200 full-time organizers in 1964. After 1965, members began to drift away, and SNCC went into permanent decline. Figures on SNCC are from Edward J. Bacciocco, Jr., *The New Left in America: Reform to Revolution* (Stanford, Calif.: Hoover Institution Press, 1974), pp. 45, 56, 60.

7. For an interesting, if finally naïve, discussion of the tensions between ordinary politics and utopian ends in the new Left—between the imperatives of the present and desires for the future—see Winifred Breines,

"The Great Refusal" (unpublished dissertation, Brandeis University, 1979).

8. Quoted in Garry Wills, "The Making of the Yippie Culture," *Esquire* 72 (November 1969):135.

9. Massimo Teodori, ed., *The New Left: A Documentary History* (Indianapolis and New York: Bobbs-Merrill, 1969), p. 4.

10. Ibid.

11. For a romantic account of the criminal as artist in America, see H. Bruce Franklin, *The Victim as Criminal and Artist: Literature from the American Prison* (New York: Oxford University Press, 1978).

12. On the distinction between exploitation and alienation, see Peter Clecak, *Radical Paradoxes: Dilemmas of the American Left, 1945–1970* (New York: Harper & Row, 1973), chap. 2, pp. 15–30.

13. A sensitive discussion of the class origins of early new Left activists can be found in Richard Flacks, "Revolt of the Young Intelligentsia: Revolutionary Class-Consciousness in a Post-Scarcity America," in Roderick Aya and Norman Miller, eds., *The New American Revolution* (New York: The Free Press, 1971), pp. 223–63.

14. By 1966, with the election of Stokely Carmichael as president, SNCC dropped its commitment to nonviolence. See "The Basis of Black Power," a position paper prepared by SNCC in the spring of 1966 and published in *The New York Times,* August 5, 1966. Reprinted in Teodori, *The New Left,* pp. 271–75.

15. Gregory Calvert, "In White America: Radical Consciousness and Social Change," *The National Guardian,* March 25, 1967. Reprinted in Teodori, *The New Left,* p. 414.

16. Evans, *Personal Politics,* p. 200.

17. Ibid., p. 205.

18. Sara Davidson, *Real Property* (Garden City, N.Y.: Doubleday, 1980), p. 191.

19. I know of no exceptions to this generalization. But there is one sensitive discussion of the power of Christian experience in the Soviet Union and the socialist nations of Eastern Europe by Erazim Kohak, a Czech Protestant: "Religion and Socialism," *Dissent* 25 (Spring 1978):174–85. Scholarly studies of the evangelical tradition in America flourished in the seventies, however. See, for example, George M. Marsden, *Fundamentalism and American Culture: The Shaping of Twentieth-Century Evangelicalism* (New York: Oxford University Press, 1980).

20. John H. Schaar, "Getting Religion," *The New York Review of Books* 23 (October 28, 1976):16.

21. Associated Press release, July 12, 1980.

22. Schaar, "Getting Religion," p. 16.

23. William G. McLoughlin posits a Fourth Great Awakening, beginning in 1960, following the first three in American history: 1730–60, 1800–30, 1890–1920. See his *Revivals, Awakenings, and Reform: An Essay on Religion and Social Change in America, 1607–1977* (Chicago and London: University of Chicago Press, 1978).

24. In 1977, 71 percent of Americans professed belief in life after death as opposed to 54 percent in Canada, 48 percent in Australia, 46 percent in Italy, 43 percent in the United Kingdom, 39 percent in France, 35 percent in Scandinavia, and 33 percent in West Germany (*Public Opinion* 2 (March–May 1979):39).

25. Ibid., p. 36. Like Schaar and many other intellectuals, Garry Wills questions the notion of a religious revival in the seventies on the dubious, or at least inconclusive, grounds that opinion polls reveal certain continuities of belief over several decades. Of course they do: how else could a *re*vival begin? See "What Religious Revival?" *Psychology Today* 11 (April 1978):74–81.

    The depth of the revival, of course, can be questioned. Opinion polls do record a widespread—and breathtaking—ignorance of doctrine and Scripture. Despite the breadth of the Christian revival, for example, "only 57 percent of the public respond at all" when asked to define *evangelical,* and nearly half of these describe an evangelical simply as a "religious person" (*The Gallup Opinion Index,* Report No. 145 (1977), p. 42).

26. *The Gallup Opinion Index,* Report No. 145, p. 19. It should be noted that prior to the recent rise, the percentage of interviewees who considered the influence of religion on the upswing had decreased from 69 percent in 1957 to 14 percent in 1969 and 1970.

27. Ibid., p. 1.

28. John Crothers Pollock et al., *The Connecticut Mutual Life Report on American Values in the '80s: The Impact of Belief* (Hartford: Connecticut Mutual Life Insurance Company, 1981), p. 17. The framers of the report conclude that approximately 25 percent of Americans fourteen years of age and older are "intensely religious." By this, they mean that respondents say they frequently "engage in or experience" at least five of the eight following items: "feel that God loves you," "engage in prayer," "attend religious services," "read the Bible," "have something you would call a religious experience," "participate in a church social activity," "encourage others to turn to religion," "listen to religious broadcasts" (pp. 42–43). Moreover, "approximately three out of every four U.S. citizens describe themselves as religious and say that religion would become a more important factor in their lives if they knew they had only six months to live" (p. 7).

29. The drop in overall church attendance since 1966 is attributable in part to the release of Roman Catholics from obligatory attendance at Mass. Old habits, however, die slowly: at the end of the seventies, Catholics still attended formal worship services more frequently than Protestants and Jews. Comparisons of Christians and Jews, however, are misleading since a large portion of Jewish worship centers on rituals in the home (ibid., p. 25).

30. In the 1977 Gallup poll, 34 percent of respondents described themselves as "born again," that is, as "having had a turning point in life" at which they formed a commitment to Jesus Christ (ibid., p. 41). In 1978 Gallup reported 40 percent born again. In 1980, the Christian Research Corporation, based in Irvine, California, found that 53.4 percent claimed to have been born again. The *Connecticut Mutual Life Report* puts the figure at 51 percent of adults. Although such polls probably ought to be taken lightly, they do suggest that a substantial percentage of the adult population is affected to one degree or another by the evangelical message. It should be remembered, however, that in recent polls more than half of those questioned professed a belief in the existence of unidentified flying objects. In this culture, most professions of faith are nearly costless items.

Indeed, the results of all public opinion polls need to be accepted tentatively. For one thing, respondents tend to give "appropriate" answers and to represent themselves as being (and feeling) closer to real or imagined norms than they probably are. For another, most opinion polls employ bivariate rather than multivariate analysis, pursuing relationships between only two rather than many variables. Finally, the data from polls can be used to overstate the case for centrist causes; small minorities, even influential ones, can exert an influence disproportionate to their numbers. Here and in subsequent chapters I use evidence from opinion polls cautiously, with these drawbacks in mind. See Lee Benson, Kevin Clancy, and John Kushma, "The Tricks of the Trade," *The Nation* 219 (November 30, 1974):553–58. See also David Gergen and William Schambra, "Pollsters and Polling," *The Wilson Quarterly* 3 (Spring 1979):61–72. "Our own experience suggests that when people answer questions dealing with *personal experience,* their views tend to be well-considered, lending the polls more credence . . . In sharp contrast, polls that ask people what the United States ought to do in a far-flung corner of the globe, such as Afghanistan, deserve little serious attention" (pp. 70–71).

31. Martin Marty, *A Nation of Behavers* (Chicago and London: University of Chicago Press, 1976), p. 106.

32. *Christianity Today*/Gallup Poll, 1980.

33. *The Gallup Opinion Index,* Report No. 145, pp. 51 ff.

34. Subsequent scriptural references are from the Revised Standard Version, *Westminster Study Bible: The Holy Bible* (New York and Glasgow: Collins' Clear-Type Press, 1965). See also Donald G. Bloesch, *Essentials of Evangelical Theology: God, Authority, and Salvation,* vol. 1 (San Francisco: Harper & Row, 1978).

35. Most evangelicals, fundamentalists, and Pentecostals cling to this exclusive version of salvation and damnation, apparently placing their faith in their Faith, thereby circumscribing the scope of divine wisdom and mercy.

36. John Macquarrie lists six "formative factors" in theology: experience, revelation, scripture, tradition, culture, and reason. Evangelicals regard Scripture as the major revelation to which all of the other formative factors are subordinated. See *Principles of Christian Theology,* 2nd ed. (New York: Charles Scribner's Sons, 1977), pp. 4 ff.

37. *The Gallup Public Opinion Index,* Report No. 145, p. 43.

38. Richard Quebedeaux, *The New Charismatics: The Origins, Development, and Significance of Neo-Pentecostalism* (Garden City, N.Y.: Doubleday, 1976), p. 4.

39. Martin Marty, *A Nation of Behavers,* p. 107.

40. On the role of independent entrepreneurs in the revival of Pentecostalism during the late forties and fifties, see the interesting study by David Edwin Harrell, Jr., *All Things Are Possible: The Healing and Charismatic Revival in Modern America* (Bloomington and London: Indiana University Press, 1975).

41. Jeremy Rifkin proceeds on this dubious assumption of the democratic character of glossolalia in his otherwise fascinating speculative study, *The Emerging Order: God in the Age of Scarcity* (New York: Putnam, 1979).

42. Edwin Scott Gaustad, *Dissent in American Religion* (Chicago and London: University of Chicago Press, 1973), p. 146.

43. See Seymour Martin Lipset and Earl Raab, "The Election & the Evangelicals," *Commentary* 71 (March 1981):25–31. For an interpretation of the interplay between right-wing political forces and fundamentalist and evangelical surges, see Seymour Martin Lipset, "The Sources of the 'Radical Right'" (1955), in Daniel Bell, ed., *The Radical Right* (Garden City, N.Y.: Doubleday, 1964), pp. 307–71.

44. Reinhold Niebuhr, "The Crisis in American Protestantism" (1963), in William R. Miller, ed., *Contemporary American Protestant Thought: 1900–1970* (Indianapolis and New York: Bobbs-Merrill, 1973), pp. 406–407.

45. *The Gallup Public Opinion Index,* Report No. 145, p. 45.

46. See Jeremy Rifkin, *The Emerging Order,* chaps. 10 and 11, pp. 211 ff.

47. Jerry Falwell's moral tour of the nation is recorded in his dismal book, *Listen, America* (Garden City, N.Y.: Doubleday, 1980). On every subject he tackles, from rock music to Marx, Falwell manages to be shallow, shrill, predictable, and often just silly. "Listen, America!" Falwell declares, attempting to buttonhole his readers, "Our nation is on a perilous path in regard to her political, economic, and military positions . . . Our nation's internal problems are direct results of her spiritual condition. America is desperately in need of a divine healing, which can only come if God's people will humble themselves, pray, seek His face, and turn from their wicked ways. It is now time that moral Americans awake to the fact that our future depends upon how we stand on moral issues. God has no reason to spare us if we continue to reject Him" (p. 243).

48. Quoted in Martin Marty, *A Nation of Behavers*, p. 106.

49. For a brilliant account of a nonexclusive interpretation of the doctrine of salvation by a Catholic theologian see Karl Rahner, *Foundations of Christian Faith: An Introduction to the Idea of Christianity* (New York: The Seabury Press, 1978).

50. *Public Opinion* 2 (March–May 1979):37.

51. Elizabeth Hardwick, "The Portable Canterbury," *The New York Review of Books* 26 (August 16, 1979):6. It should be noted also that at least from the twenties on, women were more likely to preach in Pentecostal than in mainline churches. Moreover, Aimée Semple McPherson—founder of the Foursquare Church and the most prominent woman preacher of the twenties and thirties—always managed to "look nice."

52. Makeup, of course, is not simply an instrument of social competition. It is also a great equalizer, a means by which "beauty" may be distributed among a population more evenly than it is by nature and the differing effects of social life.

53. Irving Howe, "The Culture of Modernism," in Irving Howe, *Decline of the New* (New York: Harcourt, Brace & World, 1970), p. 5.

54. Therapeutic clichés and advertising slogans have become virtually interchangeable. Indeed, one of the leading themes of the culture of consumption is the selling of enjoyment, of "gratification." Advertising thrives on images—often thin and distorted ones—of fulfillment.

55. Eva Hoffman, "*est*—the Magic of Brutality," *Dissent* 24 (Spring 1977): 212.

56. For a characterization of the languages of the therapeutic quest, see Richard D. Rosen, *Psychobabble* (New York: Avon Books, 1977).

57. Tom Wolfe, "The 'Me' Decade and the Third Great Awakening," *New West* (August 30, 1976):27.

58. The therapeutic personality was brilliantly delineated in the middle

sixties by Philip Rieff in *The Triumph of the Therapeutic: Uses of Faith After Freud* (New York: Harper & Row, 1966). See also the useful anthology of discussions of Rieff's "psychological man" edited by Robert Boyers, *Psychological Man* (New York: Harper & Row, 1975).

59. In 1980, for example, the American Medical Association granted its members the right to refer patients to chiropractors under certain circumstances. And increasing numbers of medical schools were requiring students to undergo some training in principles of nutrition. Of course, neither the techniques of holistic medicine nor the emphasis on nutrition was new. Medico-populism has a long and varied history in America. For example, the famous Hoxsey elixir, a secret compound of herbs that presumably cured Hoxsey's horse of cancer, was marketed in the 1840s by Harry Hoxsey and is still dispensed in at least one cancer clinic in northern Mexico (though not, as far as I know, to horses).

60. See Thomas C. Schelling's interesting essay, "The Intimate Contest for Self-Command," *The Public Interest* 60 (Summer 1980):94–118.

61. Quoted in Martin L. Gross, *The Psychological Society: A Critical Analysis of Psychiatry, Psychotherapy, Psychoanalysis and the Psychological Revolution* (New York: Simon and Schuster, 1978), p. 278.

62. See Donald Stone, "The Human Potential Movement," in Charles Y. Glock and Robert N. Bellah, eds., *The New Religious Consciousness* (Berkeley and Los Angeles: University of California Press, 1976), pp. 93–115.

63. Michael Rossman, "Notes on the Tao of the Body Politic," *The Self-Determination Quarterly Journal* 2 (1978):36.

64. For an interesting account of such cultural traffic patterns, see Steven M. Tipton, *Getting Saved from the Sixties: Moral Meaning in Conversion and Cultural Change* (Berkeley, Los Angeles, London: University of California Press, 1982).

65. Despite the widespread skepticism about conventional medical practice, public confidence in medicine remained fairly high in the seventies, compared with confidence in other institutions. In the 1977 Gallup survey of American religion, for example, 73 percent of the respondents expressed a "great deal" (39 percent) or "quite a lot" (34 percent) of confidence in medicine. "The Church or organized Religion" ranked a close second. Congress (40 percent, "a great deal" and "quite a lot" combined), labor (39 percent combined), and big business (33 percent combined) were the bottom three (*The Gallup Public Opinion Index,* Report No. 145, p. 14).

66. Quoted in Walter Lippmann, *A Preface to Morals* (1929; reprinted New York: Time-Life Books, 1964), pp. 150–51.

67. Daniel Yankelovich, *New Rules: Searching for Self-Fulfillment in a*

World Turned Upside Down (New York: Random House, 1981), p. 3.

68. Ibid., p. 90.

69. Frederick Crews, "Analysis Terminable," *Commentary* 70 (July 1980): 26–27. See also Lester Luborsky, Barton Singer, and Lise Luborsky, "Comparative Studies of Psychotherapies: Is It True That 'Everyone Has Won and All Must Have Prizes'?" *Archives of General Psychiatry* 32 (1975):995–1,008.

70. On social scientists' attempts to define and measure the subjective idea of happiness, see N. M. Bradburn, *The Structure of Psychological Well-Being* (Chicago: Aldine, 1969); and Burkhard Strumpel, ed., *Subjective Elements of Well-Being* (Paris: Organization for Economic Co-Operation and Development, 1974). For a popular account, see Jonathan Freedman, *Happy People: What Happiness Is, Who Has It, and Why* (New York: Harcourt Brace Jovanovich, 1978).

Chapter 10: Social Justice and the Logic of Dissent

1. On the distinction between political and cultural dissent, see Kenneth Keniston, *Young Radicals: Notes on Committed Youth* (New York: Harcourt, Brace & World, 1968), pp. 297–325. On the characteristics of protest, see Norman F. Cantor, *The Age of Protest: Dissent and Rebellion in the Twentieth Century* (San Francisco: Leswing Press, 1969), pp. 332–36.

2. *Los Angeles Times,* August 28, 1979, p. 3.

3. Two recent studies of the idea of social justice are William A. Galston, *Justice and the Human Good* (Chicago and London: University of Chicago Press, 1980); and Bruce A. Ackerman, *Social Justice in the Liberal State* (New Haven and London: Yale University Press, 1980).

4. George Katona, *Psychological Economics* (New York: Elsevier, 1975), p. 23.

5. "America" was first published in Allen Ginsberg, *Howl and Other Poems* (San Francisco: City Lights Books, 1956), pp. 31–34. All subsequent quotations of Ginsberg are from this text. For an account of the Beats, see John Tytell, *Naked Angels: The Lives and Literature of the Beat Generation* (New York: McGraw-Hill, 1976); and Bruce Cook, *The Beat Generation* (New York: Charles Scribner's Sons, 1971).

6. Throughout "America," Ginsberg writes sentimentally about his own background in the old Left: "America when I was seven momma took me to Communist Cell meetings . . ." This motif clearly is more autobiographical than political.

7. For an interesting account of the early protests, see William H. Chafe,

Civilities and Civil Rights: Greensboro, North Carolina, and the Black Struggle for Freedom (New York: Oxford University Press, 1980).

8. Martin Luther King, Jr., "I Have a Dream . . . ," in Edward Quinn and Paul J. Dolan, eds., *The Sense of the Sixties* (New York: The Free Press, 1968), pp. 211–15. This and subsequent quotations of King are from this text.

9. Frances Fox Piven and Richard A. Cloward, *Poor People's Movements: Why They Succeed, How They Fail* (New York: Vintage Books, 1979), p. 252.

10. Joseph Boskin, "The Revolt of the Urban Ghettos, 1964–1967," *The Annals of the American Academy of Political and Social Science* 382 (March 1969):8.

11. Ted Robert Gurr, "Political Protest and Rebellion in the 1960s: The United States in World Perspective," in Hugh Davis Graham and Ted Robert Gurr, eds., *Violence in America: Historical and Comparative Perspectives,* revised ed. (Beverly Hills, Cal.: Sage, 1979). Quotations are from a mimeographed typescript, pp. 102, 104–105.

12. For a moving portrait of America's handicapped people, see Sonny Kleinfields, *The Hidden Minority: America's Handicapped* (Boston: Little, Brown, 1979).

13. For an account of the tensions behind the scenes—especially the disagreement over the first draft of John Lewis's speech—see Godfrey Hodgson, *America in Our Time* (Garden City, N.Y.: Doubleday, 1976), pp. 193–99.

Chapter 11: Dissent and the Democratization of Personhood

1. E. J. Hobsbawm, "Should the Poor Organize?" *The New York Review of Books* 25 (March 23, 1978):45.

2. Vernon E. Jordan, Jr., "Introduction," in James D. Williams, ed., *The State of Black America 1980* (New York: National Urban League, January 22, 1980), p. i.

3. William Raspberry, "Denying Black Gains Is Wrong," *Los Angeles Times,* April 19, 1979, part 2, p. 15.

4. Reported in *The Chronicle of Higher Education,* March 12, 1979, p. 6.

5. Elliot Zashin, "The Progress of Black Americans in Civil Rights: The Past Two Decades Assessed," *Daedalus* 107 (Winter 1978):240, 260. Zashin, it should be noted, sensibly qualifies his generally positive account, noting that (1) the major successes of the civil-rights movement, which came in the South, could not be reproduced easily elsewhere, where patterns of discrimination and the consequences of urban isolation proved to be more subtle; (2) black inequality remained a major

American social problem at the end of the seventies; (3) future progress toward full equality cannot be predicted merely on the basis of the "forces set in motion by the developments of the sixties and seventies" (p. 260).

6. Andrew Hacker suggests that the main opposition to the Equal Rights Amendment came from women, not men. See Andrew Hacker, "E.R.A. —R.I.P.", *Harper's* 261 (September 1980):10–11, 14.

7. *Public Opinion* 2 (January–February 1979):36 (source: Surveys by the American Institute of Public Opinion [Gallup]).

8. Ibid., p. 35 (source: Surveys by Louis Harris and Associates).

9. Alice Rossi, "Contemporary American Feminism: In and Out of the Political Mainstream," paper delivered to an International Symposium on Research on Popular Movements, Stockholm, Sweden, February 7, 1978, p. 29 (mimeographed typescript, quoted by permission). See also Alice Rossi, *Feminists in Politics: A Panel Analysis of the First National Women's Conference* (New York: Academic Press, 1982).

10. Howard R. Bowen, *Socially Imposed Costs of Higher Education,* Fifth David D. Henry Lecture (Chicago: University of Illinois at Chicago Circle, 1978), p. 25.

11. Associated Press, January 29, 1980.

12. See Ralph Keyes, *The Height of Your Life* (Boston: Little, Brown, 1980).

13. On the idea of entitlements and the increasing role of government in ensuring them, see Daniel Bell, "The Revolution of Rising Entitlements," *Fortune* 91 (April 1975):98 ff. For an assessment of American attempts to enact the provisions of FDR's Economic Bill of Rights in the postwar years, see James H. Duffy, *Domestic Affairs: American Programs and Priorities* (New York: Simon and Schuster, 1978).

14. See, for example, Leo Huberman and Paul M. Sweezy, "Recovery, Stagnation, and Inflation," *Monthly Review* 10 (November 1958):241–50, and other editorials in *Monthly Review* on the American economy during these years. See also Ad Hoc Committee, "The Triple Revolution: Cybernation—Weaponry—Human Rights," in Paul Goodman, ed., *Seeds of Liberation* (New York: George Braziller, 1964), pp. 396–413. Although their economic forecasts have been wide of the mark, the framers of this manifesto clearly foresaw the emerging trends toward the democratization of personhood.

15. *Economic Report of the President* (Washington, D.C., February 1982), p. 266.

16. U.S. Bureau of the Census, *Statistical Abstract of the United States: 1980,* 101st ed. (Washington, D.C., 1980), p. 431.

17. Ibid., p. 405.

18. Ibid., p. 72.

19. *Economic Report of the President* (February 1982), p. 234.

20. Ibid., p. 261 (in constant 1972 dollars).

21. Ibid. Per capita income is, at best, a coarse index of human economic welfare. As Stanley Lebergott observes, "the simple move from using GNP [gross national product] as a measure of economic welfare to using GNP per capita tacitly implies that the birth of children reduces human economic welfare, and that death increases it." Stanley Lebergott, *The American Economy: Income, Wealth and Want* (Princeton, N.J.: Princeton University Press, 1976), p. 43.

22. John C. Musgrave, "Durable Goods Owned by Consumers in the United States, 1925–1977," *Survey of Current Business* 59 (March 1979):21.

23. I am indebted to Julius Margolis for providing these estimates, as well as for valuable advice on this section.

24. Simon Kuznets, "Notes on the Pattern of U.S. Economic Growth," in Edgar O. Edwards, ed., *The Nation's Economic Objectives* (Chicago and London: University of Chicago Press, 1964), p. 15.

25. Lebergott, *The American Economy,* p. 8. Moreover, Taylorism seems to be on the wane. According to a report issued by Theodore Barry & Associates in October 1979, the average American worker spends only about 55 percent of his or her work time being productive, as opposed to about 80–85 percent of a longer work day in 1900. Much of this form of consumption results in enriching relations with fellow workers and should be counted as a long-term gain (reported in the *Los Angeles Times,* October 17, 1979, part 3, p. 15).

26. *Economic Report of the President* (February, 1982), p. 321.

27. *Statistical Abstract of the United States: 1980,* p. 331.

28. Lester C. Thurow, *The Zero-Sum Society: Distribution and the Possibilities for Economic Change* (New York: Penguin Books, 1981), pp. 159 ff.

29. See Joel Dreyfuss and Charles Lawrence III, *The Bakke Case* (New York: Harcourt Brace Jovanovich, 1979).

30. Robert B. Hill, "Black Families in the 1970's," in *The State of Black America 1980,* p. 31.

31. *Statistical Abstract of the United States: 1980,* p. 456.

32. See Wayne J. Villemez and Candace Hinson Wiswell, "The Impact of Diminishing Discrimination on the Internal Size Distributon of Black Income: 1954–1974," *Social Forces* 56 (June 1978):1019–34.

33. *Economic Report of the President* (Washington, D.C., January 1980), p. 402. See Howard Davis, "Employment Gains of Women by Industry, 1968–1978," *Monthly Labor Review* 103 (June 1980):3.

34. Frank P. Stafford, "Women's Use of Time Compared with Men's," *Monthly Labor Review* 103 (December 1980):57–59.
35. Of course, the *idea* of equal pay for equal work has been accepted widely by the American public for decades. According to a Gallup survey taken in 1942, 92 percent of the respondents favored equal pay for equal work, as opposed to 94 percent in 1977.
36. *Economic Report of the President* (January 1980), pp. 236–38.
37. Ibid., p. 239.
38. Yankelovich's loose definition of job seeker, of course, accounts largely for the disparity between his estimates and the lower government figures.
39. U.S. Bureau of the Census, *Statistical Abstract of the United States: 1978,* 99th ed. (Washington, D.C., 1978), p. 465. The poverty line was calculated at $6,191 in unadjusted 1977 dollars for a nonfarm family of four. (It should be noted, however, that comparisons of rates before and after 1974 are not strictly accurate because of revised statistical procedures.) For an even more positive assessment of the decline of poverty in the sixties *and* the seventies, see Morton Paglin, "Poverty in the United States: A Reevaluation," *Public Policy* 8 (Spring 1979): 7–24.
40. Insofar as transfer payments are a substitute for employment, they may be considered a less than ideal means to the democratization of personhood. John Palmer presents a reasoned assessment of the jobs versus income transfers controversy that dominated discussions of social welfare policy in the seventies in "Jobs versus Income Transfers," in Eli Ginzberg, ed., *Employing the Unemployed* (New York: Basic Books, 1980), pp. 110–28.
41. The Gini index for measuring relative income inequality (created by the Italian statistician Corrado Gini) shows a slight trend toward income inequality for all earners between 1960 and 1977: .411 in 1960; .423 in 1970; and .439 in 1977. The Gini index is the ratio between complete income equality (e.g., 5 percent of the income recipients receiving 5 percent of the income, etc.) and actual distribution. Thus, the closer the Gini index comes to zero, the more equal the distribution. Several specific developments might have aided the overall postwar trend toward inequality: (1) the increase in part-time work; (2) the increasing flow of young people into the labor force, many of them with low earnings; (3) the more complex occupational structure; and (4) relatively greater increases in earnings in upper income ranges. In the late seventies, the reduced birth rates that commenced in the late fifties began to affect employment, slowing the rate of entry of young low-wage earners. Also, the increase in voluntary part-time work slowed,

as did the shift to white-collar work and the increases in earnings among higher-paid employees. Taken together, these factors may help to explain a slight retardation of the trend toward inequality, beginning in 1974. See Peter Henle and Paul Ryscavage, "The Distribution of Earned Income among Men and Women, 1958–1977," *Monthly Labor Review* 103 (April 1980):3–10.

42. *Economic Report of the President* (January 1980), p. 325.

43. For an interesting discussion of the sources of inflation and the problems of measuring this phenomenon, see Walter Heller, "Economic Policy for Inflation: Shadow, Substance, and Statistics," (mimeographed paper, 1980).

44. Howard R. Bowen, *Socially Imposed Costs of Higher Education*, pp. 16–17, 17, 18. I am indebted to Mr. Bowen for valuable advice on this and other chapters, and for permission to preview his fascinating characterization of the postwar American economy in *The State of the Nation and the Agenda for Higher Education* (San Francisco: Jossey-Bass, 1982).

45. *Statistical Abstract of the United States: 1978*, p. 455.

46. Richard Curtin, "Facing Adversity with a Smile," *Public Opinion* 3 (April–May 1980):18.

47. Ibid.

48. Reported in the *Los Angeles Times*, February 21, 1979, p. 14.

49. Among the most eloquent defenses of socialism written by an American in the seventies is Michael Harrington, *Socialism* (New York: Saturday Review Press, 1972).

50. *Public Opinion* 3 (April–May 1980):21, 22. Moreover, Seymour Martin Lipset reported that 89 percent of American university professors claim to be sympathetic to democratic capitalism (*The Chronicle of Higher Education*, June 16, 1978). See also Everett Carll Ladd, Jr., and Seymour Martin Lipset, *The Divided Academy: Professors and Politics* (New York: W. W. Norton, 1975).

51. Irving Louis Horowitz, "Race, Class, and the New Ethnicity," in Irving Louis Horowitz, *Ideology and Utopia in the United States: 1956–1976* (New York: Oxford University Press, 1977), p. 60.

52. Quoted in Godfrey Hodgson, *America in Our Time* (Garden City, N.Y.: Doubleday, 1976), p. 426. For a discussion of American attitudes toward social class, see Richard P. Coleman and Lee Rainwater, *Social Standing in America: New Dimensions of Class* (New York: Basic Books, 1978). On the basis of extensive interviews conducted in Boston and Kansas City, Coleman and Rainwater conclude that although a decisive majority of Americans believe in the equality of persons, favor schemes to broaden opportunity of the disadvantaged, and condemn

those who use unequal shares of wealth as a basis for judging personal worth, they do not advocate large redistributive schemes (apart from the vague goal of reducing poverty). Older citizens tend to favor the present class system in greater numbers than do respondents under age thirty. But overall, few dramatic changes were advocated by Americans (pp. 294–304). See also Jennifer L. Hochschild, *What's Fair? American Beliefs about Distributive Justice* (Cambridge, Mass.: Harvard University Press, 1981).

53. Richard A. Easterlin, *Birth and Fortune: The Impact of Numbers on Personal Welfare* (New York: Basic Books, 1980), p. 146.

54. See Stuart Ewen, *Captains of Consciousness: Advertising and the Social Roots of the Consumer Culture* (New York: McGraw-Hill, 1976). For a vigorous though far from subtle exposition of the view that liberal society "depoliticizes and marginalizes the political," see Alan Wolfe, *The Limits of Legitimacy* (New York: The Free Press, 1977).

55. John H. Schaar and Sheldon S. Wolin, "Campus Protests: Signals of Discontent in a Technological Society," in LeRoy Ashby and Bruce M. Stave, eds., *The Discontented Society: Interpretations of Twentieth Century American Protest* (Chicago: Rand McNally, 1972), p. 224.

56. Wolin's concerns were allowed a wider scope when he was given a journal devoted to them: *democracy: A Journal of Political Renewal and Radical Change* began publication in 1980. The journal was conceived by Max Palevsky, a wealthy radical who found none of the current literature on the left precisely to his taste. Impressed by Wolin's writings, Palevsky asked Wolin to edit *democracy*. Palevsky, the publisher, reportedly spends nearly a quarter of a million dollars a year on this venture—not an outrageous expenditure, I suppose, when compared to his contributions to such political featherweights as Gore Vidal, who in 1982 ran unsuccessfully for the Democratic senate nomination in the California primary.

57. Robert Nisbet, *The Quest for Community* (New York: Oxford University Press, 1962), pp. 28–29.

58. Christopher Jencks et al., *Who Gets Ahead?—The Determinants of Economic Success in America* (New York: Basic Books, 1979). This is the popular version of a more detailed report prepared by Jencks and eleven associates at the Harvard Center for Educational Policy Research and filed with several funding agencies as well as with the National Technical Information Service.

59. Considering the limitations of his own sort of analysis, Jencks might be expected to be gracious about the shortcomings of other modes. But his rather condescending and slightly self-serving review of Peter Steinfels's *The Neoconservatives,* which appeared shortly after Jencks's own

book, shows no evidence of such a disposition. "Mr. Steinfels's principal mistake, it seems to me, is taking his subjects too seriously . . . As magazine writers . . . the neoconservatives are among the best. Indeed, I find *The Public Interest* the most consistently interesting general-circulation magazine in America. But articles in *The Public Interest* seldom treat their subject either rigorously or exhaustively, and they frequently use evidence in a rather cavalier manner. They are also full of rhetorical flourishes that even the authors know would not withstand close scrutiny. *The Public Interest* is no worse in this respect than its liberal or radical competitors; indeed, it seems to me somewhat better. But *no* general-circulation magazine of this kind looks very good when you look to it for a comprehensive or systematic political viewpoint." Anyone who understands rhetoric as mere icing on the cake of fact (or purported fact), as Jencks seems disposed to do, probably should leave criticism of "magazine writers" to others. Christopher Jencks, "The Crisis of Authority," *The New York Times Book Review,* July 1, 1979, p. 1.

60. Daniel Yankelovich, "Who Gets Ahead in America?" *Psychology Today* 13 (July 1979):43. See also Seymour Martin Lipset, "The Limits of Social Science," *Public Opinion* 4 (October–November 1981):2–9, and Daniel Bell, *The Social Sciences Since the Second World War* (New Brunswick, N.J., and London: Transaction Books, 1982).

61. William Julius Wilson, *The Declining Significance of Race: Blacks and Changing American Institutions* (Chicago and London: University of Chicago Press, 1978), pp. 126 ff.

62. Thomas Sowell, "Ethnicity in a Changing America," *Daedalus* 107 (Winter 1978):233, 228. See also Thomas Sowell, *Ethnic America: A History* (New York: Basic Books, 1981).

63. Diana Vreeland, "Chatting About Style," in Lynda Rosen Obst, ed., *The Sixties: The Decade Remembered Now, by the People Who Lived It Then* (New York: Random House/Rolling Stone, 1977), p. 146.

64. *Statistical Abstract of the United States: 1980,* p. 44.

65. Robin Morgan, "Goodbye to All That," in *Rat,* February 6, 1970. Reprinted in David Horowitz, Michael P. Lerner, and Craig Pyes, eds., *Counterculture and Revolution* (New York: Random House, 1972), p. 95.

66. Betty Friedan, *The Feminine Mystique* (New York: Dell, 1963), p. 11.

67. Betty Friedan, "The Second Stage," *Redbook* 154 (January 1980):46. Such generalizations about mental health should not be taken solemnly, even if they are based on fairly rigorous studies. Friedan cites the Midtown Manhattan Longitudinal Study conducted by Dr. Leo Srole and Anita Kasen Fischer (1954; repeated in the early seventies) and the

study directed by Dr. Harold Dupuy within the National Center for Health Statistics (1959–62; repeated 1971–1975).

68. I am indebted to Seymour Martin Lipset for reminding me how mild the conservative and even reactionary responses of the late sixties and seventies were, compared, say, with nativist reactions to social and cultural changes in the 1920s.

69. John Crothers Pollock et al., *The Connecticut Mutual Life Report on American Values in the '80s* (Hartford: Connecticut Mutual Life Insurance Company, 1981), p. 85.

70. Daniel Yankelovich, *New Rules: Searching for Self-Fulfillment in a World Turned Upside Down* (New York: Random House, 1981), p. 89.

71. Pollock et al., *Connecticut Mutual Life Report*, p. 86.

72. Yankelovich, *New Rules*, pp. 93–96. Of the twenty changes in social norms cited by Yankelovich, more than half have to do with the freedom of persons.

73. See Everett C. Ladd, Jr., "Traditional Rights Regnant," *Public Opinion* 1 (March–April 1978):45–49.

74. Ben J. Wattenberg, "The Second Shoe Falls—and Maybe a Third," *Public Opinion* 1 (November–December 1978):3.

75. Walter Lippmann, *A Preface to Morals* (1929; New York: Time-Life Books, 1964), pp. 14 ff.

76. See, for an example, Elizabeth Fox-Genovese, "The Personal Is Not Political Enough," *Marxist Perspectives* 8 (Winter 1979–80):94–113.

77. See Jesse Lemisch, "The American Revolution Seen from the Bottom Up," in Barton J. Bernstein, ed., *Towards a New Past: Dissenting Essays in American History* (New York: Vintage Books, 1969), pp. 3–45. This shift toward social history probably enabled Marxist perspectives to enjoy a modest revival in the academy, but not in the larger society, during the late sixties and seventies.

78. See Michael Novak, *The Rise of the Unmeltable Ethnics: Politics and Culture in the Seventies* (New York: Macmillan, 1972), Chapter 10, "The Ethnic Democratic Party," pp. 267–91. See also the ambitious *We the Peoples: Harvard Encyclopedia of American Ethnic Groups,* Stephan Thernstrom, ed., (Cambridge, Mass.: Belknap/Harvard University Press, 1980). This valuable reference volume is a guide to 106 ethnic groups in America, from Acadians to Zoroastrians.

79. Quoted in Mary Claire Blakeman, "Young Protesters' New Target: Abortion," *Los Angeles Times,* September 16, 1980, part 2, p. 7. Judging from Evans's remarks, the lack of rhetorical sophistication endemic among student activists seems to have survived the decline of the Movement of the sixties.

Chapter 12: The "Rise" of Selfishness?

1. See Francesca M. Cancian, "Images of Marriage Since 1900: Trends and Cycles" (mimeographed paper, December 1980).
2. Philip Rieff, *The Triumph of the Therapeutic: Uses of Faith After Freud* (New York: Harper & Row, 1966), p. 4. Unless otherwise noted, subsequent quotations of Rieff are from this book.
3. Daniel Bell, *The Winding Passage: Essays and Sociological Journeys 1960–1980* (Cambridge, Mass.: Abt Books, 1980), p. xi. Unless otherwise noted, quotations from Bell are from this book. Portions of the section on Bell appeared in Peter Clecak, "The Pleasures of Maturity," *Dissent* 28 (Spring 1981):221–25.
4. Daniel Bell, *The Cultural Contradictions of Capitalism* (New York: Basic Books, 1976), p. 84.
5. My subsequent discussion of Bell's meditations on religion is based on his "The Return of the Sacred? The Argument on the Future of Religion," in *The Winding Passage,* pp. 324–54. This, to be sure, is only a fragment of his writings on contemporary religion, most of which either are unpublished as yet or incorporated into his two books published in the seventies: *The Coming of Post-Industrial Society: A Venture in Social Forecasting* (New York: Basic Books, 1973), and *The Cultural Contradictions of Capitalism* (1976). For a fuller exposition of Bell's views of contemporary religious phenomena at the outset of the seventies, see his "Religion in the Sixties," *Social Research* 38 (Fall 1971):447–97.
6. Dietrich Bonhoeffer, *Letters and Papers from Prison,* Eberhard Bethge, ed. (New York: Macmillan, 1978), pp. 360–61.
7. See the symposium, "The Culture of Narcissism," *Salmagundi* 46 (Fall 1979):173 ff.; and the "Special Symposium on Narcissism," *Telos* 44 (Summer 1980):49–125.
8. In *Eros and Civilization* (New York: Random House, 1962), Marcuse emphasizes the potential element of protest, of refusal, in the cultural notion of narcissism. Although *One-Dimensional Man* does not press this theme, Marcuse picks it up again at the end of the sixties in his diffident celebration of radical elements of the counterculture, *An Essay on Liberation* (Boston: Beacon Press, 1969).
9. Christopher Lasch, *The Culture of Narcissism: American Life in an Age of Diminishing Expectations* (New York: W. W. Norton, 1978), p. xv. Subsequent quotations of Lasch are from this book. Although the terms "selfishness" and "narcissism" are often used interchangeably, they do have distinct meanings. As Lasch suggests, all narcissists are selfish (even though they frequently may be unable to express this dis-

position in satisfying or uninhibited ways). But not all selfish people display the main symptoms of narcissism. Without ignoring this distinction, I have used "selfishness" as the generic term throughout this chapter. The context should clarify special uses of "narcissism."

10. Lasch follows Gulliver in another respect: he does not wish *The Culture of Narcissism* to be classified with other works on the theme of selfishness. "In order precisely to forestall the temptation to misread my book as a moralistic indictment of self-seeking or as another protest against the 'me decade,' I have cited a large body of clinical evidence which suggests that grandiose illusions of omnipotence originate in early feelings of loss and deprivation, more precisely in defenses against a boundless rage, and that narcissism must therefore not be confused with normal rapacity and greed . . . I must repudiate more emphatically than ever the suggestion that my book represents the 'latest addition to the "what's wrong with us" bibliography,' as one reviewer has characterized it." Christopher Lasch, "Politics and Social Theory: A Reply to Critics," *Salmagundi* 46 (Fall 1979):195–96.

11. U.S. Bureau of the Census, *Statistical Abstract of the United States: 1980,* 101st ed. (Washington, D.C., 1980), pp. 363, 362; and *Public Opinion* 5 (February–March 1982): 21, 22. It should be noted that although Americans believed that people were less willing to help others at the end of the seventies than in the middle sixties, they reported higher levels of voluntarism in the later years.

12. Ibid., p. 793. The big jump in percentage of owner-occupied housing units came in the early postwar period: the percentage climbed from 43.6 percent in 1940 to 55 percent in 1950 and to 61.9 percent by 1960.

13. See Anne Calamosca, "Capitalism and Housework," *The New Republic* 182 (March 29, 1980):18–20.

14. Fred Hirsch, *Social Limits to Growth* (Cambridge, Mass., and London, 1976), pp. 3, 5. See also William Leiss, *The Limits to Satisfaction: An Essay on the Problem of Needs and Commodities* (Toronto and Buffalo: University of Toronto Press, 1976).

15. For a comprehensive analysis of the essentially positive economic and noneconomic outcomes of American higher education in these years, see Howard R. Bowen, with Peter Clecak, Gordon K. Douglass, and Jacqueline Powers Doud, *Investment in Learning: The Individual and Social Value of American Higher Education* (San Francisco: Jossey-Bass, 1977).

16. Richard M. Weaver, *Visions of Order: The Cultural Crisis of Our Time* (Baton Rouge: Louisiana State University Press, 1964), p. 20.

17. Conference at University of Notre Dame, 1979.

18. Walter Lippmann, *A Preface to Morals* (1929; New York: Time-Life Books, 1964), p. 245.

19. Ernest Becker, *The Denial of Death* (New York: The Free Press, 1973), p. 88.

20. Clark E. Moustakas, "Summary: Explorations in Essential Being and Personal Growth," in *The Self: Explorations in Personal Growth* (New York: Harper & Row, 1956), p. 271.

21. In Carl Rogers, *On Becoming a Person: A Therapist's View of Psychotherapy* (Boston: Houghton Mifflin, 1961), pp. 23–24.

22. Abraham Maslow, "A Theory of Metamotivation," in Walt Anderson, ed., *The Age of Protest* (Pacific Palisades, Calif.: Goodyear Publishing, 1969), p. 246.

23. Ibid., p. 247.

24. Ibid., p. 249.

25. John Adams, *Discourses on Davilla,* quoted in Arthur O. Lovejoy, *Reflections on Human Nature* (Baltimore: The Johns Hopkins Press, 1961), pp. 200–201.

26. Russell Jacoby, "Narcissism and the Crisis of Capitalism," *Telos* 44 (Summer 1980):64–65; see also Stanley Aronowitz, *The Crisis in Historical Materialism: Class, Politics and Culture in Marxist Theory* (New York: Praeger, 1981), chap. 12, "On Narcissism," pp. 289–300.

Chapter 13: The Evolution of Authority

1. I am indebted to John Diggins's interesting work on the concept of authority. See his "Power and Authority in American History: The Case of Charles A. Beard and His Critics," *The American Historical Review* 86 (October 1981):701–30.

2. David Riesman, with Nathan Glazer and Reuel Denny, *The Lonely Crowd: A Study of the Changing American Character* (New Haven, Conn.: Yale University Press, 1964), p. 307.

3. Margaret Mead, *Culture and Commitment: A Study of the Generation Gap* (Garden City, N.Y.: Natural History Press/Doubleday, 1970), p. 91.

4. Philip Rieff, "By What Authority? Post-Freudian Reflections on the Repression of the Repressive in Modern Culture" (mimeographed paper, p. 2), in John P. Diggins and Mark Kann, eds., *The Problem of Authority in America* (Philadelphia: Temple University Press, 1981).

5. See Richard Sennett, *Authority* (New York: Alfred A. Knopf, 1980), pp. 15 ff. See also Michael Walzer, *Radical Principles: Reflections of an Unreconstructed Democrat* (New York: Basic Books, 1980). "The goal of democrats and socialists is to share and legitimize, but not to abolish

authority" (p. 10). Of course, people on the left registered reasonable views of authority in the sixties, too, but they were simply harder to make out amid the din of utopian rhetoric.

6. Sennett, *Authority*, p. 26.

7. On the historical role of the *mumi* ("big man"), see Marvin Harris, *Cannibals and Kings: The Origins of Cultures* (New York: Random House, 1977), pp. 71 ff.

8. For a fascinating historical account of varieties of authority, see Reinhard Bendix, *Kings or People: Power and the Mandate to Rule* (Berkeley, Los Angeles, London: University of California Press, 1978).

9. Harry Eckstein, "Authority Patterns: A Structural Basis for Political Inquiry," *American Political Science Review* 67 (1973):1153.

10. Sennett, *Authority*, pp. 10, 17–18, 4.

11. I would not press this speculation too far; compliance with authority is difficult to measure and even more difficult to compare over time, since sources and manifestations of social control, from authority to raw power, have occurred in different mixtures throughout American history.

12. Richard Sennett, *The Fall of Public Man* (New York: Alfred A. Knopf, 1977), p. 338.

13. Robert Bellah, "Cultural Vision and the Human Future," *Teachers College Record* 82 (Spring 1981):502.

14. John O'Neill, *Sociology as a Skin Trade: Essays Towards a Reflexive Sociology* (New York: Harper & Row, 1972), pp. 36–37.

15. Sennett, *Authority*, p. 90.

16. Kevin Phillips, "The Balkanization of America," *Harper's* 256 (May 1978):38.

17. William Phillips, "The American Establishment," *Partisan Review* 26 (Winter 1959):112, 113.

18. See Norman Podhoretz, *Breaking Ranks: A Political Memoir* (New York: Harper & Row, 1979). Several interesting discussions of the "new class," which any number of critics and social scientists have searched for diligently over the past several decades without eliciting anything resembling a generally accepted definition, may be found in B. Bruce-Briggs, ed., *The New Class?* (New Brunswick, N.J.: Transaction Books, 1979). See in particular Daniel Bell, "The New Class: A Muddled Concept," pp. 169–90.

19. U.S. Bureau of the Census, *Statistical Abstract of the United States: 1980*, 101st ed. (Washington, D.C., 1980), p. 589.

20. In the first budget year of the Reagan administration (fiscal year 1982), budgets for the National Endowment for the Arts (NEA) and the National Endowment for the Humanities (NEH) were cut by about one-third. This was some 15 percent less than administration officials

originally intended and others feared—understandably so, since many of the Reagan people initially questioned the very existence of the agencies. The NEA budget for the year ending September 30, 1981, was about $158.6 million; NEH, about $151.3 million.

21. *Statistical Abstract of the United States: 1980,* pp. 595, 594, 580 (for 1979, 36,112 new books and 9,070 new editions). Of course, many of these increases seem more salutary than they really are. For example, the rise in first-class mail may signify not a burst of sensitive correspondence but rather a rise in form letters and junk mail under first-class cover, much of it sponsored by right-wing political groups seeking funds.

22. Phillips, "The American Establishment," p. 112.

23. Subcultures can be divided indefinitely. Herbert Gans describes five "Folk Cultures": high culture, upper-middle culture, lower-middle culture, low culture, and quasi-folk low culture. He then adds such ethnic subcultures as black culture, and finally, subcultures based on age. See Herbert J. Gans, *Popular Culture and High Culture: An Analysis and Evaluation of Taste* (New York: Basic Books, 1974).

24. A particularly offensive example of the decline of deference to the idea of higher education can be found in Caroline Bird's *The Case Against College* (New York: David McKay, 1975).

25. For an opposite view of the alleged ill effects of "imposing" culture on hapless members of the middling and lower classes, see the interesting essay by John McDermott, "The Laying on of Culture," originally published in *The Nation* (March 10, 1969) and reprinted in Edgar Z. Friedenberg et al., eds., *The Cosmos Reader* (New York: Harcourt Brace Jovanovich, 1971), pp. 757–67.

26. Lionel Trilling, *Sincerity and Authenticity* (Cambridge, Mass.: Harvard University Press, 1972), pp. 171–72.

27. Rieff, "By What Authority?" p. 22.

28. Andrew Hacker, *The End of the American Era* (New York: Atheneum, 1974), p. 214.

29. See Michel J. Crozier, Samuel P. Huntington, and Joji Watanuki, *The Crisis of Democracy: Report on the Governability of Democracies to the Trilateral Commission* (New York: New York University Press, 1975).

30. Reported in Harold Rosenberg, " 'What Kind of Crazy World Are We Living In?' " *Los Angeles Times,* May 14, 1981, part 6, p. 1.

31. *Los Angeles Times,* May 13, 1981, part 4, p. 1.

32. Samuel Beer, "In Search of a New Public Philosophy," in Anthony King, ed., *The New American Political System* (Washington, D.C.: American Enterprise Institute, 1978), p. 5.

33. Everett Carll Ladd, Jr., and Seymour Martin Lipset, "Public Opinion and Public Policy," in Peter Duignan and Alvin Rabushka, eds., *The United States in the 1980s* (Stanford, Cal.: Hoover Institution, Publication 228, 1980), p. 77.

34. *Public Opinion* 4 (February–March 1981):27.

35. Ladd and Lipset, "Public Opinion and Public Policy," p. 79.

36. See Philip E. Converse, "The Nature of Belief Systems in Mass Publics," in David E. Apter, ed., *Ideology and Discontent* (New York: The Free Press, 1964), pp. 206–261.

37. Norman H. Nie, Sidney Verba, and John R. Petrocik, *The Changing American Voter* (Cambridge, Mass., and London: Harvard University Press, 1976), p. 347.

38. Christopher Lasch, *The World of Nations* (New York: Alfred A. Knopf, 1973), p. 109. A similar point of view is developed at greater length by Alvin W. Gouldner in *The Dialectic of Ideology and Technology: The Origins, Grammar, and Future of Ideology* (New York: The Seabury Press, 1976), p. 246.

39. Riesman, *The Lonely Crowd,* p. 213.

40. John Kenneth Galbraith, *American Capitalism: The Concept of Countervailing Power* (Boston: Houghton-Mifflin, 1952), p. 111.

41. Ibid., p. 109.

42. Reinhold Niebuhr, "The Crisis in American Protestantism," in William R. Miller, ed., *Contemporary American Protestant Thought: 1900–1970* (Indianapolis and New York: Bobbs-Merrill, 1973), p. 399.

43. Herbert Marcuse, *One-Dimensional Man: Studies in the Ideology of Advanced Industrial Society* (Boston: Beacon Press, 1964), p. 51.

44. Lester C. Thurow, *The Zero-Sum Society: Distribution and the Possibilities for Economic Change* (New York: Penguin Books, 1981), p. 11 (my italics). A similar point was made twenty years earlier by Daniel Bell. "The key question remains one of *political* economy. On a technical level, economic answers to the organization of production, control of inflation, maintenance of full employment, etc., are available. Political answers, in an interest-group society like ours, are not so easy. But in the long run the problems of the distribution of burdens and the nature of controls cannot be deflected" (*The End of Ideology: On the Exhaustion of Political Ideas in the Fifties* (New York: The Free Press, 1962), pp. 93–94).

45. Thurow, *The Zero-Sum Society,* p. 11.

46. Ibid., p. 12.

47. On the difficulties of assessing participation in political affairs, see Richard A. Brody, "The Puzzle of Political Participation in America," in King, ed., *The New American Political System,* pp. 278–324.

48. Sheldon Wolin, "The Idea of the State in America," mimeographed paper, March 20, 1980, p. 33.
49. Michael Novak, "The Vision of Democratic Capitalism," *Public Opinion* 4 (April–May 1981):4.

Chapter 14: Epilogue

1. See Gerald Pomper et al., *The Election of 1980: Reports and Interpretations* (Chatham, N.J.: Chatham House Publishers, 1981), pp. 97–118. For an ambitious statement of the realignment hypothesis, see Ben J. Wattenberg, "The New Moment: How Ronald Reagan Ratified LBJ's Great Society and Moved on to Other Important Items," *Public Opinion* 4 (December–January 1982):2–6, 59–60.
2. James Tobin, "Reaganomics and Economics," *The New York Review of Books* 28 (December 3, 1981):11.
3. Quoted in the *Los Angeles Times,* September 19, 1981, p. 1.
4. See the especially perceptive piece by Robert B. Reich, "Beyond Reaganomics," *The New Republic* 185 (November 18, 1981):19–25.
5. William Greider, "The Education of David Stockman," *The Atlantic* 248 (December 1981):47.
6. Tobin, "Reaganomics and Economics," p. 14.
7. This paragraph is based on Wattenberg, "The New Moment," p. 4.
8. Dennis H. Wrong, "How Critical is Our Condition? A Look at the Left and Liberals in America," *Dissent* 28 (Fall 1981):420. See comments on Wrong's essay by Tom J. Farer, Mark Levinson, Seymour Martin Lipset, and Arthur Schlesinger, Jr., in *Dissent* 29 (Winter 1982):103–112.
9. Nor does Wrong find his own argument altogether persuasive. He concludes his essay by observing that the projection of a conservative consolidation, which his reading of recent evidence seems to suggest, goes against the "weight of the liberal tradition in American history" (p. 424). Even though we cannot see the form its renewal may take, Wrong suggests, it would be foolish to discount the possibility of such an egalitarian turn.
10. The examples of successful protest are cited in H. A. Feiveson, "Thinking about Nuclear Weapons," *Dissent* 29 (Spring 1982):185. In 1982 a large number of books were published on the arms race and its possible effects. On the spring list, the most widely read and reviewed was Jonathan Schell's *The Fate of the Earth* (New York: Alfred A. Knopf, 1982).
11. The editors of *Public Opinion* have devised the "Gross National Spirit," (GNS), a measure of how Americans think they're getting on, composed of six questions concerning views of public and personal per-

formance drawn from various polls (from the National Opinion Research Center to Gallup). At first glance, the data presented for 1974–78 seem to conform to the manic-depressive cycle of public moods centered on presidential terms: the GNS was down in 1974, up from 1975 through 1977 (when Gerald Ford took over and Jimmy Carter was elected), down from 1978 through 1980, and back up again in 1981 with the election of Ronald Reagan. (Count on it to go down again.) See *Public Opinion* 4 (June–July 1981):22.

Index